Environment and Post-Soviet Transformation in Kazakhstan's Aral Sea Region

ECONOMIC EXPOSURES IN ASIA

Series Editor: Rebecca M. Empson, Department of Anthropology, UCL

Economic change in Asia often exceeds received models and expectations, leading to unexpected outcomes and experiences of rapid growth and sudden decline. This series seeks to capture this diversity. It places an emphasis on how people engage with volatility and flux as an omnipresent characteristic of life, and not necessarily as a passing phase. Shedding light on economic and political futures in the making, it also draws attention to the diverse ethical projects and strategies that flourish in such spaces of change.

The series publishes monographs and edited volumes that engage from a theoretical perspective with this new era of economic flux, exploring how current transformations come to shape and are being shaped by people in particular ways.

Environment and Post-Soviet Transformation in Kazakhstan's Aral Sea Region

Sea changes

William Wheeler

First published in 2021 by
UCL Press
University College London
Gower Street
London WC1E 6BT

Available to download free: www.uclpress.co.uk

Text © Author, 2021
Images © Author and copyright holders named in captions, 2021

The author has asserted his rights under the Copyright, Designs and Patents Act 1988 to be identified as the author of this work.

A CIP catalogue record for this book is available from The British Library.

Any third-party material in this book is not covered by the book's Creative Commons licence. Details of the copyright ownership and permitted use of third-party material is given in the image (or extract) credit lines. If you would like to reuse any third-party material not covered by the book's Creative Commons licence, you will need to obtain permission directly from the copyright owner.

This book is published under a Creative Commons Attribution-Non-Commercial 4.0 International licence (CC BY-NC 4.0), https://creativecommons.org/licenses/by-nc/4.0/. This licence allows you to share and adapt the work for non-commercial use providing attribution is made to the author and publisher (but not in any way that suggests that they endorse you or your use of the work) and any changes are indicated. Attribution should include the following information:

Wheeler, W. 2021. *Environment and Post-Soviet Transformation in Kazakhstan's Aral Sea Region: Sea changes*. London: UCL Press. https://doi.org/10.14324/111.9781800 080331

Further details about Creative Commons licences are available at https://creative commons.org/licenses/

ISBN: 978-1-80008-035-5 (Hbk.)
ISBN: 978-1-80008-034-8 (Pbk.)
ISBN: 978-1-80008-033-1 (PDF)
ISBN: 978-1-80008-036-2 (epub)
ISBN: 978-1-80008-037-9 (mobi)
DOI: https://doi.org/10.14324/111.9781800080331

Contents

List of figures	vii
List of maps	xi
Acknowledgements	xiii
Note on transliteration	xvii
Glossary and abbreviations	xix
Maps	xx
Introduction	1
1 The Aral Sea and the modernisation of Central Asia: a century of catastrophes	36
2 Seeing like a bureaucrat: problems of living standards and employment	65
3 Ocean fish, state socialism and nostalgia in Aral'sk	92
4 Rupture and continuity in Aral fishing villages	117
5 From Soviet ruins: flounder, the Kökaral dam and the return of the Small Aral Sea	141
6 Zander and social change in Bögen	175
7 Aral'sk today: fish, money, *ekologiia*	206
Conclusion	231
Appendix: sources for fish catches, 1905–80	239
Bibliography	242
Index	256

List of figures

Photographs are the author's own except where otherwise indicated.

0.1	The Aral Sea from space: (a) 1977, (b) 1987, (c) 1998, (d) 2010. Source: US Geological Survey, https://eros.usgs.gov/image-gallery/earthshot/aral-sea-kazakhstan-and-uzbekistan#earthshot-stories, accessed 18 May 2021.	1
0.2	Rusting ship on the dried-up seabed, 2004. Photograph by Vincent Robinot.	2
0.3	The Kökaral dam, 2015. Photograph by Vincent Robinot.	4
0.4	Fisherman casts his nets, autumn 2013.	4
0.5	Mosaic, Aral'sk station, 2009.	6
0.6	View towards Raiym from Nikolai Patsha's dyke, spring 2014.	20
0.7	*Qyr* country near Tastübek, spring 2014.	20
0.8	Gathering *shalang* from the dried-up seabed, summer 2013.	22
0.9	Warming up for a day's fishing, winter 2013.	23
0.10	Laying nets, winter 2013.	24
0.11	'Fish are money', winter 2013.	32
1.1	Ship sturgeon. Drawing by Amelia Abercrombie, after Zenkevich (1956).	40
1.2	Aral Sea fishermen with some vast sturgeon, c. 1900. Source: Museum of Fishermen, Aral'sk.	41
1.3	Fish catches, tonnes, in whole Aral Sea (blue), of which catches in the northern (Kazakh) part of the sea (red), 1905–80. Prepared by the author.	46
1.4	Fishing boats, 1940. Source: Museum of Fishermen, Aral'sk.	49
1.5	Ship in the ice, 1940s. Source: Museum of Fishermen, Aral'sk.	50

1.6 and 1.7	Fish factory, Aral'sk, undated. Source: Museum of Fishermen, Aral'sk.	51
1.8	Unloading from refrigerated ship, undated. Source: Museum of Fishermen, Aral'sk.	53
3.1	Cotton being unloaded from Aral'sk harbour, undated. Source: Museum of Fishermen, Aral'sk.	98
3.2	Aral'sk harbour, summer 2013.	98
3.3	Old fish plant, Aral'sk, summer 2013.	99
3.4	Shipyard, seen from harbour, summer 2013.	100
3.5	*Stanok Lenina* (Lenin's lathe), Aral'sk shipyard, summer 2013.	100
3.6	Orderly modernity? Fish plant, Aral'sk, 1983. Source: Museum of Fishermen, Aral'sk.	102
3.7	Military town, Aral'sk, winter 2013.	102
3.8 and 3.9	Smoking workshop, undated. Source: Museum of Fishermen, Aral'sk.	108
4.1	Stump of post for pontoon in former harbour, Bögen, autumn 2013.	118
4.2	Zhaqsylyq on the dried-up seabed with his *nar* camel (Bactrian camel–dromedary hybrid) on the left, winter 2013.	123
4.3	Fishing on the Aral, undated. Source: Museum of Fishermen, Aral'sk.	132
4.4	Fishing, late Soviet period. Source: Museum of Fishermen, Aral'sk.	137
5.1	Poster, Aral'sk, 2011. Nazarbayev and Kökaral: *Men Aralgha kömektesemïn degen, armanyma zhetkenïme quanyshtymyn* ('I said I would help the Aral, and I am glad to have fulfilled my dream').	141
5.2	Poster, Aral'sk, 2013. Nazarbayev and Kökaral: *Kökaral – ghasyr zhobasy* ('Kökaral – the project of the century').	142
5.3 and 5.4	Changes in sea level (above) and salinity (below) in the Small Aral Sea, 1990–2005. Prepared by the author. Data from Micklin (2010, 201) and Plotnikov (2013, 43).	149
5.5 and 5.6	Kökaral dam before and after it was breached, 14 April 1999 (above) and 23 April 1999 (below). Source: US Geological Survey, LandLook Viewer, https://landlook.usgs.gov, accessed 3 June 2021.	151

5.7	A dead sea? A selection of the aquatic fauna of the Small Aral before its restoration. Drawing by Amelia Abercrombie, after Zenkevich (1956).	152
5.8	Flounder. Drawing by Amelia Abercrombie.	152
5.9	Kökaral dyke under construction, 2004. Photograph by Vincent Robinot.	160
5.10	Restored Aral Sea, 2013. Source: US Geological Survey, https://eros.usgs.gov/image-gallery/earthshot/kazakhstan-north-aral-sea, accessed 3 June 2021.	161
5.11	Kökaral dam and Syr Dariya delta, 2013. Source: US Geological Survey, LandLook Viewer, https://landlook.usgs.gov, accessed 3 June 2021.	162
5.12	A selection of the aquatic fauna of the Small Aral following its restoration. Drawing by Amelia Abercrombie, after Zenkevich (1956).	162
6.1	Zander. Drawing by Amelia Abercrombie, after Zenkevich (1956).	177
6.2	Meirambek, fish receiver, shows off a huge zander, spring 2014.	178
6.3 and 6.4	Nauryzybai and colleagues, winter 2013.	189
6.5	Receiving station, Shaghalaly, spring 2014.	191
6.6	Receiving station, winter 2013.	191
6.7	Meirambek weighs the catch, winter 2013.	193
6.8	Loading the ZiL, spring 2014.	194
6.9	*Sortirovka*, fish plant, Bögen, spring 2014.	195
6.10	Fish in the back of the ZiL, spring 2014.	197
6.11	Aikeldï divides up a catfish, winter 2013.	200
7.1	*Aqkeme* (white ship), autumn 2013.	207
7.2	Atamcken fish factory, autumn 2013.	213
7.3	Daniiar, with dried fish, autumn 2013.	227
7.4	Child's representation of the future, November 2013.	229

List of maps

1	Central Asia. Drawn by the author.	xx
2	The Aral region. Drawn by the author.	xxi

Acknowledgements

The doctoral research this book is based on was carried out at Goldsmiths College, University of London, with funding from the Economic and Social Research Council provided through the London Social Science Doctoral Training Centre. Preparation of the book manuscript has been supported by the Leverhulme Trust as part of my Early Career Fellowship at the University of Manchester.

I am immensely grateful to my doctoral supervisors Pauline von Hellermann and Frances Pine for their guidance and friendship throughout the PhD project. The project benefited hugely from Pauline's expertise in environmental anthropology, as well as her encouragement to engage critically with dominant trends in the field, while Frances's depth of experience of socialist and postsocialist Poland proved invaluable in helping me get to grips with my own ethnography. I would also like to thank my initial supervisor, Catherine Alexander, for her generous input to the project even after she left Goldsmiths, including her much-needed encouragement during some of the more difficult moments of fieldwork. She has remained a source of inspiration for the project throughout. The thesis further benefited from feedback from other anthropologists at Goldsmiths, in particular Victoria Goddard, Sophie Day and Isaac Marrero-Guillamón, and from the support and insightful comments of my wonderful fellow doctoral students, including Aimee Joyce, Anna Wilson, Alex Urdea, Cy Elliot-Smith, Gabriela Nicolescu, Jasmin Immonen, Maka Suarez, Matteo Saltalippi, Sarah Howard, Souad Osseiran and Will Tantam.

My PhD examiners, Madeleine Reeves and Mathijs Pelkmans, offered the encouragement and rigorous feedback that helped me see how the dissertation could become a book. Since the PhD viva, Madeleine has provided unfailing friendship and encouragement, through the difficult years of postdoctoral seeming unemployability and into my current position at the University of Manchester. The book would not have been written without Madeleine's reassurance and enthusiasm at moments when I have most doubted myself. Her passion for exploring how everyday lives are lived in Central Asia, the joy she takes in anthropological theorising, and her ethical commitments to her research and to the discipline – all these have been a consistent reminder of all that is best about academia.

The Social Anthropology Department at Manchester has provided me with a welcoming and stimulating environment for completing this project; special thanks to Tony Simpson for being the most supportive and relaxed boss one could wish for. Parts of the book manuscript have benefited from comments from fellow department members, including Başak Saraç-Lesavre, Penny Harvey, Olivia Casagrande, Connie Smith, Caroline Parker and Patrick O'Hare.

A chance meeting with Niccolò Pianciola in the local archives in Aral'sk initiated a fruitful dialogue that sharpened my research and writing-up of the historical sections of the book. An invitation by Jeanne Féaux de la Croix and Tommaso Trevisani to present my work in Tübingen in 2015, and their rich and detailed feedback, provided a timely opportunity that helped me locate my research clearly in the ethnography of Central Asia. Various parts of this research have been presented at a conference on Disaster and Property Relations in Paris (2015); an Oxford Legalism seminar series on property relations (2016); the Royal Anthropological Institute conference 'Anthropology, Weather and Climate Change' (2016); a panel on Wittfogel at a European Association of Social Anthropologists conference in Milan (2016); and a Russian and East European Studies research seminar at the University of Manchester (2021). Many thanks to the organisers of all these events, and to other participants, for the fruitful discussions that followed. Special thanks to Marc Elie and Fabien Locher, to Franz Krause and Lukas Ley, and to Georgy Kantor, Tom Lambert and Hannah Skoda for their work in turning workshops into publications – all of which have been key to the development of the arguments I present.

It is hard to see how my project could have progressed without the enthusiastic input of Zhannat Makhambetova from Aral Tenizi. Before, during and after fieldwork, her practical support and the insights she has shared from her long-term work on the Aral fisheries have been invaluable. In Almaty, I was affiliated to the International Academy of Business, and I cannot thank Svetlana Shakirova and Aigerim Kaumenova enough for providing such a welcoming atmosphere for me when I was in Almaty, while also supporting me with key practicalities, especially obtaining a visa. Many thanks too to Nadir Mamilov at Al-Farabi University, Damir Zharkenov at KazNIIRKh, and Serik Timirkhanov for sharing their expertise about Kazakhstani fisheries; and to Serikbai Smailov at Kazgiprovodkhoz for his patient explanations of the details and debates surrounding hydrological projects. Various people have endeavoured to help me with learning Kazakh at different times: Säule, Alma, Baqytzhan, Nūrsultan, Botagöz: үлкен рақмет сендерге!

While huge thanks are due to all those who let me into their lives and who form the subject of this book, there are certain people in the region who deserve special mention here: Edïge, for his assistance with transcriptions and general moral support; the staff in the archives, who provided such a friendly and welcoming atmosphere; Aina, for setting up accommodation for me in the village of Bögen; and the various families who hosted me: Mūrat and Gulia, Zhaqsylyq and Gulzhamal, Sasha and Svetlana Mikhailovna, Ornyq and Samat. But to everyone who participated in my project in whatever way possible – I learnt a huge amount from you, far more than can be expressed within the bounds of this book. Арал теңізі толық болсын, балық көп болсын, халықтың жағдайы жақсы болсын деп тілеймін!

Unless otherwise stated, all photographs are my own. The black and white photographs in Chapters 1–4 are taken from the Aral'sk Museum of Fishermen – many thanks to the staff there for granting permission to reproduce them. I am also very grateful to Vincent Robinot for kindly letting me reproduce some of his extremely evocative photographs of the region, including the cover photograph.

The book has been greatly improved by the anonymous reviewers' comments on the proposal and on the manuscript. I am grateful to the series editor, Rebecca Empson, and especially to the commissioning editor at UCL Press, Chris Penfold, for his supportive, efficient and patient guidance to see the project through to its completion without any of the delays that beset so much academic publishing. Many thanks too to Jillian Bowie for her meticulous copy-editing.

Having completed this manuscript amid a global pandemic that has largely confined me at home, I have become acutely aware that producing academic knowledge is not only arduous work itself, but also a luxury that depends on tangled webs of other people's labour elsewhere. Never has our shared condition of precarity been clearer, nor the deeply uneven distribution of that precarity. It seems only right to acknowledge here all those whose labour sustains my own lifeworld through the pandemic and beyond.

Finally, I should thank friends and family for their unfailing support, in particular my sister Hannah, and my wife Millie, who, on top of everything else, was persuaded at the last minute to draw the sketches of fish and aquatic fauna that bring the underwater reality to life. Thanks to both of them for reading countless drafts and, most of all, for always being there. And, last but not least, thanks to my sons Perry and Ashley, who have brought renewed hope and joy into an ever more uncertain world. Now aged three, Perry is increasingly taking it on himself to correct me when I try to tell him about the aquatic fauna of the Aral, so it seems only right that I should dedicate this book to him.

Note on transliteration

For transliteration of Russian words, I use the modified Library of Congress transliteration. I transliterate Kazakh words from Kazakh Cyrillic. While a Latin script has been introduced for Kazakh, modelled on the Turkish alphabet, I transliterate from Kazakh Cyrillic because this is the alphabet that my informants are literate in. For Kazakh words, I therefore also use the Library of Congress transliteration as for Russian, with the following additions:

ә	*ä*
ғ	*gh*
қ	*q*
ң	*ng*
ө	*ö*
ұ	*ū*
ү	*ü*
і	*ï*

I use Kazakh versions of all place names in the region. The only exception is the town of Aral'sk, where I use the Russian form, because the Kazakh form, which is simply 'Aral', would be confusing. Where proper nouns are relatively well known in English, I use the conventional English spelling: thus Kazakhstan, not Qazaqstan; Baikonur, not Baiqongyr; Nazarbayev, not Nazarbaev; Syr Dariya, not Syr Dariia. Finally, several organisations in the region publish materials in English, so I use their own transliterations: Aral Tenizi, Aral Aielderi, Kambala Balyk.

Russian and Kazakh are abbreviated as 'Ru.' and 'Kaz.', respectively, when translations are given in parentheses.

Glossary and abbreviations

akim, akimat (Kaz.: *äkïm, äkïmdïk*): mayor, mayor's office

aqsaqal: white-beard, elder

Aralgosrybtrest (1926–60), Aralrybokombinat (1960–77), Aralrybprom (1977–98): state fishing industry on the Kazakh part of the Aral

JSDF: Japanese Social Development Fund

KazNIIRKh (Ru.: *Kazakhskii nauchno-issledovatelskii institut rybnogo khoziastva*): Kazakh Scientific Fisheries Research Institute

Kazsovmin: Kazakh Council of Ministers

kolkhoz: collective farm

Minrybkhoz: Ministry of Fisheries

Minvodkhoz: Ministry of Land Reclamation and Water Management

oblast (Ru.: *oblast'*, Kaz.: *oblys*): Soviet and post-Soviet territorial division below republic. Aral'sk is in Qyzylorda oblast.

raion (Ru.: *raion*, Kaz.: *audan*): territorial division below oblast. Aral'sk is the centre of Aral'sk raion.

sovkhoz: state farm

SYNAS: Syr Darya Control and North Aral Sea Project

tenge (KZT): Kazakh currency. For most of my fieldwork, the exchange rate was approximately 150 KZT to the dollar, though the currency was devalucd in early 2014.

Maps

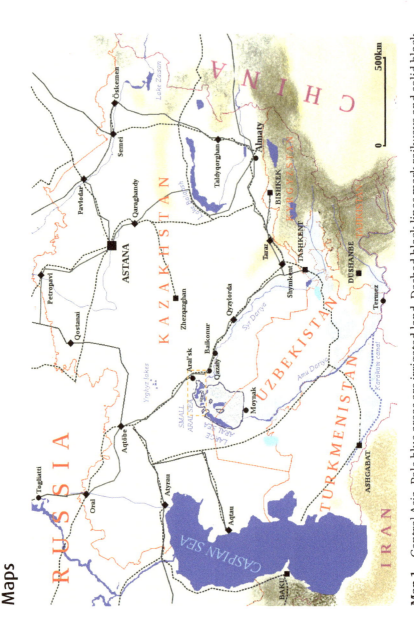

Map 1 Central Asia. Pale blue areas are irrigated land. Dashed black lines mark railways and solid black lines roads. Drawn by the author.

Map 2 The Aral region. The dashed blue line marks the pre-1960 extent of the sea. Drawn by the author.

Introduction

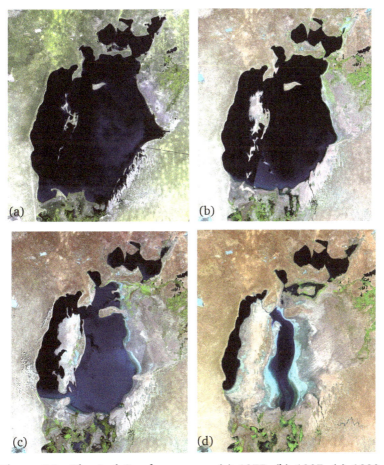

Figure 0.1 The Aral Sea from space: (a) 1977, (b) 1987, (c) 1998, (d) 2010. Source: US Geological Survey, https://eros.usgs.gov/image-gallery/earthshot/aral-sea-kazakhstan-and-uzbekistan#earthshot-stories, accessed 18 May 2021.

Figure 0.2 Rusting ship on the dried-up seabed, 2004. Photograph by Vincent Robinot.

The Aral Sea is known to the world through images like Figures 0.1 and 0.2. Ships stranded in the desert evoke a profound dissonance: the element of life has receded, leaving a sterile, barren landscape that affords a postapocalyptic look back on a modernity that has passed. The disruption of the natural order is visible from space, a matter of global concern. Before and after: a natural object destroyed. What happened is well known.[1] This was the world's fourth-largest inland waterbody, located in Soviet Central Asia between the Kazakh and Uzbek Soviet Socialist Republics. Lying amid arid steppe and desert, the sea was fed by two rivers, the Syr Dariya and the Amu Dariya, which rise thousands of kilometres away in the glaciers of the Tien Shan and Pamirs. The inflow from the rivers balanced losses to evaporation, keeping salinity levels low, and freshwater fish formed the basis of a thriving fishery. The sea softened the extremes of the continental climate and provided rainfall for pastures. However, the Soviet authorities, dreaming of making the desert bloom with cotton and, to a lesser extent, rice, diverted water from the rivers into vast irrigation projects. Aware of the consequences, they deemed cotton more valuable than the sea or the people who lived around it.

From 1960 the sea began to retreat. Salinity rose. Over the next 20 years, the fish died out. The sea separated into a Small and Large Aral in 1987–9. Windstorms blew toxic dust and salt from the desiccated seabed, poisoning the land around and its people, and spreading far beyond the region. A biological weapons laboratory on the remote Vozrozhdenie Island, abandoned after the Soviet collapse, was now connected to the mainland, posing an acute risk. Polluted water caused serious health problems. Thousands of people left. But the authorities continued to expand irrigation and failed to recognise the environmental disaster. Only in the more liberal climate of perestroika did the catastrophe become widely known across the USSR, becoming a *cause célèbre* for intellectuals and environmentalists. Popularised in the West in the 1990s, the Aral was located in Cold War categories, figuring, like Chernobyl, as a Soviet crime against people and against nature. It reads as a parable of Communist hubris: the totalitarian state seeks to control nature; nature takes its revenge. As a Canadian development worker wrote: 'The Soviets targeted, condemned and sacrificed the Aral Sea' (Ferguson 2003, 23).

After the USSR collapsed, the global notoriety of the disaster spawned scores of projects addressing the environmental degradation that stretched across the vast Aral basin. Most were unsuccessful. Locals would joke that, if everyone who had visited the Aral had brought a bucket of water, the sea would be full again. However, amid the many failures, two success stories stand out. Some Danish fishermen who visited the Kazakh shore in the early 1990s learnt that the sea was not dead, as was widely assumed: in the 1970s, as native species were dying, Soviet authorities had introduced flounder, a salt-tolerant fish; by the 1990s, flounder were thriving. Over the late 1990s and 2000s, the Danes set up a nongovernmental organisation, Aral Tenizi, and re-established a viable fishery on what was left of the Small Aral. Then, in 2005, efforts to stabilise the Small Aral finally bore fruit in the construction of the Kökaral dam by the World Bank and Kazakhstan government. As the level has risen, falling salinity has allowed the return of native fish (Micklin 2007; Micklin and Aladin 2008). The sea is now 15–20 km from the former Kazakh port of Aral'sk. The disaster is far from solved. While the acute danger posed by the exposed biological weapons laboratory resulted in a US-led clean-up operation in 2002, the Large Aral continues to shrink, and on the southern shore around the former port of Moynaq, despite some efforts to restore Amu Dariya delta lakes and wetlands, the situation remains bleak. Water is still withdrawn across Central Asia to grow cotton and rice. Nevertheless, the limited, technical solution for the Small Aral offers a hopeful, and photogenic, coda to the disaster story: images like those in Figures 0.3 and 0.4 show nature's force being channelled and contained, while fishermen turn again to their age-old occupation, interacting with their restored environment in a seemingly sustainable way.

Figure 0.3 The Kökaral dam, 2015. Photograph by Vincent Robinot.

Figure 0.4 Fisherman casts his nets, autumn 2013. Source: author.

It was with famous images like these in mind that I set off for fieldwork in late 2012. I was familiar with the extensive academic literature on the disaster, but this literature, while illuminating the causes of the sea's regression and its multifarious effects on the local environment and human health, left little sense of the lives and livelihoods of those who have stayed in the region throughout. The view from space shows the global significance of the disaster, but occludes the lifeworlds of those who lived through it: global perspectives, like all perspectives, are partial and sited (Hastrup 2013). I had visited Aral'sk twice, like many foreigners, as a tourist, a disaster voyeur. In many ways it seemed not so different from other small towns in rural Kazakhstan – remote, economically depressed, the urban landscape still marked by the crumbling remnants of the Soviet past. Academic and journalistic accounts proposed a linear causation: politics destroys the sea; environmental change causes economic collapse and social rupture, a sea change in human society. Yet I was aware that people had lived through a different sort of sea change, the disintegration and transformation that followed the Soviet collapse, the birth of independent Kazakhstan and the move from a command economy to 'wild capitalism'. How did these processes intersect with the environmental ruination wrought by the Soviet project? What futures did the restored sea offer to a region marginalised within Kazakhstan's oil economy? Though I anticipated ambiguity, I expected that the disaster would constitute a 'critical event', a totalising framework overshadowing local imaginaries (Das 1995).

The view from Aral'sk

Alighting from the train in Aral'sk, I was greeted by a mosaic depicting a story from the Civil War (Figure 0.5): in 1921, Lenin wrote to Aral fishermen exhorting them to send fish to the Volga region, which was beset by famine. One winter's night, fishermen from remote coastal villages – Bögen, Qarashalang, Qaratereng – went out onto the ice and caught a heroic haul of fish. Camels, 'the ships of the steppe' (*dalanyng kemesi*), invigorated with a swig of vodka and a chunk of pike, towed the fish by sledge to the nearest station. They filled 14 railway wagons, and the fish saved, I heard, millions from famine. Young people sometimes relate this story to the Second World War, but the point is clear: through Lenin's letter, the sea was integrated into broader spaces. It was not only a natural object, not only the ancestral property of local Kazakhs: it was also a Soviet sea.

Figure 0.5 Mosaic, Aral'sk station, 2009. The text reads: *Na pis'mo Lenina otgruzim 14 vagonov ryby*, 'In response to Lenin's letter, we will dispatch 14 wagons of fish.' Source: author.

In the 12 months I spent in Aral'sk and surrounding villages between November 2012 and June 2014, I heard this story many times. It expressed pride in local identity. By contrast, many people were tired of the disaster narrative and the stigma it carries. Some critiqued the visual construction of disaster. As one friend told me, film crews search out the oldest, poorest inhabitants and the most decrepit houses, just to make everything look catastrophic. This framing, he implied, precludes the possibility that people might lead normal lives in the region. As a totalising discourse, global visions of disaster have little space for local perspectives. Similar to what Brown (2015, Chapter 3) finds in Chernobyl, while tourists and journalists wonder at the spectacularly photogenic environmental disaster and equally photogenic recovery, the region is rather more mundane. People are puzzled by the foreign visitors: what do they want to see in Aral'sk? Indeed, in the initial months of my fieldwork, I was struck by how little people talked about disaster. They looked blank when I explained my research in terms of *Aral apaty*, the Kazakh phrase I had learnt for 'Aral disaster'.[2] Perhaps this is unsurprising. Anthropological theorisations of disasters, as 'revelatory crises' (e.g. Oliver-Smith and Hoffman 2002) that lay bare societal structures, are informed by events such as earthquakes. Lacking the temporal boundedness of an event, the gradual regression of the Aral does not work on the imagination like one-off disasters: there is no clear before and after, no dividing line at which the world was turned upside down.[3]

Certainly, there is a register for mourning the sea, expressed in the idiom *Aral qasïretï*, the 'grief' or 'sorrow' of the Aral, but this was muted by the time of my fieldwork. Moreover, I found older people sometimes blurring the disappearance of the sea with the demise of the USSR. Others would insist that, even though the sea had gone, the eighties were a good time, because there was work. I came to see that the sea's gradual regression had overlapped with processes by which the Soviet authorities sought to mitigate its effects. Though limited and uneven, these processes inflected memories of the sea's regression, which did not always figure as the sea change that I expected.

Indeed, if the environmental disaster narrative elided the lived experience of Soviet socialism and its aftermath, I found that this story loomed as large for my informants as that of environmental change, sometimes larger. Everyone agreed that the really bad time was the 1990s, when the USSR disintegrated and ecological devastation was compounded by widespread economic crisis, inflation and unemployment. Unsurprisingly, no one was keen to talk about this dismal time. There is a widespread consensus across the region that things have improved since then: people are now returning to the region. Yet I found more ambiguity than the well-worn narrative of environmental recovery implies. Images like those above depict a restored sea, but they occlude the complex mix of private and state regulation within which the post-Soviet sea is constituted; they do not show the lucrative markets for zander extending as far west as Germany, or the markets for illegal nets from China; they do not show the ailing fish plants in Aral'sk which suffer from a paradoxical shortage of fish. In short, they cannot capture the complex, variegated patterns of social change instigated by the restored sea.

Thus, rather than a singular critical event that overshadowed local imaginaries, I encountered multiple meanings ascribed to the Aral regression and partial recovery. In one register, the regression was a normal economic loss which could be absorbed by importing resources from elsewhere in Soviet space; in another, the Aral was the ancestral property of local Kazakh lineages. Some informants echoed the catastrophic accounts of perestroika intellectuals; others polemicised against all forms of disaster narrative, which they took as an affront to local pride. For some, the dam and restored sea speak hopefully of the sovereignty of independent Kazakhstan extending to a remote region;

for others, the failure of the sea to reach Aral'sk, the failure of environmental restoration to translate into widespread employment, speaks of state failure that contrasts with rosy memories of Soviet socialism.

For the ethnographer, as for Bakhtin's novelist, 'the object is always entangled in someone else's discourse (*oputan chuzhim slovom*) about it, it is already present with qualifications, an object of dispute that is conceptualized and evaluated variously, inseparable from the heteroglot social apperception of it' (Bakhtin 1981b, 330). I initially construed the ethnographic endeavour naïvely, as a quest for the pure, uncontaminated discourse of 'the local' without the ensnaring discourses of outsiders. But hacking through the thicket of discourses surrounding the Aral only multiplied the object. There was no homogeneous, bounded local. Sometimes my informants would talk of scientists discovering salt from the Aral as far away as Japan. If their point was to illustrate the global significance of the sea's demise, they equally showed how the Aral is reconstituted through this global connection: the local is inherently 'perforated' (Hastrup 2009), local discourses 'shot through' with other discourses (Bakhtin 1981b, 276).

If there was little talk of 'disaster', I quickly became attuned to discussions about *ekologiia* (Ru./Kaz.: 'ecology'), which locally signifies environmental problems affecting human health. This usage dates from the late 1980s, when the regression was finally officially recognised as an environmental disaster. In 1989 a decree of the Supreme Soviet of the USSR declared the region *zona ekologicheskogo bedstviia*, 'an ecological disaster zone' (Zonn et al. 2009, 267). Aral'sk raion, like its neighbours, became known as an *ekologicheskii raion*, 'an ecological raion'. But *ekologiia* too is ambiguous. Certainly, many acknowledge the presence of *ekologiia*, as an explanation for the myriad health problems faced in the region. However, they do not unambiguously connect *ekologiia* with the sea's regression. Just over 200 km from Aral'sk is Baikonur, from where Gagarin was launched into the cosmos. The cosmodrome, on land rented by Russia, is still active today – and on a day-to-day basis, *ekologiia* and its ill effects are blamed on the ongoing rocket launches.

Moreover, not everyone agrees there is *ekologiia*. As an outsider, I would be asked if I noticed *ekologiia*. Once a fisherman, out on the ice under pale blue skies in a howling gale, declared that people always said that there was *ekologiia* in the region, but he didn't notice it – whereas the city, *that* was where the air was dirty. Having come from London via Almaty not long before, I had to concur. Others insist that local Kazakhs, because of their nomadic past, have got used to *ekologiia* (and vodka can help mitigate it), unlike the non-Kazakhs who used to live in the region but left. Indeed, most people also talk extensively about the region's natural bounty: Aral meat and dairy products are the tastiest in the country because of the salt in the vegetation.

Environmental anthropology of Central Asia

What we make of environmental change, then, and what it makes of us, depends on the multiple ways in which it is insinuated into our lived experience. In this book, I show that the regression and partial restoration of the Aral Sea cannot be analytically separated from the processes, continuities and ruptures of Soviet socialism and postsocialism. In fleshing out this claim, I advance two sets of arguments. First, within different sets of relations, environmental change comes to mean different things. Over the course of this book, the Aral regression will emerge as a necessary economic process, a bureaucratic problem, an escalating catastrophe, a cultural loss. If environmental change assumes political agency, this agency depends on how material effects are apprehended. As a bureaucratic problem, the sea's regression prompted a specific, limited set of official responses; as an escalating catastrophe during perestroika, it prompted calls, albeit frustrated, for a far more wide-reaching transform-ation. The political agency of environmental change further depends on historical and material contingencies: if the perestroika vision was ultimately frustrated by the Soviet collapse, the Aral Sea disaster that was apprehended by the 1990s transnational development community would ultimately translate into the restoration of the Small Aral – but only after the disruptive agency of Danish activists and flounder together proved that the sea was alive.

Secondly, the capacity of environmental change to effect social change is bound up with the valuation, extraction, processing and circulation of natural resources, located within the wider political-economic context. I explore this through the history of the fishery, whose trajectory does not map neatly onto the receding and return of the sea. The sea that receded was a socialist sea: its fish were extracted and processed within the command economy, and would circulate across Soviet 'gridded space' (Brown 2015) – and when the sea receded, this same gridded space facilitated the import of ocean fish for processing in Aral'sk, and the sending of fishermen to other lakes in Kazakhstan.[4] The survival of the Soviet fishery even without the sea afforded, amid en-vironmental devastation, a measure of continuity, and is even sometimes remembered as strengthening the social contract. The sea that has returned is a postsocialist sea, subject to new forms of regulation, and fishing and fish processing depend on the divergent values ascribed to fish on transnational markets, driving variegated patterns of social change across the region.[5]

In making these arguments, I will be making a case for an environmental anthropology of post-Soviet Central Asia.[6] Despite widespread ecological degradation, environmental concerns have been marginal to the regional ethnography. Foregrounding them, I suggest, enriches the wider field of environmental anthropology in three ways. First, a political ecology shaped by the state-socialist legacy provides a valuable counterpoint to accounts of environmental change in Western contexts or contexts shaped by Western colonial legacies. Indeed, if anthropologists are increasingly recognising the multiple ways in which nature is 'done', the state-socialist/postsocialist context shows how not all 'versions' of nature are equal, as the informal exercise of power has prioritised some over others. Secondly, the region's ambiguous enrolment in modernity, whereby modernist models of nature were *both* imposed from outside *and* internalised, has resulted in heterogeneous ways of doing nature that cannot be reduced to compliance with or resistance to modernist projects. Finally, I will suggest that the intersection of large-scale political-economic transformation following the Soviet collapse with environmental change demands that we rethink concepts of adaptation and resilience.

A political ecology of socialism and after

The demise of the Aral Sea speaks to core concerns of contemporary environmental anthropology. The unceasing expansion of irrigation and cotton plantations is an instance of what Tsing calls the 'scalable' projects of modernity, premised on the quantitative growth of abstracted commodities, 'as if the entanglements of living did not matter' (2015, 5). Operationalising nature as a resource to be mastered to serve human progress, Soviet modernity violently reordered environments and human–environment entanglements, leaving ruination. No less than Tsing's (2015) ruined industrial forests of Oregon, the dried-up bed of the Aral stands witness to the ruination inherent in modernist projects. After all, as Buck-Morss (2002, xi) reminds us, both socialist and capitalist systems were premised on similar dreams, with comparable catastrophic human and environmental outcomes.

However, while global comparisons are significant, there was something distinctive about Soviet modernity. If this story forms part of 'the history of the human concentration of wealth through making both humans and nonhumans into resources for investment' (Tsing 2015, 5), how investments were made, how wealth was concentrated – and redistributed – differed between East and West. I thus take up Peet and Watts' (1996, 10) call for a political ecology of state socialism. Such a political ecology starts, on the one hand, from the quantitative growth of fixed assets that maximised the power of the state apparatus (Fehér, Heller and Márkus 1983; cf. Weiner 1999, 15–16) and, on the other, from the 'economics of shortage' (Kornai 1980) that frustrated centralised control. Both these tendencies drove ecological degradation in Central Asia: quantitative expansion of irrigation maximised central control, which was simultaneously undermined by leaks, waste and competition over water at every level. So too with the Aral fisheries, labour and resources were largely controlled by a single state enterprise, but efforts to intensify fishing practices were undermined by lack of investment, poor labour discipline and pilfering. This legacy is critical for understanding postsocialist transformations. While I am not proposing a unitary 'political ecology of postsocialism', the continuities with, as well as differences from, the socialist fishery help in understanding how the contemporary fishery has emerged as a 'pericapitalist' (Tsing 2015) formation within a heterogeneous terrain of new global connections.

These political ecologies are crucial for understanding not only what drives environmental change, but also what it comes to mean. Thinking through these questions, I will draw on approaches in environmental anthropology which, moving beyond modernist assumptions of a singular nature to be controlled by human society, explore how nature is 'done' in different contexts. Exemplary in this regard is Lien's (2015) ethnography of Norwegian salmon farming. Despite the apparent singularity of the context, she shows that, as salmon are enrolled in heterogeneous assemblages of people and things, they emerge as different, if partially connected, entities – now as biomass, now as sentient beings, now as hungry, now as alien invaders. In what follows, I show how the Aral emerges at different moments in history as a multiple object as it is entangled in different configurations of space and time, infrastructures, structures of value and regimes of nature – although, while Lien (2015) is inspired by science and technology studies (STS), my theoretical pathway to multiplicity shall be, as I elaborate later in this Introduction, through Bakhtin and his concept of the chronotope.

However, where Lien (2015, 23) writes of 'a multiplicity of ever-emergent human-natural worlds that sometimes rub up against one another, sometimes cause controversy and friction, and sometimes unfold quietly side by side', in the post-Soviet context, multiple worlds coexist less comfortably. As Richardson (2014) notes, STS approaches are often couched within liberal assumptions about politics: the suggestion that reality can be multiple is a democratising force (e.g. Mol 1999). By contrast, in Richardson's (2014) ethnography of a failed irrigation project in Ukraine, activists' efforts to establish that the waterbody was toxic and valueless, and thus in need of environmental restoration, were frustrated by powerful interests that multiplied some connections while suppressing others, such that alternative, economically valuable, versions of the waterbody emerged: a drinking water reservoir, and a fishery. As Richardson (2014, 6) remarks, the STS focus on human–nonhuman symmetry risks occluding 'which asymmetries among humans may affect which reality can exist'. If, then, multiple versions of the Aral have emerged before it receded, during its recession and since its partial restoration, not all have been equal; we will focus not only on the connections, but also the disconnections, the obfuscations, the cultivated ignorance that prioritise certain versions over others.

Ambiguous modernity

A further potential for environmental anthropology lies in the ambiguous relationship of Central Asian peoples to modernity, and to modernist paradigms of nature. Soviet modernisation processes both were and were not an alien imposition, leaving a legacy between postcoloniality and postsocialism (Abashin 2015; Kandiyoti 2002). This is evident in the recent historiography of the devastating famine that Bolshevik collectivisation policies unleashed in Kazakhstan in 1931–4 when 'backward' Kazakh nomads were to be modernised by being forcibly settled in collective farms and their livestock requisitioned to feed urban centres outside Kazakhstan. In Cameron's (2018) environmental history, as the Bolsheviks sought to remake the Kazakh nation and the steppe environment together, rigid economic plans ignored the ecological instability to which the flexibility of nomadic life had been adapted. In the appalling hunger that killed around 1.5 million people, pre-existing clan structures were shattered as the steppe descended into violence. And yet, both Cameron (2018) and Kindler (2018) stress that the famine cemented Soviet rule by leaving the survivors totally dependent on the state. Indeed, Kindler draws out how survival depended on complicity, compromise and silence. The networks necessary for survival during the famine, deeply implicated with Party-state structures, lived on in post-famine collective farms, kolkhozy, what Kindler (2018, 2) calls 'Sovietization by hunger'.

The recent environmental historiography of the Aral Sea basin similarly draws out both the violence of early Soviet rule and the degree to which Central Asian people came to have a stake in, and desire, infrastructures and technologies of mastering nature. Peterson (2019) documents the tragic irony of the supposedly emancipatory Bolshevik project reconstituting that epitome of capitalist oppression, the cotton plantation. However, she also shows how what was, materially, a continuation of the colonial-extractive project came to be cast as liberation from the dual oppression of Tsarist rule and of the arid environment. Indeed, Obertreis (2017) describes how the proliferating technical and scientific networks that sustained the expansion of irrigation at any cost were deeply indigenised, and how the legitimacy of the entire Soviet project in Central Asia came to rest on irrigation, especially after economic growth accelerated in the 1960s. Thus, in Uzbekistan today there is deep ambivalence about cotton: while ecologically and socially damaging, it is nevertheless felt to represent modernity (Trevisani 2010; Zanca 2010).

More broadly, Central Asia's place in the Soviet economy was premised on export of agricultural goods and, especially in Kazakhstan, minerals, with little development of heavy industry (Gleason 1991; Rumer 1989). However, not quite balancing this quasi-colonial extractive relation was a countervailing tendency to redistribution: the social contract of socialism promised a gradual rise in living standards – especially as post-Stalinist economic growth saw the Soviet welfare state extend into remote rural locations (Kalinovsky 2018). Modernity increasingly came with 'expectations' (Ferguson 1999). If, in Brown's (2015) evocative description, space was organised into 'gridded matrices', the grid facilitated the flow of raw commodities to the centre and the redistributed fruits of modernity back into the periphery. In this way, people came to live 'gridded lives'.

Certainly, Soviet space was not homogeneous. Recent ethnography has highlighted the diverse modes of connection between Moscow and Central Asia: some sites, of more material value to the centre, were more incorporated than others (Mostowlansky 2017; Pelkmans 2013; Reeves 2014, Chapter 3). Yet, while the fulfilment of the promise embedded in the social contract was wildly uneven, the promise itself is significant (Reeves 2014, 138). This ambiguous enrolment in Soviet modernity also involved enrolment in Soviet ways of 'doing' nature. Thus, in Mostowlansky's (2017, 27–9) ethnography of the Pamir Highway in Tajikistan, an engineering feat that materialised modernity in the

Pamirs, 'the roof of the world', he describes how the road facilitated the stocking of a mountain lake with Siberian carp in the 1960s: what was a sacred lake is now a valued fishpond.

As Mostowlansky (2017) poignantly describes, amid material disintegration, there is a sense that modernity has passed, echoing Tsing's (2015) and Buck-Morss's (1999) evocations of the demise of dreams of mass utopia East and West. Yet, Mostowlansky also shows how ongoing state discourses and projects of modernisation continue to promise bright futures premised on new global connections. This is evident in the contemporary appeal of vast dam projects in Kyrgyzstan and Tajikistan (Féaux de la Croix 2016; Suyarkulova 2015). In Kazakhstan too, sovereignty is projected in official modernisation strategies: first Kazakhstan-2030, formulated in 1997, offered a vision for the long-term development of the country; in 2012, this future was superseded by the Kazakhstan-2050 Strategy. These visions of the future do not offer mass utopias, but rather the economic stability within which to realise private consumerist utopias (Adams and Rustemova 2009; Laszczkowski 2011, 90). Unlike the Soviet social contract, compliance with authoritarian rule depends on modernisation which promises the conditions for private citizens to acquire wealth (Kudaibergenova 2015). Critically, this promise depends on the oil economy, which continues to exploit environments across Kazakhstan (e.g. Zonn 2002).[7]

However, processes of modernisation past and present are not unidirectional. Central Asian socialities cannot be reduced to the shadow of the 'gridded lives' of Soviet modernity. Indeed, Mostowlansky (2017, 33–4) describes first encountering the sacred-lake-turned-fishpond while travelling to pilgrimage sites (*mazar*) that have developed along the road. The road, he thus argues, has reshaped local socialities in ways that exceeded the ideological expectations of its planners, reconstituting cultural forms that resist the teleology of modernisation. This is not to suggest a dichotomy between 'modernity' and recalcitrant 'tradition'. As Kandiyoti (1996; 2002) argues, Soviet 'modernisation without the market' resulted in a complex transformation: formal dysfunction of the command economy necessitated informal practices, which reproduced pre-existing identities but transformed them in the process. Similarly, in his monumental historical ethnography of a village in Tajikistan, Abashin (2015) describes how modernisation processes embedded 'Sovietness' in everyday life, while simultaneously reconstituting local cultural practices, which increasingly became understood as national tradition. Showing how people moved without contradiction between spaces deemed 'Soviet' and spaces deemed 'our own', 'national' or 'Muslim', Abashin thus replaces dichotomies of modernity/tradition, compliance/resistance with a heterogeneous picture of Soviet Central Asian society as a 'mosaic' or 'kaleidoscope'.

Féaux de la Croix (2016) draws out the geographical implications of this ambiguous modernisation in her exploration of the dams, sacred shrines and mountain pastures that coexist in the Kyrgyz countryside. Contrasting her material with the coherent landscapes described by ethnographers of Mongolia, she describes a heterogeneous 'moral geography' where different understandings of value and worth, often held by the same people, are anchored in sites that are variously associated with resource politics, religious belief and the pastoral good life. If modernist dam projects seem to be located in an abstract space, this space 'is not an *a priori*, but a vision', and an achievement; it is the '*quality* of a place', and as such, for Soviet nostalgics, it can even have a certain 'romance' (Féaux de la Croix 2016, 295). Thus, weighing various theoretical approaches to space/place, she concludes that different places 'have more space-like or more landscape-like qualities' (Féaux de la Croix 2016, 34). What emerges is a coexistence of different ways of doing space and nature which, though perceived as more 'modern' or more 'traditional', are coeval and mutually constitutive. This is a different sort of multiplicity to, say, Lien's (2015) multiple salmon, which all emerge within a recognisably modernist paradigm, albeit a heterogeneous one. Thus, if Lien (2015, 22–3) opposes her practical ontological multiplicity to the radical alterity proposed in some non-Western contexts (e.g. Pedersen 2011), post-Soviet Central Asia forces us to think between the two: heterogeneous ways of doing nature within an ambiguous modernity where modernisation processes have repeatedly reconstituted their 'traditional' other.

Adaptation over a century of catastrophes

The final contribution this book will bring to environmental anthropology is to understandings of adaptation. '[E]nvironmental changes', write Hastrup and Rubow (2014, 4), 'cannot be kept apart from social life in general, or isolated as changes-in-themselves.' Not only on the Aral, but across Kazakhstan, the ruination wrought by Soviet modernity intersects with the ruins *of* Soviet modernity. This offers a rich terrain for thinking through the analytical challenge of integrating our accounts of environmental change with a social that has been repeatedly, and traumatically, remade over the last century. Intertwined with what Grant (1995), in Siberia, describes as a 'century of perestroikas' was a century of catastrophes: the implosion of imperial space amid world war and Civil War, the violent disentangling of the nomadic economy during collectivisation, the Great Patriotic War, nuclear testing in eastern Kazakhstan, the Virgin Lands programme, the Aral regression and the Soviet collapse, each followed by a rebuilding that reshaped social worlds and local environments. In the terms proposed by Alexander and Sanchez (2019), my informants have been dealing both with the wastes, environmental and human, produced by socialism, and with the new indeterminacies, between waste and value, of postsocialist disintegration and transformation. This is evident in Stawkowski's (2016) ethnography of the former nuclear testing sites of eastern Kazakhstan, where 'biological' subjectivities emerge from the intersection of radioactivity with postsocialist marginalisation. Describing themselves as 'mutants', Stawkowski's informants claim to have adapted to radiation (as with Aral residents' encounters with *ekologiia*, vodka helps). This mutant subjectivity, Stawkowski proposes, helps reassert local pride in face of the dual stigma of victimhood and rurality.

Both the Aral Sea and the nuclear Polygon are rhetorically located as victims of the Soviet project, thus stressing their value to independent Kazakhstan, founded on the equal value of all Kazakhs. However, the uneven development of the oil economy marginalises peripheral territories, producing surplus populations suspended between waste and value. How, then, are we to think about a concept like 'adaptation' to environmental change in a context where people have also had to adapt to the disintegration of material infrastructure, to the collapse of socialist frameworks of meaning and value, and to the emergence of new ideologies and actualities of the market? What happens to the concept of 'resilience' when local worlds have been repeatedly 'perforated' (Hastrup 2009) not only by environmental degradation, but also by integration into Soviet space, the disintegration of that space and reintegration into circuits of global capital?

In the following section, I introduce my fieldsites. Homing in on an ethnographic vignette about a fishing net, I will then lay out my particular theoretical approach, which integrates contemporary interest in material agency with a Bakhtinian approach to discourse, human history and political economy. I close the introduction by applying this approach to the history of the fisheries.

Locating the Aral

I flew to Kazakhstan's former capital, Almaty (formerly Alma-Ata) in November 2012, the plane full of members of Kazakhstan's new middle classes, beneficiaries of the country's oil wealth. I spent some time in Almaty, where the old gridded Soviet city was still just about legible amid glass office blocks and luxury flats. I found that 'the Aral Sea' was an object of curiosity among older inhabitants who remembered its fame in the 1980s and 1990s. However, amid present concerns about economic crisis, perestroika-era concern for the environment had largely faded, and the Aral region was marginal to most imaginings of contemporary Kazakhstan. My Kazakh teacher warned me of the dangers of going to such a polluted region, insisting that I wear a mask at all times, while simultaneously waxing lyrical about how I would find the most 'authentic' Kazakhs, their traditions still intact.

While in Almaty, I turned to the solid grey building which houses the state archives, seeking details and thickness to the Soviet past, about which official discourse today is muted. Indeed, though lip service is paid to the country's sufferings (the Aral Sea, nuclear testing, the Virgin Lands programme), this does not constitute a strong anti-Soviet postcolonial narrative. After all, in an ethnically diverse country, the authorities have avoided encouraging strong ethnonationalist sentiment (Cameron 2018, Epilogue; Davé 2007; Kindler 2018, Chapter 7). Moreover, the then president, Nazarbayev, and the country's elite all rose through the Soviet system. So, while Kazakhstani statehood is legitimised by claims of cultural authenticity and continuity, based on symbols from the pre-Soviet past (Alexander 2004b; Buchli 2007; Dubuisson and Genina 2012; Privratsky 2001), there is little narrative arc encompassing the recent past. Kazakhstan-2030 makes hardly any mention of Soviet legacies; Kazakhstan-2050 makes none. The overwhelming orientation is to the future: sovereignty is imagined in Astana, Kazakhstan's shiny new capital since 1997, which promises a bright future for an imagined collectivity (Laszczkowski 2011; 2014; 2016).[8]

From Almaty I travelled by train to Aral'sk, a journey of 30–40 hours across 1,600 km of relentlessly flat snow-covered steppe and semi-desert. Fellow passengers included large families on their way to weddings; shift workers on their way to or from work on oilfields or in uranium mines (often drinking their way through the brief freedom between the constraints of home life and work life); students; parents visiting children working in oil on the Caspian; and Astana migrants visiting families in Qyzylorda. I took this journey several times over the following year. Conversations captured all the ambiguities of early 2010s Kazakhstan: the beauty of Astana; the pervasive corruption; the morality of the Soviet past; the bright future that might lie ahead if Kazakhstan could diversify its economy; the need for the younger generation to move away from

Soviet-era practices; the threat and opportunity posed by increasing dependence on China. Sometimes as we passed through the heavily salinised land in Qyzylorda oblast, older people would talk about the damage of the Soviet legacy – not just the damage to the Aral Sea, but the destruction of the nomadic way of life.

Aral'sk is the raion centre, a town of some 30,000 inhabitants, 450 km from the oblast capital, Qyzylorda. In many ways, it is a typical small post-Soviet town. The old Soviet buildings are decaying; the closed factories are rusting. Sand swirls everywhere. Camels stroll up and down the streets, and cows graze off rubbish heaps. There are no cinemas and no supermarkets. There is, however, a bustling market and a range of bars and cafes; if the public space can seem depressed, new private houses abound. Clean drinking water from a vast aquifer in the desert was brought here in 1990. In the mid-2000s it was piped to individual households, and it now reaches all villages in the raion. There is no centralised sewage in Aral'sk, and during my fieldwork there was no piped gas, though it was promised soon. There is a perception that there are no jobs in Aral'sk, which relates to its peripherality within Kazakhstan. However, Astana is strikingly visible, depicted on billboards around the town and beamed into households in daily TV news – a constant reminder both of Aral'sk's peripherality and of what its residents might aspire to.

I stayed with various families during my fieldwork. My first host-family kept livestock, and my obligations as a guest included feeding the animals, mucking out and keeping dung for fuel. My landlady worked in school administration; my landlord worked informally as a taxi driver. Later I lived with a retired Russian couple, among the few non-Kazakhs left in Aral'sk. On my final trip I lived with a couple who worked as an accountant and a vet. Much of my data from the town comes from conversations with my hosts, their relatives, friends and colleagues, and others I got to know: kitchen conversations over countless bowls of tea while Kazakh or Russian news played in the background. Daily comings and goings of relatives, friends and colleagues spoke of the connections people maintain both within the town and beyond, and the various means of sustaining these relationships: one day we would be drinking beer with a colleague among the tulips on the steppe for 1 May; another day there would be a feast with kin and the Mullah to commemorate a dead relative, involving *bauyrsaq* (fried dough), fried carp, *qazy* (sausage) and the Kazakh speciality *besbarmaq*.

I would travel to the village of Bögen in a rattling Soviet-era bus crammed with sacks of flour, potatoes and other goods. As the bus leaves

Aral'sk, it climbs to the main road above the town, where there is a large cemetery. Everyone wipes their hands over their faces and says *Äumin*, 'Amen'. As the bus joins the main road south, the under-construction Western China to Western Europe highway, modern container lorries thunder past. Freight trains laden with oil snake through the undulating dunes. Apart from the large herding village of Aralqūm, settlements are sparse and small.

A hundred kilometres from Aral'sk, the bus reaches the village of Qamystybas ('reedy lake'), situated by the lake of the same name, which forms part of an extensive delta lake system. Fields of cereals lay here until the eighteenth century, when irrigation channels burst in spring floods and the lakes formed.[9] At Qamystybas, one road branches to the south, towards Raiym, formerly a kolkhoz, which lies between a lake and a steep hill of mud and gravel. At the top of the hill, barely visible, are the traces of a fort built by Tsarist explorers in 1848. A view extends over expanses of interconnected lakes, deep blue amid the yellows and greys of the surrounding steppe. A mud dyke runs across the marshes, placed there by Nikolai Patsha (Tsar Nicholas II), to bring a water pipe to Aral'sk from the Syr Dariya (Figure 0.6). To the south the view extends to Lake Aqshatau, where the *ülken ata* (ancestor) of the Zhaqaiym lineage (*ru*) is buried; descendants from all over the country visit the shrine.

My bus does not go to Raiym, but turns off onto a road along the southern shore of Lake Qamystybas. This road has been tarmacked recently, some say because oil will be extracted. A few hundred metres from the road there are some mud structures: Stalin kolkhoz, established in the 1930s, later abandoned; the structures are the remains of the *zemlianki*, mud huts which passed for housing when Kazakhs were sedentarised. The next stop is Qoszhar, on the shores of Qamystybas, where the state fish-hatchery, established in 1966, hatches valuable carp species. Next the bus arrives in Amanötkel, a large village where livelihoods are based on herding, fishing and some cultivation. This is *syr* country, where the soil is not salty, and is suitable for cattle. Around the sea's northern shores, towards Zhalangash, Tastübek and Aqespe, away from the freshening influence of the river, is arid *qyr* country (Figure 0.7), the land heavily salinised and full of wormwood, suitable pasture for camels.

The bus now heads away from the river and lakes, across rolling steppe. Twenty kilometres from Amanötkel, we pass the eastern end of Lake Tūshchy. Tūshchy was restored as part of the Small Aral restoration project, when weirs along the Syr Dariya were renovated. Until the 1960s millet was grown here, but today around the lake all is bare. Beyond the

Figure 0.6 View towards Raiym from Nikolai Patsha's dyke, spring 2014. The fort was on top of the hill in the distance. Source: author.

Figure 0.7 *Qyr* country near Tastübek, spring 2014. Source: author.

lake the bus drives up a hill into Bögen, a village of 140 houses; from the hill, the traveller would once have seen the sea stretching out to the west. Down the hill there is a war memorial and a shrine to Zhamanköz, the *ülken ata* of a small lineage. The village cemetery is at a high point behind the village, overlooking Tūshchy. At the foot of the hill, the scrubby sand runs down to meet a strip of salinised mud – once the bottom of the harbour. Nearby stands a decrepit compound, once the headquarters of the Bögen State Fishing Base. Today the akimat (mayor's office) stands in this compound. On a wall, the painted Kazakhstan-2030 logo is fading, but a poster depicts the new future which has replaced it, Kazakhstan-2050. Bögen has had electricity since Soviet times; piped water to every household is more recent. In the last few years, phone lines were installed in all villages in the region; mobile connection remains patchy. The main economic activity in Bögen today, as in Soviet times, is fishing. The sea is 12 km away by rough track. The recovery of the fishery since 2005 has brought an influx of money to the village; most villagers now have UAZ jeeps, and many have built new houses.

After Bögen, the crumbling tarmac terminates and the bus will turn to the south, to Qarashalang ('black seaweed'). Beyond Qarashalang the road crosses the river at Aghlaq, where a recently renovated sluice regulates the river flow. In Soviet times, after the sea had been written off, a dam was placed here, so that the trickle of water in the river would water lakes further upstream. Twenty kilometres to the south is Qaratereng ('the black deep'), a large village once lying amid sea, lake and marsh; just a few small lakes remain. Soon after Qaratereng, the gravel track turns west onto the Kökaral dyke towards Aqbasty. To the south, along the former shoreline and on former islands, lie remains of abandoned villages, far from water sources: Ūzyn Qaiyr, Qasqaqūlan, Ūialy. It is three to four hours from Aral'sk to Bögen, depending on weather conditions, and another hour to Qarashalang. Previously, they would all have been connected to Aral'sk by sea – and in Soviet times Bögen, Qaratereng and Ūialy were even connected to Aral'sk by air.

Fishing and daily life

In Bögen, I stayed with Zhaqsylyq, an important figure in the contemporary fishery. His family lives in a large house near the former shoreline. The house looks onto a courtyard, also enclosing the *sarai*, the shed which acts as summer quarters. Zhaqsylyq and his wife Gulzhamal live with their eldest son Zikön and his wife Gulnar, who, as *kelïn* (daughter-in-law), is responsible for most household chores. Two younger unmarried sons also live at home, Maqsat and Mūkhtar. The daughters are all married, most outside Bögen, as is usual in a strictly exogamous society. My access while in the village was predominantly to male worlds.

During fishing seasons, I spent most days accompanying Zhaqsylyq to the receiving-station, observing fish being handed in, chatting to fishermen as they sorted their nets, helping move sacks of fish. Periods of boredom would be spent squatting near the ground eating sunflower seeds (*semechki*), a habit which suspends time. During my first winter, evenings were passed drinking in Zhaqsylyq's *sarai* while fishermen sorted their nets, divided up fish and quizzed me about prices in the UK.

When fishing was impossible in the summer, I was told that fishermen would be 'relaxing'. But apart from the occasional tasty *besbarmaq* of newly fattened lambs, I have seldom spent a less relaxing time than those hot days in Bögen. I was enlisted into building projects: dusty seaweed (*shalang*) had to be gathered from the dried-up seabed (Figure 0.8), which was then laid on the roof as insulation with the collective help (*asar*) of a large group of men, rewarded with a *besbarmaq*; or hundreds of bricks had to be made from sand, clay and reeds in the baking sun while Enrique Iglesias sang from someone's mobile phone.

Early in my fieldwork I watched the process of laying nets (*au salu*) through the ice with Zhaqsylyq's sons and their fellow fishermen: two of their cousins, Bolat and Zhüman; Zhaqsylyq's *bazha* (wife's sister's husband) from Amanötkel, Müsïlïm; and a neighbour, Aikeldï. The day begins as usual with Gulnar waking us with a brusquely repeated *Tūr!* ('Get up!'). After some bread, butter and tea, and after swathing ourselves in layers of clothes, we are off. Zikön drives the UAZ; Müsïlïm, the oldest, sits in the front; the rest of us are crowded into the back,

Figure 0.8 Gathering *shalang* from the dried-up seabed, summer 2013. Source: author.

sitting uncomfortably on a plank which jumps around as we bounce over sand and snow. The air is thick with cigarette smoke, the smell of fish, Kazakh pop music blaring from an MP3, and Russian curses at the discomfort of an extra body in the cramped UAZ. Out on the sea, where it is bitterly cold with a howling wind, we encounter another group of fishermen and there is boisterous discussion. They have just made a hole in the ice, and Maqsat, the youngest brother, offers a little token help shovelling ice out. They tell us that yesterday they were unlucky here. We drive on, and stop about 5 km offshore. The older fishermen have a draught of vodka (Figure 0.9). Everyone except the two youngest brothers discusses where to lay nets.

Most fishermen have a handheld metal bar (*lom*) for breaking the ice, but we have a Soviet-era petrol-powered drill, towed behind the UAZ. Ice is removed from the drill and pole with a petrol-burner. Aikeldï and Zikön drill holes through the 45-cm-thick ice at 20-m intervals. Meanwhile, a long pole has been lowered into the water, and Zhüman manoeuvres it along under the ice with a two-pronged fork (Figure 0.10). A string is attached to the pole, and once this is pulled through, Bolat extracts it with the hook, and Mūkhtar uses it to haul the net through from one hole to the next. The net is a 100-m fixed gillnet, with stones tied to one edge to anchor it. Meanwhile, back at the first hole, Maqsat

Figure 0.9 Warming up for a day's fishing, winter 2013. Source: author.

Figure 0.10 Laying nets, winter 2013. Source: author.

and Müsïlïm feed the net into the water. Maqsat does most of the work; Müsïlïm checks for tangles – as the oldest person, he is not engaged in onerous work. At the fifth hole, the whole net has been hauled through. Maqsat and Mūkhtar plant some sticks in the snow as markers, and tie them to the end of the net with a piece of string. Then the next net is started. The whole process is entirely seamless. No one directs operations. When a net is pulled through, this is communicated with a gesture or shout of *OOO*, or *Boldy!* ('That's it!'). A line of 12 nets, each 100 m long, is laid today, and holes are prepared to lay a further eight tomorrow.

Tangled nets

Such is one mode of engaging with the environment. It involves skill and local knowledge, which is acquired socially through daily embodied engagement with the sea (Knudsen 2008; Pálsson 1994; Vermonden 2013). Though fishing has changed immensely over the years, there is a certain continuity to fishing as a way of life. Fishermen's understandings of the environment, and of environmental change, are grounded in this daily interaction with it, and this description should inform the reading of Chapters 4 and 6. However, this embodied engagement with the environment is just one link in a web of connections linking Aral fish to German consumers and Chinese net manufacturers. Indeed, as Howard (2017) shows in her ethnography of Scottish fishers, daily embodied encounters with the sea are directed and shaped by the shifting opportunities and constraints of capitalist markets. By exploring this web of connections, I will now introduce my approach to the relationship between people, materialities and political economies.

The net is a material technology through which two or three fishermen abstract fish from their marine surroundings. Dependent on these fish for their livelihoods, the fishermen are also tangled in a set of human dependencies. They are dependent on their employers for the right to fish and remuneration (while their employers are dependent, but rather less so, on them to go out and fish). Within Bögen, fishermen's wives and children also depend on fishing for their livelihood, while fishermen depend on female household members for other forms of labour, including preparing some fish for domestic consumption. Fishermen and their families further depend on money from fishing to sustain ritual expenditure.

Beyond Bögen, others depend on fish for a different sort of labour, in processing plants in Aral'sk and Qazaly. Many others, whether or not connected to the fishery, consume fish, incorporating the protein and vitamins into their bodies during shared meals that reproduce relations with friends and family. Though meat is always preferred, my informants would particularly enjoy fatty fish like carp and bream: a carp *besbarmaq* is a local twist on a Kazakh speciality; *qarma* from bream is another local delicacy. Or smoked fish might be eaten with beer, as across the former USSR. However, the market is mostly driven by demand elsewhere in the Commonwealth of Independent States and, for zander, in Germany and Poland. As my Russian host, Aleksandr (Sasha), explained, zander is a 'capitalist fish' because it can be filleted and served in restaurants, while Soviet man (*sovetskii chelovek*) prefers gnawing at smoked bream full of bones. Fish thus link different local worlds – their ecosystem, Bögen, Aral'sk, German supermarkets. These linkages, entangling fish and people in different ways and to different degrees, shape the meaning of environmental change: without the German supermarkets, the sea's return would mean something different.

Thinking about entanglements as the messy mutual dependencies among things and people across different scales (Hodder 2012) helps us move beyond simplistic notions of 'resource dependency'. It also allows us to bring in the agency of the material. The word 'tangle' entered the English language from the Norse word for seaweed, something

INTRODUCTION   25

that entangles technologies such as nets, oars and rudders. There is a pervasive sort of seaweed in the Aral Sea, *shalang*. If possible, fishermen avoid laying their nets where there is *shalang*. However, despite their best efforts, nets move in high winds, and may get tangled in *shalang*. This is what Hodder (2012, 158) calls 'the unruliness of things': they lie beyond the perfect control of humans. The net entangles human relations with natural forces beyond human intentionality. Different processes unfold according to their own logic and at their own tempo, but as they are entangled, they influence each other in contingent ways (Hastrup 2013; 2014; Tsing 2015).

If the net is a monofilament 'Chinese' net, as most are, it was cheap, so can be abandoned. But, tangled up with the *shalang*, it will not decompose. Because of the low price, the temporal span of fishermen's engagement with the net is of a different order from the perdurance of the physical substance of monofilament nylon. It will go on entangling fish, without any human intention, awareness or use.

As Chinese nets accumulate, scientists worry that fish stocks will be depleted. Chinese nets are therefore illegal: unruly in the water, they are an object of regulation out of the water, mediating relations between fishermen and inspectors. However, Chinese nets are no less unruly out of the water than in the water, and go on being used – and abandoned. If fish stocks are depleted, and catches fall, fishermen's income will fall. But the German consumers of Aral fish will simply buy their zander from elsewhere: there are varying degrees of 'tautness' within an entanglement. Even the fishermen would not starve if resources were depleted, as most keep livestock too: their entanglements with the environment are 'dispersed' across livestock and fish (Hodder 2012). Despite widespread use of Chinese nets, fish catches continue to grow in the restored sea, which itself is the contingent, ever-shifting outcome of entangled hydrological, biological and human histories across the whole Aral basin.

Materiality and discourse

Environmental anthropologists use 'entanglement' to break down the nature/culture dichotomy that has dominated Western thought for centuries. By attending to entanglements between different organisms, with their heterogeneous experiences of reality, or 'lifeworlds', we puncture human exceptionalism and decentre the human subject. The ethnography that follows is deeply sympathetic to this project. After all, the fate of the Aral speaks powerfully of what happens when we treat nature as an object that can be subjected to human control. As the description above makes clear, I do not approach the net simply as a piece of technology for mastering nature: by attending to the relational materialities of the net and seaweed, we see how the net entangles fishermen in 'more-than-human' worlds.

Nevertheless, although the insight that everything is entangled decentres the sovereign human subject, I maintain a focus on human discourse. I approach entanglements as not only material but also discursive: through our social utterances, spoken and written, we produce images of the world. These images are consequential – the sea today has been materially shaped by Soviet understandings of nature and global visions of disaster. Discursive entanglements are open-ended, never finalised: objects are 'conceptualized and evaluated variously' (Bakhtin 1981b, 330) within different systems of ideas, seen within different 'horizons'. If Chinese nets are evaluated as an object of regulation in the authoritative discourse of the state, in Aral'sk they are located within a discourse about danger from China. But in fishermen's horizons, they are a matter-of-fact technology, cheap and effective, so they go on being used. These horizons are not fixed: they are themselves inflected with processes of environmental and political-economic change.

I contrast this approach with a passage in Lien's (2015) text that is emblematic of a 'more-than-human' anthropology. Like Aral fishermen, Norwegian salmon farmers have trouble with nets getting fouled up. Lien describes how the function humans ascribe to nets, containment, is frustrated by algae growth, which has to be countered by laying the nets out to dry in the sun:

> The work that the netting performs unfolds instead along the temporal ebb and flow of biofueling (algae growth) and human labor (*tromling*). Each of these heterogeneous practices relies on and enrolls either netting fibers or the sun and wind in order to achieve their opposite futures: a netting that is either lively with algae, relatively impermeable and incompatible with salmon growth, or relatively "dead," permeable and conducive to salmon growth and well-being. (Lien 2015, 59)

While downplaying human agency, Lien talks up the agentive capacities of things by importing the language of human purpose. As her 'view from nowhere' posits a symmetry between human and (anthropomorphised) nonhuman worldmaking capacities, the social is extended to encompass the more-than-human. My concern is that this 'view from nowhere' (itself a site of ethnographic privilege) can risk leaving little space for the subjective lives of our human informants. I would maintain that we can decentre the exceptional human subject while still attending to what it feels like to be human, what is distinctive about human experience, in a world that lies beyond human control. If, then, I take seriously the agentive capacities of things in relation to human lives, I shall be looking at how things exert agency as they are mediated through discourse.

I take the Soviet theorist Bakhtin here as my guide, as a thinker deeply attuned to the materiality of the word, and to the dialogical relationship between human subjects and the world around them.[10] Amid the intellectual ferment of 1920s Leningrad, and the progressive monopolisation of discourse by the Party state over the late 1920s and 1930s, Bakhtin elaborated his ideas about dialogism, the non-finalisability of discourse, the many voices present in every utterance – ideas which resonate with contemporary concerns in environmental anthropology about multiplicity, indeterminacy and polyphony. Indeed, Bakhtin's (1981b, 351) critique of the way scientific discourse approaches things as 'mute objects, brute things' seems to speak of a 'vibrancy' of matter (cf. Bennett 2010). However, where new materialists insist on the autonomy of matter, Bakhtin would insist that there are no unspoken objects. While he is alive to the creative, generative potential within nature, he also sees all nature as dialogically mediated (Last 2013). This is not to propose a discontinuity between the human subject and the material world: rather than taking discourse as a realm of abstract meaning, Bakhtin instead insists on the social and material sitedness of the speaking subject in the world.[11] Between word and world stands the body, which for Bakhtin – as he was well aware from his experiences of disease and disability – is not sealed off from the world as a self-contained entity, but is continuous with it (Hitchcock 1998). If, then, I maintain more focus on speaking subjects than is customary in contemporary environmental anthropology, I approach these subjects as taking shape through their material, bodily encounters with a changing environment, and through their shifting social position within Soviet and post-Soviet political economies.

Chronotopes and political economy

In thinking through how our experience of the world is mediated, I am particularly inspired by Bakhtin's 1937–8 essay on the 'chronotope', where he explores the structuring functions of time and space in narrative (Bakhtin 1981a). Though the essay primarily lays out a monumental history of the novel, I suggest that it also holds a rich potential for linking embodied experiences of entangled lifeworlds, material historical change and discursive representation – domains which are often treated separately within environmental anthropology. Over the course of the essay, Bakhtin explores how the various constellations of space and time in narrative do not merely make up the background setting for action, but produce different kinds of person, different possibilities for action, different forms of causality – and, what has been little remarked upon, different conceptions of nature. Thus, in one passage, he shows how eighteenth- and nineteenth-century novels oppose an idyllic, particularised space and time that generates an organic connection between persons and nature, to 'a great but abstract world, where people are out of contact with each other, egotistically sealed-off from each other, greedily practical, where labor is differentiated and mechanized, where objects are alienated from the labor that produced them' (Bakhtin 1981a, 234). This opposition is echoed in Chapter 4, where I contrast fishermen's narratives structured around the abstractions of Soviet plans with those structured around *tughan zher*, or homeland.

However, the relevance of Bakhtin's essay to environmental anthropology goes beyond the structuring role of time and space in representation. In a tantalising footnote, Bakhtin (1981a, 84, n. 1) informs us that he came across the chronotope in 1925 in a lecture by the biologist Ukhtomsky. For Ukhtomsky, living organisms experience time and space variously, which defines how they perceive and act upon their environment (Chebanov 2015). Fascinated by contemporary advances in biology, Bakhtin was evidently deeply struck by Ukhtomsky's take on Einsteinian ideas about relativity. If, as he tells us in a second footnote, Bakhtin (1981a, 85, n. 2) takes time and space as 'forms of the most immediate reality', he seems to be suggesting that reality is relative, encountered heterogeneously through different bodies' diverse experiences of time and space. The resonances with contemporary anthropology's attention to heterogeneous lifeworlds are striking.[12]

What the essay brings to this literature is the role of political economy, not only reordering times and spaces, but, in doing so, restructuring embodied experiences of reality. Crucially, the Ukhtomsky-derived time and space as the 'forms of the most immediate reality' and the cultural representations Bakhtin tracks in the novel are connected through processes of material historical change that, as they reorder time–space constellations, reconstitute persons, labour, nature and value. The increasing abstraction of time, space and nature, Bakhtin shows, accompanies the growth of class society.[13]

Bakhtin was no stranger to such processes of historical change. Before writing his chronotope essay, he had been exiled to Kazakhstan, where he had worked as an economist in a District Consumers' Union and in 1934 had written an article, very different from his more famous work, about growth in consumer demand among newly collectivised farm workers (Bakhtin 2019; cf. Balysheva 2019). In the early 1930s, kolkhozy were just emerging from devastating famine brought about by the violent integration of Kazakhs into Soviet gridded space during collectivisation. My informants' parents and grandparents lived through this same period, expected to provide the state with ever greater quantities of fish while their livestock were confiscated and grain provisioning collapsed. Unsurprisingly, Bakhtin did not write about the famine in his article about growth in consumer demand. Nor, however, did he celebrate the successes of collectivisation, and, reading between the lines of his text, the abject state of kolkhozniks is plain to see.

In his chronotopes essay written later in that tumultuous decade, Bakhtin speaks of his hero Rabelais's healthy chronotope of organic growth based on direct proportionality of body, world and value, where things were brought into organic relation with one another. In doing so, the Renaissance writer challenged official medieval versions of the world based on 'false connections that distort the authentic nature of things', on 'false hierarchical relationships' between objects and ideas (Bakhtin 1981a, 169). There are evident historical echoes with Bakhtin's own time, when hierarchies of value were being established that prioritised quantitative growth of commodities abstracted from lifeworld entanglements.

What I take from this is that within heterogeneous orderings of time and space, the world emerges as multiple – but that not all 'versions' are equal, nor are all equally true. To relate this insight to contemporary environmental anthropology, modernist abstractions of nature as a manipulable domain of discrete entities, and of human bodies as fungible units of labour, misrepresent lifeworld entanglements (recall Tsing's [2015, 5] phrase on abstraction cited above, 'as if the entanglements of living did not matter') – but these abstractions, their dominance reproduced by powerful interests, are materially consequential, reshaping natural environments and human relations with them. While multiple versions of the Aral emerge in the ethnography that follows, some have emerged out of 'false connections that distort the nature of things', and they have jostled awkwardly against one another as powerful interests have dictated which version has more capacity to exist (cf. Richardson 2014). I shall therefore pay particular attention to political economy, to how, as the Soviet plan and post-Soviet market variously order times and spaces, fish are abstracted as different kinds of value, both misrepresenting their watery entanglements with the marine environment and materially reshaping them.[14] It is to the fishery that I now turn.

Approaching environmental change through the fishery

Running throughout this book is the story of how environmental change has been entangled in the history of the fishing industry, whose demise and rebirth have not mapped neatly onto the water levels in the sea. Building on the approach outlined above, my account of the fishery will be attentive both to the materiality of fish and to the structuring role of political economy.

As fish are invisible beneath the water, it is hard for humans to lay claims to ownership before they are extracted. Once out of the water, they are quick to spoil. So there is a certain immediatism about fish, connected with the here and now, as testified in the Kazakh proverb *egenshï zhylda armanda, balyqshy künde armanda*, 'the sower dreams for the year, the fisherman dreams for the day'. In the past, and to some extent today, there is therefore a sort of hunter-gatherer attitude towards fish, in contrast to livestock. Sometimes when I went to Bögen, my hosts in Aral'sk would encourage me to demand fish from Zhaqsylyq. Sometimes this worked. Sometimes I would be met with a *Balyq zhoq*, 'no fish' – even when I was confident that this was not the case. But Zhaqsylyq had no connection with my hosts in Aral'sk, and no obligation to give them fish. They would never ask me to bring back meat from the village. When I asked Zhaqsylyq if I could *buy* fish from him, he was adamant that I could not. This seems to bear some relation to the hunter-gatherer ethic of claiming shares in environments of natural abundance.[15] Myers (1988) relates how he became frustrated with this ethic among the Pintupi as they constantly demanded cigarettes from him; he only managed to keep his cigarettes when one helpful Pintupi told him to hide them. I suspect something similar was going on with Zhaqsylyq's *balyq zhoq*.

The same material features also mean that, in Soviet times and today, fish are closely associated with money. As one young fisherman declared as he pointed to a heap of fish on the ice: *Bïzge balyq aqsha!*, 'Fish are money for us!' (Figure 0.11). Like money, they are impersonal and fungible. Moreover, because they are quick to spoil, integration into wider time-spaces than the here and now – becoming scalable – requires some sort of 'time machine' (Lien 2015, 120–4), involving salt, ice and

Figure 0.11 'Fish are money', winter 2013. Source: author.

processing infrastructure.[16] In Aral'sk in particular, then, fish are associated with factory labour, mostly here female. Finally, invisible in the water, fish are also hard to pin down once out of the water: in an extensive landscape of sea, lakes and marsh with few roads, fisheries are hard to regulate. Another proverb plays on this tension: *balyqshy aitpaidy rasyn, künde alady bir asym*, 'the fisherman does not tell the truth, every day he takes a portion'. Indeed, lots of actors, not only fishermen, are creative in their accounting of fish. Within the command economy, this opacity further undermined centralised control, while today it shapes the movement of fish so that they largely bypass Aral'sk.

Within both state socialism and capitalism, natural resources, and the time-space within which they circulate, are homogenised. Both plans and market exchange require the commodification of nature: diverse natural objects are abstracted from their ecosystemic contexts as numbers, so that they are commensurable (Carrier 2001). As commodities, fish are arranged in a hierarchy of value that bears no relation to their lifeworld entanglements. This hierarchy of value also shapes fishing practices: as labour is commodified, the intentionality of embodied engagement with the environment is directed towards maximising value extraction (Howard 2017). However, plan and market organise materialities differently, which has consequences for what the sea's retreat and partial return have come to mean. To return to our net: in Soviet times, generally seine nets were used, which were much more selective. They involved different social relations, as they required more people to lay them; and they materialised a connection with the state, in the form of the local fishery managers, who provided equipment. The connection to the state was crucial: social entitlements depended on the practice of fishing. As we will see, the partial capacity of the creaking structures of the command economy to hold this set of relationships together afforded a level of continuity even when the sea disappeared. In this economy, money had less pressing value, so, despite rewards for overfulfilling plans, there was no strong incentive to fish without limit. This contrasts with the present, where, in the absence of the state as an 'over-arching structure of connection' (Alexander 2004, 271), money acquires increasing value, creating high incentives to fish. Moreover, the circulation of fish out of the water differs within the plan and within the market: the fishery sustained by the gridded time-space of the USSR once supported a major processing plant in Aral'sk itself, but today, within the flexible, opaque time-space of the contemporary market, fish largely bypass factories in Aral'sk, frustrating widespread hopes of a return of employment.

This is not to claim that the meanings of the sea's demise and partial return can be reduced to its political-economic entanglements. But amid the multiplicity that I will describe, I will afford a structuring significance to the point that it was a socialist sea that receded and a postsocialist sea that has returned.

Outline of chapters

The first four chapters explore the sea's regression. In Chapter 1, I weave a narrative from secondary and archival sources about colonial and Soviet transformations of the Aral Sea itself, and the wider Aral basin. I locate the Aral regression in a century of catastrophes, involving dispossession, disaster and development: interdependencies of people and environments were reshaped as cotton, water and fish were enrolled in colonial and Soviet visions and, ultimately, integrated into gridded Soviet space. Chapter 2 looks at how the sea's regression emerged as a bureaucratic 'problem', and the resultant efforts to mitigate it, especially by importing ocean fish and sending fishermen to other lakes. In Chapter 3 we see how these efforts inflect perspectives in Aral'sk today: in nostalgic memories of gridded Soviet space, ocean fish are felt to have sustained relations between Aral'sk and the centre, while 'bad' Soviet pasts are partitioned off. Chapter 4 turns to the meanings of the sea's regression in Aral villages, which I locate in the broader history of transformation of understandings of nature. I show how hunter-gatherer ethics about fish are overlaid with visions of fish as exchange-values, and a discourse of homeland (*tughan zher*) oscillates with one based on labour and abstract space – with implications for understandings of the regression.

The three final chapters examine how the sea has been restored, and its divergent outcomes. Chapter 5 shows how the Aral disaster became an object for international development, culminating (though not inevitably) in the restoration of the Small Aral. The chapter tells a story of post-Soviet transformation that foregrounds the lively contributions of nonhuman actors, from flounder and mussels to wind, sand and concrete, to processes of 'hegemonic fragmentation and reconstruction' (Brandtstädter 2007). Chapter 6 shows how entanglements of restored environment, postsocialist property rights and regulations, and lucrative but opaque markets shape the extraction and circulation of fish, driving new-found prosperity and socioeconomic differentiation in Bögen. Fish, I argue, are both reproducing and transforming moral landscapes and local structures of value. As fish bypass Aral'sk, Chapter 7 explores the marginality of the fisheries to the town, and its economic marginality within Kazakhstan today. Economic marginalisation, I show, intersects with *ekologiia* as environmental affect to shape local subjectivities. Finally, the Conclusion draws out the multiplicity of environmental change, before critically relating my ethnography to theories of adaptation, and to the wider anthropology of the Anthropocene.

Notes

1 See Glantz (1999a), Kostianoy and Kosarev (2010), Micklin (1988; 2000; 2007), Micklin et al. (2014), Weinthal (2002) and Zonn et al. (2009) for some of the vast academic output on the issue.
2 Used in formal writing about the Aral, *apat* means 'accident' or 'disaster'.
3 While ethnographers are well placed to draw out the processual quality of disasters like floods and earthquakes (e.g. Hoffman and Oliver-Smith 2002; Simpson 2013), we should nevertheless distinguish between what is materially experienced as a temporally bounded event and environmental change whose material effects are themselves processual.
4 Brown (2015, Chapter 6) introduces the phrase 'gridded space' in her comparison of Soviet Qaraghandy (Kazakhstan) and Billings (USA). While the metaphor stems from the similar urban layout of the two towns, Brown deploys it to talk about how space – and time – are abstracted, commodified and carved up into discrete, exploitable units. In her account, which focuses on the early Soviet period, gridded infrastructures facilitate the flow of resources to

the centre; as I elaborate in Chapter 2, in the postwar period they would also facilitate the redistribution of resources by the centre.

5   My project is geographically limited. The Uzbek (Karakalpak) shore is particularly marginal within contemporary Uzbekistan. In Soviet times, there were similar processes of importing ocean fish and sending fishermen to other lakes there (Karimov et al. 2005; Karimov et al. 2009). Recent efforts to restore Amu Dariya delta lakes and wetlands have been reasonably effective, but less so than the Kökaral dam (Karimov et al. 2005; Micklin 2014b). Environmental problems are of course not restricted to the sea itself: throughout Central Asia, continued use of monoculture is linked to ongoing environmental degradation.

6   During my fieldwork more than 20 years after Kazakhstani independence, I still found 'post-Soviet' a relevant category. Although trajectories across Central Asia have been diverse, and although the category makes less sense to a younger generation, social, political and natural landscapes are still heavily marked by Soviet legacies. While Ibañez-Tirado (2015) argues that such a label risks casting the region as temporally other, I hope that this charge is evaded through my attention to the Aral's contemporary integration into transnational markets and independent Kazakhstan's state-building processes. Indeed, given the historical amnesia of Kazakhstan's elites, it is important to stress continuities with the near past. I concur with Trevisani's (2014) proposal of a 'second phase' of postsocialism: after the disintegration of state socialism in the 1990s, something new has been built, albeit influenced by Soviet legacies.

7   Kazakhstan-2050 is supposed to involve a transition to a 'green economy', based on market mechanisms like pricing and regulation of common-pool resources, and diversification away from oil (Brown 2014).

8   In 2019, Astana was renamed Nūr-Sūltan in honour of the recently retired president, Nursultan Nazarbayev.

9   Director of the scientific fisheries station V. O. Kochkarev, 'Otchët o gidrotekhnicheskom obsledovanii rybougodii pri ust'e reki Syr-Dar'i', 19 June 1930, Aral'skii filial gosudarstvennogo arkhiva Kyzylordinskoi oblasti [hereafter AFGAKO], f. 5, o. 1, d. 1, ll. 70–87.

10 Despite the materiality of Bakhtin's thought and his focus on the body, Bakhtinian approaches within anthropology are often restricted to linguistic anthropology (e.g. Blommaert 2015; Smith 2004). Cruikshank (1998) draws on Bakhtin to oppose the dialogic quality of oral narratives about the environment with the monologic discourse of the state, but her focus remains on discourse itself. In the wider social sciences, there have been some attempts to think with Bakhtin about environmental change and political ecology (Gardiner 1993; Hitchcock 1998; Last 2013; Sandywell 2000), but these remain underdeveloped.

11 If some new materialist approaches downplay discourse, this arguably relates to the association of language with a realm of abstract meaning where human intentions are negotiated, which ironically risks reinscribing the mind/matter dualism that such approaches (rightly) seek to overcome.

12 Chebanov (2015) notes the connection between Ukhtomsky and Uexküll's notion of Umwelt, which has been influential in the development of multispecies ethnography (e.g. Ingold 2000; Tsing 2015).

13 Cf. Hornborg's (1996) suggestive connection between Polanyian 'disembedding' of economy from society and the separation of nature and society. Cf. also Thompson's (1967) arguments about a shift from 'task-oriented time' to 'industrial time'.

14 New materialist and historical materialist approaches are sometimes presented as if they have to be in competition (e.g. Bennett 2010, xv–xvi). It does not have to be so: Tsing (2015) masterfully integrates the structuring work of alienation of both persons and things into a thick description of 'indeterminate assemblages', while Li's (2014) fine-grained account of shifting class relations among Indonesian highlanders includes in the analysis of the conjuncture close attention to materialities of different sorts of trees.

15 Similar ethics of sharing fish are found in various cultural contexts: northern Russia (Nakhshina 2011), the Canadian Cree (Berkes 1987), Somalia (Dua 2017), southern India (Hoeppe 2007, Chapter 5).

16 Lien (2015) describes how canning processes of wild Alaskan salmon and desiccated anchovy pellets to feed farmed Norwegian salmon both act as 'time machines' that make production 'scalable'.

1

The Aral Sea and the modernisation of Central Asia: a century of catastrophes

Accounts of modernist destruction of environments often assume that premodern nature existed in equilibrium. Such is also the case with the Aral Sea: 'And the Aral lived its natural life, practically undisturbed by man's interference, until 1960' (Kosarev and Kostianoy 2010b, 46). Yet, in 2001, a medieval mausoleum was discovered on the dried-up seabed, providing clear evidence that the Aral had receded before (Oberhänsli et al. 2007). Geographers and scientists had suspected this since the nineteenth century, and, as we will see in Chapter 4, local people have long been aware of it. This wider temporal perspective troubles assumptions about 'man's interference' in premodern pristine nature.

The Aral Sea first emerged a mere ten to twenty thousand years ago, the blink of an eye in geological time, when the Amu Dariya happened to change course towards a shallow dip caused by wind erosion two million years earlier (Zonn et al. 2009, 21, 27). Throughout its existence, the sea's level has varied, and several times the diversion of the Amu Dariya into the Caspian via the Uzboi channel has led to major regressions comparable to today's, the most recent ending only in the mid-seventeenth century. Archaeologists debate the causes, but four factors have been involved: climate, earthquakes, irrigation, and wartime destruction of dykes – notably by Genghis Khan in the early thirteenth century, then by Timur in the late fourteenth century. Evidently, since the advent of irrigation in the region some three thousand years ago, the landscape has been profoundly shaped by human interventions. Indeed, the area of irrigated land in antiquity was comparable to that today (Oberhänsli et al. 2007).

Over the millennia, then, the lives of those living by the sea have been affected by distant happenings elsewhere in the Aral basin. Even in the nineteenth century, the level fluctuated by several metres, fuelling theories that the whole of Eurasia was drying up (Kropotkin 1904). In part, this chapter offers a genealogy of the processes, far upstream from the sea itself, which culminated in its twentieth-century regression, processes rooted in histories of Tsarist colonialism and Soviet socialism, and also in the global history of cotton.[1]

If the sea itself has never been stable, nor have societies around it. I also therefore present an overlapping narrative, centred on fish, of the reshaping of social and environmental relations around the northern shores of the Aral, from the beginnings of Russian colonial rule to 1960, when the sea started to dry up. These transformations are crucial for understanding what the sea's regression would come to mean. I put these two stories in the same interpretive frame, as two strands of the modernisation of Central Asia. Across imperial and Soviet Central Asia, there are homologous histories of dispossession. The sea's regression was another episode in what might be termed a century of catastrophes. Peoples were deemed backward, and landscapes empty or wasteful. Beginning in the imperial period and accelerating under Soviet rule, human–environment relations were reorganised to make agricultural production 'scalable' (Tsing 2015). The promises of modernity rested on the quantitative increase in production of fungible commodities by fungible human labour, while new infrastructural connections integrated the region into wider imperial/Soviet space. As people came to live 'gridded lives' (Brown 2015), their dependency on their environment was mediated by a matrix linking them to the centre via flows of goods to and from it.[2]

However, the precise form that modernisation processes took depended on the diverse environments and societies that imperial and Soviet administrators encountered, from the pastoralists of the steppe, desert and mountains to the settled agriculturalists along the rivers and in the oases. The stories told here, of irrigation development and fisheries construction, may be homologous, but the heterogeneous material conditions, offering variable possibilities for scalability, shaped development in different ways. Nor was each afforded equal weight. As in many modernist visions, mastering water particularly captured both imperial and Soviet imaginations (Obertreis 2017; Peterson 2019). Development was therefore premised on irrigation projects, dams and canals. Beyond the massive Aral basin, there were plans, only dropped in the perestroika period, to bring the Siberian rivers Ob' and Enisei to Central Asia (Bressler 1995).

These parallel stories about irrigation and fish diverged after the sea began to shrink in 1960: while irrigation expansion continued, the fishery contracted. We pick up the story of the contracting fishery in Chapter 2. Later in the present chapter, however, I will ask why irrigation continued to grow even after its escalating consequences were evident. While it may seem to be an instance of the high modernist myopia described by Scott (1998) – seeing like a state – I root this myopia more specifically in a political ecology of state socialism in Central Asia.[3] This entails a broader interpretation of Central Asia's place in the USSR. As the underdeveloped Central Asian periphery produced primary commodities (especially cotton) cheaply for processing in the centre, where living standards were higher, some scholars at the time of the USSR's demise, picking up on interpretations by Central Asian intellectuals, characterised the relationship as colonialism or dependency (Gleason 1991; Rumer 1989). What this perspective misses is the patronage relations both between republican elites and central leadership, and throughout Central Asian society (Kandiyoti 2002; Spoor 1993; Weinthal 2002). It also misses the (albeit limited) redistribution by the centre, and the concomitant enrolment of local populations in Soviet visions. I therefore suggest that we recast 'dependency' as a web of interdependencies of varying tautness, which resulted in spatially uneven rates of development, and uneven distribution of vulnerability to ecological damage (cf. Hodder 2012).

From nomads to fishers

Kazakhs first came to the sea's northern shores in the eighteenth century, deprived of access to their pastures by Russian and Dzungar incursions, and driving the Karakalpaks who were living there to the south (Jacquesson 2002). Though Kazakhs, like their predecessors, practised some small-scale irrigated agriculture and fishing on rivers and lakes, the economy centred on livestock (Khazanov 2012; Tolybekov 1959, 95–6). In a decentralised political ecology, constant movement allowed flexibility in negotiating the changing environment, a flexibility that helped mitigate crises such as drought or *zhūt*, late-spring frosts that trapped fodder below a crust of ice (Campbell 2018). Like agriculture, fishing was subsidiary, practised by the poor, those with few or no livestock. Fish, unlike livestock, were not a source of prestige. It is unclear to what extent fish caught on the Aral's northern shores were marketed in Central Asian cities far to the south, but without processing infrastructure, it seems unlikely that they were a source of accumulation of wealth.[4] A proverb testifies to what fish meant in this economy: *balyqshynyng bailyghy etek zhengï kepkenshe*, 'the fisherman's wealth lasts until his sleeve dries'. Livestock brought wealth and power; fish were about sustenance and immediate return. Nor did fishing require the careful husbandry of scarce resources that livestock demanded. *Aulau*, 'to fish' or 'to hunt', derives from the noun *au*, 'trap/net'. When they fished, employing basic technologies, Kazakhs encountered natural abundance, lakes and rivers teeming with fish.[5]

Russian interest in the northern Aral was, initially, military. A fort was built above Lake Raiym in 1847 when the naval officer Butakov conducted an exploration of the sea. Next, a fort was built at Qazaly (Kazalinsk), the starting point for a gradual advance up the Syr Dariya. This culminated in the capture of Tashkent in 1865, a key moment in Russian expansion into Central Asia. Although Russian eyes were focused on the rich settled lands to the south, the Russian presence on the lower Syr Dariya and around the northern Aral had immediate consequences for local inhabitants. Russian settlers, themselves fleeing upheavals in Russian agriculture, were encroaching on the best pastures. Tsarist policy cast them as a progressive force in the 'backward' economy of the steppe.[6] This resulted in dispossession of local Kazakhs: as migration routes were curtailed, the fragile economy of nomadic life was disrupted and livestock numbers fell (Beknazarov 2010, 39–40). As Cameron (2018) describes, settler incursions rendered Kazakhs more vulnerable to climate variability, and increasingly dependent on Russian grain. Increasingly, winter quarters were established around Russian forts. After a *zhūt* in 1879–80 and again in 1892–3, increasing numbers of impoverished Kazakhs settled along the Syr Dariya, turning to fishing for survival (Tolybekov 1959, 299–300).

When the Tsarist authorities deported rebellious Ural Cossacks to the region in 1875, they brought new technologies for catching, smoking and curing fish, especially ship sturgeon (Pianciola 2019; see Figure 1.1). Increasingly, Kazakhs began to fish for the market, and fish were exported overland by caravan in winter to the railhead at Orenburg (Beknazarov 2010, 31; Plotnikov et al. 2014, 56). Partially integrated into a market stretching across the whole Russian empire, the sea acquired a new sort of economic value. Integration into imperial space, and thus value, depended on infrastructure that could overcome the perishability of fish, so Russian industrialists opened ice houses and plants for smoking and curing Aral fish, taking advantage of nearby salt deposits.[7] Those Kazakhs who were dispossessed of livestock had little choice but to subscribe to this vision of fish as value, and were increasingly hired to fish for Cossacks.

As the fishery grew, the Tsarist authorities recognised the need for science-based management to guarantee the future of the sea's resources.

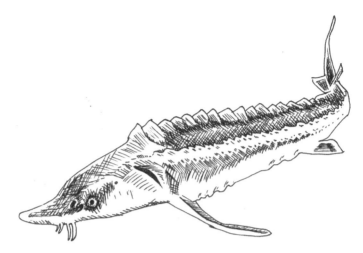

Figure 1.1 Ship sturgeon. Drawing by Amelia Abercrombie, after Zenkevich (1956).

From 1886, access was regulated by permits; there was a banned zone around the Syr Dariya delta and bans on fishing during spawning season (Plotnikov et al. 2014, 56). Cossacks mediated the generation of environmental knowledge: science-backed regulation focused on sturgeon (Figure 1.2), the key fish of interest to the Cossacks, while Kazakhs and Karakalpaks were pushed into 'cognitive irrelevance' (Pianciola 2019, 629). Nevertheless, rich scientific studies emerged, notably the monumental monograph of L. S. Berg (1908), which detailed the sea's geology, hydrology, flora and fauna, as well as exploring the oscillations in sea level and opposing the widespread theory of the ongoing desiccation of Eurasia. As Pianciola (2019, 667) suggests, the authority that administrators granted to scientific knowledge perhaps rested, paradoxically, on the Aral's relative political and economic marginality within imperial projects.

A crucial moment in the fishery's development was the construction in 1905–6 of the Orenburg–Tashkent railway, which passes the sea's northeastern corner, where the sheltered Saryshyghanaq bay was deemed a suitable site for a port. The station was named *Aral'skoe more* (Ru.: 'Aral Sea'), and a village grew between station and sea. The railway opened new markets, and catches rose rapidly. The railway also dramatically expanded the fishing population, facilitating widespread immigration from western parts of the empire, especially the Danube delta and the Sea of Azov. Intensive fishing severely undermined fragile attempts at regulation (Pianciola 2019). On the eve of the First World

Figure 1.2 Aral Sea fishermen with some vast sturgeon, c. 1900. Source: Museum of Fishermen, Aral'sk.

War, some 15,000 were working in the industry, and 44,000–50,000 tonnes of fish were caught and exported from the region annually.[8] First the market, then the railway: both reconfigured human entanglements with the sea. As fish integrated local populations into imperial markets, new dependencies emerged. Fishermen were advanced equipment and food, in return for handing over all their catch to pay off the debt. A 1968 book celebrating the glorious construction of the Soviet fishery waxes lyrical about colonial oppression: 'And the family of the fisherman-Kazakh struggled in hopeless destitution, entangled in debts like a fish in a net' (Turmagambetov et al. 1968, 1).

Cotton famine, cotton fever

Meanwhile, a vision was taking shape centred on water and cotton, which decades later would be consequential for the sea. Though its roots dated to the 1820s, distant events gave it fresh impetus in the 1860s. As the American Civil War starved global markets of raw cotton, cotton manufacturing across the world was devastated by 'cotton famine' (Beckert 2014, 140). The crisis sparked swathes of accumulation by dispossession across the globe. The British, whose Lancashire mills were paralysed, began to turn over swathes of their empire, especially India, to cotton cultivation; driven away from subsistence farming, primary producers became vulnerable to the vicissitudes of the global market, and to extreme climate events, resulting in devastating famines later in the nineteenth century (Davis 2001, Chapter 10; cf. Beckert 2014, Chapter 9).

Russian industrialists and administrators keen to secure the empire's cotton independence looked to the warm lands of newly colonised Central Asia (Obertreis 2017; Peterson 2019).[9] As in other expanding European empires, colonial eyes saw indigenous people as backward and the landscape as wasted. Indeed, ruined irrigation systems spoke of a region which had gone backwards from its medieval glories (Voeikov 1949b [1908], 157). The dream of turning the Amu Dariya again to the Caspian offered the opportunity both to connect Europe and Asia by water, and to restore the region's glory through irrigation (Peterson 2019). Scientific theory supported this vision: the geographer Voeikov (1949a [1909], 149) argued that 'Man must strive to ensure that water, when it evaporates, performs work that is useful for him, i.e. that it evaporates from the surface of plants'. Flowing into the sea, water was wasted. The Aral's area could therefore be drastically reduced, if the water was used 'usefully' instead (Voeikov 1949b [1908]).

However, while colonial reforms undermined indigenous irrigation practices, Tsarist dreams of expanding irrigated area came to little: only two major irrigation works were completed, and the amount of water withdrawn from the Amu and Syr Dariya did not increase dramatically (Peterson 2019; Thurman 1999). Even so, amid 'cotton fever', the area cultivated with cotton grew and raw cotton exports from Central Asia to Russia increased dramatically. Central Asian farmers became entangled in debts, and the best irrigated lands were appropriated (Joffe 1995; Peterson 2019). Nevertheless, even at this stage, cotton was not just a colonial imposition: Penati (2013) stresses the active involvement of Central Asian entrepreneurs and farmers in the cotton boom.[10] Meanwhile, the sea acquired significance as a shipping route, linking the cotton-growing regions of Karakalpakstan to textiles factories in European Russia via the railway at Aral'sk.

Soviet dreams in Central Asia

Rapid growth in both fish and cotton production was abruptly halted by distant events again reverberating across the globe. Integrated into

Russian imperial space, dependent on imperial markets, the Aral region was vulnerable to the implosion of that space during world war, revolution and civil war. The fishery rapidly unravelled as provisioning collapsed, fishermen were conscripted into the army, and hastily built infrastructure crumbled. The stressed populations of sturgeon were, for now, saved, while the human populations around the sea faced famine (Pianciola 2019; 2020). Upstream, irrigation systems fell into disrepair and the area of irrigated land halved.

The Bolsheviks in Central Asia blended Tsarist visions with their own emancipatory and anti-colonial agenda (Obertreis 2017; Peterson 2019; Teichmann 2007). Colonialism, they supposed, had exacerbated backwardness. In exploiting the wealth of the Aral to the full, men and women were to be freed from the bonds of debt and exploitation. Upstream, conquering nature through mastering water was at the heart of the Bolshevik decolonising vision (Peterson 2019; Teichmann 2007). However, another logic would crystallise during collectivisation: value created in agriculture would subsidise the industrialisation of the USSR as a whole, termed 'primitive socialist accumulation' (Spoor 1993). Central Asia remained, as in Tsarist times, a producer of agricultural commodities that would flow to the centre, a status that was in sharp tension with the anti-colonial vision (Peterson 2019; Teichmann 2007). Indeed, across the USSR, the promised utopia of industrial abundance, premised on the scalable production of commodities, came to override other utopian goals. Voices for nature conservation that had been present in the 1920s were silenced (Weiner 1988). Thus, because of decisions favouring modernisation by industrialisation, Buck-Morss (2002, 115) argues, 'the Soviets missed the opportunity to transform the very idea of economic "development" and of the ecological preconditions through which it might be realised.' Development, directed by the centre, was to proceed at maximum scale, entailing new forms of dispossession. In Tsing's (2015) terms, entangled lifeworlds were destroyed to make way for scalable monocultures.

The consequences of this shift in policy for Central Asian irrigation, and thus, ultimately, for the Aral, are well documented. Previously, irrigation systems had been decentralised, access to water embedded in a range of social relations. After collectivisation, plans were dictated by the centre, and cotton monoculture displaced old patterns of crop rotation which had guaranteed food security and improved soil productivity (Micklin 2000; Peterson 2019; Teichmann 2007). With the completion of the Turksib railway in 1929, Central Asia was provisioned with Siberian grain, allowing more irrigated land to be devoted to cotton.

Despite promises of mechanisation, as Peterson (2019) stresses, irrigation projects were achieved chaotically through the mass deployment of forced labour. Deportations of enemy peoples (Pohl 2007) and, later, resettlements from mountain regions (Bichsel 2012; Loy 2006) also brought people to work on the reclaimed land. In this matrix, flows of water, cotton and labour were directed by the apparatus.

Scalability under state socialism, and its ruinous ecological and social consequences, has a different dynamic from its capitalist variant. Indeed, Fehér, Heller and Márkus (1983, 65) argued that the goal-function of state socialist economies was not, as under capitalism, profit, but 'the maximization of the volume of the material means (as use-values) under the global disposition of the apparatus of power as a whole'. Scaling up the resources under the control of the apparatus took priority over scaling up production of exchange-values. Legitimacy was based on the countervailing tendency to redistribute, but, as this would diminish the power of the apparatus, these tendencies were in tension (Verdery 1996). Furthermore, different branches of the apparatus identified with their sector or region, as the source of their power, and competed to expand their allocated share of scarce resources by expanding their economic activity (Kornai 1980). This led to huge-scale development, as in the giant steel complex at Magnitogorsk (Kotkin 1995). In agriculture, there was a tendency towards centralisation and monoculture, regardless of economic efficiency or ecological sustainability (Weiner 1999, 15–16). As Wittfogel (1957) saw, because water flows, and can be manipulated, the urge to accumulate material assets could be satisfied by constantly expanding irrigation infrastructure (Wheeler 2019). Irrigation offered the opportunity to reshape landscapes so that fixed assets, agricultural output and the labour of millions of people were under the control of the apparatus.[11]

Nevertheless, the apparent rationality of the grid was belied by chaos on the ground. Control was, *pace* Wittfogel (1957), incomplete: as in modernisation processes the world over, it was belied by the unruliness of things and people involved. State power was limited both by local ecologies and by the recalcitrance of the local population, and projects proceeded more by improvisation than by planning (Teichmann 2018). Indeed, cotton yields only recovered from the shock of collectivisation when the level of coercion dropped: the resultant system was premised on complicity, so that informally arranged 'accidents' and 'inefficiencies' would provide enough water for personal plots (Teichmann 2007). Meanwhile, irrigation projects, delivered by mass manual labour, were built with rudimentary technologies. Though the effects were not immediately evident, high losses to evaporation and seepage meant that large volumes of water that might have reached the sea were wasted.

Yet, despite the chaos and coercion, cotton became integral to Central Asian imaginings of modernity. As Peterson (2019) describes, propaganda cast 'people's construction projects' like the Great Ferghana Canal as popular initiatives based on the Central Asian institution of *hashar*, the collective labour of the people propelling the region into modernity. Proliferating technical water management cadres were indigenised, and Central Asian elites at all levels acquired an interest in irrigation and cotton (Obertreis 2017). The First Party Secretary of Uzbekistan mobilised Voeikov's theories for a patriotic socialism: 'We cannot resign ourselves to the fact that the water-abundant Amudarya River carries its waters to the Aral Sea without any use, while our lands in the Samarkand and Bukhara regions are insufficiently irrigated' (cited in Zonn 1999, 159). The task, he said, was 'to bridle the Syrdarya and Amudarya rivers, to control them and to make their water serve the cause of socialism, for the purpose of raising the living standards of the population and developing the country' (cited in Zonn 1999, 159). If steel represented the urbanist values of the USSR as a whole (Kotkin 1995), cotton represented development for much of Central Asia. As the state-socialist social contract took shape, compliance was secured by the promise of rising living standards and full employment (Verdery 1996), a promise that came to be imagined through cotton. This was a web of dependencies more complex than the flow of raw resources from periphery to centre.

Constructing a socialist fishery

Meanwhile related, but distinct, processes were playing out in the fisheries. During the 1920s, the fishing industry was gradually rebuilt. In 1925, the Aral State Fishery Trust, Aralgosrybtrest, was established, its aims to harness the natural wealth of the sea and emancipate local people. Aralgosrybtrest provided credit for cooperatives to create independent fishermen, albeit bound to the state by debt.[12] These cooperatives also engaged in salting and cottage production of smoked fish, and, in one case, in melioration work on a lake, which, according to the umbrella organisation of cooperatives, Aralrybaksoiuz, fishermen did enthusiastically.[13] By 1930, catches were approaching their prewar peak (see Figure 1.3). But there was little centralised control: Aralgosrybtrest managers competed with Aralrybaksoiuz for fish; and semi-nomadic fishermen were liable to migrate away from the sea in spring.[14]

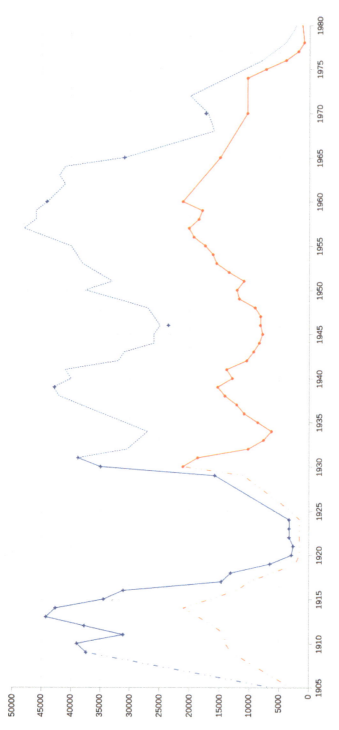

Figure 1.3 Fish catches, tonnes, in whole Aral Sea (blue), of which catches in the northern (Kazakh) part of the sea (red), 1905–80. Prepared by the author. The dashed lines (whole sea 1905–9; northern part 1905–30) mark informed estimates. Notice the timings of the four catastrophic falls in catches: the First World War, collectivisation, the Second World War and the sea's regression. See Appendix for sources.

The cooperative model was enthusiastically defended when collectivisation of the fisheries was discussed at an all-Union level in 1929: fishing should not, it was argued, be an industry where 'raw material' (*syr'ë*) is later processed industrially; the seasonal variability of inland fisheries necessitated small-scale and decentralised cooperatives, with processing carried out within households.[15] There are parallels with recent ideas about community co-management (see Chapter 5). But this was no time to defend the small-scale. Stalinist ideology was premised on the abundance of nature, and natural resources were to be exploited to the full. In fishing regions, Kazakhs were to be forcibly settled in kolkhozy, herdsmen were to become fishermen, to address the mismatch between 'the lack of fisher population and the natural riches of the water-bodies of Kazakhstan'.[16] Female emancipation would be achieved by women fishing. Nomadic movement was replaced with a centrally ordered movement of people: populations were relocated, especially from delta lakes to the sea, where their labour was more useful. Deportations of 'enemies of the people' further served to fill the labour deficit. Settled in poor conditions on the far-flung Vozrozhdenie Island, these *spetspereselentsy*, 'special settlers', were regarded as an 'obedient labour force'.[17]

If sedentarisation and collectivisation in the Aral region were directed at exploiting fish resources to the full, across Kazakhstan, as Cameron (2018) argues, the same policies sought, in a stroke, to turn the steppe into a reliable source of grain and to modernise 'backward' Kazakhs. The results were disastrous. Livestock were confiscated, and when wildly unrealistic grain procurement targets were compounded by drought, devastating famine resulted (Cameron 2018; Kindler 2018; Pianciola 2004; 2020). A third of the Kazakh population died, others fled to other parts of Soviet Central Asia and beyond – to China, Afghanistan, Iran. As Pianciola (2020) shows, the northern shores of the Aral were particularly vulnerable because the railway facilitated the transport of requisitioned livestock to feed urban centres in Russia. By contrast, the Karakalpak southern shores, in 1930 administratively detached from Kazakhstan, benefited from their relative marginality.[18] While grandiose plans far exceeded the likely capacity of the sea, actual catches collapsed. In late 1932 fishermen were receiving 25 kg of flour per quarter, against a regulation 73 kg.[19] In the Aral region, according to an oblast inspection, from Bögen 86 out of 264 households fled, while from settlements on the northwestern shores, 300 households fled; the inspection euphemistically blamed inadequate housing and low pay.[20] The region was also a transit route for returning famine refugees (*otkochevniki*) who had fled to Uzbekistan and Turkmenistan (Pianciola 2020). Some attempted to settle in Aral kolkhozy, although they knew nothing about fishing, while at the same time people were still fleeing the northern coastline.[21]

The period of collectivisation was thus the violent culmination of a decades-long disentanglement of local social and ecological relations. The process was chaotic, rapidly escaping central control. Yet, as Kindler (2018) argues, although the famine was unplanned, it consolidated Soviet rule, breaking resistance by forcing the population to become dependent on the state. The outcome was a reorganisation of local society: human relations with the environment were reconfigured according to a gridded matrix whereby labour was directed and forcibly relocated, and the circulation of fish was controlled by the apparatus. Nature was 'disembedded' from society (Hornborg 1996). In the new system, fishing was an industry (*promyshlennost'*), with extraction (*dobycha*) of raw materials (*syr'ë*) separated from processing (*obrabotka*). Output by type of production was centralised, and processing facilities came under the disposition of the apparatus. The labour of fishing was reduced to the mechanical extraction of resources. Goals of mechanisation and deep-sea fishing on ships were slow to materialise; but in the sense that the time and space of fishing were micromanaged by the apparatus, *dobycha* was industrialised no less than *obrabotka*.

The shift from cooperatives to kolkhozy reconstituted the fishing population. Confiscation of livestock also amounted to confiscation of the time devoted to them, time which was now to be given to the state in fulfilling the plan. Though kolkhozy had subsidiary agriculture and herding to give them a semblance of autarky, their primary function was fishing. Nets and equipment were kolkhoz property. Kolkhoz management received the plan from Aralgosrybtrest; the plan would be split between brigades and units who would be assigned to specific spaces; brigadiers would pass the plan on to individuals. Pay was defined by amount of fish caught, and there were rewards for overfulfilling the plan. Fishing labour was directed by the numbers imposed by the plan. If, during the colonial period, fish were increasingly translated into money under conditions of extremely unequal exchange, now, in addition, fish mediated the hierarchical, dependent relations between the fishing population and the state.

Central control was, again, undermined by the unruliness of people and things, as the material constraints of the environment intersected with the inherent difficulties of operating in a shortage economy, where managers' authority was always constrained (Humphrey 1998). The relevant means of production could be formally put under the control of the apparatus, but bureaucrats' capacity to actually control them was limited. Bad weather disrupted the micromanagement of the plan.[22] Regulations about storing kolkhoz property like nets in centralised stores were routinely flouted.[23] The military-style arrangement of brigades, and exhortations to fish systematically across the sea, were ignored in favour of easily accessible inshore waters.[24] The capacity of the state to see what was happening along hundreds of kilometres of shoreline was limited.

Over the 1930s, plans were gradually relaxed; livestock numbers recovered slightly; and catches rose, though the centre of the industry shifted to Karakalpakstan in the south, which had been less affected by the famine (Pianciola 2020). In this new configuration, inhabitants of the region were dependent on provisioning with equipment and foodstuffs. Nevertheless, although local agency was thus constrained, in the archives there are glimpses of how these conditions enabled agency in other spheres. A report in the newspaper *Priaral'skaia Pravda* tells of how overfulfilment of the 1936 plan has brought a 'prosperous (*zazhitochnaia*) life'; 'European-style houses' have replaced the 'dark Asiatic *zemlianki*', and some Stakhanovites – who, following the widely publicised example of the coal miner Aleksei Stakhanov, were rewarded for exceeding production norms – own gramophones and silk suits.[25] Though the claim of a 'prosperous life' is doubtless exaggerated, there was clearly an expectation that fishing should be connected to rising living standards. It was through fishing (Figures 1.4 and 1.5) that the

Figure 1.4 Fishing boats, 1940. Source: Museum of Fishermen, Aral'sk.

Figure 1.5 Ship in the ice, 1940s. Source: Museum of Fishermen, Aral'sk.

people of the region were entitled to redistribution from the state; as a result, local people had a stake in Soviet visions of nature.

While Kazakh kolkhozy gradually recovered, the region continued to be transformed by arrivals from elsewhere in the USSR. Many were fleeing famine or repression in the European parts of the USSR. From the late 1930s and throughout the Second World War, Koreans and a range of 'enemy peoples', including Volga Germans, Chechens and Kalmyks, whose loyalty to the Soviet state was doubted, were deported en masse and settled across Central Asia. Those deported from fishing regions in particular were settled in the Aral region. According to the 1939 census, out of a total population of 65,295 in Aral'sk raion, 7,731 were *spetskontingent* (i.e. deportees).[26]

Meanwhile, Aral'sk was growing, an important connecting node between the sea and railway, and an industrial centre. It was upgraded from a village to an 'urban-type settlement' (*posëlok gorodskogo tipa*), and then to a town (*gorod*) in 1938, when it became the raion centre. The cotton economy elsewhere in Central Asia did not result in the development of manufacturing centres, because raw cotton could be shipped to existing factories in European Russia. By contrast, since there were as yet no refrigerated railway wagons, fish had to be processed immediately, resulting in an integrated industry within the Aral region

Figures 1.6 and 1.7 Fish factory, Aral'sk, undated. Source: Museum of Fishermen, Aral'sk.

(Figures 1.6 and 1.7). There was a major plant in Aral'sk, where Aralgosrybtrest's headquarters were. Fish processed elsewhere on the sea would be brought to Aral'sk for distribution. Aral'sk was also the hub for provisioning remote fishing settlements. Other enterprises contributed to the industrial character of the town: in the port, Karakalpak cotton was unloaded and transferred onto the railway, while grain from Russia would be loaded onto ships for the return journey; there was also a shipyard, building vessels for the transport and fishing fleets. Until after the Second World War, the town was predominantly non-Kazakh.

Nevertheless, while collectivisation was directed towards quantitative growth in fisheries production, the sector did not offer the same possibilities for scaling up as irrigation. Indeed, while planners talked of the sea's natural 'wealth', ichthyologists deemed the sea poor, in terms both of limited species composition, and of biomass of fish, zooplankton and zoobenthos. As Berg (1908, 449–59) explained, the sea's 'poverty' related not to its chemical composition, but to its geological history. Its aboriginal fauna dated from the distant past when it was connected with the Caspian. Since its separation from the Caspian basin, it had been freshening, so most of the Caspian fauna had been dying out; but, as a relatively young freshwater lake, it had not had time to 'be populated' (*zaselit'sia*) with new freshwater species.[27] This suggested the possibility of acclimatising new species, to maximise the sea's potential. Results were disastrous: most notably, stellate sturgeon introduced from the Caspian, while failing to reproduce, brought with it a parasite which proved fatal to the local ship sturgeon, which died off in large numbers (Plotnikov et al. 2014, 59–68).

At the same time, institutions to manage nature were developed. Their logic was not reducible to the economic vision of nature as wealth, and they acted as a brake on the constant demands to scale up. A conservationist vision lived on in the circumscribed territory of a nature reserve (*zapovednik*) established on Barsakelmes Island in 1939.[28] Even fisheries management, based on scientific research conducted by a research station, KazNIIRKh (established in 1928), was not just about unrestrained quantitative growth. A separate body regulated the fishery, introducing new rules to guarantee reproduction of stocks (Plotnikov et al. 2014, 57). Spatial and temporal bans were expanded to protect spawning grounds. Inputs were regulated, as were sizes of fish caught (Mitrofanov et al. 1992, 399). Further management measures included amelioration works such as clearing spawning grounds, dredging channels to connect lakes and clearing reeds which choked water of oxygen.

The Second World War led to yet another catastrophic collapse in catches, as women and children were left to fulfil the plan. Only by the late 1950s were catches approaching the levels of the late 1920s and the early 1910s. Some mechanisation had taken place, notably the introduction of motors and refrigerated ships (Figure 1.8). But the

Figure 1.8 Unloading from refrigerated ship, undated. Source: Museum of Fishermen, Aral'sk.

fisheries were never thriving. In the late 1950s, people in many remote fishing settlements still had to drink sea water. Leprosy had not been eradicated. Villages lacked electricity and housing, and other amenities on which the USSR prided itself.[29] Centralised control was still weak: fishermen, allowed 100–120 kg of fish per year for their families, often took home that quantity every month without paying for it.[30]

Finally, there was ongoing financial crisis. Kolkhozy had bought new ships to master deep-sea fishing and finally develop the fishery to its full potential. But this expenditure had saddled them with debt, and they suffered chronic lack of circulating assets. The majority of the kolkhozy were liquidated and replaced with state fishery bases (*bazy goslova*), directly subordinate to Aralgosrybtrest, leaving only kolkhoz Zhambul (today Zhalangash village) and kolkhoz Raiym.[31] But Aralgosrybtrest too was saddled with debts, and fish production was consistently of a low quality. Indeed, the main processing plant in Aral'sk, built in the 1930s, was in a state of decay.[32] Supplies of equipment were hoarded throughout the system, contributing to financial difficulties. Most of the industry was not mechanised. In a shortage economy characterised by interdepartmental competition, inland fisheries were not prioritised, so investment tension (Kornai 1980) precluded the growth that was always planned. This, then, is the preceding history of the twentieth-century regression of the Aral Sea, in which movements of fish, people and capital were reconfigured and integrated into the gridded time-space of the USSR.

The region was integrated in darker ways too, into the Soviet military-industrial complex. After the Second World War, military bases were established in Aral'sk. One provisioned the highly secret biological weapons laboratory on the remote island of Vozrozhdenie. After the construction of the cosmodrome at Baikonur, other bases ran search-and-rescue missions for cosmonauts who landed in the sea. Formally, these bases were not connected with the rest of the region: the secretive space of the military-industrial complex was distinct from the space of the command economy.

'The needs of agriculture'

Meanwhile, irrigation expansion took off. As Soviet plans to modernise Central Asia were renewed in the post-Stalin era, living standards were to be raised by economic development premised on irrigation and cotton.[33] In 1954 work began on the Karakum canal, leading across the deserts of Turkmenistan towards the Caspian, as Tsarist colonialists had dreamed. As economic growth accelerated in the 1960s, the legitimacy of Soviet rule came to rest on water infrastructure (Obertreis 2017). From 1960 the sea began to retreat as a cycle of low rainfall years accentuated the effects of irrigation withdrawals: in the 1960s the level fell by nearly 2 m, in the following decade by 5.3 m (Micklin 2014a, 121–4). Development around the sea itself now began to take a different path, as we see in Chapter 2. Ironically, inland fisheries were one sector which was relatively well managed across the Soviet Union, but they always bore the brunt of development priorities in agriculture (Berka 1990).[34] From 1960 the Kazakh Fisheries Ministry shifted its emphasis from intensifying existing fisheries to establishing new fisheries on remote lakes and reservoirs (Mitrofanov et al. 1992, 400). In 1965 the Presidium of the Council of Ministers of the USSR made a resolution, 'About measures for the preservation of the fishery significance (*rybokhoziaistvennogo znacheniia*) of the Aral Sea.'[35] An integrated plan (*kompleksnaia skhema*) was to be drawn up for the rational use of the water resources of the whole Aral basin, taking into account the interests of the fishery.

However, the integrated plan was slow to materialise, and water withdrawals continued to grow. In the Brezhnev era, patronage relationships between Moscow and Central Asian elites facilitated the flow of investment into agriculture. Republican leaders, despite their awareness of the damage wrought by cotton, were also aware that their political capital with Moscow depended on it. Irrigation specialists, recognising the widespread wastage of water, stressed the need to raise efficiency, but to little avail as farm managers continued to waste water (Kalinovsky 2018, 110–15). At the same time, low levels of mechanisation, coupled with rising wages on cotton farms, tied people to the land. In what Kalinovsky (2018, 177) describes as 'involution', the amenities of modernity, in the form of schools and hospitals, reached cotton-growing kolkhozy, even as practices like child labour persisted. As the cotton monopoly transformed local formal and informal economic relations right down to the level of the kolkhoz, all levels of society in cotton-growing regions came to have a stake in irrigation, and developments were thus not always top-down. Describing how one kolkhoz chairman played on his political connections, with dubious legality, to develop irrigation schemes that would attract investment into his kolkhoz, Abashin (2015, 359–64) shows how local actors, standing up for local interests, played their role in shaping policy.

The environmental scientist Glantz (1999b) explains the Aral regression as a 'creeping environmental problem'. Because the onset is gradual, there is no objective threshold after which behaviour might change: postponement is always possible. Rather than seeing this, as Glantz (1999b, 16) does, as a problem of 'human nature', the previous sections suggest instead that we should locate this particular creeping environmental problem in the specific path of development taken in Soviet Central Asia. As expectations of modernity were invested in a tangled web of dependencies linking centre and periphery via cotton, any change of policy was increasingly difficult – which Hodder (2012) calls 'entrapment'. This was accentuated by the labour surplus (Lubin 1984): most state-socialist economies faced an overall deficit of labour (Kornai 1980), but in predominantly rural Central Asia, provision of work was outstripped by population growth. The authorities proposed more of the same: expanding irrigation and hastening the Siberian rivers diversion, dubbed *proekt veka*, 'the project of the century' (Lubin 1984, 131–4). As population growth outstripped the provision of work on kolkhozy, and as irrigation continued to be the easiest way to satisfy bureaucrats' urge to accumulate fixed assets, development continued as before.

There was also a wilful myopia: planners refused to take into account the escalating effects of the sea's regression. As we will see in Chapter 2, a limited vocabulary developed over the 1960s and 1970s to talk about the sea's retreat as a 'problem', but it was not acknowledged as a disaster or catastrophe until perestroika. This myopia echoes Scott's (1998) famous account of 'seeing like a state': from a synoptic but myopic utilitarian viewpoint, things and people are seen out of context, with disastrous consequences. Indeed, the Aral's global notoriety lies in the way planners weighed the costs and benefits: the economic value of cotton exceeded that of fish (e.g. Ellis 1990; Zonn 1998). But the thrust of my narrative so far suggests that this viewpoint lies not in 'the state', but in powerful departmental and regional interests that were backed by central decision-making bodies in Moscow. From an abstract cost–benefit perspective, raising the efficiency of existing irrigation infrastructure would have been more beneficial than building new infrastructure with diminishing rates of return. The unfinished integrated plan for the water resources of the whole basin could also have made water use more efficient – which required a *more* synoptic viewpoint. If the roots of the Aral regression lie in the competitive urge to accumulate use-values, the cost–benefit rationality which weighed the sea against cotton emerges as less abstract than it may seem.

Take this 1971 resolution about 'the problem of the Aral Sea' issued by the all-Union scientific council 'Integrated Use and Preservation of Water Resources'.[36] I do not suggest that this particular document played any major instrumental role, but it illustrates the sort of discourse used pervasively to justify political decisions as rational necessity. The resolution begins:

> The problem of the Aral Sea is acquiring ever greater importance in relation to the development of the national economy in its basin. Water withdrawals from rivers feeding the sea for the needs of irrigated agriculture and other branches of the economy are growing continuously, which is leading to (*vedët*) a fall in the level of sea. The problem is made sharper in connection with the presence of a significant fund of lands suitable for irrigation, the possible prospective water demands of which exceed the available water resources of the basin.[37]

Sentence structure precludes debate. 'Irrigated agriculture needs a lot of water'; 'significant funds of lands are suitable for irrigation': compressed into noun phrases, these questionable claims cannot be questioned. The verb *vedët* mechanically connects the falling sea level with 'water withdrawals', eliding the causation which reaches back to a political decision about the definition of the needs of agriculture. Later comes the cost–benefit analysis:

The fall in the level of the Aral Sea will cause specific adverse economic consequences: there will be radical changes in shipping, reproduction of fish stocks of the sea, muskrat-breeding, livestock-herding and other branches of the economy in the neighbouring regions. Nevertheless, the national-economic (*narodno-khoziaistvennoe*) and economic (*ekonomicheskoe*) effectiveness of the development of irrigation and agriculture on the basis of irrigation in the basins of the Syr Dariya and Amu Dariya by far exceeds the damages which can be expected from the fall in the level of the Aral Sea.[38]

Notice how costs and benefits are weighed: adverse consequences are determinate and separate; they are also postponed to the future, which in 1971 was a basic misrepresentation. Rising salinity, which was more destructive to fish stocks than the shrinking of the sea, is absent from the analysis. By contrast, the benefits are a tautologically interconnected whole. The author goes on to note: 'It is also necessary to take into account factors not measurable by direct economic evaluation: the influence of the changes in the regime of the sea on the nature of the surrounding territories.'[39] But these are only 'factors': they are not acknowledged as 'consequences', though they would become famous visual symbols of disaster.

Such monologic discourse establishes a particular constellation of logical connections, silencing other voices, closing down other perspectives. Form ('the needs of irrigation') conceals the arbitrariness of the content ('we've decided irrigation is more important than the sea'). Like all discourse, and like other decontextualising visions the world over, it is sited.[40] This is not the abstract rationality of a monolithic state. The claim of abstract rationality – the claim to follow fixed rules – may be the foundation of bureaucratic legitimacy (Herzfeld 1992). However, as Bakhtin (1986) argues, rules do not precede discourse but are produced by it, sited in social practice. Powerful interests defined the question in a particular way, drawing on scientific theory going back to Voeikov to discursively abstract people and resources from their contexts. The centralising tendencies within Soviet political economy had, as Bakhtin (1981b, 270–2) arguably saw, a centripetal corollary in discourse. This discursive abstraction of resources legitimised extraction and accumulation under the disposition of the apparatus. This discourse was a key element of the 'creeping environmental problem'. The 'needs of irrigation' provided what Herzfeld (1992, 81) calls an 'ethical alibi', justifying bureaucratic indifference by presenting the interests of particular bureaucratic departments as the common good. Within this discourse, the Aral was a 'mute object', a 'brute thing' (Bakhtin 1981b, 351).

Aral-88 and the emergence of the Aral catastrophe

In the 1970s, a handful of scientists were trying to draw attention to the ecological crisis, to establish that a threshold had been reached (Obertreis 2017; Weiner 1999, 417–19). These voices were stifled by bureaucratic discourse, which lacked resources to speak up for the Aral. The regression remained a 'matter of fact' (Latour 2004): determinate effects which could be known and accounted for. As a 'matter of fact', the regression was addressed in a limited, circumscribed way, as we will see in Chapter 2. However, during perestroika, environmental activists, building on those earlier efforts, turned the Aral into a 'matter of concern' (Latour 2004): a proliferation of interconnected crises involving humans, water, salt and dust, far beyond scientific and bureaucratic control (Obertreis 2017; Wheeler 2016). Environmental protests were erupting across the USSR and, alongside Chernobyl, the Aral catastrophe became a *cause célèbre*. In response to public pressure, the long planned Siberian Rivers scheme was cancelled in 1986, in what was deemed an important victory for the environmental movement. The dried-up Aral was first shown on television in 1988. As the materiality of the crisis was mediated through images and texts, the Aral acquired a voice in Soviet society. In the freer discursive environment of glasnost, the sea's regression became a 'revelatory crisis', laying bare uncomfortable truths about Soviet society (Hoffman and Oliver-Smith 2002). At last, it was officially recognised as a disaster.

In 1988 a well-publicised expedition of environmental activists, scientists and writers, including Central Asian intellectuals, was organised by *Novy Mir* and the Central Asian newspaper *Pamir*.[41] They travelled across Central Asia, seeking the truth about the causes and consequences of the catastrophe. In a diary of the expedition published in *Novy Mir* the following year, the expedition director, G. I. Reznichenko (1989, 83), described the devastation they found, the sea now 60–90 km from its former ports, which were full of rusting boats. Yet his description extended far beyond the sea itself:

> On our journey we constantly encountered women and children, gathering cotton from dawn till dusk. In the Kyzylkum and Karakum deserts we would often stumble upon lakes filled with salty drainage water. The majority do not have a name. But they should, perhaps,

for clarity, be labelled one hundredth, one fiftieth or one twentieth of the Aral. For in them is now accommodated a good half of all the waters of the Aral Sea. And these lakes are useful for absolutely nothing. (Reznichenko 1989, 183)

If the scientific council resolution analysed above fixed the drying sea as a knowable, containable waste of the progress of modernity, these countless unnamed lakes spoke of indeterminacy, destabilising the metanarrative of Soviet progress (Alexander and Sanchez 2019). The picture is one of modernity gone disastrously wrong. The expedition's painstaking research across Central Asia found that colossal wastage occurred as water seeped through, and evaporated from, rudimentary earth canals. Without proper drainage, water laden with pesticides was reused, polluting the soil; yet more water was needed to flush chemicals out. The land became less fertile, and productivity fell.[42] Intertwined with wastage of water was wastage of money, which the expedition located in the same systemic source: the competition for centrally allocated resources engendered by the command economy. The Aral regression was therefore just part of a complex ecological crisis across the region.

Not only did they find unemployment and proliferating health problems by the sea's former shores: the human crisis too extended across the whole basin. While cotton had seemed to promise progress, it had facilitated clientelism and entrenched corruption, most notably the infamous cotton scandal in Uzbekistan, implicating the entire political class.[43] The expedition concluded that the scandal was rooted not, as was widely assumed, in backward cultural practices, but in the economic unviability of cotton. Soviet cotton was of poor quality, and prices were too low to sustain kolkhozy, which necessitated falsification of accounts in the practice known as *pripiska*. After *pripiska* was stamped out, plan fulfilment increasingly rested on coercion. Farm workers were malnourished. If cotton purported to be the vehicle of Central Asian modernisation, perestroika activists found a negation of the urbanist values of the Soviet Union.

As a catastrophe, the crisis was extended spatially from the sea itself to the whole of Central Asia and indeed the entire USSR; and it was extended temporally, involving a rereading of the Soviet past, and eschatological hope that the moment might prove a turning point for a better future. As Reznichenko (1989, 194) wrote, '[t]he Aral and, together with it, man too, can be saved by a new ecological way of thinking and glasnost, which give hope – albeit small, but urgent for all of us; they offer a chance for survival'. Soon after the expedition commenced, a decree by the Central Committee of the Communist Party of the Soviet Union set out measures to guarantee an inflow of 21 km^3/year to the Aral by 2005, ensure safe drinking water supplies, improve ecological conditions in delta lakes and improve the efficiency of irrigation systems (Micklin 1998, 404). For activists, this was too little too late. The expedition materials published in *Novy Mir* and distributed to relevant ministries culminate in a wide-ranging proposal for reform by the economic journalist Seliunin (1989), centred on land reform: land was to be rented to peasant households.[44]

For a brief moment, the sea's regression acquired major political agency, prompting radical systemic change. Yet, as environmental concerns were displaced amid the escalating crisis of late perestroika, a major paradigm shift faded from view (Ianitskii 1995; Sigman 2013). Over the next few years, there were further decrees about the Aral, but there was, as yet, no reduction in the area sown with cotton. In 1991 the newly formed State Commission for the Aral proposed diversifying the economy away from cotton and irrigation, but these recommendations were immediately frustrated by the collapse of the USSR (Micklin 1998, 404).

Conclusion: uneven development in Soviet Central Asia

Travelling the length and breadth of Central Asia, the Aral-88 expedition concluded that socialism had never existed in peripheral areas (Reznichenko 1989, 192). For these writers, the catastrophe revealed the uneven development of state socialism. The tangentially related stories I have told in this chapter, about fish and irrigation, entangled local populations in multiple dependencies, with spatially divergent outcomes. Space was homogenised by the plan; natural resources and labour power were abstracted as numbers and rearranged in a gridded matrix. However, space was also differentiated by the uneven investment of capital, which related to the apparatus's urge to accumulate fixed assets and to the hoarding and blockages inherent in the shortage economy. Thus space and nature were differentiated according to their divergent political value to the apparatus.[45] The materialities of the assets involved (fisheries, irrigation systems), offering different possibilities for scaling up, shaped processes of accumulation and the sorts of infrastructures which were developed.

Entangled in different sets of relations, two incompatible versions of the Aral emerged within the project of Soviet modernity. Within an assemblage involving railway, processing plants and fishing kolkhozy, it was an object of economic value; in an assemblage of irrigation systems and cotton plantations, it was an aberration, wasting water that could be fuelling progress. Concomitantly, discursive resources were unevenly distributed: as the centralising tendencies of Soviet political economy were matched by a centripetal tendency in discourse, more powerful branches of the apparatus were able to define the terms of the question, making it all but impossible to speak up for the Aral. Sustained by radically asymmetrical human interests (cf. Richardson 2014), the coexistence of the two versions of the sea was impossible.

The modernisation processes described in this chapter both drove the sea's regression and radically reshaped the relations between people around the Aral and their environment before the sea dried up. People in the Aral region were doubly vulnerable. First, the consolidation of the sea as economic value involved the region in an extractive relationship with Moscow. People were dependent both on fish as a resource and on the centre for provisioning. While Aral people were dependent on the Soviet centre, the centre was much less dependent on them. Central Asian Fisheries Ministries were subordinate to the USSR Fisheries Ministry, whose jurisdiction extended from the Baltic to the Pacific and for whom the Aral was a drop in the ocean. Within the region this vulnerability was unevenly distributed: the port of Aral'sk, because of its strategic location, attracted much more investment than the villages scattered along the remote shoreline, which were of little political value to anyone, and remained underdeveloped into the 1950s.

Secondly, the region was vulnerable to the uncompromising logic of ever-expanding irrigation, according to which the sea was an aberration. After all, the few hundred thousand people around the Aral were a small fraction of the tens of millions living in Central Asia. The Aral fisheries were relatively marginal in republics whose economies were based on agriculture and (in Kazakhstan) mineral extraction. Constant quantitative growth in cotton and rice meant more strategic resources for the apparatus to accumulate, and Central Asian cotton fed the Russian textiles industry. Though the same urge towards centralisation drove development in the fisheries, this was never a capital- or labour-intensive industry. Whatever improvements could be made by mechanisation, management and amelioration, expansion would always be limited by the total stocks in the sea. By contrast, expansion of agriculture could only be limited by water availability, and there was always the expectation of diverting the Siberian rivers to Central Asia. This promised to solve the region's water issues altogether, and, in doing so, massively increase the fixed assets under the disposition of Central Asian elites and the Ministry of Land Reclamation and Water Management (Minvodkhoz) in Moscow (Bressler 1995).

If the centralising tendency of state socialism drove uneven development, I have also suggested that compliance was secured, in part, by the countervailing tendency within state socialism towards redistribution which somewhat equalised Soviet space, as sympathetic observers argued at the time (Khan and Ghai 1979; Nove and Newth 1967). While these two tendencies were sharply asymmetrical, the equalising tendency would, as the following chapter shows, dictate the authorities' responses to the Aral regression.

Notes

1   Beckert (2014) persuasively argues that the history of cotton is the history of capitalism. However, his 'global' history focuses on western Europe's relationship to the rest of the world; he has little space for the rather different story of Soviet cotton, and the postcolonial experiments in India and Egypt which it in part inspired. All these he reduces to 'state-led capitalism', another moment in the unilinear evolution of capitalism (Beckert 2014, 435–6). Apart from a glancing comment (Beckert 2014, 431), he also ignores the environmental impacts of cotton monoculture.
2   As environmental historians stress, such processes were hardly unique: Peterson (2019) stresses parallels with other European empires; Brown (2015, Chapter 6) provocatively compares Montana, USA, and early Soviet Qaraghandy, Kazakhstan, two similar environments emptied of indigenous inhabitants and thoroughly transformed over just 30 years. Compare also Cronon (1992) on the role of narratives about modernisation and conquering nature in the disastrous formation of the dust-bowl in the American west.
3   In the historiography of Central Asian irrigation, Scott's work has had a mixed reception. Obertreis (2017) finds the model, though empirically questionable, helpful for exploring the dreams of technical elites. Peterson (2019), focusing on the retreat from mechanisation in the Stalinist period in favour of forced labour, argues that methods were not modernist, but nevertheless highly modern. Teichmann (2018) also rejects Scott's model, instead offering a thick description of the (chaotic) modes of administration through which the state came into being in the Stalinist period.
4   Beknazarov (2010), like Tsarist and Soviet ethnographers before him, maintains that fish were not caught for exchange. Pianciola (2019) suggests that Tsarist sources underestimated the degree of marketisation of fish both by the Kazakhs of the northern Aral and the Karakalpaks in the Amu Dariya delta, although he acknowledges that evidence is at present wholly lacking. Either way, whether caught for sale or for immediate consumption, fish constituted a very different sort of resource from livestock.
5   Dua (2017) finds a similar contrast between livestock and the 'gifts of the sea' in the pastoral economy of Somalia.
6   See Campbell (2012), though he emphasises the ambivalent attitude of many of the agents of colonisation towards this vision.
7   In Lien's (2015) terms, salt acts as a 'time machine', extending the temporal and spatial reach of fish flesh.
8   Plotnikov et al. (2014, 57), Evseev, n.d. but 1925, 'Perspektivnyi piatiletnii plan rybnoi promyshlennosti KazSSR', AFGAKO, fond 4, op. 1, d. 8, ll. 1–17 (7).
9   Colonial visions were not uniform: Peterson (2019, Chapter 2) tells the story of Grand Duke Romanov, who, while believing in the benefits of Russian rule for indigenous people, was also fascinated with local cultures; his irrigation projects on the Hungry Steppe sought to create

harmonious Russo-Asiatic relations. Nor, as Obertreis (2017) stresses, were relations between capitalists and the state harmonious.

10   Indeed, highlighting the pivotal role of the tax break on land sown with American cotton in driving the growth in cotton production, Penati (2013) stresses that this policy was not the result of economic planning from St Petersburg, but developed in response to demands from below.

11   Thus, for Weinthal (2002, Chapter 4), cotton was, and is, a form of 'social control'. This point also emerges in Bichsel's (2012, 98) discussion of resettlements of mountain populations to irrigated lands: the constraints of the mountain environment meant that people were not always engaged in 'socially useful labour', but worked on their personal plots; that is, their labour was not fully under the disposition of the apparatus.

12   e.g. Communication from Aralgosrybtrest deputy manager Iurtvenson to the Muinak fishery, copied to all Aral fisheries, 14 April 1927, AFGAKO, f. 4, op. 1, d. 15, ll. 46–8.

13   'Otchëtnyi doklad pravleniia Aralskogo soiuza rybakov za 1928 god', n.d. but 1929, Tsentral'nyi gosudarstvennyi arkhiv respubliki Kazakhstana [hereafter TsGARK], f. 759, op. 1, d. 39, ll. 1–42.

14   Protokol soveshchaniia orgotdela pri Aralrybaksoiuze po voprosu osedaniia rybatskogo naseleniia, 8 November 1930, AFGAKO, f. 7, op. 1, d. 16, l. 124.

15   'Tezisy po dokladu "Gosudarstvennaia rybnaia promyshlennost' i lovetskii vopros"', 25 January 1929, 7th–8th sessions of the council of Vsekopromrybaksoiuz, TsGARK, f. 759, op. 1, d. 1, ll. 150–5.

16   Letter from Kazrybaksoiuz chairman Kolnyshev and economist-planner Petrenko to Komitet Osedaniia pri KazSNK, 5 September 1930, TsGARK, f. 759, op. 1, d. 31, l. 56.

17   Brigada Obkoma VKPb i Obl KK RKI, 'Vyvody i predlozheniia brigady Obkoma i Obl KK-RKI o rezul'tatakh obsledovaniia Aralrybtresta', n.d. but 1932, AFGAKO, f. 7, op. 1, d. 12, ll. 2–12 (4).

18   Later, in 1936, the Kara-Kalpak ASSR was transferred to the Uzbek SSR.

19   Postanovlenie Biuro Ar-More raikoma VKP/b/ i prezidiuma KK RKI 'O dolgosrochnom zavoze prodovol'stviia na putinu khraneniia poriadke iskhodovaniia putinnykh fondov', 24 October 1932, AFGAKO, f. 7, op. 1, d. 32, ll. 34–7.

20   Brigada, 'Vyvody i predlozheniia' (3).

21   Aralrybakkolkhozsoiuz, 16 December 1934, AFGAKO, f. 7, op. 1, d. 51, ll. 12–14.

22   e.g. Aralgosrybtrest manager Sel'demirov, chief accountant Razdoborov, 'Ob'iasnitel'naia zapiska k otchetu "ARALGOSRYBTRESTA" za 1933g.', n.d. but 1934, AFGAKO, f. 4, op. 1, d. 98, ll. 2–37 (11).

23   e.g. letter from chairman of the board of Rybakkolkhoztsentr Mazhonov to the chairman of Aral'sk mezhrairybakkolkhozsoiuz, 27 March 1936, AFGAKO, f. 7, op. 1, d. 62, ll. 85–6.

24   e.g. Postanovlenie biuro Aktiubinskogo Obkoma VKP(b) ot 27 maia 1934 g., 27 May 1934, AFGAKO, f. 7, op. 1, d. 42, ll. 60–2.

25   Raikom VKP(b), 'Ob itogakh vypolneniia plana dobychi ryby za 1936 god i o plane dobychi na 1937 god po kolkhozam Aral'skogo raiona', *Priaral'skaia Pravda*, 15 February 1937, AFGAKO, f. 7, op. 1, d. 75, l. 4.

26   'Vsesoiuznaia perepis' naseleniia 1939g.: Chislennost' nalichnogo naseleniia SSSR po raionam i gorodam', published online by Demoskop Weekly, http://www.demoscope.ru/weekly/ssp/rus_pop_39_2.php, accessed 7 May 2021.

27   This vision of the sea would be long-lasting: in 1975, the ichthyologist Karpevich (1975, 331) would describe the Aral as a 'biocenotic "semi-desert"'. On Karpevich, see further Chapter 2.

28   See Weiner (1999) on the conservationist visions of *zapovedniki*. Barsakelmes suffered from the sea's regression as the island joined the mainland, pastures became depleted and herds of saigaks and kulans migrated away. Today, the reserve is thriving, having been awarded more land to reflect the distribution of its animals; it is also well funded, as part of recent moves towards 'greening' Kazakhstan's economy.

29   e.g. Vice chairman of South Kazakhstan Sovnarkhoz D. Dzhumaliev, 'Meropriiatiia po razvitiiu rybnoi promyshlennosti Aral'skogo basseina', n.d. but 1962, TsGARK, f. 1874, op. 1, d. 23, ll. 7–20 (13).

30   Rasporiazhenie po Aral'skomu rybokombinatu No. 54 ot 13 iulia 1960 g., 13 July 1960, AFGAKO, f. 4, op. 2, d. 8, ll. 125–7.

31   Letter from Aralgosrybtrest director Kh. Musagaliev to obkom secretary, oblsovet chairman, chairman of South Kazakhstan SNKh, 6 March 1961, TsGARK, f. 1874, op. 1, d. 38, ll. 8–12.

32   'Rybnaia promyshlennost", n.d. but 1961, TsGARK, f. 1874, op. 1, d. 37, ll. 147–55.

33 Kalinovsky (2018, 244–5) describes the Khrushchev era as a second postcolonial moment, tackling the legacies of colonialism and also of Stalinism.

34 In contrast to the management measures outlined above, most Western fisheries management regulates only by biomass, a much blunter management instrument, widely critiqued, e.g. by Larkin (1977) and Wilson et al. (1994). Today, such authors suggest parametric management, e.g. of conditions for reproduction, food base, species interactions etc. – all parameters which Soviet management did, in theory, take into account. Of course, things went wrong (as with overfishing of sturgeon on the Caspian, and with acclimatisations), but catches were reliably higher across Kazakhstan than today. Often, problems stemmed from not enough science, and from conflicts between industry and scientists (Mitrofanov et al. 1992).

35 Referenced in a letter from Kazsovmin vice-chairman M. Iskanov to the USSR fisheries minister A. A. Ishkov and USSR minister of land reclamation and water management E. E. Alekseevskii, 17 June 1969, TsGARK, f. 1130, op. 1, d. 843, ll. 96–9.

36 Chairman of scientific council P. Neporozhnyi, 'Reshenie biuro Nauchnogo soveta "Kompleksnoe ispol'zovanie i okhrana vodnykh resursov" po dokladu Vremennoi podkomissii o probleme Aral'skogo moria', 4 June 1971, AFGAKO, f. 4, op. 2pr, d. 272, ll. 1–7. The scientific council reported to the Science and Technology Committee of the USSR Council of Ministers. The resolution, based on a report of a subcommission on the Aral Sea, made a series of recommendations about water management in the Aral basin. Only one recommendation mentioned the sea itself: Minrybkhoz USSR and republican authorities were to take into account the fall in sea level in their plans.

37 Neporozhnyi, 'Reshenie' (1).

38 Neporozhnyi, 'Reshenie' (4).

39 Neporozhnyi, 'Reshenie' (4).

40 Cf. Carrier (2012), who extends Scott's argument away from the modernist state to capitalist investment: things are seen schematically, out of context, when powerful interests, motivated by profit, have the discursive resources to define the terms of the question.

41 My analysis is based on the published accounts in *Novy Mir* (Reznichenko 1989; Seliunin 1989). See further Obertreis (2017), Wheeler (2016).

42 The expedition's analysis tallies with the accounts of Micklin (1998), Obertreis (2017) and Weinthal (2002).

43 See also, for example, Weinthal 2002, 101–2; Kandiyoti 2002, 241–2.

44 Seliunin's proposals should not be approached uncritically: assuming a sharp distinction between society and the state, he arguably placed too much hope on instating the family as a unit of production. Purporting to speak for the Soviet public, he relied on a romantic image of the Central Asian family as a vehicle for utopian hope (Wheeler 2016).

45 Dynamics thus differ from capitalist uneven development, where, as Smith (1984) describes, space is, on the one hand, homogenised by the market and, on the other, differentiated through the investment of capital where it is most profitable. Soviet uneven development was further exacerbated by the specialisation of production and interdependence between regions (Humphrey 1995, 3–4).

2
Seeing like a bureaucrat: problems of living standards and employment

A 1962 document signed by the vice-chairman of the South Kazakhstan Sovnarkhoz, outlining measures for the development of the Aral fishery, begins:

> As a result of (*v rezul'tate*) the deterioration of the hydrological regime of the sea and the rivers Amu Dariya and Syr Dariya, [and] the sharp contraction in flow of fresh water into the sea, the raw-material stocks (*syr'evye zapasy*) of the Aral have been under great strain in recent years, and catches of such valuable species of fish as barbel, bream and shemaya are sharply contracting.[1]

Scientists, he continued, predict that annual catches on the North Aral will fall from 21,300 tonnes to 15,800 tonnes by 1966. He made no explicit mention of the cause. Instead, he blamed fisheries managers: rapidly falling catches were due to their failure 'to take effective and immediate measures to restore the raw-material stocks of the water-bodies'.[2] He therefore instructed them to carry out amelioration measures, construct artificial spawning grounds and acclimatise new species. He also urged mechanisation of the fleet in order to maintain catches at 19,500 tonnes.[3] This document is typical of official responses to the sea's regression over the coming years: further regulation and reorganisation of people and environment, continuing policies of previous decades. As the sea contracted, deep-sea fishing, with newly acquired ships, assumed more importance, especially in remote western waters. However, there was no paradigm shift in fisheries management, nor could those responsible for the fishery officially voice complaints against irrigation policies.

Environmental historians have offered rich accounts of the processes driving irrigation expansion and environmental degradation in Soviet Central Asia. This chapter focuses on the branches of the state that bore the brunt of these processes, asking how fisheries managers and regional bosses responded to the sea's retreat. The quotation above is indicative of the limited framing of the issue. Narrative arc is kept to a minimum, as causal connections ('the hydrological regime is deteriorating, so stocks are under stress, so catches are falling') are syntactically reduced to parenthetic background factors through the subordinating phrase 'as a result of'. There is no possibility of asking *why* the hydrological regime is deteriorating. Such language obscures the root cause of the problem, irrigation. It is hardly surprising that no paradigm shift occurred.

Indeed, in the documents lying in the dust of the archives, at every level of the state, there are scant discursive resources for speaking up for the sea. The state of fish stocks could be described as 'catastrophic' (*katastroficheskii*); the state of the region, or its human population, could not. The 'sharp fall in the sea level' is related to 'the withdrawal of water for the needs of irrigation', which has raised 'difficulties' for the fishing industry to fulfil its plans. Clauses are articulated through mechanical connecting phrases, so that isolated causes and effects are abstracted from their contexts. This is typical of the 'contorted redundancy of bureaucratic speech' (Brown 2015, 31).[4] Narrative, the basis of moral evaluation (Cronon 1992), is reduced to bureaucratic formula.

Ostensibly, these documents reveal bureaucratic indifference to the plight of the Aral region and its population at every level and in every branch of the Soviet state, the myopic focus on irrigation providing an 'ethical alibi' (Herzfeld 1992). The language of the state seems to close down meaning, restricting other ways of talking about the sea's regression (Cruikshank 1998, Chapter 4). The forms of discourse within which the issue was framed precluded the emergence of a 'critical event' (Das 1995) or 'matter of concern' (Latour 2004).

However, many bureaucrats were far from indifferent to the Aral's plight. Insofar as the receding sea impinged on their domain, they had no choice but to respond. The next part of the chapter examines efforts to maintain the productivity of the sea through introducing salt-tolerant species. However, these had no immediate positive effect. The rest of the chapter, therefore, explores how bureaucrats responded to a rapidly deteriorating environment and the loss of the sea's 'fishery significance'. As we shall see, investments were made during the 1970s to develop infrastructure that responded to what was described as a crisis in living standards. Despite the Aral's specificity, this story is part of a broader picture of intense investment across rural Central Asia, as the institutions of the Soviet 'welfare state' were to modernise local society (Kalinovsky 2018).[5]

Furthermore, while the port closed, other enterprises kept going, including the fishery itself. After a sharp contraction in the 1960s and early 1970s, the fishing industry stabilised and continued to operate even after fishing became impossible on the sea itself after 1978. Like many stagnation-era enterprises, it was in permanent crisis, but continued to operate by importing frozen ocean fish and sending fishermen to fish elsewhere in Kazakhstan. The population of the raion fell from nearly 80,000 in 1970 to 70,000 in 1979 as the non-Kazakh population in particular left – but this fall halted in the 1980s.[6] In the Moynaq fishery on the Karakalpak shore too, ocean fish were imported (Karimov et al. 2005, 90), while the fishing operation moved away from the sea to newly created reservoirs across Uzbekistan, where aquaculture yielded 20,000–25,000 tonnes per year (Karimov et al. 2009, 3).

This chapter therefore adds further nuance to the political ecology of state socialism developed in Chapter 1. If ecological damage derived from state socialism's centralising tendency, this chapter focuses on the redistributive tendency of late socialism which, in limited, prescribed ways, mitigated some of that damage. Interventions did not simply respond to material changes but to how these material changes emerged as a bureaucratic 'problem'. As we saw in Chapter 1, the irrigation vision was, *pace* Scott (1998), not so much that of the state as that of specific bureaucratic interests, albeit backed by the Communist Party leadership in Moscow. However, other bureaucrats, with their own interests, had their own ways of seeing the Aral. No state is a monolith, and, while bureaucrats might write like cogs in a machine, the Soviet state was not a homogeneous cohesive machine. Bureaucrats encountered the deteriorating environment through the web of dependencies, obligations and constraints that made up the Soviet state. Managers were obliged to fulfil plans set by superiors, but were dependent on superiors for inputs, and on those beneath them to fulfil the plan. They were also constrained by endemic shortages, which set bureaucrats in competition over the allocation of scarce resources (Kornai 1980). For the bureaucrats discussed here, the constraints of the shortage economy were compounded by the constraints of a deteriorating environment.

These structural constraints and dependencies have discursive implications: the 'speech will' (Bakhtin 1986) of bureaucrats derived, at least in part, from their position within the apparatus. The Aral may have been doomed by the dominance of irrigation interests, but there were plenty of actors at different levels of the state who cared about it: whether or not they cared about 'nature', or the livelihoods and health of the people working and living there, they were structurally inclined to care about their domain. Of course, they may also have been interested in their personal enrichment, but their departmental interests cannot be reduced to their personal interests. For these bureaucrats, then, the sea's regression, insofar as its material effects impinged on their domain, emerged as a 'problem'.

Thus the 'needs of irrigation', while an ethical alibi for some, were a discursive constraint for others. Bakhtin (1986), critiquing the Saussurian view of language as an abstract set of rules, introduces the notion of 'speech genres', which are marked by varying degrees of constraints on what may be said. While some are very free, even the strictest contain some freedom. The speech genres open to bureaucrats writing to higher authorities about the Aral's regression were particularly constrained, as they had to follow the 'authoritative utterances' of superiors which 'set the tone' (Bakhtin 1986, 88). There were constraints not only on what might be said but on who might be addressed: there was no official speech genre for fisheries managers to complain to water-management organisations. However, although discursive resources were unevenly distributed across different departments and regions, some speech genres offered certain affordances. Bureaucrats could appeal to other rationalities than the cost–benefit analysis, or they could use the sea's regression as a rhetorical tool for seeking investment or negotiating a lower plan.[7]

As bureaucrats were constrained both by the deteriorating environment and by the linguistic resources to address it, the sea's regression emerged as a limited, circumscribed fact – a problem of living standards and of employment. Certain crucial material effects were occluded from view: the proliferating dust storms, or the damage to human health. Nevertheless, even in this limited form, the fact of the sea's regression would be materially consequential. It assumed a degree of political agency, prompting measures to maintain the overall shape of the assemblage of fish, infrastructure and labour even as the sea at the heart of the assemblage vanished from sight.

This chapter is necessarily limited to official discourse: the archives I examined did not include the 'hidden transcripts' (Scott 1990) that doubtless played a role in negotiations between different branches of the state. A Tastübek fisherman once showed me a huge dried-up channel that previously led to a pool for keeping sturgeon. When a gift was needed for a minister, the sturgeon would be taken out and dispatched by train to the ministry in Alma-Ata (Almaty). Similarly, when my host in Bögen,

Zhaqsylyq, caught a large carp, he would tether it by its gills to a reed until he needed to present it as a gift for a visiting dignitary. Such practices are not recorded in the archives; nor are offstage communications like angry telephone conversations between local bosses and the fisheries minister. Privately, officials may have been appalled at what was happening to the sea. The documents I saw offered only tantalising glimpses of this offstage discourse, when bureaucrats endeavoured to drag it onstage, as we will see at the end of the chapter. But even within official discourse, there is space for heterogeneity, competing claims and hence some agency.[8]

Making full use of the sea's biological resources

Before embarking on this story, an excursus is necessary into efforts to preserve the sea's productivity by introducing salt-tolerant species, which would have profound effects on the species composition of the sea (Plotnikov et al. 2016). The full significance to humans of these efforts would only become evident after the Soviet collapse, as we will see in Chapter 5. In the short term, they did not halt the catastrophic decline in catches and, indeed, some interventions accelerated it. If prewar acclimatisations had sought to address the 'poverty' of the Aral's ichthyofauna, the expected decline in sea level and rise in salinity after the war heightened the need to acclimatise new species. Before the sea started to retreat, mullet were introduced from the Caspian in the mid-1950s. Unused to the cold Aral waters, they failed to reproduce. Accidentally introduced with them were gobies and atherines, as well as a shrimp, *P. elegans*, which established itself as part of the benthic fauna. While the mullet failed to reproduce, the population of gobies and atherines exploded. Shortly afterwards, Baltic herring were introduced, but, contrary to scientific recommendations, without any measures to increase the 'poor' planktonic food base. The herring multiplied rapidly, ate all the zooplankton and then starved. Meanwhile, the gobies, of no commercial value themselves, were competing with native fish over benthic fauna. Commercial catches of fish like bream and carp fell, but gobies provided food for predator fish such as asp and zander, catches of which rose.

Ichthyologists were not deterred by these results. As Karpevich (1960b, 77), an ichthyologist at the All-Union Research Institute of Fisheries and Oceanography, VNIRO, wrote, 'To maintain the fishery significance of the Aral Sea as far as possible in the future, it is necessary even now to introduce to its fauna more euryhaline, eurythermal species of fish and non-fish objects, capable of making full use of its food resources.'[9] Thus, after 1960, as salinity levels rose, more systematic measures were taken to reconstruct the whole ecosystem. Elaborating the new approach, Karpevich (1960a, 11) started from Michurin's principle of 'the unity of the organism with its conditions of life (*edinstvo organizma i uslovii ego zhizni*)' to view acclimatisation as a complex process of organisms adapting to their new habitat. Successful acclimatisation depended both on the survival of the individual organisms and on the growth of the species population to occupy an 'ecological niche'. Thus, whereas the Azov Sea, rich in small fish, was suitable for the introduction of predators, the Aral, deemed 'poor' in biomass, first required the introduction of invertebrates at the base of the food chain. This was a 'utilitarian' (Karpevich 1960a, 25) project, its goal the scalable growth of commercial fisheries (cf. Lien 2015; Tsing 2015). However, acclimatisations were not about abstracting fungible commodities from their lifeworlds: the quantitative growth of species of commercial value was premised on the interrelations between different species throughout the food chain.[10]

Karpevich (1960b) recognised that it was initially preferable to enrich the food base (*kormovaia baza*) of native fish rather than introduce new fish, which might compete with existing ones. Thus, in this period, only silver carp and belyy amur, plant-eating species from the Far East with no local competitors, were introduced. However, a range of euryhaline invertebrates were introduced, some more successful than others. To replace the zooplankton wiped out by Baltic herring, a small crustacean, *C. aquaedulcis*, was introduced, quickly spreading across the sea. To enrich the benthic fauna, under stress from rising salinity and from the voracious gobies, the bivalve mollusc *A. ovata* and a polychaete worm, *N. diversicolor*, were introduced from the Azov Sea. In previous decades, they had already been introduced to the Caspian with positive results. Amid rising salinities, they became dominant species in the Aral's invertebrate population. Indeed, as salinity rose, biomass of benthic fauna increased tenfold (Krupa and Grishaeva 2019). Biodiversity, however, fell, with many species wiped out by the rising salinity; chironomid (midge) larvae, a key benthic foodstuff, probably also suffered from predation by the polychaete worm (Plotnikov 2013).

In the 1970s, rising salinity levels and shrinking spawning grounds made it impossible for native species to reproduce. By the late 1970s, only gobies, atherines and a few Baltic herring were left. Yet, in terms of its invertebrate population, the sea was far from dead. In her major work on the acclimatisation published in 1975, Karpevich affirmed that, with the expected diversion of Siberian rivers, the Aral regression would not last long; in the meantime 'it is necessary to continue both theoretical and practical works to maintain life in this difficult period for the sea, and to preserve its biological and economic significance, however small' (Karpevich 1975, 356). Recognising the uncertainty surrounding the sea's future as it continued to shrink, Karpevich proposed a range of experiments, following which efforts were made to introduce euryhaline fish species: two types of flounder, Caspian sturgeon, Pacific salmon.[11] Of these, flounder glossa, introduced from the Azov Sea in 1979–87, thrived, feeding on *N. diversicolor* and two bivalve molluscs – *A. ovata* (introduced) and *C. isthmicum* (aboriginal).[12] Flounder faced competition for food only from gobies. Able to cope with salinities of 15–50 g/l, the flounder quickly adapted to its new environment, shortening its spawning time in response to the more rapid ice melt than on the Azov (Ermakhanov et al. 2012). It also, throughout the 1980s, faced no predation from humans, who were now fishing elsewhere. We will pick this story up in Chapter 5.

Problems of living standards and of employment

In the short term, these efforts did not halt the fall in catches. Despite the Presidium of the USSR Council of Ministers' 1965 resolution to preserve the sea's fishery significance (*rybokhoziaistvennoe znachenie*), the amount of water reaching the sea continued to decline. In 1969 the Kazakh Council of Ministers (Kazsovmin) referred to the resolution when they sought investment in the Aral region from the USSR Fisheries Ministry (Minrybkhoz) and the USSR Water Management Ministry (Minvodkhoz).[13] However, their attempt to use the resolution to bolster the case for investment failed.[14] Critically, the decision to preserve the sea's economic significance did not trump the needs of irrigation. So in their letter, Kazsovmin asked Minrybkhoz USSR and Minvodkhoz USSR to petition Sovmin USSR 'about hastening the resolution of the question of preserving the Aral Sea by means of diversion of the flow of Siberian rivers'.[15] It was thus possible to talk about preserving the sea itself only on the basis of diverting Siberian rivers; otherwise, within the limits set by the necessity of irrigation, it was only possible to talk about saving the Aral's 'fishery significance'. In practice, this related only to delta lakes – and talk did not easily translate into action. As one arm of the state continued as normal, water continued to be withdrawn for irrigation and the sea receded further; for other state organs, preserving even the economic significance of the Aral was a race against time. By the early 1970s, the situation was worse than foreseen: a 1973 Union-level commission forecast, accurately, that the 'industrial significance' of the sea would be almost entirely lost by 1980.[16]

The Kazakh authorities now began to talk about the regression as a problem of employment (*trudoustroistvo*) and of living conditions (*sotsiial'no-bytovye usloviia*). One solution to the problem of living standards was *pereselenie*, deportation/relocation. Over the course of the 1970s populations of former islands were relocated to Qaratereng, while inhabitants of the villages Ūialy and Ūzyn Qaiyr, far to the south of the delta, with no fresh water, were relocated to Aral'sk, continuing earlier policies of settling and concentrating populations. While the USSR Fisheries Ministry suggested relocating *all* the coastal villages to another region altogether, this met stiff resistance from both the Kazakh authorities and local people.[17] In contrast to the deportations of the Stalinist era, it is a mark of the less repressive atmosphere of the late Soviet period that this resistance was successful.[18] With mass relocation out of the question, the focus fell on improving living conditions. As outlined in a 1973 directive of Kazsovmin, living conditions in villages were to be improved through construction of water pipes, field hospitals, schools, nurseries and shops; and villagers were to be provided with feed for livestock and Ural motorcycles.[19] Work was also conducted to create lake fish farms (*ozërno-tovarnye rybokhoziaistva*), while investment was sought for other sorts of employment, most importantly a canning factory in Aral'sk.

That the sea's regression should emerge on the political agenda as a problem of employment and living standards – rather than, say, an ecological problem, or a problem of falling economic output – relates to the tacit social contract of state socialism, which rested on full employment and steadily rising living standards. Living standards in the Aral region had always lagged far behind those of metropolitan regions of the USSR. As the sea receded, the worsening living standards, falling pay, and layoffs further jeopardised the social contract. The sea's regression thus became bureaucratically known through these effects, and investment was sought to mitigate them. As Kornai (1980) explains, 'investment hunger' was characteristic of socialist economies. Amid perennial shortages, both fisheries bosses and regional officials had to seek investment from higher bodies to ensure the functioning of their sector or region, the locus of their political authority and prestige. The sea's regression exacerbated the difficulties of functioning within the shortage economy, prompting further investment hunger. Since the violation of the social contract threatened regional and fisheries bosses' own legitimacy, investment hunger was expressed in the politically acceptable terms of living standards and employment.

Allocative bodies tended towards postponement, because savings from postponement were immediate, certain and quantifiable, even if in the long run this meant higher social costs, requiring more investment to resolve the problem (Kornai 1980). Furthermore, most spare funds were being used for investment in cases which had reached the tipping point. Investments therefore would only be made after 'tolerance limits' had been reached, after a problem had become a crisis. However, Kornai (1980) argues, recognition of tolerance limits was not automatic, but required bureaucrats to forcibly voice them. This point was particularly salient in a 'creeping environmental problem' where change was incremental and thresholds were not objectively given (Glantz 1999b). Many of these documents show bureaucrats struggling, within constrained speech genres, to establish that tolerance limits had been breached, while higher-level authorities sought to downplay the problem to avoid assigning funds. In this process of toing and froing, in an economy that was, on the one hand, legitimised by a social contract of full employment and rising living standards and, on the other, hampered by endemic shortages, the Aral Sea regression emerged, haltingly, as a 'problem' demanding specific sorts of action.

Improving living standards by decrees

Accordingly, Kazsovmin passed a series of resolutions about living conditions and employment. Each was preceded by correspondence between Kazsovmin, the planning body (Gosplan KazSSR), the fisheries ministry (Minrybkhoz KazSSR) and the Qyzylorda oblast authorities (obkom/oblispolkom). Minrybkhoz and oblast authorities sought investments, with varying degrees of success. For example, in 1974 Minrybkhoz KazSSR tried to insert a clause to ask Minrybkhoz USSR for investment for hatcheries in the Syr Dariya delta and a fish farm on the Aqshatau lake system, and for assistance in relocation of villages, which 'cannot stand further delay since the social conditions of the existing villages are difficult'.[20] This attempt to establish tolerance limits was unsuccessful: when the resolution was drafted, there was no reference to investment from Minrybkhoz USSR (although the Kazakh Minrybkhoz was told to allocate funds for construction of water pipes).[21]

The following year, a letter from Qyzylorda obkom/oblispolkom prompted another Kazsovmin resolution. As the regional authorities strove to make their voice heard, they began with some flourish, and an unusual sense of narrative arc:

> The Aral water-body is one of the oldest fishery basins in the country. In the past on the Aral Sea up to 500 thousand tsentners [50,000 tonnes] of high-quality table fish were extracted (zander, asp, carp, barbel, bream, roach). However, since 1965 the Aral Sea and the fishery lakes of the oblast, because of the sharp increase in the abstraction of water from the rivers Syr Dariya and Amu Dariya for agricultural needs, have been shallowing, which has led to a serious deterioration in the natural reproduction of fish stocks in the basin and reduction in the volume of fish catches.[22]

As usual, the needs of agriculture are a parenthesis (indeed, the oblast authorities themselves had an interest in the development of irrigation in Qyzylorda oblast for rice). However, the emplotment in the glorious past, though exaggerating both quality and quantity, rhetorically boosts the claim for investment. The authors note efforts to maintain water levels and fish stocks in lakes, but stress that these measures cannot solve the problem of employment. They therefore make a series of requests, 'in the interests of preserving a contingent of fishermen and workers in the fishing industry and making full use of the labour resources existing in the region'.[23] Most ambitiously, they demand the construction of a canning factory in Aral'sk, processing 20,000,000 cans per year, employing 500 people – a clear case of investment hunger. Other requests include hydrological installations on lakes, and the hastening of the construction of Qamystybas fish farm; funding for flats in Aral'sk for relocated families; and money for loans for fishermen to build new houses. There are also smaller requests relating to the increasing difficulty of reaching the receding sea, including refrigerated lorries for receiving fish, mobile banyas (steam baths), Ural motorbikes for fishermen and trucks to transport drinking water.

The final resolution of Kazsovmin, 'About measures for labour organisation (*trudovoe ustroistvo*) of fishermen of the Aral region and improvement of their living and cultural conditions', was more muted than the florid tone of the oblast authorities: 'In the interests of improvement of everyday cultural conditions of fishermen of the Aral region and employment of workers in the fishing industry who have been released (*vysvobodivshiesia*) in connection with the contracting fishery on the Aral Sea, the Council of Ministers of Kazakh SSR resolves: [...]'.[24] The constraints of the speech genre are evident: the participle phrase 'the contracting fishery' conceals both the glorious past described by the oblast authorities and the reasons for its contraction, while the euphemistic *vysvobodivshiesia* casts the problem of employment as the natural consequence of a normal economic process. Not all the demands of the oblast authorities were met. The resolution approved the construction of the Qamystybas fish farm and other interventions in delta lakes, and instructed Gosplan KazSSR to assign necessary equipment. It also included a range of measures to improve living conditions, including water pipes and field hospitals. It approved the decision to relocate 520 families from remote villages to the town of Aral'sk, and instructed Minrybkhoz KazSSR to house them, and Gosplan 'to provide measures for improving the use of labour resources of the Aral region'.[25] Despite this vague gesture towards providing employment for the relocated families, however, the oblast authorities' central demand for a canning factory was ignored.

In 1976 the pattern was repeated. A letter from the oblast authorities stressed the effects of the sea's retreat on water provisioning, transport, fisheries, the shipyard and the port. The effects are stark:

> This has led to the reduction of workers in the last 10 years by 2,000 people. At the present time in the whole Aral region it is not possible to provide with work 10,500 people capable of work (including 6,000 women), of whom in the town of Aral'sk 6,600 people (including 2,300 women).[26]

These figures represent approximately 30% of the working-age population, a proportion that was in fact broadly typical of Central Asia (Lubin 1984, 58). Occluded from this picture are the informal means by which people supported themselves, whether by keeping private livestock or by trading. However, statistics baldly demonstrate that tolerance limits have been reached, presenting a severe problem of employment that requires investment.

The resulting decree from Kazsovmin, 'On urgent measures for the further development of the economy and improvement of everyday-cultural conditions of the population of the Aral raion of Qyzylorda oblast',[27] included only some of the oblast authorities' requests. The canning factory was now included in the decree, as well as new fish farms. However, funds were not allocated: Minrybkhoz KazSSR was to 'discuss' funding with Minrybkhoz USSR. New enterprises in Aral'sk were planned, including a sewing factory and a meat processing plant; but other requests, such as a glass factory and a brick factory, were not included. According to the decree, fishermen's pay also rose to compensate for falling catches. The oblast authorities had requested that, in accordance with a previous directive, Minvodkhoz KazSSR be obliged to deliver 50 m^3/s (1.57 km^3/year) of water below Qazaly, for lakes and fish farms.[28] In the final decree, this figure was to be defined each year by Minvodkhoz, in dialogue with Minrybkhoz.

In sum, although Kazsovmin recognised that tolerance limits were reached, not all the demands were fulfilled, and many measures were tacitly postponed simply by not allocating resources. Nevertheless, according to later reports on the progress of implementing these resolutions, some concrete action ensued.[29] Relocated populations from islands were housed in Aral'sk, and hospitals, shops and schools were built in villages. A stud farm was established at Qūlandy to provide employment. Water pipes were, eventually, built to most villages, while others were provided with wells. A water-purifying station was built at Amanötkel in 1977, although this could not mitigate the heavy mineralisation of drinking water caused by agriculture (Elpiner 1998). Electricity was provided to many villages for the first time. In other words, some basic aspects of state-socialist development, new forms of gridded connection, which had long been absent from the region, finally arrived.

However, not all measures were fulfilled. Two fish farms were created, but Minrybkhoz USSR refused to assign funds before water provisioning for the lakes was guaranteed in the integrated plan for water use in the whole Aral basin – which never materialised. Indeed, the decree stipulated that Minvodkhoz KazSSR define the quantities of water to be delivered to the lower reaches of the Syr Dariya, and this varied from year to year. In 1981–2 total flow below Qazaly was more than the oblast authorities had requested, 1.63 km^3 and 2.04 km^3 respectively, in 1983 much less, just 0.39 km^3.[30] Some of the enterprises to provide work were cancelled: the sewing factory was never built; the canning factory, for which funds had been unsuccessfully sought from Minrybkhoz USSR, was cancelled by decree of Kazsovmin in 1982; and the meat-processing factory was cancelled. The 'problem of employment' was not resolved.

In 1984 another letter from the oblast authorities to Kazsovmin sought help for the Aral region. Gosplan carried out investigations, focused on the village of Qaratereng, where they found that, despite some positive results of the measures taken, there was still a labour surplus comparable to that identified in the region nearly 10 years earlier. The investigation also found that, while some families had been relocated to rice-growing sovkhozy (state farms) elsewhere in Qyzylorda oblast, most of the population categorically refused to leave, for reasons we explore in Chapter 4. Gosplan's solutions were more of the same: Minvodkhoz was to guarantee 30 m^3/s (0.95 km^3/year) below Qazaly; the Ministry of Agriculture was, in compensation for the damage done to the fisheries, to allot funds for building a dam on a delta lake; electricity lines were to be built to power pumps for the lakes.[31]

Even when investment was allocated, it could never resolve the root cause of the region's problems, lack of water. Critically, because of the discursive constraints of these speech genres, the problem could only be constructed in a limited way, disaggregating cause and effect. In a mechanical chain of consequences, regulation of rivers is a parenthetic background factor. The end consequence is a problem of 10,500 surplus workers. Through the statistic, the problem of employment is abstracted from the complex set of material effects brought about by the sea's regression. A problem of living standards entailed some investment in basic infrastructure, but dust storms and their effects could not be recognised as problems. As a problem of living standards and employment, the regression did not constitute a critical event mobilising large-scale transformation. Entering the political sphere through this very limited optic, the sea's regression prompted a limited set of actions that broadly sought to maintain the status quo.

Nevertheless, as we will see in the following chapters, Soviet times are remembered as a period of full employment. Employment *was* provided even in the late Soviet period, if not the full employment which was promised. Certainly, the fishery shrank dramatically. In the postwar period, about 8,000 people were working in the industry, including 2,000–3,000 men and women fishing on the sea, lakes and lower reaches of the Syr Dariya.[32] Over the coming years, the fishery upstream on lakes in Qazaly raion sharply contracted as irrigation systems were developed to grow rice. Fisheries in uninhabitable villages like Ūialy and Ūzyn Qaiyr were liquidated. By 1970 the number of people fishing had fallen to about 650.[33] Women were the first to stop fishing as the fishery contracted over the 1960s, though they continued to work in processing plants. In 1976 Avan' fish plant was liquidated, and some of the fishermen from Aqespe and Aqbasty villages were laid off and transferred to the nearby Qūlandy stud farm.[34] However, this was the last case of workers being laid off until perestroika. If challenging the needs of irrigation was politically unconscionable, so was suggesting layoffs – a point forcibly voiced by an Aralrybprom accountant at a Minrybkhoz meeting in 1986.[35] The function of the enterprise shifted from exploiting the wealth of the sea to supporting the workers in the region, and Aralrybprom went on employing some 2,000 people: fishermen mostly in coastal villages, and workers, mostly women, in processing plants in Aral'sk, Bögen,

Qaratereng, Qazaly, and Aqtöbe to the north. Although the port closed, analogous processes maintained employment in the shipyard and other enterprises in Aral'sk.

Fish farms

As the industrial character of the Aral Sea disappeared, attention turned to developing fish farms (*ozërno-tovarniia rybokhoziaistva*) on delta lakes, which seemed to promise a sustainable supply of fish, and employment, over the years.[36] If they were provided with fresh water, cleared of weeds and stocked with valuable carp species, lakes promised up to 4,500 tonnes of fish per year.[37] Even as the environment deteriorated, the *ozërno-tovarnoe rybokhoziaistvo* offered a form to be regulated. Yet the promise of control was, as ever, frustrated. Aralrybprom decrees reiterate the need for the 'rational use' of the farms, involving stocking, cleaning canals and pumping in fresh water.[38] Weeds and low-value fish like pike were not in fact removed.[39] All lakes were supposed to be assigned to a single enterprise or kolkhoz, which would be responsible for the lake, but poaching was rife, and inspectors and managers did little to stop it. An order from 1981 found enterprises fishing on forbidden lakes; in one instance, a local manager was complicit.[40] Given the difficulties of fulfilling the plan in the deteriorating environment, such behaviour is unsurprising.

The biggest constraint on the development of fish farms was, of course, lack of water, which lay far beyond fisheries managers' control. But within official speech genres, blame could only be passed downwards, not upwards and/or sideways, to Minvodkhoz for example. Thus a 1984 Minrybkhoz USSR commission sternly instructed Minrybkhoz KazSSR to ensure that lakes were supplied with water – although the commission explicitly recognised that water-management institutions were failing to assign water for fishing. The commission also found an absurd situation whereby Qamystybas, an important fish farm, was being used by subsidiary enterprises based in Aral'sk, who were growing watermelons along its shores, withdrawing water and polluting with pesticides.[41] Local fisheries managers, as well as the ministry, were aware of this practice – and had complained to the raion authorities, who, it turned out, had been organising it! People from Aral'sk had even been keeping boats and nets by the lake – a hint of the informal practices lying behind the official statistics of dire unemployment.[42]

Meanwhile, Aralrybprom managers blamed those below them for failing to stock lakes and supply them with water. In 1984, they complained that Lake Aqshatau, managed by kolkhoz Zhambul, had not been watered since 1970.[43] They also found that kolkhoz Raiym had taken things into their own hands: their lake was separated from Lake Qamystybas by a dam, which the kolkhoz managers had destroyed, to raise the level of their own lake. This behaviour prompted the ministry to remove the lake from the kolkhoz's control. But a delegation of kolkhozniks to the ministry successfully requested that it be returned to the kolkhoz; the ministry even agreed to put in a sluice to improve water supply to the lake.[44]

In the late 1970s the Syr Dariya was dammed at Aghlaq, so that what little water there was would not flow into the sea but could be used on the lakes and provide drinking water (Plotnikov et al. 2014, 160). But there was never enough water. In 1985 a famous brigadier fisherman and Party member, Narghaly Demeuov, wrote to the oblast newspaper *Put' Lenina* criticising Aralrybprom. The managers defended themselves by blaming water-management organisations, in particular for their failure to build a dam at Qarashalang which would provide for the 'rational use of limited water resources'. Kazsovmin had decreed that water-management organisations build this dam, but five years later they had failed to do so.[45] However, although fisheries managers could make these points to defend themselves in the press, there was no official channel for them to address the water-management organisations directly.

Expeditionary fishing and ocean fish

Nevertheless, these fish farms were not futile. In 1979 the total caught in the lakes of Qyzylorda oblast was 1,153 tonnes; in 1988, 1,540 tonnes.[46] However, they could not provide enough work for fishermen or processors. Fishermen were therefore sent to fish on lakes hundreds or thousands of kilometres away elsewhere in Kazakhstan: if earlier in the century labour had been forcibly relocated to places where resources were abundant and labour in deficit, surplus labour was now dispatched to regions where there were resources left to exploit. But *all* major lakes in Kazakhstan were damaged by the insatiable demands of agriculture, and fish stocks across the republic were under pressure.[47] The Caspian was out of bounds, as it was not managed by Minrybkhoz KazSSR but by a trans-republican authority. Most promising were the lakes on the Yrghyz river in Aqtöbe oblast, some 300 km north of Aral'sk. Though initially poor in ichthyofauna, they were successfully stocked with carp – loaded into oak barrels from the Aral and flown to the Yrghyz by AN-2 aircraft – which grew rapidly and proved the basis of a successful fishery.

The other two biggest lakes in the country, Balqash and Zaisan, had their own fisheries. Even more isolated than the Aral, their 'poor' ichthyofauna had also been 'enriched' by acclimatisations of carp, bream, zander and so on. Kolkhoz Zhambul fished on Balqash from 1976, and in 1978 a Minrybkhoz decree allocated Aralrybprom a sector of northeastern Balqash, 'in the interests of the full development (*osvoenie*) of the lake'.[48] In this remote region Aralrybprom set up a receiving station with a salting workshop. *Ekspeditsionnyi lov*, 'expeditionary fishing', was contingent on permission from Glavrybvod, a regulatory body directly subordinate to Minrybkhoz USSR, not Minrybkhoz KazSSR. As a practice of providing employment, it was therefore constrained institutionally, and by the limits of a damaged environment. This was not full-time work, though fishermen were paid extra for the time away (*komandirochnye raskhody*). When not fishing, they would be employed in 'subsidiary enterprises', gathering hay, tending to Aralrybprom livestock.

In 1979, 1,887 tonnes were caught from other oblasts; in 1988, 3,420 tonnes.[49] However, the majority of fish processed in Aralrybprom factories was from the oceans – vast enterprises deploying factory ships in the Pacific (Dal'ryba), the Arctic Ocean (Sevryba) and the Baltic (Zapryba). Pollock, capelin, herring, sardine, sardinella, mackerel, horse-mackerel: all were brought in refrigerated railway wagons to Aral'sk and small plants in Bögen, Qaratereng and Qazaly for smoking or curing. This was common practice in all fish plants in Kazakhstan as catches fell. From the late 1970s, up to 5,000 tonnes a year were imported to Aral'sk. But ocean fish had their own problems, connected with the dysfunction of the Soviet economy: despite their abundance in the ocean, deliveries were highly irregular, and rarely conformed to what was promised, still less to Aralrybprom's annual plans. There was a tendency to dispatch fish such as pollock, which was unprofitable to process, being as unpopular in the USSR as it is in Britain.

Because of the cost of importing fish and sending fishermen thousands of kilometres to fish, the enterprise went from being profitable to loss-making, dependent on subsidies from Minrybkhoz KazSSR, which itself was subsidised from the republican budget. Even so, there were almost constant financial difficulties. While output plans tended to be met (after some tweaking), cost of production was generally higher than planned. So, while planned losses were automatically covered by the ministry, there were also over-plan losses; and there was a chronic shortage of circulating assets (*oborotnye sredstva*). From the late 1970s onwards, losses oscillated between 500,000 and 1,000,000 roubles per year.[50]

Trouble with the bank

Despite chronic difficulties, the industry kept functioning – in which sense, this is also a typical story of a struggling stagnation-era enterprise. Indeed, while 'financial difficulty' was a result of all the constraints which we have explored, it was not, in itself, an insuperable constraint. In Kornai's (1980) terms, because state-socialist enterprises were always bailed out, budget constraints were 'soft', and enterprises therefore treated money as 'passive': their behaviour was not affected by how much money they had. While the material below supports that point, bailouts still required negotiation. After all, only in the 1950s most Aral kolkhozy had been liquidated precisely because of financial difficulties. Thus, fisheries managers were caught up in various constraints and dependencies: the ministry set the plan, and they were dependent both on the ministry and on their workers to fulfil it. They also depended on the local branch of the state bank (Gosbank) for financing everyday operations, including purchasing ocean fish.[51] They were constrained both by the dysfunction of the shortage economy and by the deteriorating environment. However, certain forms of agency were open to them as they negotiated their awkward situation. After all, their superiors also depended on them to maintain the industry and prevent the crisis worsening.

When negotiating bailouts, all the discursive constraints we have looked at applied: fisheries managers could not protest officially about the loss of the sea or claim compensation from water-management or agriculture ministries. There was no official idiom for expressing the severity of the crisis, or for addressing anything other than the economic symptoms. Take this 1975 letter to Minrybkhoz KazSSR. Seeking to raise the limits for production costs and personnel, managers cite several reasons, including costs of ocean fish. Only the fifth reason touches directly on the drying up of the sea:

> As a result of the deterioration of the industrial significance of the Aral Sea and lakes belonging to it, as in fact the first quarter showed, to fulfil the state plan we have been forced (*vynuzhdeny*) to carry out expeditionary fishing in the 2 and 3rd quarters of 20,000 tsentners [2,000 tonnes] of fish on the lakes of Aqtöbe oblast, which are delivered to Aral'sk and Aqtöbe fish-plant by auto-transport, which just for the additional transport costs requires more than 450,000 roubles.[52]

The complex ecological crisis is reduced to a single-stranded economic problem – deteriorating industrial significance, a technical problem obstructing fulfilment of the state plan. Within these discursive constraints, what can be claimed from the higher organ is also limited. Nevertheless, claims can be made. Highlighting constraints allows the authors to disavow agency ('we have been forced to'), thus forestalling any charge of mismanagement, and bolsters their claims for leeway. The speech genre thus also has its affordances: reductions in plans and economic assistance could be negotiated by highlighting environmental constraints.[53] Indeed, Minrybkhoz KazSSR and Gosplan KazSSR gave the enterprise considerable leeway, often on that very basis.[54] In turn, Kazakh fisheries ministers would try to negotiate with USSR ministers and with their colleagues in Kazsovmin. Of course, while local managers would highlight only the constraints within which they operated, communications from the ministry would, as well as acknowledging the 'objective reasons' for their difficulties, also blame mismanagement, especially hoarding, and would instruct them to take measures to improve management.[55] But this was a generic feature, part of the performative aspect of the document. It never translated into sanctions from the ministry. Doubtless informal pressure, involving other ways of talking about the problem offstage which are not recorded in these documents, also played its part, particularly when Sarzhanov, former director of Aralrybkombinat, was Fisheries Minister in the 1980s.

Relations between Aralrybprom and Gosbank were more fractious, and a file of correspondence between them from 1979 offers insight into the (dys)functioning of the fishing industry.[56] Gosbank was less interested in Aralrybprom's plan fulfilment than in resolution of its chronically dire financial situation and improving its 'economic efficiency'. Thus further bargaining was necessary to secure loans to cover shortages in working capital and purchase of ocean fish. On Aralrybprom's side, correspondence draws attention to a permanent state of 'temporary financial difficulty', which managers blame on various factors beyond their control: irregular delivery of ocean fish; the high expense of fishing on Balqash; the failure of the ministry to top up their working capital as promised; and shortage of railway wagons delaying dispatch of finished production. Managers also voiced the measures being taken to rectify the financial situation: sending their fishermen to the southern Aral (before 1978) and Balqash, and making full use of the delta lakes. They stressed that the factory was working as hard as possible to process all the fish which had arrived to avoid accumulating excess stocks, and that they were trying to get hold of profitable fish.

In reply, Gosbank would never mention the sea's regression – although the sea's retreat from the town would have been perfectly visible to Aral'sk Gosbank managers. They focused on the overdue loans owed by Aralrybprom; their over-expenditure on pay and travel expenses; their hoarding of materials, especially fish; and their failure to call in debts owed to them. Threats would involve 'special regimes of financing', which aimed to reduce indebtedness. Faced with such threats, Aralrybprom managers would write to the ministry for help. There would be less explanation of the root causes of the problem than in letters to the bank – a sign, perhaps, of a more sympathetic addressee. The standard format was simply to state the shortfall in working capital, the various overdue loans and the threats from Gosbank, before requesting a loan or subsidy. A particularly desperate telegram from 1978 adds that deliverers of ocean fish are refusing to deliver because of problems in paying them, and that the enterprise will be 'paralysed' without the ministry's help.[57] In this instance, the Aralrybprom director requested that the minister petition the republic office of Gosbank for a one-million-rouble loan.

Generally, special regimes of financing would be avoided. But when one such regime was applied, in 1979, the director and accountant of Aralrybprom wrote to the local manager of Gosbank: 'The experience of recent years has shown that when the association Aralrybprom has experienced tough financial difficulty, Minrybkhoz has always come forward and through the Ministry of Finances has paid off all the debt on Gosbank loans.'[58] They note that the fishery on local lakes and on Balqash is going well; that an agreement has been reached with Zaprybsbyt about more marketable ocean fish like mackerel and horse-mackerel; 'experienced comrades' are being sent all over the USSR to choose suitable fish for processing. A week later the regime was cancelled.

Gosbank was also under constraints. Their goal was to make the enterprise run more efficiently, but the only pressure they could apply threatened the working of the enterprise altogether, and in the stagnation era the rationality of meeting plans – not to mention keeping people in work – trumped that of economic efficiency. An internal Aralrybprom document from 1979 mentions that the local bank has applied to the oblast office of the bank to apply the most serious sanction of all: forced sale, implying the dissolution of the enterprise and the distribution of its assets to other enterprises.[59] But there is no mention of it anywhere else. From a strictly economistic perspective, it may have seemed the only solution to a chronically failing enterprise, but it was politically and socially unconscionable: the rationality of economic efficiency was subordinate.

The limits of bureaucratic discourse

And so the industry limped on. In the local archives, after a flurry of correspondence in 1978–9, there is no more about financial difficulties until 1985, but there is no reason to suppose that they went away. Indeed, files from 1985 containing the correspondence between Aralrybprom, Minrybkhoz and Gosbank follow the same pattern as earlier documents.[60] However, in some letters from Aralrybprom managers there is a shift in the language used, a new level of exasperation, and bureaucratic discourse almost breaks down. In late 1985 Gosbank applied a credit sanction without warning and cut off all forms of credit. In outrage, the director and accountant of Aralrybprom wrote to the Gosbank oblast office, sending copies to the ministry, and to the Gosbank republic and local offices.[61]

After explaining how the regression of the sea has led to the necessary reorganisation of the fishery so that it is based on ocean fish and expeditionary fishing, they state bluntly: 'The sharp retreat of the sea has caused anxiety (*vyzval bespokoistvo*) for the local inhabitants, and they have started moving to other life favourable regions of south Kazakhstan (*drugie zhiznennye blagopriiatnye raiony iuga Kazakhstana*).'[62] This is the most evident expression of concern for the local population that I found in the archives – and the closest to their voices. But the Russian is strange. As Bakhtin (1986, 80) notes, even people competent in a language may lack the generic repertoire to partake in certain forms of discourse. Here the writers, native Kazakh speakers, are well schooled in official bureaucratic genres of Russian, but the Russian becomes ungrammatical as their speech incorporates other forms of discourse about the sea, exceeding the limits of those genres. They then refer to a further constraint, imposed by higher authorities in line with the social contract:

> In the interests of supporting the indigenous fishermen and processing workers of the Aral, the TsK KP Kazakhstan and Kazsovmin have adopted a special decree, where it is categorically forbidden to dissolve any sections, brigades, units, both of fishermen and processors. Accordingly technical-economic assistance has been given, both of an individual and societal character of production (we adduce these facts for the information of the employees of the bank who are not acquainted with the exhausted [?] situation of the Aral and with its labourers [*s istomnym* [?] *polozheniem Arala i s ego truzhenikakh*]).[63]

The parenthesis at the end of the paragraph is sarcastic: the employees of Aral'sk Gosbank would have been well acquainted with how Aral's situation far exceeded the limits of official discourse. With this phrase, the authors, usually restricted by generic rules to talking just about the 'loss of industrial character' or 'deterioration of hydrological regime', gesture towards the whole complex of ecological, economic and social effects, and the sorts of discourse with which people were talking about them. Official discourse holds a trace of hidden, offstage transcripts.

The authors go on to complain that, although the plans have been fulfilled and Minrybkhoz is helping, the financial situation has deteriorated. At this point, their frustration bubbles over:

> Consequently, just for the normal work of the Association, a constant overdraft limit of no less than 1.5 million roubles is necessary; factually the matter far from corresponds to what was expected, since ocean raw-material from the main basins of the USSR arrives with interruptions (*s pereboem*); everyone knows that fish is not ore, or coal; suppliers dispatch whatever they have in stock. Here we are forced to accept without analysis of species of fish, whether they are included in the plan, whether they are profitable or not; the fact is that if we refuse, because the goods are not foreseen in the delivery plan or for some other reason, then we will be left without raw materials, and the 2000-strong workforce collective will be left with nothing. We have been through that bitter experience (*gor'kii opyt*) several times. Actually in recent years by seasons there is a practice of stocking up with raw materials 3–4 times more than the required norm. And the sequence of shipping to customers, in contrast to a combination of regional fish, dictates its own: they demand ordinary species of fish from local water-bodies, which we often don't have.[64]

The language breaks down here. The sense is clear: consumers want local fish, not fish from the oceans. But there is some odd phraseology, punctuation is lacking, and the syntax is unclear, with verbs lacking clear subjects. The sheer frustration of trying to function in the shortage economy boils over in a discourse lacking the resources to express such frustration. They continue to point out that supply is seasonal, and processing is also seasonal since it is impossible to process fish in the summer heat, before highlighting another constraint, the 'law of socialism': 'At that time, we present the workers with leave without pay, however we do not reduce the whole collective, since that is not stipulated in the law of socialism.'[65] Thus, they explain, materials and debts accumulated together. When production was ready to be dispatched in September, all the railway wagons were busy transporting watermelons. This explains the current financial difficulties. The bank has ignored their letters and imposed a regime of special crediting. The authors further remark that the bank has omitted to consider Aralrybprom's early overfulfilment of the Eleventh Five-Year Plan, and the overfulfilment of the plan for the first nine months of this year. On this basis, they urge, the bank is obliged to help. The managers have also appealed to the minister, Sarzhanov, both orally and in writing, but still the special regime of financing has been imposed. The sense of outrage accumulates as more arguments are adduced.

Finally, the authors spell out the consequences of Gosbank cutting off credit: 'Production is on the verge of final paralysis (*na grani okonchatel'noi paralizatsii*), since in days suppliers can refuse to deliver raw materials and other materials necessary for production, which will sharply influence the fulfilment of the state plan and without doubt will disrupt the pre-Congress obligations of the association.'[66] While bureaucratic discourse may be at its limit, the authors are still writing according to the rules of the genre, drawing attention to their legal obligations before the state. They use the genre's affordances to strengthen their hand in fulfilling what remains a relatively modest 'speech will'. They indicate clearly that tolerance limits, 'the verge of paralysis' of the fishery, have been reached. After this letter, and a phone conversation with the oblast bank manager, the credit sanctions were lifted.[67]

Conclusion

Over the coming years, in the climate of perestroika, central subsidies were cut, and the ban on layoffs was breached, with the remaining fishermen in Aqbasty transferred to the Qūlandy stud farm.[68] But 1988 saw some success: a new refrigeration unit was purchased from Denmark, a storage facility from Japan, and new lines of production, including spiced kippers, were mastered; that year saw an extraordinary above-plan profit.[69] Nevertheless, the basic pattern of financial difficulties, resolved at the last minute by intervention from the ministry, persisted. At the same time, as we saw in Chapter 1, the freer political atmosphere of glasnost brought a new way of talking about the sea, as activists' work established that tolerance limits or thresholds – economic, social, ecological and medical – had been passed years ago.

The story lying in the archives is rather different. In a century of catastrophes that included the destruction of the pastoral economy, the sea's disappearance both was and was not a sea change. As the sea's regression emerged as a 'problem', in a process of top-down adaptation to environmental change, the assemblage of people, fish and infrastructure was maintained, even once the sea at its centre had gone. Of course, this top-down adaptation introduced new dependencies and new vulnerabilities – as became clear when the Soviet Union collapsed. Nevertheless, this story of top-down adaptation casts further light on the relationship between the Soviet periphery and the centre, and on the political ecology of Soviet socialism. Chapter 1 demonstrated how interdependencies characterised by unequal exchange resulted in spatially uneven development. When the sea receded, the Aral region's dependence on gridded space was accentuated, but the unequal exchange was now reversed. In the less authoritarian context of the late USSR, rather than imposing forced relocation or deportation, bureaucrats at different levels were able, in limited, prescribed ways, to stand up for the local population. As the increasingly uncontrollable environmental consequences of uneven development threatened the social contract, and as the sea's regression emerged as a problem of living standards and employment, the equalising, redistributive tendency of late Soviet socialism became prominent, mitigating some of the damage wrought. Hence the financial subsidies, the redistribution of ocean fish, and the redistribution of the right to fish on other lakes to Aral fishermen. Tendencies towards centralisation and redistribution, though contradictory, were connected, resting on integration into Soviet space: the capacity of Minrybkhoz to redistribute depended on centralisation of resources. Had Balqash been managed by local communities, or the ocean fish managed by their own fishermen, this would not have happened.

Nevertheless, bureaucrats always struggled to deal with even the limited problem of employment and living standards. Indeed, the uneven distribution of discursive resources and the constraints of official speech genres circumscribed how the sea's regression could emerge as a fact, and hence limited the possible official responses. Surplus labour or a paralysed fishery could constitute a tolerance limit; more complex problems could not. Indeed, these contradictory tendencies, towards centralisation and towards redistribution, were sharply asymmetrical: redistribution could not make up for the escalating damage wrought by irrigation projects, even in the very limited terms in which this damage was understood. The following two chapters explore what these processes look like to people in the region today.

Notes

1. Vice-chairman of South Kazakhstan Sovnarkhoz, D. Dzhumaliev, 'Meropriiatiia po razvitiiu rybnoi promyshlennosti Aral'skogo basseina', n.d. but 1962, TsGARK, f. 1874, op. 1, d. 23, ll. 7–20 (7).
2. Dzhumaliev, 'Meropriiatiia' (7).
3. Dzhumaliev, 'Meropriiatiia' (16).
4. I am inspired by Yurchak's (2005) notion of the 'redundancy' of late Soviet ideological discourse, which I find helpful also for approaching bureaucratic discourse. Such redundancy is of course not unique to Soviet bureaucratic discourse: the quotation from Brown above describes a US context.
5. There were also similar patterns of relocation and consolidation among remote Russian fisheries that had not seen large-scale environmental problems (Grant 1995; Nakhshina 2011; E. Wilson 2002).
6. This is according to census data from 1970, 1979 and 1989 (published online at http://www.demoscope.ru/weekly/ssp/ussr70_reg1.php, http://www.demoscope.ru/weekly/ssp/ussr79_reg1.php, http://www.demoscope.ru/weekly/ssp/sng89_reg1.php, accessed 8 May 2021). The population of the town of Aral'sk itself fell from nearly 38,000 to 32,000 over 1970–9, but was just below 31,000 in 1989.
7. Similarly, Kalinovsky's description of the role of Central Asian economists and social scientists in the planning process reveals how 'planning became a field of political struggle as much as a technocratic process, allowing different groups to make arguments for or against investments, targets, and so forth' (2018, 89). If ethnographies of bureaucracies focus on the mismatch between claims to abstract rationality and the arbitrariness of bureaucratic action (e.g. Alexander 2002; Graeber 2015; Gupta 2012; Herzfeld 1992), I focus on the different sorts of rationality which particular interests appeal to.
8. Similarly, Kotkin (1995) and Yurchak (2005) challenge totalitarian accounts of the Soviet state by breaking down the opposition between compliance and resistance, agency and passivity. For Kotkin, getting by in the Stalinist USSR depended on 'speaking Bolshevik'. In Yurchak's account of the late Soviet period, voicing ideological pronouncements that were devoid of semantic meaning was neither a matter of belief nor cynical public conformity, but a performance which enabled a wide array of meanings to emerge in everyday life. However, while for Kotkin and Yurchak conforming with official discourse is the precondition for agency, my argument is that even within the constraints of official discourse, some agency is possible. Cf. also Abashin (2015), who builds on the work of Kotkin and Yurchak to show how local actors like kolkhoz chairmen both acted as agents of Soviet rule and stood up for local interests, sometimes adopting policies emanating from the centre, sometimes subverting them, sometimes pushing back and negotiating them.
9. Euryhaline and eurythermal species are those tolerating a wide range of salinity and temperature, respectively.
10. The history of Soviet ichthyology is a history waiting to be written, a distinctive instance of scientific modernism. As a project of scalability, it is difficult to assess: since acclimatisations took place in environments already damaged by agriculture, they could only combat decline, rather than foster growth.
11. These attempts were rather more limited than Karpevich's (1975, 356–8) proposals, which involved experimenting with 18 different fish species, as well as further interventions in the phytoplankton and planktonic and benthic fauna.
12. Though aboriginal, *C. isthmicum* fared better in higher salinities.
13. Letter from vice-chairman of Kazsovmin, M. Iskanov, to the USSR Fisheries Minister, A. A. Ishkov, and USSR Minister of Land Reclamation and Water Resources, E. E. Alekseevskii, 17 June 1969, TsGARK, f. 1130, op. 1, d. 843, ll. 96–9.
14. A. Romanov, 'Spravka o khoziaistvenno-finansovoi deiatel'nosti Ministerstva rybnogo khoziaistva Kazakhskoi SSR za 1969 god', March 1970, TsGARK, f. 1130, op. 1, d. 910, l. 93.
15. Letter from Iskanov to Ishkov and Alekseevskii, 17 June 1969, TsGARK, f. 1130, op. 1, d. 843, ll. 96–9 (99).
16. Referenced in communication No. 30-11-07 from Glavrybvod to Uzbekrybvod and Kazakhrybvod, 18 August 1976, TsGARK, f. 1130, op. 1, d. 1692, l. 26.

17 Letter from USSR Fisheries Minister A. Ishkov to Kazsovmin, 20 June 1974, TsGARK, f. 1130, op. 1, d. 1484, ll. 66–7; letter from chairman of Kazsovmin B. Ashimov to USSR Sovmin, 'O perebazirovanii rybopromyshlennoi bazy i nekotorykh pribrezhnykh rybatskykh poselkov Aral'skogo moria', 13 December 1974, TsGARK, f. 1130, op. 1, d. 1484, ll. 91–3.

18 Even so, in the same period, villagers from the mountain regions of Tajikistan *were* being relocated to the cotton-growing regions in the valleys, with at least some degree of coercion – in part, as Kalinovsky (2018, Chapter 7) argues, because it was logistically easier to deliver the institutions of the welfare state in the valleys than in remote mountain settlements. Arguably, the successful resistance to the relocation of northern Aral fishing villages was due to their backing by the Kazakh republican authorities.

19 Vice-chairman of Kazsovmin A. Vartanian, 'Rasporiazhenie ot 15 ianvaria 1973 goda No. 21-r', 15 January 1973, TsGARK, f. 1130, op. 1, d. 1484, l. 2.

20 Letter from Fisheries Minister KazSSR, Utegaliev, to Gosplan KazSSR, 'Zamechaniia k proektu pis'ma v Sovet Ministrov Kazakhskoi SSR "Ob uluchsheniia sotsial'no-bytovykh uslovii naseleniia pribrezhnykh poselkov Aral'skogo moria"', September 1974, TsGARK, f. 1130, op. 1, d. 1484, ll. 68–71 (69).

21 Postanovlenie SM KazSSR 'O dopolnitel'nykh merakh po uluchsheniiu sotsial'no-bytovykh uslovii naseleniia pribrezhnykh poselkov severnoi chasti Aral'skogo mor'ia' (proekt), September 1974, TsGARK, f. 1130, op. 1, d. 1484, ll. 78–80.

22 Letter from Kzyl-Orda obkom secretary I. Abdukarimov and ispolkom chariman Sh. Bakirov to TsK KP Kazakhstana, Sovet Ministrov Kazakhskoi SSR, 'O sostoianii i perspektivakh rybnogo khoziaistva v Aral'skom more', 23 May 1975, TsGARK, f. 1137, op. 1pr, d. 4721, ll. 163–6 (163).

23 Abdukarimov and Bakirov (164).

24 Postanovlenie SM KazSSR ot 15 avgusta 1975 goda No 414 'O merakh po trudovomu ustroistvu rybakov Aral'skogo raiona i uluchsheniiu ikh zhilishchnykh i kul'turno-bytovykh uslovii', 15 August 1975, TsGARK, f. 1137, op. 1pr, d. 4721, ll. 139–40 (139).

25 Postanovlenie SM KazSSR ot 15 avgusta 1975 goda No 414 (139).

26 Letter from Kzyl-Orda obkom secretary I. Abdukarimov and ispolkom chairman Sh. Bakirov to TsK KP Kazakhstana, Sovet Ministrov Kazakhskoi SSR, 'O merakh po obespecheniiu zaniatosti i uluchsheniiu kul'turno-bytovykh uslovii naseleniia Aral'skogo raiona Kzyl-Ordinskoi oblasti', 12 June 1976, TsGARK, f. 1137, op. 1pr, d. 5145, ll. 161–71 (162).

27 Postanovlenie TsK KP Kazakhstana i SM KazSSR ot 6 avgusta 1976 goda No 368 'O neotlozhnykh merakh po dal'neishemu razvitiiu ekonomiki i uluchsheniiu kul'turno-bytovykh uslovii naseleniia Aral'skogo raiona Kzyl-Ordinskoi oblasti', 6 August 1976, TsGARK, f. 1137, op. 1pr, d. 5145, ll. 118–19.

28 Before 1960, annual inflow to the sea from the Syr Dariya was 13–16 km^3 (Asarin et al. 2010, 119).

29 Progress on implementation of the resolutions is summarised at: letter from fisheries minister Utegaliev to comrade N.N. Irtazin 'Informatsiia o khode vypolneniia postanovleniia Soveta Ministrov Kazakhskoi SSR ot 15 avgusta 1975 No 414 "O merakh po trudovomu ustroistvu rybakov Aral'skogo raiona i uluchsheniiu ikh zhilishchnykh i kul'turno-bytovykh uslovii"', 20 March 1978, TsGARK, f. 1130, op. 1, d. 1830, ll. 17–20; M. Dzhekbatyrov, 'Informatsiia o khode vypolneniia postanovleniia TsK KP Kazakhstana i Soveta Ministrov Kazakhskoi SSR ot 6 avgusta 1976 g. No 368 "O neotlozhnykh merakh po dal'neishemu razvitiiu ekonomiki i uluchsheniiu kul'turno-bytovykh uslovii naseleniia Aral'skogo raiona Kzyl-Ordinskoi oblasti"', 26 March 1984, TsGARK, f. 1130, op. 1, d. 2484, ll. 44–54.

30 Dzhekbatyrov, 'Informatsiia' (48). Over the 1980s, water reaching the Syr Dariya delta averaged 1.1 km^3/year, none of which reached the sea itself (Micklin 2014a, 125).

31 Gosplan chairman T. G. Mukhamed-Rakhimov, 'Prilozheniie No 3 k protokolu soveshchaniia ot 9 avgusta 1984 g.', 9 August 1984, AFGAKO, 4, op. 2, d. 719, ll. 8–12.

32 B. Musafirov et al., 'Meropriiatiia po koreinnomu uluchsheniiu raboty rybnoi promyshlennosti Kzyl-Ordinskoi oblasti Soveta Narodnogo Khoziaistva Iuzhno-Kazakhstanskogo ekonomicheskogo raiona', 16 June 1960, TsGARK f. 1874, op. 1, d. 18, ll. 1–29 (1); A. V. Volodkin, 'Fakticheskoe uchastie rybakov v dobyche ryby po Severu Aral'skogo moria', 8 July 1960, AFGAKO, f. 4, op. 2, d. 10, l. 43.

33 Communication from deputy fisheries minister M. T. Tairov to Kazsovmin (Otdel legkoi i pishchevoi promyshlennosti), 'Osnovnye pokazateli raboty Aral'skogo rybokombinata za 9-iu piatiletku i perspektivy na 1976-1980 gody', 8 August 1975, TsGARK, f. 1130, op. 1, d. 1484, ll. 188–91 (189).

34 Prikaz po Aral'skomu rybokombinatu No 316r, 'O peredache osnovnykh sredstv Avan'skogo rybozavoda Kulandinskomu konezavodu', 26 October 1976, AFGAKO, f. 4, op. 1pr, d. 516, l. 33.

35 Vystuplenie Glavnogo bukhgaltera Trakhanova Amangel'di na vyezdnoi kollegii Mynrybkhoza Kaz.SSR s uchastiem Ministra tov. Sarzhanova K.S., 'O finansovoi deiatel'nosti za 9 mesiatsev 1986 goda, o sostoianii ucheta i otchetnosti i mery po uluchsheniiu etoi raboty', 1986, AFGAKO, f. 4, op. 2, d. 802, ll. 38–42.

36 On the southern shore, similar efforts were made to rehabilitate the Amu Dariya delta (Micklin 2014b, 376).

37 e.g. Aralrybprom general director K. Sarzhanov et al., 'Perspektivnyi plan sotsial'no-ekonomicheskogo razvitiia Aral'skogo proizvodstvennogo ob'edineniia "Aralrybprom" na 1981-1985 gody', 1980, AFGAKO, f. 4, op. 1pr, d. 666, ll. 1–11 (5).

38 e.g. Chief specialist K. Aryngaziev, 'Meropriiatiia po organizatsii i ratsional'nomu vedeniiu Kamyshlybashskogo ozerno-tovarnogo khoziaistva', 26 May 1975, AFGAKO, f. 4, op. 1pr, d. 479, ll. 107–9.

39 Minrybkhoz KazSSR – Prikaz No 117 'Ob itogakh khoziaistvenno-finansovoi deiiatel'nosti Aral'skogo rybokombinata za 1976 god', 8 April 1977, AFGAKO, f. 4, op. 1pr, d. 549, ll. 16–27 (17). See also Mitrofanov et al. (1992, 401), who blame both the shortcomings of fish farms themselves and the 'objective' factor of lack of water.

40 Prikaz po proizvodstvennomu ob'edineniiu 'Aralrybprom' No 22r, 15 January 1981, AFGAKO, f. 4, op. 1pr, d. 660, ll. 27–8.

41 Letter from head of the department of fish-farming and fishing on internal water-bodies, V. S. Belov, to the Kazakh fisheries minister, K. S. Sarzhanov, and head of Kazakhrybvod, I. M. Utegaliev, 21 February 1984, AFGAKO, f. 4, op. 2, d. 718, ll. 16–17.

42 Letter from deputy minister M. N. Duisenov to Aralrybprom general director S. Sermagambetov, copied to the First Secretary of Aral'sk raikom, B. U. Ualiev, and chairman of ispolkom, A. T. Medetbaev, 14 February 1984, AFGAKO, f. 4, op. 2, d. 718, l. 15; letter from general director Sermagambetov to chairman of Aral'sk ispolkom A. Medetbaev, 1 March 1984, AFGAKO, f. 4, op. 2, d. 718, l. 23.

43 Minrybkhoz KazSSR – Prikaz No 72 'O vozvrashchenii oz. Dzhalanash v sostav Kamyshly-Bashkogo ozërnogo tovarnogo rybnogo khoziaistva ob'edineniia "Aralrybprom"', 5 March 1984, AFGAKO, f. 4, op. 2, d. 707, ll. 1–3.

44 Letter from minister K. S. Sarzhanov to chairman of Aral'sk ispolkom A. Medetbaev and Aralrybprom general director S. Sermagambetov, 7 May 1984, AFGAKO, f. 4, op. 2, d. 718, ll. 40–1.

45 Letter from Aralrybprom general director S. Sermagambetov to the editor of the Kzyl-Orda newspaper *Put' Lenina*, copied to Brigadeer N. Demeuov, 26 June 1985, AFGAKO, f. 4, op. 2, d. 760, ll. 45–9.

46 General director K. Sarzhanov, head of planning department Sh. Zhumakhmetov, chief accountant B. Sharapadinov, 'Analiz khoziaistvenno-finansovoi deiatel'nosti proizvodstvennogo ob'edineniia "Aralrybprom" za 1979g.', 2 February 1980, AFGAKO, f. 4, op. 1pr, d. 622, ll. 47–68 (49); general director Zh. Sapiev, head of planning-economic department V. F. Posina, chief accountant K. Tleulesov, 'Analiz khoziaistvenno-finansovoi deiatel'nosti PO "Aralrybprom" za ianvar'–dekabr' 1989 [sic] goda', 26 January 1989, AFGAKO, f. 4, op. 3pr, d. 935, ll. 8–21 (13).

47 e.g. 'Doklad "O sostoianii ispol'zovaniia proizvodstvennykh moshchnostei predpriiatii rybnogo khoziaistva respubliki po proizvodstvu pishchevoi rybnoi produktsii i merakh ob ego uluchshenii na 1970-1975 gg."', n.d. but 1970, TsGARK, f. 1130, op. 1, d. 913, ll. 43–5.

48 Minrybkhoz KazSSR – Prikaz 'Po osvoeniiu severnoi chasti oz. Balkhash rybakami ARPa v 1978g.', No. 285, 8 September 1977, TsGARK, f. 1130, op. 1, d. 1710, ll. 296–8. The policy is usually described in terms of employment, but in the late 1970s in particular other rationalities explained this practice, such as sorting out the finances of the industry, more profit, etc.

49 Sarzhanov, Zhumakhmetov, Sharapadinov, 'Analiz', AFGAKO, f. 4, op. 1pr, d. 622, ll. 47–68 (49); Sapiev, Posina, Tleulesov, 'Analiz', AFGAKO, f. 4, op. 3pr, d. 935, ll. 8–21 (13).

50 Aralrybprom's total production output was around 10 million roubles per year, that of Minrybkhoz KazSSR as a whole around 40 million roubles per year.

51 Enterprises were maintained on a minimum of working capital, and short-term loans from Gosbank were crucial to everyday operations, which allowed Gosbank to monitor everyday management (Garvy 1977). The local branch of Gosbank in Aral'sk was subordinate to the oblast bank, ultimately subordinate to Gosbank in Moscow, not to Kazsovmin.

52 Letter from Aral'sk rybokombinat director K. Sarzhanov to fisheries minister I. M. Utegaliev, 31 March 1975, AFGAKO, f. 4, op. 1pr, d. 504, ll. 6–8 (7).

53 e.g. letter from general director of Aralrybprom, Sermagambetov, to deputy fisheries minister KazSSR, M. N. Duisenov, n.d., but 1984, AFGAKO, f. 4, op. 2, d. 718, l. 20.

54 e.g. Letter from deputy fisheries minister, M. Tairov, to director of Aralrybokombinat, K. Sarzhanov, 25 August 1975, AFGAKO, f. 4, op. 1pr, d. 504, l. 110.

55 e.g. Minrybkhoz KazSSR – Prikaz No 198 'O merakh po povysheniiu ekonomicheskoi effektivnosti proizvodstva v ob'edinenii "Aralrybprom"', 14 June 1977, AFGAKO, f. 4, op. 1pr, d. 549, ll. 32–7.

56 *Perepiski s Aral'skim otdeleniem Gosbanka, po voprosu finansirovaniia na 1979g.*, AFGAKO, f. 4, op. 1pr, d. 631.

57 Telegram from Aralrybprom General Director K. Sarzhanov to Fisheries Minister Utegaliev, 7 September 1978, AFGAKO, f. 4, op. 1pr, d. 592, l. 90.

58 Letter from Aralrybprom general director K. Sarzhanov, chief accountant B. Sharapadinov to Aral'sk branch of Gosbank manager Zh. Alimbetov, 5 February 1979, AFGAKO, f. 4, op. 1pr, d. 631, l. 8.

59 Letter from head of finance department A. Trakhanov to Aralrybprom acting director B. Dzhienbaev and secretary of the enterprise's Party committee B. Turmagambetov, 22 November 1979, AFGAKO, f. 4, op. 1pr, d. 630, ll. 62–3.

60 *Zhoghary zhaqtan kelgen qatynastar*, AFGAKO, f. 4, op. 2, d. 760, 761.

61 Letter from general director S. Sermagambetov, chief accountant A. Trakhanov to manager of the Kzyl-Orda oblast office of Gosbank B. Sh. Tadzhniakov, 4 November 1985, AFGAKO, f. 4, op. 2, d. 761, ll. 24–8.

62 Sermagambetov and Trakhanov, 25.

63 Sermagambetov and Trakhanov, 25.

64 Sermagambetov and Trakhanov, 25–6.

65 Sermagambetov and Trakhanov, 26.

66 Sermagambetov and Trakhanov, 28.

67 Letter from general director S. Sermagambetov, chief accountant A. Trakhanov to manager of Aral'sk branch of Gosbank I. O. Ospanov, 27 November 1985, AFGAKO, f. 4, op. 2, d. 761, l. 33.

68 Letter from general director of Aralrybprom, Zh. Sapiev, to First Secretary of Aral'sk raikom CP Kazakhstan, B. U. Ualiev, and the chairman of the Aral'sk raisovet, B. N. Akpenbetov, 13 August 1987, AFGAKO, f. 4, op. 2, d. 857, ll. 22–3.

69 General director Zh. Sapiev et al., 'Godovoi otchet predpriiatiia za 1988 god', 26 January 1989, AFGAKO, f. 4, op. 3, d. 935, ll. 11–21.

3
Ocean fish, state socialism and nostalgia in Aral'sk

Mūrat Sydyqov is a poet and musician known across Kazakhstan. My friend Edïge, who is in his early thirties, suggested I visit him. Edïge had been telling me how little he had heard about the sea from his parents, saying that everyone in Aral'sk today is mostly concerned about money and everyday pressures. He recommended I talk to Mūrat, as a fund of cultural knowledge, someone who truly cares about the sea and the region. Mūrat was born in 1941 to a fishing family in Qarashalang. His descriptions of his childhood emphasise the heroism of Aral fishermen, the wealth and holiness of the sea, the natural wonders of the landscape. His talent, he maintains, comes from being washed in the sea as a baby. Injured in an accident on the ice as a child which left half his face paralysed, he moved to Aral'sk, and later studied in Kazakhstan's then capital Alma-Ata (now Almaty). He and his wife Bazar worked on the *kul'tsudno*, the 'culture ship', performing national music for fishermen at sea. Since the sea dried up, he has composed songs lamenting its loss and expressing hope for its return. In the early 1990s, he raised money through his concerts in the region, and donated them to a fund for saving the Aral Sea.

Our conversations reflected the topics of his songs, and accorded with what I had been expecting before I went to the field – integrated narratives of the sea's regression, encompassing issues about politics, ecology, morality and personal health. In our recorded interviews, Mūrat presented his public self, an artist who stands up for and defends the people (*khalyq*). He talked extensively about Kazakhstan's bright future as a sovereign state, its success in restoring the sea, and his hope for further restoration of the sea in the future. His account of the sea's regression spoke of the proper, divinely ordained, relations between humans and their environment: 'We have an enemy, *ekologiia* … the sea is disappearing, wealth is disappearing, but nature – if you defend it, such a disaster (Ru.: *bedstvie*) won't happen. Wealth wasn't valued.' He cited the Koran, saying that God had given all the wonders of nature on condition that humans should only take what was needed. He stressed the need for *qanaghat*, meaning 'sufficiency' or 'moderation': 'Between heaven and earth there will be wealth, but if someone destroys *qanaghat*, there will be suffering, you spoil nature, you spoil wealth, *ekologiia* comes.' Weaving together ecology, economy and health, Mūrat posits the failure to observe *qanaghat* as a breach of the divinely ordained relations between humans and their environment. But I did not hear anyone else use *qanaghat* in this context, and whereas Mūrat, in his public voice, talks in abstract terms about 'wealth' (*bailyq*), others, including the unofficial Mūrat, talk more concretely about money and work, and connect them to the political economy of contemporary Kazakhstan.

More typical was a conversation with the grandmother in the house where I initially stayed in Aral'sk. She told me how her husband had sold dried fish illicitly from their household in the 1960s, as well as deer, ducks and geese which he hunted. She concluded: 'There was a lot of wealth in the sea. We lived very well in those days, under Communism, but now we've gone past that.' There was no contradiction between the informal practices endemic to lived socialism and the abstract idea of Communism. Most striking was her equation of natural abundance, a good life, and Communism. She did not mention that in the 1960s the sea was already shrinking and fish catches were falling dramatically. I tried to clarify the date. She said something vaguely about the sixties and seventies, before declaring firmly that it was in 1990 that the crisis started. I tried to press her about what life was like in the town in the 1980s, when the sea was already long gone, but she contradicted me: 'It didn't go suddenly – it went gradually, gradually …' This is certainly true, but even so most people agree that the sea had disappeared from the town by 1978. Her memory collapsed the loss of the sea and the fall of the USSR: both are periods of abundance defined against the indisputable scarcity of the 1990s.

Indeed, during my time in Aral'sk, I did not encounter integrated narratives of total disaster, a critical event touching on all aspects of people's lives. People are certainly aware of the global disaster narrative, but, as something that is felt to have come from outside, it is often felt to be stigmatising. People who grew up in the USSR remember the late Soviet period as a time of stable employment, facilitated by ocean fish; a time of relative abundance, of cinemas and workers' clubs in the town, of powerful industrial enterprises (*krupnye predpriiatiia*), even a naval college (*morskoe uchilishche*); a time when people's lives were integrated into the encompassing, gridded space of the USSR, which sustained a sense of belonging (Ferguson and Gupta 2002; Jansen 2014). While talk about the loss of the sea tends to be muted, the collapse of the USSR is narrated as a sea change: a contraction of space, a loss of connections and belonging – of the 'expectations of modernity' (Ferguson 1999). These memories of the late Soviet period are in stark contrast to outsiders' impressions at the time: for the Aral-88 expedition, the town was 'the epicentre of an ecological disaster' (Reznichenko 1989, 191), a chaotic and disordered sprawl that negated the urbanist values of Soviet socialism.

This is not to say that the sea itself is not mourned. However, while nostalgia for the USSR prompts litanies about jobs, the cost of groceries and pensions, nostalgia for the sea is invariably compressed into memories of swimming: 'We swam, where the restaurant "Aral" is today, we swam there.' Memories of the sea are memories of leisure. After all, while the town's growth had depended on the sea's economic significance as a transport route and a fishery, the livelihoods of many in the town did not depend directly on the sea: they interacted with it as a space of leisure. My landlady Ornyq happily told me how her mother forbade her to go to the sea; when she came back covered in salt (salinity levels were rising then!), her mother scolded her. These memories of leisure tend to be private, happy reminiscences of childhood. Although most people understand why the sea dried up, there is little sense of contradiction between the two sorts of nostalgia. Indeed, often the demise of the sea and the demise of state socialism are blurred: the two sorts of nostalgia leak into each other, both expressing longing for a time-space of abundance, or just for a time-space away from the stresses and concerns of the present. Memories of being Soviet are of course not the only meaningful framework of belonging, and may be less salient for recent migrants to the town; like the villagers of the next chapter, most Aral'sk inhabitants are deeply attached to the region, the home of their ancestors and of most of their kin today. But the memories of being Soviet are the key focus in this chapter.

Postsocialist nostalgia

The official efforts to mitigate the sea's regression, described in Chapter 2, partly explain why it can seem less than the sea change one might expect. Ocean fish, realising the abstract promise of employment, are often narrated as *strengthening* the state-socialist social contract. Nevertheless, as I stressed, there was a gap between the escalating material effects on the ground and the limited emergence of the Aral regression as a 'problem'. Moreover, the centralising (environmentally devastating) and redistributive (mitigating) tendencies of state socialism cannot be separated, at least at the level of analysis. How, then, to explain the nostalgia for late socialism among the older generations? Why does nostalgia for the Soviet Union often overshadow nostalgia for the natural environment? How is the moral content of the nostalgia for Soviet space sustained despite awareness that the sea was destroyed by Soviet development projects? This chapter argues that the nostalgia for the Soviet project, focused on labour and livelihood, speaks to the present, and offers an implicit critique of the present (Boym 2002). Nostalgia for the sea does not easily lend itself to articulation, and, when it does, it does not speak to the present. Nor are political explanations of the desiccation, or outsiders' narratives of an environmental disaster, salient to present concerns.

However, the past is not simply reconstructed from scratch to suit the needs of the present. Certainly, the content of nostalgic narratives is often the loss of the promise of socialism rather than of its actuality. Certainly, memories are selective, and there is a degree of (conscious or unconscious) 'memory management' (Sorabji 2006). But I also take seriously the reality of the past to the people who lived through it. Perspectives on the past today derive, in the first instance, from lived experiences of the sea's retreat. If the consolidation of the Aral as an object of economic value had integrated the town into Soviet space, the provision of ocean fish as the sea receded maintained the town's integration, inflecting the meaning of the sea's demise for those working in the industry, as well as the wider population. Perspectives on the past have also been reshaped by layers of change in the intervening period, particularly the rapid unravelling of the 1990s. These past experiences are further interpreted through tangled discourses past and present, which constitute shared (but not all-encompassing) frameworks within which people use the past to make sense of present and future. These frameworks may be variously rooted in pre-Soviet understandings of nature, or in the authoritative utterances of the Soviet state, or in the critical perspectives of perestroika intellectuals, or even in the global disaster vision. I do not propose a singular 'official' framework which people either resist or conform to. Certainly, the Soviet state's monopoly on many forms of discourse engendered oppositional private narratives or counter-memories (Boym 2002, 61; Pine et al. 2004; Watson 1994), while in many postsocialist contexts, nostalgia is a way of resisting new hegemonic narratives (e.g. Berdahl 1999). But the relative absence of strong official narratives about the Soviet period today means that remembering is taking place in something of a historiographical vacuum. There is little sense of an authoritative or hegemonic discourse about the late Soviet period.

Postsocialist nostalgia is not unique to Aral'sk: across the former Soviet bloc, the disintegration of Soviet space produced a defensive nostalgia, as people sought to stabilise the past amid rapid change (Boym 2002, Chapter 6). Reeves (2014, Chapter 3) emphasises the sense of loss and disorientation that accompanied the disintegration of the manifold modes of connection by which Central Asia was incorporated into the USSR. Thus, even in a small town like Aral'sk, people are nostalgic for an urbanist identity based on order and legibility, which allowed people to imagine their futures and pasts within the future and past of the Soviet Union (Alexander and Buchli 2007; cf. Buck-Morss 2002; Kotkin 1995, 18). Across Central Asia, ethnographers find similar litanies about employment and pensions – from urban Almaty (Alexander 2004a; 2007; 2009a), to decollectivised rural Kazakhstan and Kyrgyzstan (Féaux de la Croix 2014; McMann 2007; Toleubayev et al. 2010, 363–5), to postindustrial Kyrgyzstan (Pelkmans 2013), to urban Uzbekistan (Dadabaev 2010). These laments point to a moral connection between state and citizens that has been breached. When memories of being Soviet focus on the measures taken to mitigate the sea's demise, ocean fish are remembered as materialising this moral connection between state and citizen.

However, when I was doing fieldwork more than 20 years after the collapse of the USSR, differences across the region had widened. In much of Central Asia, 'memories of having been modern' (Reeves 2016, 4) centre on the material markers of modernity, such as constant electricity supply and decent roads which integrated far-flung locales into Soviet space; but in Aral'sk, much of the infrastructure has improved, most notably the clean drinking water which arrived on the eve of the USSR's demise and since then has been piped to all households. Nor is the pace of change the same as in the 1990s. There is a sense of chronic instability, but it is possible to get by and imagine a future for oneself and one's family, even if hedged around with uncertainty and financial tension. My informants are not stuck in the past: certain aspects of Soviet rule, notably the lack of variety in the shops, are contrasted negatively with the present; and there is a broad recognition that things have got better since the disastrous 1990s. Sovereign Kazakhstan provides a new sort of belonging, which is certainly meaningful for many, though it does not preclude regret at the loss of the older, more encompassing sense of belonging. A further question, then, is why postsocialist nostalgia persists in these circumstances – particularly when the ecological devastation wrought by the Soviet project might be expected to destabilise the longing for a return to the Soviet 'home'.

Ruins

When I look back on my time in Aral'sk, I see the cranes which loom, rusting, over the dried-up harbour. From almost anywhere in the town they are visible, rising like dinosaurs' heads above the skyline – fossils, metonyms of a lost world. Ships bearing raw cotton would arrive from Karakalpakstan, and the cotton would be unloaded and loaded onto trains to be sent for processing to Ivanovo, in the Russian Soviet Federative Socialist Republic. In the museum a grainy black-and-white photograph shows cotton being unloaded (Figure 3.1, cf. the later scene in Figure 3.2); a caption states what is happening but makes no comment. Ships would then be laden with grain from the northern parts of the Soviet Union, for the return journey to Moynaq and Nókis to feed the cotton-growing regions of Central Asia. The port was kept open until 1978 by dredging a channel through the Berg Strait that separated the Small and Large Seas, and along Saryshyghanaq bay. When this too dried up, the port closed. Over the course of the 1970s, most of the non-Kazakh population left. Many moved to Togliatti, where AvtoVAZ (the car plant which was to make the famous Zhiguli, or Lada) was being constructed – and today former Aral'sk residents meet up in Togliatti. For many older Kazakh inhabitants of Aral'sk, the loss of the sea is associated, with regret, with the departure of the non-Kazakh population, and a loss of the cosmopolitan, urban nature of Aral'sk.

The area around the former harbour, once a hive of activity and a focal point of the town, is today peripheral. Cement is sold out of the back of the port. The enterprises connected with the sea are largely ruined. Sometimes, when at a loose end, I would be drawn to these spaces. I would walk past the Hotel Aral, past the fishermen's museum and the crumbling fisheries research institute, past a large new school which overlooks the harbour, round the corner and towards the remains of the fish processing plant (Figure 3.3). Though a new fish plant has opened in the old building (see Chapter 7), there is an overwhelming sense of

Figure 3.1 Cotton being unloaded from Aral'sk harbour, undated. Source: Museum of Fishermen, Aral'sk.

Figure 3.2 Aral'sk harbour, summer 2013. Source: author.

abandonment. The former shore is today littered with rubbish. Once, there were pontoons where fish would be unloaded for processing. Old residents reminisce about children stealing fish from these pontoons, and no one cared because there were *so many* fish; about fish being used as

Figure 3.3 Old fish plant, Aral'sk, summer 2013. Source: author.

fuel because the fish were abundant and worthless; about catfish so large that they could feed an entire village.

Across the harbour from the fish processing plant stand the long sheds of the shipyard (*sudoremontnyi zavod*; Figure 3.4), where vessels for the fishing industry and the transport fleet were built and repaired. It now stands largely empty. An attempt to install a plant for repairing railway wagons was unsuccessful. Inside the shipyard stands *stanok Lenina*, 'Lenin's lathe' (Figure 3.5), donated to the people of the region in thanks for the 14 wagons of fish. This event is also commemorated in the mosaic in the station, and in the central square. Even for young people who never saw the sea full, this story functions as a metonym for the golden age of the Aral fisheries.

To return to the shipyard: like the fish processing plant, it was kept open even when the sea had dried up. My host Sasha worked there as an electrician until it went bankrupt in 1995, leaving him unemployed. He talks enthusiastically about how, once the sea had gone, the principal activity of the shipyard shifted to the construction of barge sections. These would be loaded onto trains and assembled in Siberia into 200-tonne barges, used to transport oil and other key goods in a remote region. In the winter, Sasha explained, shipyard workers would go on 'business trips' (*komandirovki*) to Termez, where the Amu Dariya forms the border between Uzbekistan and Afghanistan. They would repair barges used for ferrying goods up and down the river and across the border. Locals, Sasha added, lacked the expert knowledge of the Aral shipyard workers. In this typically Soviet solution to the problem of employment, space is abstract,

Figure 3.4 Shipyard, seen from harbour, summer 2013. Source: author.

Figure 3.5 *Stanok Lenina* (Lenin's lathe), Aral'sk shipyard, summer 2013. Source: author.

and production is divorced from place. But this in itself becomes part of local identity: as the productive labour of shipyard workers incorporated Aral'sk into Soviet space, Sasha is proud of his role in maintaining infrastructural connections elsewhere.

Near the end of my fieldwork, I was talking with Ornyq, who is in her forties, about these measures to maintain employment. She said that all the same it would have been better to have the sea. She proceeded in the subjunctive, imagining what it would be like if the sea was still there:

there would be a beach, and tourists would come here rather than go to the Black Sea; the port would be open and ships would sail on the sea; the *rybokombinat* would be working (she ignored the several fish plants that are open in the town today); young people would all become sailors. This longing for the sea was strikingly distinct from a longing for socialism. While her words drew on her childhood memories of the remnants of the sea in the harbour, she was imagining what the present-day town would look like if the sea was there. Capitalism and socialism were irrelevant to that vision. But then the subjunctive slipped into past historic:

> Before, the fish plant operated, and the shipyard ... And every morning there would be a siren from the shipyard: WOOOOOAAAAAAA! We would all check our watches and say, 'Time for work!' And off we'd go, in buses, big buses, not these taxis that we have today ... Not like today, now ... what? People just sit in the market and trade.

Her longing for the sea slipped into a straightforward reminiscence about the late Soviet years, with no reference to the sea. The content of the reminiscence is instructive: she recalls order, rationality, the labour discipline of industrial time, in contrast to a present of small-scale market trading. Ornyq came of age in the mid-1980s, her working life began when the sea was already long gone, and the siren sounded from a shipyard which was making barges for Siberia. Yet it was the sea that prompted this reminiscence. Brown (2015, 52) suggests that one reason why the Chernobyl catastrophe was so unexpected was that the 'orderly modernity' in towns like Pripiat lulled any sense of danger. Given the chronic difficulties of the Aral fishing industry explored in the previous chapter, it is questionable whether there was a sense of orderly modernity, yet, looking back, Ornyq produces a narrative of orderly modernity, of gridded lives, which precludes reading the past as catastrophe (Figure 3.6).

There is another, much more ambivalent, ruined space in Aral'sk – the old military town, where just a few crumbling apartment blocks remain (Figure 3.7). This was part of the Soviet military-industrial complex, built for provisioning the top-secret biological weapons laboratory on Vozrozhdenie Island. This is an eerie space, nearly always deserted – though it has been plundered for building materials. My friend Mūrat took me there with his young son, saying that it was important for him to see it. As we drove, Mūrat told us stories about accidental deaths when people took bricks and the buildings collapsed on them; he talked

Figure 3.6 Orderly modernity? Fish plant, Aral'sk, 1983. Source: Museum of Fishermen, Aral'sk.

Figure 3.7 Military town, Aral'sk, winter 2013. Source: author.

about the thieves and prostitutes loitering there after dark. He stressed that they had not known what happened in here in Soviet times.

For the most part, however, this space is marked off with silences, oblique remarks that it was all secret. Nowadays, people are aware of the weapons laboratory. Ornyq told me of reading in the press during perestroika about lepers being taken there. Soldiers sent there were blindfolded, she went on, so they would not know where they were; she had later read on the internet how those sent there remembered the smell of chlorine for the rest of their lives. They should not have used Kazakh land for all that, she concluded. This is the bad Soviet past, the unspoken and unspeakable. But 25 years on, this bad past was, in general, partitioned off in memory, just as the space is largely avoided. Contradictions between good and bad pasts are, usually, smoothed over: potentially troubling memories do not disturb cherished memories of good Soviet times. Indeed, even this eerie space is sometimes reintegrated into fond memories of the informal side of socialism: sailors would signal when they needed alcohol, and children would row it over to trade for lemonade; the military was provisioned with high-quality foodstuffs, which the soldiers' wives would bring into the town to exchange. In such stories, the unspeakable is domesticated. Nevertheless, it is a significant space, significant for its abandonment, and for the way in which it is avoided in stories about the good Soviet past.

Indeed, such horrors are not always neatly partitioned off from nostalgia, as became clear in the following conversation with Sasha. He started out his normal jolly self, reminiscing about the other nationalities that had lived in the town, the cosmopolitan past which defined Aral'sk as an urban Soviet space. As he fleshed out his narrative, however, he talked about their status as enemy peoples, forbidden to talk about what had happened to them. I mentioned a line I had heard from others, that Aral'sk was a site of exile for some and a 'heaven on earth' for others. But I was being naïve, and had missed the seriousness of his tone. He immediately cut in that it only seemed like heaven on earth because there was famine all over the country at that time. He explained how his mother had fled here in the 1930s, before asking if I knew about the famine all over the Volga region, all over Ukraine. He was now visibly distressed, and said slowly: 'What a story! The Communist Party! Lenin ... Stalin ... Fucking hell ...'. He paused – the air thick with the horrors he had left unsaid – before adding half-heartedly, as if from force of habit: 'Of course, there were benefits ... free education, free healthcare ...', but he trailed off. The collective framework of nostalgia which so often affords meaning in the present could not be sustained here. In other contexts, as when talking about the shipyard, Sasha would reminisce happily about life under socialism, but this flood of memory recalled the terrifying arbitrariness of Soviet space. Different elements of the Soviet state could not be compartmentalised, and the contradiction was untenable.

Both Alexander (2009a) and Pelkmans (2013) find that nostalgia can, as here, be destabilised by memories of dark pasts. Alexander describes the sense of spiralling disintegration in the rapidly changing city of Almaty in the late 1990s, while Pelkmans evokes a context of despair and stagnation in a postindustrial mining town in Kyrgyzstan in the 2010s. If nostalgia in Aral'sk does not tend to be destabilised by darker memories, this is perhaps because, despite the dissatisfaction with the present, there is a sense that things have stabilised since the collapse of the 1990s, and a sense of future. Accordingly, the object of nostalgia itself is more stable, and the good past can, for the most part, be separated from bad pasts.

'To provide work': remembering the state-socialist social contract

If the sea's recession had emerged as a problem of employment and living standards, it is employment that is remembered as the locus of state paternalism. Former employees of the *rybokombinat* stress that importing ocean fish was loss-making (Ru.: *ubytochno*). But they equally stress that 'the state' did this so as 'to save *rybprom*' and 'to provide work' (Ru.: *chtoby obespechivat' rabotu*). Former managers describe their role as providing work for people. This narrative, then, provides a collective framework of memory. There is little reflection on where the ocean fish came from: their provenance is thought of not as an issue of natural resources but of allocation, not a question of what nature gives but of what the state provides. No one suggests that sending frozen fish from, for example, Riga for processing in Aral'sk was economically irrational. On the contrary, people imply a certain rationality to the practice, describing the USSR as *odin kotël*, 'a single pot/cauldron', highlighting its capacity to absorb the losses of any industry. In these narratives, as ocean fish circulate around the unitary, homogeneous space of the USSR, they materialise the moral connection between state and citizens via Minrybkhoz and factory managers. Paradoxically, the sea's regression gives shape to the social contract in these memories.[1]

As we saw in Chapter 2, provisioning of fish, the prerequisite of employment, was fraught. Daniiar, a friend of Sasha's, worked in Aralrybprom in the 1980s – one of the 'experienced comrades' mentioned by Aralrybprom managers as they negotiated with Gosbank. When Sasha first took me to meet him, Daniiar declared: 'I personally loaded fish in Kaliningrad, in Riga, Sakhalin, Murmansk ... I personally was there ...'. At this point Sasha interjected, relating Daniiar's personal narrative to the collective framework of the town: 'So there would be work.' Daniiar's list of places takes us to the furthest corners of the USSR, as the state's abstract promise to provide work is personalised in himself. When I met Daniiar on other occasions, he expanded on his role in procuring fish. Before working in the fishing industry, he had already established networks of acquaintances across the country while working as a lorry driver in the 1970s, apparently unaware that the cargoes of nuts and tomatoes he was driving from Uzbekistan and Tajikistan were concealing narcotics. Networks of acquaintances were to prove crucial in his work in the fisheries:

Daniiar:	You put in an application, and if they aren't your acquaintances (*znakomye*), they send your orders to Sakhalin! Understand?! How can you get fish from Sakhalin? You need to get across to Vladivostok, then from the ship to the railway, and from Vladivostok to here – it's 13, 14 days by freight train ... I travelled! Then I started to understand, I started ... Russians, those who work in deliveries, I started to get to know them, in Moscow I had good acquaintances, I went through them and so ... they started to stand by me.
William:	So to get fish, you needed acquaintances?
Daniiar:	But of course ...
William:	You needed connections (*sviazy*) ...
Daniiar:	Of course. Without that you won't get anywhere ... In Kaliningrad, the director of the *rybzavod* ... I couldn't go in for *three days* ... Busy, busy, busy ...
William:	Nightmare ...
Daniiar:	Nightmare! Then I had to treat (*ugoshchat'*) the secretary ... there was French eau de cologne, er, Chanel, French eau de cologne, yes ... and flowers, for the secretary ... and she let me in! There, you see?!
William:	What else did you treat people to?
Daniiar:	Well it wasn't about money then, nothing like that ...
William:	In the eighties?
Daniiar:	Yes. Flowers, eau de cologne, or *shampanskoe* [Soviet Champagne] – a bottle ... or cognac. It was enough. Understand? And now – only dollars.

The gridded space of the USSR is crisscrossed with networks of acquaintances fostered by Daniiar on his travels. As he recalls the informal connections necessary to procure fish, he portrays himself as the cosmopolitan man of the world, with the charm and cultural knowledge to navigate the informal channels of the Soviet economy with the appropriate gifts.[2] In this account, then, informal practices were embedded in ideas about gift exchange, in moral relations between persons. Today, he implies, everything is mediated only by the abstractions of dollars: moral informal practices give way to damaging corruption, carried out through the impersonal medium of money.

I again mentioned the lack of the sea in the 1980s, at which Daniiar responded:

Daniiar:	Well, the sea had gone away ... there were few fish ... somehow it was necessary to maintain the people (*narod*) ... that's why we went off to other republics, from there –
William:	Looking for fish?
Daniiar:	So as to maintain workers here, there was work ...
William:	So it was loss-making?
Daniiar:	It was loss-making, but they were maintained, the workers ...
William:	Quite right ...
Daniiar:	The state was socialist. Not capitalist.
William:	It was necessary to help people?
Daniiar:	Socialist. And when the socialist state was ruined, we proceeded (*pereshli*) to a capitalist one, but the capitalist one isn't working out for us.

He explained that the local capitalists have not read Marx, and do not understand that they should reinvest capital rather than pocketing their profits: 'They don't know what capital is.' Again, the past acts as a commentary on the present. Notice the seamless transition from the personal narrative about the procurement of fish to the abstract state–citizen relation – there is no sense of contradiction between the two. Socialism, in this account, was both the abstract, ordered, rational promise of the state to provide work for its citizens, and the chaotic, disordered, contingent processes by which the promise was delivered, which necessitated the fostering of personal relations. In Daniiar's account, as in the archival documents, the sea's disappearance is just a fact, devoid of human agency, which sharpens the need for the state to fulfil its moral obligations. It is the 'transition' (expressed in the verb *pereshli*) to capitalism which is the major rupture.

As we saw, despite Daniiar's best efforts, deliveries of fish from the oceans were sporadic, with lengthy periods of no fish at all, followed by the arrival of more than could be handled. Aqshabaq was born in the kolkhoz Zhambul and is now in her early fifties. In 1980 she started working for Aralrybprom in Aral'sk (Figures 3.8 and 3.9). After it collapsed in the late 1990s, she was instrumental in setting up the nongovernmental organisation Aral Tenizi. She now works in the management of a shiny new, but chronically failing, fish factory in Aral'sk (see Chapters 5 and 7). When I visited her in the factory, our conversations would veer unpredictably between these three periods of her life. Whether reminiscing about her time working for an apparently successful state enterprise, or about her quite different work setting up a nongovernmental organisation with Danish assistance, the past featured in a positive light compared to the present of working in a failing private enterprise. The contrast in her tone was marked: world-weary, disjointed remarks about the present; animated, engaging narratives about the past. Picking up on my finds in the archives about irregular deliveries of ocean fish, I asked whether deliveries were reliable:

> Yes! Distribution, deliveries: it was all according to contract (*dogovor*). If they didn't deliver, then there would be a fine. Everything was according to plan: annual and five-yearly plans. They were obliged to deliver, and if they didn't deliver, the director in Vladivostok or wherever would be sacked … and we were *obliged* to process it! Everyone chased the plan – by quantity and quality. Everywhere it was written [chuckling]: THE PLAN IS THE LAW – TO FULFIL IS A DUTY, TO OVERFULFIL IS AN HONOUR.

Given her position today, it is unsurprising that Aqshabaq should miss a time when everything was planned, and unsurprising that she claims that things went according to plan rather more than they may have done in fact. Unlike Daniiar's account of the informal practices and relations through which the enterprise functioned, she remembers a congruence of moral and legal obligations. In other contexts, or differently framed, obligations to fulfil the plan might imply an absence of agency. But in this context, they are precisely the inverse of state paternalism: the state supported citizens, and in return citizens played their active part. Again, ocean fish materialised this relationship. The authoritative discourse of the Party state, picked up in dialogue more than 20 years later, is treated

Figures 3.8 and 3.9 Smoking workshop, undated. Source: Museum of Fishermen, Aral'sk.

with affectionate humour; evoking an overarching rationality connecting the obligations of a director in Vladivostok with the obligations of the Aralrybprom workforce, it is recontextualised as an implicit comment on a present of chaotic, unplanned capitalism.

One paradoxical consequence of irregular deliveries of ocean fish was that, despite the overall problem of surplus labour, when several big deliveries arrived at once, Aralrybprom lacked the labour resources to unload and process them all. Here the functioning of the economy through informal relationships became noticeable in the interstices of Aqshabaq's narrative: there was never any labour shortage, she said, because soldiers from the military bases could be enlisted to help with unloading, the boss of the factory being an acquaintance of their commander. Soldiers enjoyed it, she emphasised, especially because they could take some fish for their wives and children. She also told me, with much hilarity, that schoolchildren were forced to work: 'Anyone in the town will tell you about it!'

Indeed, Ornyq enthusiastically reminisced with her sister about their *praktika* ('work experience') in the fish factory while at school, recalling how they would steal fish and take them home; they remembered capelin and mackerel (nowadays unavailable in Aral'sk) as particularly tasty. Ocean fish, then, not only incorporated Aral'sk into Soviet space both formally and informally; they also became part of the identity of the town. Reminiscing together, Ornyq and her sister reproduced their Aral'sk identity by affirming a shared past, characterised by material abundance. As much as the formal channels of redistribution, affectionate memories of the lived experience of socialism include such informal practices as pilfering.

After Aqshabaq had told me about all that, I made an inconsequential remark about my surprise at there being jobs even when the sea went away. This prompted a lengthy dreamy reminiscence, unconnected to my remark, about the town when the sea *was* there: about ships in the port unloading cotton from Karakalpakstan (she made no comment on the role of cotton in destroying the sea); about the floating restaurant in the harbour; how people relaxed by the harbour; how when she was a little girl they would swim all day every day, and when they came home their parents would shout at them. Nostalgia for the sea, and for the innocence of childhood, here seeps into the nostalgia for late socialism.

More often, however, nostalgia for the sea is submerged in nostalgia for the Soviet Union. This is because, I suggest, the contrast between the supposed full employment of Soviet times and the low employment of the present acts as a commentary on the present in a way in which nostalgia for the sea does not. This is a yearning for encompassment within wider, gridded space (Jansen 2014). Nevertheless, people are also broadly aware that the sea's regression related directly to the region's unequal integration into Soviet space – Aqshabaq's silence on the role of cotton in the sea's demise should not be mistaken for unawareness. How, then, do people who yearn for the Soviet past account for the sea's regression?

Understanding the sea's regression

I first went to the old processing plant one eerily still and warm winter's day, the sun veiled behind hazy cirrus; the light was watery and the air heavy with silence, punctuated only by the distant barking of dogs. A man was standing gazing up at a red metal skeleton which was part of the plant. He asked me for matches, and we got talking. Aslan was born in the mid-1960s and remembers the sea, though he never saw it full. He studied in Orenburg, Russia, but is long-term unemployed. I asked him if he had understood at the time why the sea was drying up. He said: 'There were different versions. They said that there is another channel from the bottom of the sea, connecting it to the Caspian … That was the scientific version.' But, he said, the 'fundamental reason' was the Uzbek authorities' withdrawals of water for cotton and the Kazakh withdrawals for rice. We chatted a bit more and then I asked who was guilty for the sea going away. His reply was surprising: Gorbachev. Why? He let the Soviet Union be divided into 15 republics. Had the Soviet Union continued, the Siberian rivers project would have been carried out; the Ob' and Irtysh would have been brought to Central Asia and the sea would have been saved. I was taken aback: what about irrigation? He reiterated that irrigation was the 'fundamental reason' why the sea had dried up. As in the archival documents, the needs of irrigation are taken for granted; Aslan did not question the political decisions that lay behind them.

Indeed, official accounts in the late Soviet period, which are still taught in schools today, primarily blamed the Uzbeks for taking all the water. In Aral'sk today, most people relate the irrigation explanation, without mentioning Moscow's role. It is told blandly, usually as a matter of objective fact, without resentment or a sense of victimhood. Younger people say that this is what their parents told them. The scientific theory about the Caspian which Aslan alluded to responded to the unexplained rise in the level of the Caspian in this period: the theory, long since discredited, posited that as one fell, the other rose. Accordingly, people in Aral'sk often supplement the irrigation thesis with the Caspian theory, and occasionally reject the irrigation explanation altogether. I even heard that boats from the Caspian resurfaced on the Aral, *proving* the existence of extensive underground waterways. There is also a near-universal belief that the desiccation was hastened or even caused by rockets being released from the nearby cosmodrome, Baikonur, which apparently bring about evaporation and cause *ekologiia*. These accounts bear some similarity to explanations of climate change in post-Soviet Siberia, which is ascribed either to local projects, such as a nearby reservoir, or to people going into the cosmos disturbing a natural balance, or to the agency of nature itself (Crate 2008). The Baikonur explanation alludes both to ongoing local concerns (see Chapter 7) and to anxiety about destabilising cosmic relations, while the Caspian explanation alludes to an agency greater than human agency, without which it is hard to make sense of such massive changes in the environment. Because none of these accounts blame the Soviet system itself, they do not destabilise the object of nostalgia.

However, there are also political explanations, blaming the Communist Party leadership and their ideology of nature. Such explanations tend to be voiced by well-educated older people, who would have been immersed in the critical perestroika discourse of disaster. Iura, a laboratory technician in a school, is one of the few Koreans remaining in Aral'sk. Talking about those who left, he told me in hushed tones how everyone who remembers the sea sees it in their dreams, and the sea 'draws them to itself'. Iura's parents were deported from the Vladivostok region in the 1930s, and his father worked as a fisherman in Ūialy and Bögen before moving to Aral'sk in the 1950s. This deportation was part of *stalinskaia politika*, 'Stalinist policy', he said. His account was hedged with silences, *stalinskaia politika* gesturing to the unspeakable horrors of that period. Although for his parents the Aral region was a place of exile, Iura sees the region as his homeland (*rodina*), and recalls a childhood of long summer days spent on the sea, perpetual good health and abundant fish. While serving in the army in 1976, the sea came to him in his sleep. But on his return from the army, he immediately noticed that the sea had gone away.

His account for the sea drying up was overtly political:

William:	Did you know why the sea was going away?
Iura:	Yes of course. Everyone knew.
William:	Knew what?
Iura:	That they were taking water. There are records … They were taking water in the 1930s, *in the time of Stalin* …

While 1960 is usually cited as the year when the sea started to recede, Iura went back to the hydraulic projects of the Stalinist era: as with his parents' deportation, the name of Stalin gestured at a catalogue of horrors, commonly known but not voiced beyond allusion. Later in the interview he told me of the utter powerlessness of local people: 'It was the Communist Party then. That was *something* (*eto bylo* chto-to).' He did not elaborate: like the name of Stalin, 'the Communist Party' stood for something vast and unspeakable.

Later he discussed more explicitly Soviet ideology and nature, talking about his reading on the subject – and his account was shot through with other people's discourses: he quoted the language of planners and scientists, polemicising with them and holding them up to critical scrutiny in the manner of perestroika intellectuals. He cited contemptuously a famous line of the Soviet scientist Michurin: 'We cannot expect favours from nature: our task is to seize them.' He juxtaposed it with the line of another scientist, Vavilov: 'For every such victory, nature will take a cruel revenge.' At this he reeled off the health problems that the sea's desiccation had caused, as instances of the revenge that nature had taken. Finally, he leant forward and said slowly and quietly, emphasising every word:

> Everyone needed cotton and rice. That's all. And the fact that they destroyed the sea: they didn't care … [raising his voice, gesturing] There were lots of grandiose projects: the Enisei – they wanted to bring the Enisei to fill the Aral! If they'd done that we'd all have been underwater! It was stupidity, idiotic!

The Siberian rivers scheme, the ever-deferred future, stood as the final proof of megalomania and heroic disregard for nature.

Madi is the director of the town museum and a friend of Iura. Both his parents were Party officials, and his father established the museum in 1988. He was brought up in a street on the seafront inhabited by Russians and other nationalities, and he relates his good education to the Russian and Ukrainian intellectuals who were exiled to Aral'sk. He maintains active links with the remaining non-Kazakh families in the town, and his everyday talk over beer and dried fish with other old inhabitants is full of nostalgia for the cosmopolitan Soviet past.

One day he took me on a tour of the dried-up seabed outside the town. Although he talked a little about the final abandoning of the ships when the port closed, on this occasion he focused on when the sea *was* there. His manner was celebratory, without regret. It was only later on in our acquaintance that I asked him directly about the causes behind the sea's regression. On that occasion his account was strikingly similar to Iura's: the command was in Moscow; the Communist Party always knew best; man should not have interfered with nature. This narrative, however, did not surface before or after. After all, it has less relevance to Madi's daily concerns than post-Soviet decline, and it sits uneasily with his rosy memories of the Soviet period. Different memories are compartmentalised.

Indeed, at the time of my fieldwork in the early 2010s, this political narrative has little salience to everyday concerns. People who grew up in the 1980s and 1990s say that they were *informed* that the water was used for irrigation elsewhere; then after a pause, or when pressed by me, they declare that in their opinion it was the fault of the authorities, or of the Communist Party; that 'up top' (*sverkhu*) they knew what was going to happen to the sea. This is presented as personal, private knowledge, inferred from their awareness of the Soviet system and the gaps in official stories. Such knowledge is not related to the present. The dark side of socialism is relegated to the unknowable upper reaches of the Soviet state, distinct from (and not in contradiction to) the lived actuality of socialism (cf. Dadabaev 2010, 44). In late Soviet times, when the monologic utterances of the state were everywhere, such stories may have been a locus of opposition to the state (Watson 1994), but in the historiographical vacuum of contemporary Kazakhstan, they are less pertinent.

There are hints, however, that the political narrative had more salience before, and with it a sense of victimhood. The director of the local archives, Bolatbek, told me about the region's glorious history, and the fish they gave to the state when the rest of the Soviet Union was starving in the 1920s, before remarking bitterly, 'But no one helps us now.' It is not a phrase I heard in any other context – and indeed, it was contradicted by the rest of our conversation, in which Bolatbek told me about the positive effects of the Kökaral dam, and the beneficial role the Kazakh government plays today. His 'no one helps us now' seemed to be an echo of a now submerged discourse of political victimhood.

Indeed, political accounts of the sea's desiccation can take unexpected forms, blurring with nostalgia for the grandeur of the Soviet project itself, as we saw with Aslan. Daniiar talked in detail about Stalin's plans to connect all the rivers and lakes of the Soviet Union with canals so that it would be possible to transport cargo from the Far East to the Black Sea by water, enthusiastically drawing a map in the sand as he explained it. If this had been implemented, he said, vast swathes of desert would have been irrigated, and moreover the sea would have been saved. 'But,' he said regretfully, 'the war got in the way.' When I asked about the promise of the Siberian rivers scheme in the 1970s and 1980s, he declared that the Soviet Union was no longer at full strength: since Stalin's death it had been taken over by rogues (*zhuliki*) and weakened by American rock music. If for Iura the name of Stalin gestures towards the unspeakable, for Daniiar it signifies a time of greatness, looked back to wistfully after years of decline and collapse. The problem was not the ideology, but the failure to implement it, and the loss of the long-promised utopia. The loss of the sea is blurred with the loss of the Soviet dreamworld (Buck-Morss 2002), the lost promise of a utopian hydraulic civilisation (cf. Wittfogel 1957). If the sea's demise related to the uneven integration of the Central Asian periphery into Soviet space, for Daniiar, as for Aslan, the problem was rather a *lack* of integration, a failure to develop the grid to the full through hydraulic connections.

Even so, in another register, Daniiar would distinguish between 'those up there' who knew that the sea was being destroyed and the ordinary citizen, suggesting a disconnect within Soviet space which did not quite tally with his nostalgia for Stalinist hydraulic despotism. Indeed, from his family history he was keenly aware of the repressive side of Soviet power: his mother was from a wealthy family in southern Kazakhstan and had fled to Aral'sk in the 1920s, where she had lived with a disguised identity. Daniiar keeps this private past separate from his nostalgias both for the lived space of socialism and for the utopian promise of Stalinism.

Conclusion

As should be evident from my perhaps too ready agreement with Daniiar's assessment of socialist employment policies, I suggest that we take seriously not only the function but also the content of postsocialist nostalgia in Aral'sk. After all, environmental change did not come alone: Aral'sk residents' encounter with the changing environment was mediated by the measures taken by the Soviet authorities. Limited as those measures were, they are today recalled as meaningful. The critique of the present which nostalgic voices articulate will become clearer in Chapter 7, when we look at the town today. Critically, rather than breaching the Soviet social contract, environmental change is felt to have strengthened it, so that ocean fish became the means by which the promise was delivered, connecting state and citizens within a moral space of belonging. It is the promise of these connections which has been lost. The inefficiency of the Soviet state in making investments and the chaotic and, ultimately, incomplete manner in which work was provided are not remembered: it is the promise of socialism – the promise of providing employment in response to ecological crisis, the promise that local resilience can lie in integration into broader, gridded spaces – which is remembered, and which forms a critique of the present. Insofar as the informal relations which crisscrossed gridded space are remembered, they are not remembered in resistance to the grid; rather, they are felt to have sustained moral relations between persons within an encompassing space of belonging.

However, this nostalgia, and the critique it contains, are maintained at the expense of social forgetting, compartmentalising the good past from the various bad pasts which threaten to subsume it – and as these are not transmitted, memory of them fades, just as the military town, embodying another dark Soviet past, gradually crumbles. Political accounts of why the sea dried up, or other Soviet horror stories, which would destabilise the nostalgic reconstruction of the USSR, are seldom voiced. Accordingly, what is also suppressed is Aral'sk's vulnerability within Soviet space. This social forgetting, I have argued, depends on the relative stability of the present, and the sense of a future. The disconnection of the 1990s has been replaced with new forms of connection within contemporary Kazakhstan: under circumstances of greater uncertainty, this compartmentalisation may be less effective. Ultimately, the social forgetting will be more encompassing. This is not a 'restorative' nostalgia (Boym 2002): no one foresees (or even wants) a return to the Soviet system in the future. It is not a project. Perhaps as a result, the content has little traction for the post-Soviet generation. Though young people are aware of Soviet times as a period of abundance, and proud of the town's role in providing 14 wagons of fish (even if they tend to associate it not with the Civil War but with the Second World War), the specifics of how employment was provided are of less interest in a context where no one foresees the Soviet Union returning, or an alternative to the present of deregulated capitalism.

At various moments in this chapter, memories of the sea overflow nostalgic commentary on the present. But while experience may be resilient, some experiences resist narration. Even if they are narrated, there are certain embodied experiences that cannot be verbalised – except in the elliptical 'we swam', which says so little and hints at so much. The difficulty of transmitting those embodied experiences to a generation that never partook in them emerged poignantly when my friend Edïge told me that his parents had not told him anything about the sea, except that they had swum. Without transmission of meaningful memories, Edïge and his friends would, he told me, play on the rusting ships, trying to imagine what the sea had been like.

Notes

1 By contrast, Trevisani (2010, 217) argues that decollectivised Uzbek farmers do not miss the social contract so much as the decent standard of living and the possibility of moving forward. Again, the sense of a future in Aral'sk today perhaps makes people here focus more on the *promise* of socialism.
2 Gifts like cognac and French perfume were appropriate symbolic tokens to acknowledge favours, being of low monetary value but hard to obtain (Ledeneva 1998, 152–5).

4
Rupture and continuity in Aral fishing villages

One summer's evening, I was sitting in the sand on the edge of Bögen with Aikeldï and two other men enjoying some well-earned drinks after a hard day's work on Aikeldï's new house. All are in their forties. As usual, Aikeldï was doing most of the talking. At one point he wanted to know about meat in England, and asked if we ate pork; the answer, as always, attracted much hilarity.[1] Aikeldï then started talking about how important pigs were to Russians, before asking rhetorically: 'And what is our *bailyq*?' *Bailyq*, literally 'wealth', here suggests cultural property. The answer was obvious: fish. Eighty per cent of the fish eaten in the USSR, he declared, were from the Aral Sea. The others then told me about Bögen's glorious past, about the factory which had stood very near where we were sitting. Today barely a trace remains (Figure 4.1). Slipping from Aikeldï's talk of the natural wealth of the sea, they told me about how fish were sent here from the Far East for processing. In this display of local patriotism, there was no narrative of loss, or sense of rupture between Aral fish and the ocean fish which replaced them. Aikeldï did not mention that he first fished several thousand kilometres away on Balqash and had never seen the sea when it was full, its shore at the edge of the village. There was no mention of the disaster by which outsiders know the region, or of the many who left the region.

On another occasion, I was talking with Zhūbatqan, who was born in 1936. At 14, Zhūbatqan started fishing, working first for the kolkhoz, then for the state fishing base until retiring in the 1990s. He worked on ships travelling all over the sea, before fishing mainly on Balqash. Today he lives in Bögen with his son, daughter-in-law and small grandchildren. He has another son in the village; his other children have all left for Aral'sk, Qazaly, Aqtöbe, Almaty. One son fishes, and has just bought a UAZ jeep. Although Zhūbatqan is well liked and respected, he does not

Figure 4.1 Stump of post for pontoon in former harbour, Bögen, autumn 2013. Source: author.

command the authority that many men of his age command, and while he often recounts tales about the Soviet fishery, he is not always listened to – except by me, and I draw on his stories in this chapter. On this occasion, Zhūbatqan began by telling me about the different sorts of vessel which came to the region, how 'we fished' (*auladyq*) first with wooden boats then with fibreglass boats, how Kawasaki engines were brought from Japan in 1954, gradually replacing sails and oars. He told me about the ships that came to the kolkhoz in the 1950s; how small fishing boats would be loaded onto them by crane and how they fished for months at a time in distant waters.

Zhūbatqan:	Then in 65 the water receded (*qaitty*).[2]
William:	In 65?
Zhūbatqan:	It receded, the water … disappearing, disappearing, disappearing (*qūryp, qūryp, qūryp*) … 75, it stopped. Then we left for Balqash, we fished on Balqash (*Balqashta auladyq*).

In this narrative of gradual change, in which the constant is fishing, the retreat of the sea forms a rupture. But unlike events like earthquakes, the retreat of the sea insinuates itself into the everyday, and the rupture is immediately covered over by the repetition of 'we fished'. Everything changed – but still fishing went on. In such stories, the sea's disappearance is less of a sea change than one might expect.

In this chapter, I contextualise the sea's regression in local notions of space, place and nature, which, in a century of catastrophes, had been transformed long before the sea dried up, as commodified understandings of fish as exchange-values overlaid, but did not fully displace, older ideas about natural abundance. As we saw in Chapters 1 and 2, the unevenness of state-socialist development, consolidating two incompatible versions of the sea, positioned Aral villages ambiguously within Soviet Central Asia. They were extremely marginal to the irrigation complex, which was sustained by powerful interests that prioritised cotton over the sea. But within the socialist fishery, the sea connected them to the state via Minrybkhoz: daily bodily interactions with the marine environment were embedded in a relationship that was both extractive and redistributive. Both marginality and connectedness within Soviet space emerge in villagers' narratives of Soviet times. Yet the sense of place that emerges is not reducible to the political-economic relationships within which Aral villages were positioned. People also stress the relationship to the land going back generations, embodied in graveyards and shrines. In this register, the sea figures as ancestral property. Indeed, there is an oscillation between a discourse based on place and belonging, and one based on labour and livelihood. While not contradictory, these discourses are distinct. To understand local meanings of environmental change, then, requires attention to how the Soviet project had already reconfigured indigenous relationships with the environment. Drawing on Bakhtin (1981a), I explore how persons and nature are variously constituted within different 'chronotopes', or orderings of time and space: the abstract chronotope of the plan, and the particularised chronotope of *tughan zher*, or homeland. Within these different time-space configurations, the sea's retreat holds different meanings.

My account of the interplay between rupture and continuity will offer an intervention into theories of resilience. Deriving from ecologists' accounts of the capacity of ecosystems to absorb shocks (Holling 1973), resilience has been applied by social scientists to understanding flexibility and adaptation within 'socio-ecological systems' (Adger 2000; Berkes and Folke 1998). In the next part of this chapter, I present seemingly opposing narratives: if the Aral emerges as vulnerable when it can be arbitrarily exchanged for rice plantations, narratives of attachment to *tughan zher*, embodying continuity that transcended the changes to the environment, suggest a local resilience. However, the material that follows throws that dichotomy into question, suggesting that resilience lay both in the local attachment to land and in the wider political-economic structures that facilitated it. Indeed, the later parts of the chapter show how local identity was Sovietised, and how fishermen internalised the state's gridded divisions of space and time, and the concomitant understanding of nature.

The chapter also speaks to concerns of political ecology. If, for some political ecologists, the Aral case might seem to present a lack (why did no one protest?), it would be tempting to appeal to the total nature of Soviet power. Certainly, many narratives stress the constraints on agency, a point that is reinforced by documentary evidence of the very limited contestation that was possible. However, although the nostalgia we saw in Chapter 3 is much less marked among villagers, they were enrolled in the Soviet project, and in its ways of dealing with the problem. Rather than starting from an absence of protest, I instead explore how shifting understandings of nature informed experiences of ecological change. In keeping with other accounts of Soviet Central Asia, I stress the ambiguous compliance with the Soviet modernising project, which did not so much destroy 'traditional' identities as transform them in their articulations with Soviet modernity (Abashin 2015; Kandiyoti 1996; 2002; Kandiyoti and Azimova 2004; Tett 1994).

A subtheme running through this chapter is the question of how past difficulties and suffering are socially forgotten in a present filled with hope about the restored sea. As an old man in Qaratereng announced after listing the benefits of Communism: 'We've passed the former time of Communism, but *now* ... now we don't slander ourselves, we are a sovereign country, Kazakhstan ... now we are good ... we're good now.' Communism is not the ever-deferred endpoint of history, but another stage which has been passed on the way to sovereignty. Traumatic memories are fading as they are not transmitted. When I asked people born in the 1940s and 1950s if they had heard about the period of collectivisation from their parents, they would say 'we didn't ask', or 'they didn't say'. The same is true, I think, of more recent traumas. As a result, many of the narratives which emerged in formal interviews, often in response to my questions, did not emerge in other contexts, and some of these stories are alien to young people. This does not mean that individuals do not hold memories. Nor is it to suggest that there is no register for mourning the sea; but, as in Chapter 3, I suggest that register has little salience today amid high fish catches. This is in part, therefore, a story about how the immense traumas of a century of catastrophes are smoothed over.

Vulnerability

As in Aral'sk, everyone knows that the sea dried up because water was used elsewhere for agriculture, and the most common account blames Uzbekistan for 'not giving water', so that 'the Amu Dariya and Syr Dariya didn't flow properly (*dūrys qūmaidy*)'. Nevertheless, many older people are aware of Moscow's role in the sea's regression, although, also as in Aral'sk, this would only emerge when I asked directly who was responsible. Most strikingly, some accounts allude to the cost–benefit analysis we saw in Chapter 1, like this interview with an aqsaqal (elder), Rai, in Raiym:

> Someone was looking at the sea and said, 'In place of the Aral Sea it's necessary to sow rice' ... One minister from there (*ana zhaqtaghy*) said it. Then they divided the water. Rice doesn't grow at all, and now they can't fill it again. Now they can't fill it with water again. They transferred it all to Karakalpakstan, and our river is left dried up.

The phrasing captures nicely the arbitrariness of the synoptic viewpoint from which a sea can be exchanged for rice: local particularities are abstracted in a political ecology whereby natural resources can be dispatched across homogeneous gridded space. This account is theodical, locating agency far away from the individual (Herzfeld 1992) – and far from the local. Bureaucratic structures are reduced to the figure of a capricious minister who has the power to divide the water. In this narrative, local people are vulnerable to a state optic which is blind to the Aral region. Looked at in this light, the silence of other informants on the political context of irrigation may be read as misinformation by the authorities, who cast all the blame on Uzbekistan; moreover, overtly critical narratives about Moscow were risky in Soviet times, hence their mutedness even today. This suggests a further dimension to vulnerability: an inability to voice what had happened. As in other remote parts of post-Soviet space, Soviet modernity is felt, in this register, to be something which has happened *to* people, changes on the local wrought by distant, powerful forces (Alexander 2004b, 54; Grant 1995; Humphrey 1998, viii).

There is no sense of communication between the two levels. The minister was 'from there', from elsewhere. As we saw in Chapter 2, throughout the Soviet state, the resources to raise the issue of the sea's regression with higher authorities were limited. Discursive resources were even more sparsely distributed at the village level: it was impossible, my informants would tell me, to complain to anyone. In fact, there is evidence of a letter in 1977 from inhabitants of Bögen to Qonaev, the First Secretary of the Communist Party of Kazakhstan, demanding better use of the delta lakes and improvement of living conditions. The letter also protested against the transfer of a melioration station, along with all its machinery, to another village. This caused a flurry of communication between Minrybkhoz and the Central Committee, in which the fisheries minister blamed Minvodkhoz for failing to deliver 50 m³/s below Qazaly. The villagers received a reply only from the vice-minister of fisheries, who noted the measures being taken to improve their living standards, including a water pipe and a banya (steam bath); he also noted that measures were being taken to exploit the delta lakes but that these could not, owing to the 'low water level of 1974–77', be implemented in full. But some glimmer of hope was promised, as the vice-minister noted that the integrated scheme for use of the Aral water resources should be finished in 1978 (it was not, of course). The letter stated that the melioration station had to be moved to a region where there was more water. The only positive response to the villagers' attempt to protest their plight was compensation with a single bulldozer.[3] It is hardly surprising that the letter should today be forgotten. The locality and 'higher up' are thus felt to have been unconnected. When I asked Zhūbatqan directly whether the government helped, he replied: 'They didn't. They said "move (kösh)". If we moved, where would we go?' In this way of talking, then, villagers were vulnerable to the optic of the distant and uncaring state, which sees only abstract space and reorders environments accordingly, blind to local lives and local meanings.

The resilience of local identity?

Many, of course, did leave, and narratives of the sea going away often slip into narratives of people leaving. First, the non-Kazakh population left over the 1950s and 1960s: while ecological conditions deteriorated, a freer political climate allowed 'enemy peoples' to return to their homelands. Later, local Kazakhs began to leave, seeking work elsewhere, with some being resettled in rice plantations elsewhere in Qyzylorda oblast. Yet, though many did leave, most of my informants did not. Indeed, as we saw in Chapter 2, the refusal of the majority of the population to leave was another constraint for the authorities dealing with the Aral. Early in my fieldwork, a conversation with my host Zhaqsylyq suggested a reason why they stayed. We were driving over the dried-up seabed towards the sea, when he stopped beside a rusting heap of metal, the remains of a ship, which Zhaqsylyq pointed out with a laugh. But we had stopped to look at his camel, which was grazing with the village herd. Zhaqsylyq stood for some time gazing at it (Figure 4.2). As we walked back to the UAZ, I asked him how he had felt when the sea disappeared. He replied: 'We always thought it would come back.' When I asked why, he explained: 'Because we knew that long ago, the sea wasn't there, then it came back.' I had read about the previous regressions, but I had not suspected that local people would have been aware of these even before the archaeological discovery in 2001. In this temporal framework, the sea is a transient object which comes and goes. Hence this knowledge about the deep past was oriented towards the future. It is striking that Zhaqsylyq spoke in the first-person plural. At an earlier time, when many were leaving the village, such a story may have maintained a shared sense of hope.

This local knowledge is no closed tradition, but has been reproduced through encounters between people and environment. Fishermen describe dredging up with their nets bits of saxaul (a desert shrub),

Figure 4.2 Zhaqsylyq on the dried-up seabed with his *nar* camel (Bactrian camel–dromedary hybrid) on the left, winter 2013. Source: author.

remains of jugs, cradles, parts of yurts. People also cite the recent discovery of the mausoleum as further evidence of what had long been known. Although this provided the definitive proof for archaeologists that the sea had gone away and come back before, locals make no distinction between legend (*angyz*) and archaeological proof. During my fieldwork, I often heard versions of this story, presented as something that had been passed down through the generations, local knowledge transmitted by the elders (*aqsaqaldar*). When I would ask if they had thought the sea would return one day, people might reply in the past tense, saying that the sea had disappeared and reappeared before. This is the third time that it has gone away, they would say. This story alludes to a time span far beyond that of the human life, a time span in which, in the narratives of older people, the sea itself assumes agency: I was told that the sea 'slept'; that it 'came to itself'; that when it returned, it came 'in a single day'. Sometimes, when people mention the populations living on the dried-up seabed who were wiped out when the sea returned, the sea's agency transcends that of humans.

If these stories provide one explanation for why my informants stayed, a further answer lies in the strong local identity connected with place. When I asked people why they did not leave, the dominant response was that this is *tughan zher*, 'homeland', 'land of birth'. This phrase captures the relationship between people, place and ancestors. Important sites indexing the land as *tughan zher* include the shrines of *ülken atalar*, founders of lineages, where rituals bring together descendants now scattered across the country. There are also the cemeteries on the high ground above villages, a visible reminder of the dead. Whenever anyone passes them, they pass their hands over their faces, a gesture which embodies a connection to the past; longer prayers evoke the more recent dead. This connection to the land emerged most clearly in a conversation in Aqespe, a village on the northwest of the sea, far from the delta, far from Aral'sk and paved roads, where ecological conditions continue to deteriorate owing to an advancing sand dune. Only 40 houses remain today. One fisherman, Zhengïs, told me how all his brothers and sisters had left and gone to Aral'sk, Qazaly, Qyzylorda; but, he said as he pointed at the hillside opposite, their ancestors are buried here and someone needs to stay to watch over them. In addition to this sense of moral obligation, many, as in Aral'sk, also insist on their emotional, even bodily attachment to the land where they were born, despite the ecological devastation: some from Qaratereng who were relocated to rice farms elsewhere in Qyzylorda oblast could not cope with the climate, I was told, and died there. Ancestors are not restricted to sacred sites. In the home, before a *besbarmaq* for example, a verse from the Koran recited in Arabic is followed by a Kazakh blessing (*bata*) invoking the spirits of the ancestors. Indeed, the ancestors link people in the present through their relatedness within a particular lineage.

The importance of *tughan zher* to Kazakhs as ancestral homeland is attested by Privratsky (2001), Post (2007) and Dubuisson and Genina (2012).[4] In contrast to the abstractions of the plan that rendered villagers vulnerable, *tughan zher* is a chronotope in which the permanence of sites connects people to the ancestral past; persons are constituted through their connections to the land and to each other. Taken together, stories of previous regressions and the discourse of *tughan zher* seem to point to the resilience of the local, making connections between people and place which transcend the visible changes in the environment wrought by the abstractions of the Soviet project. By drawing attention to temporal connections far beyond the reach of individual lifetimes, and indeed that of the projects of the Soviet state, they suggest compelling reasons why people stayed, despite the rupture of the disappearing sea.

Things are not, of course, that simple. The story about previous regressions is not unambiguous. Many draw the same conclusion as Zhaqsylyq, that the sea will come back again. But not everyone grants this knowledge the same significance. Some say straightforwardly that if the Syr Dariya and the Amu Dariya flow into the sea again, then the sea will return; if not, it will not. Although Zhaqsylyq seemed to affirm a collective sense of hope in his use of 'we', he was by no means talking for everyone. Indeed, I found that some younger people did not know about the previous regressions. Given the sea's partial return, and its renewal of community relations, this story has lost its social function. Furthermore, although there is certainly an ideology of *tughan zher*, and although stories of previous regressions provided some sort of hope, for those who did leave, economic exigency trumped attachment to place.

Even those who stayed do not always account for their decision in terms of *tughan zher*. As Zhūbatqan said, 'Where would we go?' In the 1970s and 1980s, the authorities were encouraging Qaratereng villagers (including those resettled from the now abandoned islands and villages to the south) to work on rice plantations elsewhere in Qyzylorda oblast, but those who stayed stress that they knew nothing about rice: they only knew fishing. They stress the limits of their knowledge, the limits of their horizons. Others wanted to leave, particularly in the 1990s when the situation was increasingly dire, but they stress the constraints they faced – they lacked money to leave, or perhaps an elderly family member needed to be looked after. More than the moral connection to the land

and ancestors, obligations to actual family relations in the present needed to be sustained.

Batyrkhan was born into a fishing family on the island of Qasqaqūlan. His family was relocated to Qaratereng in 1974. Today, he is an important figure in the Qaratereng fishery and, on the basis of his success, has built a huge house in the village. But he had never wanted to stay in Qaratereng: in 1980 he left school and entered a railway college; in 1982 he went to serve in the army in Hungary (he showed me his tank unit tattoo with pride) and decided he wanted to become a professional soldier. We were talking in Russian, which he spoke fluently from his experience in the army:

> **William:** Many say that this is *tughan zher*, their homeland (Ru.: *rodina*) –
>
> **Batyrkhan:** Well, homeland, homeland (*rodina, rodina*) … If there's no water here, no food, then it's not a homeland! This is people's emotion, that this is *tughan zher* … Well, I stayed here with my father, my youngest brother was little, our mother had died, I had little brothers and sisters at school.

In contrast to others who stress the limitedness of their horizons, Batyrkhan presents himself as someone who had seen the world, and could see through the ideology of *tughan zher*, distancing himself from it by citing the Kazakh phrase in a Russian sentence. He too knew the legend of the previous desiccation, telling me how settlements had been wiped out when the sea returned; after the flood, just one kulan (a wild horse), with a white spot on its head, had been left alone on Qasqaqūlan, giving the island its name.[5] But he insisted that there had been no hope of the sea returning, and that he had stayed only to fulfil family duties.

Batyrkhan rejected the power of *tughan zher* when the environment has been ruined. Others, however, would dispute the idea that the environment *has* been ruined: after all, people have gone on living there. Certainly, the damaging effects of *ekologiia*, visible in the salt which lies on land, are acknowledged. When the sea receded, villagers explain, salt went up into the air, creating *ekologiia*. Understood as salt and dust in the air from the dried-up seabed, *ekologiia* is a transitory phenomenon, and indeed, around Bögen and the lakes, some assert that *ekologiia* has gone away. Crucially, fluctuations in numbers of livestock are related to political-economic factors as much as to ecological factors: immediately after collectivisation, people had few or no private livestock, and only after the war did they start acquiring more livestock, though seldom more than a few heads. The bankruptcy of the fishing industry in the 1990s is related to an *increase* in private livestock, when working animals were distributed to fishermen as pay. Meanwhile, large herds, especially those belonging to the fishing kolkhozy Zhambul and Raiym and the large livestock sovkhozy elsewhere in Aral'sk raion, were massively depleted as collective and state farms went bust. At the same time, while salt is acknowledged to have damaged the pastures, the region has always been salty (especially around the northern coast), which is why Aral meat is deemed the tastiest in the country. Indeed, today the dried-up seabed around Bögen is considered good pasture for camels.

Attachment to place, therefore, needs to be contextualised in the significance of the landscape within socialist and postsocialist spaces. In the following sections, I show how, before the sea's retreat, colonial and Soviet regimes of nature had transformed local structures of value, and the meaning of the sea itself. *Tughan zher*, I suggest, was thoroughly Sovietised, its reproduction resting on the gridded chronotope of the plan. This transformation, coupled with Soviet practices to maintain the fishery in the 1970s and 1980s, helps in understanding how the rupture of the sea's regression is smoothed over.

The sea, famine and mutual aid

On one occasion, I asked Zhūbatqan whether there would be fish in the future, given current intensive fishing practices. To my surprise, his reply was couched in the past: 'There will ... The Aral Sea in 32, in 41, in the war, fed all people. You eat fish, and it's enough.' Another chronotope thus emerged, one of timeless natural abundance, in which the sea directly sustains the human body. Zhūbatqan collapsed temporal differences: throughout the years of collectivisation and war, the constant is that the sea fed people – and this is a guide to the future of the sea, the years of the sea's absence notwithstanding. He continued:

> Then how many people flocked (*auyp*)[6] here from other places: this place fed them. They ate fish, they drank *sorpa* [stock], they ate it fried, they ate it boiled, they put it in a pan, made *qarma* and ate it ... you don't die. Far away, they were people from far from the sea, they don't have fish. They came to the Aral Sea, lots of people. It fed them, this is what feeds them (*osy asyrady ghoi, būl asyraidy*).

Mass migrations of famine refugees from other parts of Kazakhstan in the early 1930s, deportations of enemy peoples from all over the USSR before and during the war: all are blurred in a narrative where the sea is the centre, the source of sustenance for all, assuming agency in feeding the bodies of those who flocked around it. This image of natural abundance, I suggest, originates in precolonial practices of fishing, when, in a pastoral economy predicated on scarcity and differentiated ownership, fish were abundant, a common resource owned by no one. Hence the representation of the sea as centre, sustaining all people, regardless of their attachment to the locality.

In this narrative there is no trace of the famine in the Aral region itself, and Zhūbatqan, like many others in Bögen and other villages in the delta, explicitly denied that there had been famine, drawing a contrast with other regions in Kazakhstan. As Rai put it: 'At that time, if a man came to this lake and laid two nets, his stomach would be full.' Stories of people coming from other regions are also common: 'food was necessary' (*tamaq kerek qoi*). In Aqespe on the northwestern shore, I heard a slightly different story from Tasbolat, who was born in 1949. When I asked explicitly, he at first said that he did not know anything about famine because his parents had not told him about it. But later in our conversation, he mentioned how all his parents' livestock had been confiscated 'when there was famine'. He told me that his parents had moved away, to Bögen, where his mother had relatives. Although people were fleeing Bögen too, this is consistent with the documentary evidence which suggests that the famine was more severe on the northwest shores, where, with no fresh water, nothing grew.[7]

Interwoven with these links between the sea and famine are stories about other nationalities coming in the 1930s and 1940s – Koreans, Chechens, Kalmyks, Germans. Explanations for why they came are vague. Sometimes it is because of famine, sometimes because 'Stalin brought them'. Stories about other nationalities emphasise reciprocity: the help that the local Kazakhs gave them, inviting them into their houses; how they learnt Kazakh while Kazakh children learnt Russian and Kalmyk; how they fished together. Most left in the 1950s, after Stalin's death, when enemy peoples were allowed to return; the rest left when the sea began to retreat. The arrival of deportees is not presented as an intrusion or rupture. The narrative format is: 'they came … and then they left, to their own countries (*öz elderïne*)'.

In the chronotope of abundance, the sea transcends economic valuation. This became clear when I asked Zhūbatqan about the famous story of Lenin's letter. He told me that 'our fathers' had fished and loaded the fish onto sledges, and camels had dragged them to Qamystybas, where they were cleaned, processed and stored, before being loaded onto trains:

> There had been a call for help. The old men [here] had seen poverty (*zhoqty*, lit. 'nothingness') before, and those guys there [in the Volga region] were on the brink of death … so they said, 'Come on, send something, food is needed.' So they fished and fished, saying 'We won't take money, this is our help, we're giving those guys help' … By camel, lots of camels … they brought it and loaded into wagons.

There is a sense of generalised reciprocity between the Aral region and the outside. The refusal of money suggests that the sea's wealth is more than an economic resource: the sea as a source of sustenance connects the locality with the outside through help (*kömek*). There is a parallel with hunter-gatherer ideologies of sharing natural abundance, rejecting calculated exchange (e.g. Woodburn 1982). At the same time, this account establishes a moral connection between the sea and elsewhere in terms compatible with the utopian ideology of Communism.[8]

Nevertheless, this relationship between the sea and the Soviet outside would transform what the sea was. The commodification of nature started well before the Soviet period: stories about Russians, stories about encounters between different sorts of knowledge, already establish an association between fish and money. Such stories describe a period when the local – and local understandings of nature – was becoming increasingly 'perforated' (Hastrup 2009). Yet these early encounters are still couched in terms of reciprocity. The gradual process of colonisation, which from the outside looks like a rupture of local knowledge, is domesticated, and rendered in local idioms: Zhūbatqan told me that before the kolkhoz was constructed, Russians and Ukrainians 'came to help', because Kazakhs had not known about fishing and did not have nets. They had brought nets and hooks and had installed ice houses. Zhūbatqan described them as *bai* (rich men, kulaks), emphasising that they were private (*zheke*), paying the Kazakhs money. But he framed this in terms of 'help' rather than exploitation: they helped by giving money, clothes and boats. The tangle of debts and exploitation which the Bolsheviks saw was, in Zhūbatqan's account, a relationship embedded in reciprocity. The new vision of the sea as an economic resource was, in this account, assimilated to local understandings of mutual aid. Thus, if, according to Zhūbatqan, fishermen refused to accept money for the fish they gave in response to Lenin's letter, it was because fish were not yet pure commodities.

Kolkhoz construction

Collectivisation, as we saw in Chapter 1, was to bring fishers into the industrial, homogeneous time-space of the Five-Year Plan. The clan structures of Kazakh society were to be broken down, and people and nature were to be separated, mediated by the numbers of the plan. Policies of sedentarisation, collectivisation and deportation instigated a political form of movement which treated space and time as abstract, overriding the ecological movements of people in tune with geographical particularities, clan affiliations and the rhythm of the seasons. Chapter 1 showed this moment to be a significant rupture, the official Soviet narrative of a glorious socialist construction contradicted by archival evidence of chaos and collapse.

Zhūbatqan's take was different. He said that the kolkhoz was founded 'when the government was constructed', explaining that before the 1930s 'the kolkhoz couldn't be organised'. But he did not mention the reasons, or the chaos of relocations and sedentarisation. He explained that the private employers had to leave when the kolkhoz was constructed, because it would not allow them to work privately, but he did not pass judgement on either. Rather, he explained the practical advantages of the kolkhoz: 'The government gives you money, it gives you a boat for free; your boat, nets, it gives them for free. The kolkhoz, the committee maintains it. They don't ask money from you. *Koptit'* (Ru.: smoking), sale, the Trust does that. Then ... for free they give nets to the kolkhoz.' Indeed, some accounts of the period of collectivisation and famine stress not natural abundance, but state provisioning.

Möngkebai, another Bögen villager slightly older than Zhūbatqan, told me about the confiscations, emphasising that they were 'not right' (*dūrys emes*). In his telling, this encounter with the outside ('the government') produced a sense of rupture, and, unlike Zhūbatqan and many others, he did say that there was famine in the region. He continued to tell me that when people started fishing for the kolkhoz, 'the Soviet government took the fish and brought groceries, Lenin-Stalin gave money'. After this, he said, things got better. In this phrasing, it is not just natural abundance that is important, but the encounter with the outside, embodied in 'the Soviet government' or 'Lenin-Stalin', which provisioned the region (eventually) with foodstuffs. The state is personalised in the figure of Lenin-Stalin, and the relationship is one of reciprocal exchange. Crucially, the sea is a source of money as well as a sustaining centre. Möngkebai added with a laugh that this was before his time, but 'the aqsaqals told us'. Though I was often told about the people who came to the region, I was never told about the 84 households that left Bögen in 1931: either this was not something the aqsaqals told Möngkebai, or it was something which he, himself an aqsaqal now, omits from his narratives. He smoothed over other traumas with laughter, joking about how he had first fished during the war, when women and children were fishing to fulfil the plan in a time of 'shock work' (Ru.: *udar*).

When rupture is smoothed over, collectivisation does not figure as an alien imposition on the native *tughan zher*. Family histories express pride in generations who fished first for the Russians, then for the kolkhoz, then for the state fishery base (Figure 4.3). This Sovietisation of the local landscape comes out particularly clearly in a famous *terme*, a sort of song, which I first heard blaring from an MP3 player in the UAZ while fishermen drew their nets through the ice. It begins:

> My Aral's endless surface, mine (*Aralym aidyn shalqarym*) – land
> blessed with abundance (*qūt-bereke qonghan zher*).
> Land which left its mark in history, land where Nūrtughan[9] wrote
> my precious *zhyr* [poem].
> My Aral (*Aralym*), land thus blessed with happiness and wealth
> (*däuletpen bailyq*).

As the *terme* stresses the connections between the singer and the land with the repeated possessive suffix *-ym/-im*, the Aral emerges as a place of natural wealth and abundance compatible with the accounts above. Yet the rest of the *terme* lists labour heroes, war veterans and writers from the region famed across the Soviet Union. The patriotism expressed is for a Sovietised *tughan zher*.[10]

Indeed, while collectivisation marked an assault on the clan structure of Kazakh society, the kin-based ordering of space and time was not destroyed, but was articulated with socialist logics. Clan identity remains salient today, with particular *ru* (lineages) rooted in specific villages, even if the *ru* no longer constitutes a corporate unit of production.[11] Although the economic functions of clan institutions were formally replaced with the institutions of Soviet governance, industrial space and time provided the conditions for the perpetuation, and transformation, of family space and time. After all, given the difficulties of the shortage economy, state-socialist time was in practice arhythmic

Figure 4.3 Fishing on the Aral, undated. Source: Museum of Fishermen, Aral'sk.

(Verdery 1996, 57); and, while space was formally homogenised, development was, as we saw in Chapter 1, uneven, with widely heterogeneous distribution of resources over space. As Humphrey's (1998) classic ethnography of a Siberian Buriat kolkhoz demonstrates, the concomitant formal difficulties of fulfilling the plan necessitated informal practices, which were organised according to kinship logics.[12] Hence, local, place-based identity is neither autonomous of, nor opposed to, the gridded time and space of state socialism: the two are articulated.

Rybatskii zhizn': the fisherman's life in the late Soviet fishery

> 'We had food to eat, vodka to drink [flicking throat][13]... it was Communism.' – Tolpash, fisherman

After camping in the back of a draughty GAZ-66 truck for several days by Kökaral in spring 2014 (see Chapter 6), Zhaqsylyq and I were travelling back to Bögen in driving sleet. Zhaqsylyq asked me, not for the first time, what I thought of the 'fisherman's life', using a Russian phrase, *rybatskii zhizn'*.[14] I had not been fishing, but I had lugged sacks of fish around and dragged boats over the mud and loaded them onto the roof of the truck, and was cold, wet and exhausted, so I replied, as I was expected to reply, that it was 'difficult' (*qiyn ghoi*). He concurred with a hearty laugh. But when I asked if it had been the same in the past, he said that it was much easier today: until recently, there had been no jeeps and trucks, only camels. Older people remember still more difficult times, when there were no motors and they had to row for hours against strong winds. Recall Zhūbatqan's narrative at the opening of this chapter: the regression of the sea formed a rupture in the progressive arrival of newer sorts of technology. *Rybatskii zhizn'* has changed dramatically since Zhūbatqan's youth, both because of environmental change and because of technological improvements. It still, however, provides narrative continuity even in the late Soviet years after the sea had gone away.

Narratives of fishing in the late Soviet period should be contextualised in memories of the period as one of abundance. Indeed, my incessant questions as to how things were different before and after the sea went away would elicit comparisons between an often undifferentiated 'Soviet time' (*kenges kezi*) and today. As in Aral'sk, the presence of the sea becomes blurred with the late Soviet period in general. Fuel was free, groceries were abundant, everything was affordable because 'money had value': all this is characterised as 'Communism', understood as a historical stage in the Brezhnev era, now passed. Small factories in Bögen and Qaratereng continued to function, where women worked processing ocean fish delivered by lorry from Aral'sk; through such factory labour many local women participated in the public sphere. This was also, as we saw in Chapter 2, a period of infrastructural development: water pipes, electricity cables, field hospitals. Although these changes are not narrated by villagers, it is significant that the period when the sea finally retreated was also the period when some, albeit limited, amenities of modernity reached many of the villages in the region. This also helps us understand why there is no clear narrative of decline. Much of the infrastructure remains or has been improved. Some elements, like the public banya, the canteen, the factory and the wireless station, have gone, along with the stable currency and efficient provisioning. As the public sphere has sharply contracted, women's roles are increasingly restricted to the household.

Against this backdrop of late Soviet abundance, accounts of fishing elsewhere in Kazakhstan smooth over the rupture of the sea's regression. Indeed, litanies of places fished are often woven into official presentation of biography, as seen with this Qaratereng fisherman, who announced, as soon as my dictaphone was turned on:

My name is Küntughan, Tūrghanbaev Küntughan. I started fishing on the sea in 73, I worked in this fish system (*balyq sistemasynda*). It was good. When the sea went away, after it disappeared, in the Aqtöbe region there is a place called Yrghyz, the fish on the sea was becoming scarce (*azaidy*), when it became scarce they sent us (*zhïberdï*) on *komandirovka* (Ru.: business trip) to Aqtöbe ... We fished from this place. There is a place called Yrghyz. Baitaq. So we fished. There are lots of names of the lakes. There's Baitaq, there's Lake Qarmaq ...

He went on to talk of fishing on Zaisan (east Kazakhstan) and Qapshaghai (south Kazakhstan), expressing pride in a life spent fishing all over Kazakhstan. Such stories reflect the hierarchical structure of the fishery: 'they sent us' is a recurring phrase. Sometimes it is the local director who is said to have sent them, sometimes the *kombinat*. Sometimes it was the minister himself, an emphasis that personalises the distant state. However, there is less emphasis on the state providing work than we saw in the previous chapter, less sense of a moral space affording an encompassing sense of belonging than we saw in the last chapter.

My informants stressed the importance of labour discipline, and of fulfilling the plan. By contrast, documents from the late Soviet period are full of complaints about poaching and about poor labour discipline. Sometimes in the 1970s fishermen refused to go out and fish. On one occasion, Bögen fishermen wrote to the chairman of Kazsovmin complaining about not receiving the minimum pay grade in the winter of 1977–8, when fishing on the sea was nearly impossible; a Minrybkhoz investigation found that they had been breaking labour discipline by not going fishing at all, so were not entitled to the minimum salary – indeed, they should have been punished.[15] If this may be interpreted as a minor act of resistance against their plight in a situation where agency was severely constrained, it is not remembered today. Indeed, in contrast to the archival evidence, fishermen today insist that the fishery was well managed: poaching was minimal, and banned seasons were respected. Both people and nature were, they say, better managed than today: lakes were stocked with fish and provided with water, and monitoring deterred poachers. The Yrghyz lakes are said to have deteriorated dramatically since Soviet times because now they are private, so there is no water; within the Aral region, there are complaints that Lake Aqshatau also does not have enough water and is not stocked with fish, while on Lake Raiym stocks are declining because of poor monitoring and no possibility for villagers to fish legally. Crucially, labour discipline and plan fulfilment are associated with economic security, as this exchange with Zhūbatqan shows:

William: So discipline was good?

Zhūbatqan: We were OK. The Soviet government looked after us. They didn't let anyone eat up [i.e. embezzle] our salary, they didn't allow it. If you tell the *raikom*, they'll get it, if you say they've eaten up your salary. They can't eat it up, back then they can't eat it up. If you say I'm going to work, *pozhaluista* (Ru.: 'by all means' [lit. 'please']). You must fulfil the *plan* (Ru.: 'plan'). *Plan*, if you fulfil the *plan*, that's enough.

William: And did you fulfil the *plan* on Balqash?

Zhūbatqan: We fulfilled it, we overfulfilled it! We overfulfilled it, twice over.

In such accounts, fishing for the plan materialises a connection with the state, albeit one more limited than the encompassing incorporation that we explored in the previous chapter. However, Tasbolat, from Aqespe, talked much more critically about the connection with the state materialised through fishing for the plan. He had fished all his life under Narghaly Demeuov, a brigadier and labour hero (and Party member) famous across the region. There was a clear contrast between Demeuov's discipline and Tasbolat's irreverent views of the system. Edïge, my friend from Aral'sk, had accompanied me to help with the interview. Tasbolat mixed Russian and Kazakh, but seemed to prefer speaking to me in ungrammatical army Russian, partly sensing that it was easier for me to follow, but partly also because it offered him the opportunity to show off his swearing:

William: And when you fished then, did you always fulfil plan?

Tasbolat: Yes, we fulfilled the plan.

Edïge: (in Kazakh) There was no *perevypolnenie* (Ru.: overfulfilment)?

Tasbolat: (in Kazakh) There is ... (in Russian) there was *perevypolnenie* ... ninth, tenth five-year plans, there was ... they'd give a little medal – fucking cheating us! No gold for fuck's sake, just metal crap ... Bullshit. Crap. All politics cheats. It's state politics, of

	course they cheat people, all of them … bullshit, they gave money …
Edïge:	(in clean, grammatical Russian) They rewarded them with medals, they claimed that this is gold but it was ordinary metal he says, not gold.
Tasbolat:	They gave a certificate … utter crap … paper … it's all fucking shit, they clap and say 'go on, work'. Fuck it … There, William … And now it's the same too!

Yet, in the same interview, Tasbolat also talked of the benefits of Soviet modernity, and did not question Soviet conceptions of the environment. Indeed, over the generation or so since collectivisation, subjection to the plan, which situated fishermen as resource extractors, had transformed local understandings of fish, advancing the colonial-era process of commodification. The political ecology of numbers was internalised, with implications for conceptions of space and time. When I asked how they would decide where to lay their nets, Zhūbatqan told me simply: 'You fish where you're taken.' Others point to some agency, albeit constrained and within a limited space. This is how Rai put it:

> From dawn till dusk you go on laying the seine. In the end you have to go over the whole surface of this lake [Raiym] and find fish. If you sit in the middle, the fish won't come. Now if I've fished from this place, tomorrow I must fish from Qoszhar. I have to fish from Qambash. I have to go right round and fish. *Then* the fish will enter [the net].

In this description of fishing labour, the plan structures the everyday embodied practice of fishing. Fishermen are constrained to extract the requisite amount of fish from the lakes, and the lakes are reduced to resources. Local knowledge is applied according to the logic of fulfilling the plan. Lakes are, in this register, homogenised. This is not, of course, to say that fishermen did not have local knowledge or agency in their fishing activities. However, in narratives like these, they present themselves as extracting resources to fulfil the plan; their bodily engagement with the environment is constrained by higher agency.

This same logic applies on the much larger scale of the Kazakh republic. After Zhūbatqan had told me about overfulfilling the plan on Balqash, I asked if they were sent there specifically to fulfil the plan: 'If there's no fish here, you have to fish in that place (*ana zhaqta*). They're all Kazakhstani lakes. Then... There was a single minister, in this place (*myna zhaqta*) there's no fish, *davai* ... in this place the fish are disappearing, and it's necessary to fish.' When people say, for example, 'Stalin sent Kalmyks here', there is a clear sense of bounded locality, an inside and an outside. Here Kazakhstan is an undifferentiated space, united by a single minister. When the plan must be fulfilled, there is no difference between lakes: fish are equivalent wherever they are. When I pressed fishermen further, they would, of course, talk about the differences between places fished: Balqash fish are thin, because the bottom is rocky and lacking in *shalang*; zander on Balqash had scabs; some of the fish on Zaisan had worms; the Yrghyz system on the other hand, after it was stocked with new species, was rich in fish, especially carp. However, these differences are subsumed in the continuity provided by the phrase 'we fished': the logic of the plan just demands fish. Indeed, when I suggested that life must have become much harder after the sea went away, Zhūbatqan responded: 'There was work. We fished from Balqash, then we'd take our salary.' From this perspective, the association of fish with money means that it is not significant where one fishes, so long as one has work and money (Figure 4.4).

Figure 4.4 Fishing, late Soviet period. Source: Museum of Fishermen, Aral'sk.

Conclusion

In the narratives explored in this chapter, the sea's regression both is and is not a sea change. Amid devastating environmental change, there is also continuity. If resilience is about the endurance of a set of relationships even when some of those relationships have been ruptured, it makes sense to talk about resilience. However, this chapter suggests that resilience does not lie solely in the local, beneath or in resistance to the externally imposed grids of the state.[16] If long-term relationships between people and place were resilient, this lay in their incorporation into gridded time and space, via fish, money, infrastructure and entitlements. Local resilience depended on the top-down adaptation described in Chapter 2. This is not simply a matter of linkages between scales. Incorporation into the imperial and then the command economy transformed local conceptions of time, space and nature. The colonial and Soviet periods saw a new meaning of *bailyq*, whereby fish were abstracted as exchange-values. Translated into money and linking the region to gridded infrastructure, fish came to be associated with rising living standards. This conception overlaid but did not quite displace a local conception whereby the sea is valued as an agent sustaining life itself. Within the new conceptualisation, fish and water are both fungible, so it does not matter where you fish, so long as you fulfil the plan, hence the level of continuity which fishing provides. Space becomes homogeneous, place loses meaning and local agency is limited. The locality is connected to broader spaces by ministers and authorities giving money, making orders, sending fishermen here and there. When Aikeldï spoke of the *bailyq* of the region, both understandings of wealth could be signified.

Crucially, as *tughan zher* itself was Sovietised, there is no clear opposition between a 'traditional', cultural landscape and a 'modern' space of economic gain. As Abashin (2015, Chapter 9) shows in his discussion of the development of wedding rituals in Tajikistan, as wages rose, the lack of opportunities for financial investment resulted in investments in social capital in the form of increasingly lavish weddings and extravagant gift-giving. Indeed, even from the late 1930s, money from fishing was reinvested in livestock, which circulated in the ritual economy. Rai, who married in the 1950s, remarked laconically that the wedding feast was great because there were lots of fish and lots of money. The association of connections is instructive: social reproduction, which is rooted in place, and which also reproduces place, is dependent on the abstraction of nature and its transformation into monetary value. Local resilience – the maintenance of relationships among people and between people and place despite the loss of the sea that lay at the heart of these relationships – depended on the articulation of chronotopes of plan and *tughan zher*. If *tughan zher* suggests a permanence that transcends the rupture of the sea's retreat, this ongoing connection between people and place was maintained by the abstract chronotope of the plan, within which the sea was a replaceable economic resource.

Nuances of past narratives are fading. One day I was sitting with Zhūbatqan near Zhaqsylyq's house. Elzhas, a recent arrival in the village, was repairing a truck. Zhūbatqan was telling him in detail where the kolkhoz had been, how the management had given nets and clothing, where fish had been received. I was (of course) listening to all this avidly, but Elzhas devoted most of his attention to repairing the truck. Younger people in Bögen know that the sea came up to the village, that there had been a quay and a factory in the village; they told me how 'the old men (*shaldar*) said' that the sea dried up when Uzbeks did not give water; when it dried up, salt spread up into the air and into foreign countries, then there was *ekologiia*. Narratives about the past are being transmitted, and when prefaced by 'the old men say', there is a sense of a homogenised narrative, crystallised local knowledge. But the texture of the past, with all its trauma, is not transmitted, just as, at an earlier stage, other traumas were not transmitted.

Notes

1 Kazakhs do not generally eat pork on religious grounds, though many fishermen are partial to *salo*, salted pork fat, a Russian and Ukrainian delicacy.

2 The verb *qaitu* means, primarily, 'to return', but also means 'to be lost' and is used as a euphemism for 'to die'; with water it means 'to fall, recede'.

3 This story emerges from correspondence between the ministry, TsK KP Kazakhstana, Aralrybprom and the Bögen villagers: letter from deputy minister Duisenov to TsK KP Kazakhstana (General'nyi otdel), 16 June 1977, TsGARK, f. 1130, op. 1, d. 1722, l. 39; letter from deputy minister Duisenov to comrades A. Baitakhanov, T. Balkybaev, T. Zhopaev, S. Sydykov, I. Ibraimov, Zh. Zhanuzakov, 1 July 1977, TsGARK, f. 1130, op. 1, d. 1722, ll. 40–1; letter from deputy minister Duisenov to ARP director K. Sarzhanov, 1 July 1977, TsGARK, f. 1130, op. 1, d. 1722, l. 42; letter from minister Utegaliev to secretary of TsK KP Kazakhstana A.I. Klimov, 20 July 1977, TsGARK, f. 1130, op. 1, d. 1722, ll. 43–4.

4 Privratsky argues that landscape embodies Kazakh collective memory and, in the relative absence of mosques, defines Kazakh Islam. While his argument about a teleological development towards universal, global Islam, and his suggestion that this form of Islam is linked specifically to ethnic (as opposed to local) identity, are problematic, this particular point is well taken. Both Post (discussing Mongolian Kazakhs), and Dubuisson and Genina (discussing Kazakhstani Kazakhs), argue that *tughan zher* is more real to people than the macronarratives of the state.

5 *Qasqa*, 'white spot'; *qūlan*, 'kulan, wild horse'.

6 The verb signifies 'to move en masse, migrate'.

7 The social forgetting of the famine here and elsewhere in Kazakhstan contrasts strikingly with memories of the famine in Ukraine, which is integral to nationalist narratives. This forgetting is evidently linked both to the official Soviet silence on the famine and to the danger of speaking out, as well as the muteness of official discourse about it today. Kindler (2018, Chapter 7) suggests a darker possibility, that silence is, beyond fear of the state, the outcome of an inability to come to terms with the complicity that survival had depended on.

8 The nuances about not exchanging fish are absent from most accounts of this story. For younger people, as in Aral'sk, the story simply expresses local pride in the connection between the region and the outside.

9 Nūrtughan Kenzheghūlūly: an *aqyn*, musician/poet, of the Aral region in the early twentieth century.

10 Cf. Beyer (2012) on the connections between descent, place and relatedness in the present in rural Kyrgyzstan. Beyer argues that the process of 'settling descent' is inflected with Soviet (and post-Soviet) modes of governance which have transformed but not destroyed clan identity. Conversely, Beyer argues, villagers 'customised' collectivisation, relating to it through genealogy and landscape. There is thus no clear opposition between a Soviet landscape and a resistant 'traditional' landscape. By contrast, Privratsky (2001) ignores the Sovietisation of Kazakh landscapes (and indeed of Kazakh identity and religion in general): he only sees Soviet modernity as a threat to a resilient local identity.

11 See further Chapter 6. Cf. also Cameron (2018, 173) on the persistence of clan identities within kolkhozy.

12 See Kandiyoti (2002) and Abashin (2015, 398–400) for the relevance of Humphrey's argument to Central Asia.

13 A symbol for drinking ubiquitous in the former USSR.

14 Like many who learnt their Russian in the army, Zhaqsylyq has a cavalier attitude towards gender: in formal Russian the phrase would be *rybatskaia zhizn'*.

15 Prikaz po proizvodstvennogo ob'edineniia 'Aralrybprom' No.161r 'O faktakh narusheniia trudovoi distsipliny, oplaty truda rybakam i slabyi kontrol' nad raskhodami sredstv na gosudarstvennom love Bugun'skoi bazy goslova', 26 May 1978, AFGAKO, f. 4, op. 1pr, d. 584, ll. 98–100. Fishermen received pay per amount of fish caught, but in case of poor catches, they were entitled to a minimum salary.

16 Cf. Hastrup (2009) for a critique of the tendency in much of the social science of adaptation and resilience to locate resilience in local 'socio-ecological systems'.

5
From Soviet ruins: flounder, the Kökaral dam and the return of the Small Aral Sea

Figure 5.1 Poster, Aral'sk, 2011. Nazarbayev and Kökaral: *Men Aralgha kömektesemïn degen, armanyma zhetkenïme quanyshtymyn* ('I said I would help the Aral, and I am glad to have fulfilled my dream'). Source: author.

This chapter tells of how, amid Soviet ruins, a small part of the Aral returned, of how fish populations recovered and of how a fishery was rebuilt, stories that are entangled with broader processes of post-Soviet transformation. There are different ways of narrating the Small Aral's return. The posters in Figures 5.1 and 5.2 link the sea's recovery to

Figure 5.2 Poster, Aral'sk, 2013. Nazarbayev and Kökaral: *Kökaral – ghasyr zhobasy* ('Kökaral – the project of the century'). Source: author.

the benevolent desires of the president, mastering water through the completion, in 2005, of the Kökaral dam.[1] A more modest account is offered in a 2010 *National Geographic* article:

> For many years, the Aral – the infamous sea-turned-desert, the one historians and environmental scientists still place among the worst ecological disasters ever – gave [local fishermen] nothing to celebrate. The fishery died in the 1980s, after the Soviet government drained the sea to feed thirsty cotton fields planted in the inhospitable landscape surrounding it ... But with help from the government, the World Bank, and scientists, the northern part of the Aral has started to make a recovery. There are fish in the water again, and for the past four years, fishermen have gathered to celebrate. (Walters 2010)

This, then, is a technopolitics that, in implicit contrast to Soviet megalomania, works with nature. With 'help' from the new hegemonic actors – unlike the billboards in Aral'sk, Walters includes the World Bank and scientists in their number – nature has started to recover. The sea that has been saved is only a small fraction of the former Aral, but some of the mess left by the Soviet regime has been cleared up.[2]

I will tell a rather different story. Contrary to the reassuring certainties of both the state-centred and the World Bank-centred narratives, there was nothing inevitable about the sea's restoration. After all, the disaster was popularised in the West in a *National Geographic* article that proclaimed: 'a Soviet sea lies dying' (Ellis 1990). Indeed, to most of the many development workers rallied by this disaster narrative to the Aral's former shores, the distant sea was dead or dying. Even at the end of the 1990s, a World Bank annual environmental review described the sea as 'biologically dead' (World Bank 1999, 21). The disaster narrative was a monologic form of discourse, fixing the sea as a knowable, determinate 'mute object, brute thing' (Bakhtin 1981b, 351), a waste of the defunct time-space of the USSR. What changed? How did the sea come to speak, to offer an alternative future for itself? Two factors were key: as the sea separated in two in 1987–9, the level of the Small Sea stabilised somewhat, offering hope that it might be preserved, while at the same time, the flounder population introduced over 1979–87 had grown significantly, offering a possible basis for a fishery. These developments were bolstered by local efforts to dam the strait between the two seas and a Danish aid project to encourage people to fish for flounder.

As an 'indeterminate assemblage' (Tsing 2015) of nonhuman and human processes, what the Small Aral *was* was not a given. The sea's indeterminacy posed a question: could the waste of the Soviet project become a source of value for the future? To be an entity worth saving, the 'biologically dead sea', the Soviet ruin known through the disaster narrative, had to be cast in a set of relations within which it could become a living sea, and a future object of post-Soviet fishery. Amid heterogeneity, openness, uncertainty, this required the cooperation of flounder and mussels, of wind and sand, of water flow and salt. It also required holding together a rapidly disintegrating fishery. Indeed, compounding the indeterminacy of the sea's existence was the heightened precarity of those living on its former shores following the Soviet collapse. As previous chapters suggested, local resilience had depended on the circulation of goods, subsidies and entitlements across Soviet gridded space. As all this disintegrated over the 1990s, the fishery, which had staggered on despite the sea's demise, gradually unravelled. This was the context that the Danish project intervened in, focusing on basic material provisioning to get people fishing again.

As Brandtstädter (2007, 138) claims, 'the postsocialist transition is best explored as a period of hegemonic fragmentation and reconstruction'. Brandtstädter's (2007, 133) comparison of the project of postsocialist 'transition' to the 'hegemonic discursive formation' of international development is helpful for exploring how the Aral, through the disaster narrative, became an object of transnational governmentality in the post-Soviet period. However, attending also to *material* disintegration and restoration highlights the contingency and heterogeneity of this 'hegemonic fragmentation and reconstruction'. This chapter juxtaposes two very different projects, responding to different sorts of instability and operating at different temporal scales: the Danish project to restore the fishery in the immediate term through basic material provision of nets, boats and so on; and the World Bank/Kazakhstan government project of stabilising the sea level into the future through the Kökaral dam. These two projects participated in very different forms of hegemonic reconstruction: if the Kökaral dam has come to materialise the Kazakhstani state, the Danes' urgent material provisioning facilitated, for a time, the emergence of a small-scale, relatively equitable fishery.

Indeed, in the early postsocialist years, the region diverged from other agrarian postsocialist settings that were marked by increasing inequality (Hann 2003; Hivon 1998; Shreeves 2002; Toleubayev et al. 2010; Trevisani 2010). Nevertheless, despite the very specific shape of post-Soviet transformations in the Aral region, by the time of my fieldwork the 'hegemonic reconstruction' resembled other postsocialist settings more closely, with the fishery increasingly dominated by a few big players. Explaining how this came about requires attention to a final sort of indeterminacy surrounding the post-Soviet Aral: the legal uncertainty surrounding property rights over the sea following the demise of Aralrybprom. Over the 1990s and early 2000s, this legal uncertainty did not provide an obstacle to the reconstruction of a small-scale flounder fishery. In the final part of the chapter, however, we see how this indeterminacy was resolved, in a way that contradicted the hopes of the Danes and their local colleagues, and how, as a result, patterns of social change came to conform more closely to other postsocialist settings.

Disaster development

We saw in Chapters 1 and 2 how, after decades when the Aral struggled to figure as anything more than a 'problem' of living standards and employment, during perestroika the sea became a 'matter of concern', a crisis that revealed the catastrophic outcome of the Soviet project. We closed Chapter 1 with belated official measures to tackle the crisis, which were almost immediately frustrated by the Soviet collapse. The Aral basin was divided between five successor states, whose interests over the sea's feeder rivers diverged dramatically: downstream Uzbekistan and

Turkmenistan, dependent on cotton, still needed water for irrigation, while the mountainous, energy-poor Tajikistan and Kyrgyzstan needed water for hydroelectricity.

At the same time, the famous disaster rallied a vast array of actors, including national governments in the region and beyond, international institutions, nongovernmental organisations (NGOs) and scientists. In the 1990s, over a thousand books and articles were published on the Aral and more than 30 international projects initiated (Kosarev and Kostianoy 2010a). This emerging 'global' vision, driven by the famous 'before and after' pictures from space and images of rusting ships, was embedded in the post-Cold War imaginary. The Aral was an environmental problem 'left over from the Communist era' (World Bank 1999, 23). As Western eyes focused on post-Soviet environmental crises, the USSR was situated as the unsustainable, destructive other, incapable of mitigating destructive effects (Oldfield 2005). Melodramatically entitled works like *Ecocide in the USSR* (Feshbach and Friendly 1992) featured the Aral, along with Chernobyl, in prime position.

As the Aral disaster was positioned as a problem of the Soviet past, there was also a blindness to the economic crisis unfolding amid the promised 'transition' to capitalism. For most development workers, the unemployment that beset the region stemmed directly from environmental disaster. Moreover, many aid projects, particularly in the densely populated Ferghana Valley, were based on the spectre of interethnic conflict fuelled by water scarcity.[3] Unlike the perestroika vision of disaster as a catalyst for radical transformation from within, the global vision was one of technical solutions from outside, through knowledge transfer from the 'normal' West to 'backward' post-Soviet space.

The United Nations Environment Programme, invited by the Soviet authorities to address the problem in 1990, completed a diagnostic study for conserving the Aral in 1993. Its scope was the whole Aral basin. It did not offer concrete proposals for preserving any of the sea itself. Flounder – key actors in this chapter's narrative – were mentioned only in passing (UNEP 1993). In 1992 the International Fund for Saving the Aral Sea was established, comprising all post-Soviet Central Asian republics. In 1994 the Aral Sea Basin Program was launched by the post-Soviet Central Asian republics together with the World Bank. Its objectives were rehabilitating the disaster zone around the sea, improving international water management and building institutional capacity. An initial goal of stabilising the sea level was rapidly dropped as too difficult (Micklin 1998, 406). Although deltas were identified as sites for intervention, no future was seen for the sea itself.

Weinthal (2002) relates the proliferation of development initiatives in the region to an elective affinity between Central Asian leaders and 'third-party actors', including Western governments and international institutions. National leaders could enhance their legitimacy, while third parties, by helping solve a 'global' disaster, could raise their prestige in the region. Weinthal's argument can be pushed further. For Brandtstädter (2007), 'transition', like international development, was a utopian project that fixed an idealised construct of 'the West' as the centre, the only viable future to which peripheral others could aspire. With Soviet governmental practices now cast as backward, development would be managed by a 'transnational apparatus of governmentality' (Ferguson and Gupta 2002). As the environment was identified as a priority for transnational development in postsocialist space (Wedel 1998, 33–4), and as the Aral disaster so clearly showed the 'backwardness' of Soviet environmental policy, it was an obvious area for international institutions to intervene in. The region was positioned not as 'underdeveloped', but 'misdeveloped' (Wedel 1998, 21).

Despite vast global interest, results were slow (Micklin 1998; Sievers 2003; Weinthal 2002). Central Asian leaders still talked about restoring the whole sea through diverting Siberian rivers, while international lenders advised that the whole sea could not be saved, stressing instead institutional reform and poverty alleviation. The only other 'solution', stopping cotton cultivation, was unconscionable for governments dependent on cotton. Meanwhile, energy-poor Kyrgyzstan and Tajikistan started using reservoirs, which had been built for irrigation, for hydroelectric energy instead. Fraught negotiations took place about water, or about water and energy, but agriculture was never discussed (Weinthal 2002, Chapter 7). Although international consultants' dire warnings about conflict did not materialise, there was little improvement. In 2003 Médecins Sans Frontières researchers identified a second disaster, a 'disaster of international assistance', a landscape littered with the ruins of unfinished projects, as donors retreated from earlier goals of environmental rehabilitation and abandoned the sea to its fate (Small and Bunce 2003).[4]

For Brandtstädter (2007, 138), the inevitable failure of grand plans of transition lies in the 'dissonance between administrative spaces and local worlds'. On the Aral, the discourse of environmental disaster did not resonate with local worlds partly because it ignored the compounding effects of post-Soviet economic breakdown. However, there was a further dissonance. The disaster narrative fixed the Aral as a stable, knowable entity, a ruin left by the Soviet past. The view from space of a dying sea, the rusting ships and the collapsing fishing industry all pointed to an environmental disaster that had profound impacts on human livelihoods. However, some of those closer to the sea itself saw a more lively sea, with a possible future.

Salvaging the sea from Soviet ruins

In contrast to the dead sea known to development actors, the Small Aral of the 1990s resembled what Tsing (2015) calls an 'indeterminate assemblage', its elements precarious and vulnerable, but full of potentiality and, indeed, of life. Let us first focus on hydrological processes. The ruination left by the Soviet project involved escalating nonhuman forces. As water was withdrawn from the rivers, evaporation from the sea exceeded inflow. The sea receded from its shores and the level fell. By 1988 it had fallen to 40 m above sea level (asl) from its 1960 level of 53 m asl, and salinity had increased from an average of 10 g/l to 30 g/l, killing off native species. The Berg Strait, between the mainland and the former island of Kökaral, which connected the Small Sea with the much larger body of water to the south, now dried up. This coincided with a reduction in water withdrawals in the late perestroika and early independence years, and in 1988 the Syr Dariya again reached the sea (Plotnikov et al. 2014, 164). Previously, this water would have spread across the whole sea, but now it flowed only into the Small Aral. Less water evaporated from the much smaller waterbody, so, in 1990, the Small Aral rose. As it rose, however, it overflowed back through the Berg Strait.

The ichthyologist N. V. Aladin had first suggested damming the Berg Strait in 1988. However, unable for several years to visit the strait, it was only in spring 1992 that he witnessed what was happening – and he foresaw disaster. In the late 1970s, to maintain navigation across the sea, a channel had been dredged through the strait. Though this was silted up, the water flowing through was washing the silt out. By spring 1992 it was 2 m deep and 100 m wide, stretching for 5 km, with 100 m³/s flowing through it, raising the fear that the 'self-deepening channel (*samouglubliaiushchiisia kanal)*' (Aladin and Plotnikov 1995, 8) might reach the mouth of the Syr Dariya just to the north, which could divert the river entirely into the Large Sea. In this dire prognosis, the 'self-deepening channel', an outcome of the ruination left by the Soviet project, was an actant that, unchecked, could lead to the Small Sea's disappearance.

After Aladin took his warning to the local authorities, permission was granted to construct a dam, though central government funding was not forthcoming. After an initial attempt to block the channel failed, an earth dam was constructed in July–August 1992. Rudimentary though it was, the sea level stabilised (Figure 5.3). The Syr Dariya now exerted a freshening influence in its estuary, and freshwater fish could forage in the sea (Figure 5.4). Reeds began to grow again in the delta, and pelicans, ducks, swans and cormorants began to nest.

The following spring, the Syr Dariya was swollen with meltwater. The sea level rose, breaching the dam. Even so, the outflow from the sea was less than previously. In the short time of the dam's existence, other materials had reinforced its effect: to the south, the wind had formed sand dunes 2–3 m high, while to the north, wave action had formed sandbanks – processes Aladin and Plotnikov (1995, 14) describe as 'natural reinforcement (*estestvennoe ukreplenie*)'. Over the coming years, local authorities rebuilt the dam, eventually extending an earth dyke across the Berg Strait in 1996–7. The structure remained fragile: as it was made only of earth and reeds, there was a high level of filtration; meanwhile, waves driven by the prevailing northerly wind eroded the structure. Amid acute economic crisis, continuous efforts to reinforce the dyke were hampered by a shortage of resources. Much machinery stood idle, lacking spare parts.

Shifts in human–hydrological relations upstream had mixed effects. Independent republics, no longer supported with grain from Russia, shifted somewhat from cotton to wheat cultivation. Less water was withdrawn from the Syr Dariya, leaving more to flow into the Small Aral. However, upstream reservoirs in energy-poor Kyrgyzstan, constructed in the 1970s to provide water for irrigation in summer, now shifted to continuous use for hydroelectricity. What had been a summer flow river became a winter flood river, for which hydrological installations were not designed. Bottlenecks formed, and water was lost to desert sinks (World Bank 2001).

Throughout the 1990s, the existence of the Small Aral remained very fragile: the interventions of local dam builders were a small part of a precarious assemblage of human, hydrological and climatic processes. Holding the assemblage together was the hybrid object of a 'naturally reinforced dam'. Despite its precarity, the sea's level stabilised. The Syr Dariya began to form a new delta slightly to the north, diminishing the risk of it being sucked through the Berg Strait. Critically, as the fresh water brought by the river exceeded evaporation, salinity fell dramatically. Freshwater fish were foraging in the sea, although it was still too salty for

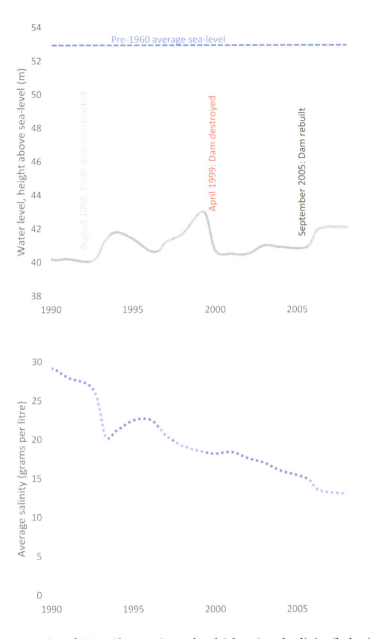

Figures 5.3 and 5.4 Changes in sea level (above) and salinity (below) in the Small Aral Sea, 1990–2008. Prepared by the author. Data from Micklin (2010, 201) and Plotnikov (2013, 43). The shaded areas mark periods when dams are present.

them to reproduce. Aladin and his colleagues noted with delight how invertebrates not seen in the sea for decades were reappearing, such as the planktonic crustacean *Moina mongolica*, seed shrimps (ostracods) and midge larvae (Chironomidae), blown in by the wind from nearby lakes. These increased the nutritional value of the benthic fauna, with potential benefits for freshwater fish species (Aladin et al. 2000; Aladin et al. 2004).

Yet throughout this period, investments from either the Kazakh government or international institutions were not forthcoming, despite lobbying from the regional authorities. The World Bank was considering the project from 1994, but a 1995 report on the Aral Sea Basin Program concluded that, with the current water availability, the sea level would remain well below its 1960 level, 'and the benefits of such a project would be limited' (World Bank 1995, 7). A later report was more positive but identified lack of water and low economic impact as substantial risks (World Bank 1997, 7). Amid the pervading sense that the sea was dead, the project held little appeal. After all, the fishery was lying in ruins, and there was no guarantee that, even if the fish returned, a fishery could recover on a much smaller sea.

In spring 1999 meltwater pouring down the river raised the sea level by nearly 2 m. On 20 April a northerly gale breached the dyke in three places (Micklin 2014b; Figures 5.5 and 5.6). Two workers carrying out emergency repairs were killed, and the akim of Aral'sk was fired. The nonhuman had intervened spectacularly in human affairs. The dyke was irreparable, and the sea level fell rapidly.

However, at this lower level, outflow through the Berg Strait decreased again, and the following spring the sea began to grow again, only to recede over the course of the summer. In 2001, after increased precipitation across the Syr Dariya watershed, the sea level did not fall so far in the autumn. As water flowing through the Berg Strait was replenished by the Syr Dariya, the sea oscillated around 40–41 m asl. Continued inflow of fresh water meant that salinity levels went on falling, even though the sea was leaking. The presence or absence of a dam did not map directly onto sea level or, crucially for the fish, salinity levels.

Following the dam's collapse in 1999, local and regional authorities lobbied intensively for a more stable structure. After a draft report for the 'Syr Darya Control and North Aral Sea project phase 1' (SYNAS-1) was submitted in 1999, the World Bank finally approved the project in 2001. What had changed since 1995, when the project was deemed to have 'limited' benefits? To understand how the 'biologically dead' sea had become a living sea that could sustain a viable fishery, we need to explore

Figures 5.5 and 5.6 Kökaral dam before and after it was breached, 14 April 1999 (above) and 23 April 1999 (below). Source: US Geological Survey, LandLook Viewer, https://landlook.usgs.gov, accessed 3 June 2021.

three further elements of the Small Aral assemblage: the flounder introduced by the Soviet authorities; the unravelling fishing industry; and the Danish activists drawn to the Aral by the famous disaster narrative.

The flounder and the Danes

After native fish had died out, flounder, a salt-tolerant species, had been introduced over 1979–87 (see Chapter 2). A bottom-feeder, flounder had a wealth of benthic fauna to feast on: the native bivalve mollusc *C. isthmicum*; the accidentally introduced shrimp *P. elegans*; and the deliberately introduced bivalve mollusc *A. ovata* and the polychaete worm *N. diversicolor* (Figure 5.7). Benthic fauna, though less diverse than before the sea's regression, was substantially greater in terms of biomass (Krupa

Figure 5.7 A dead sea? A selection of the aquatic fauna of the Small Aral before its restoration. Drawing by Amelia Abercrombie, after Zenkevich (1956). 1. Bivalve mollusc *C. isthmicum*, 2. Shrimp *P. elegans*, 3. Bivalve mollusc *A. ovata*, 4. Polychaete worm *N. diversicolor*, 5. Copepod *C. Aquaedulcis*, 6. Flounder, 7. Baltic herring, 8. Goby.

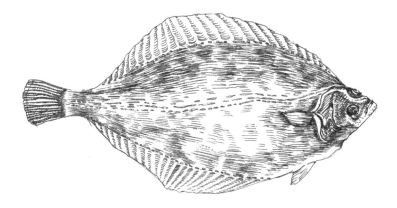

Figure 5.8 Flounder. Drawing by Amelia Abercrombie.

and Grishaeva 2019). Native fish having died out, flounder (Figure 5.8) faced competition only from the gobies and atherines that had been accidentally introduced in the mid-1950s.[5] Amid the ruins wrought by Soviet irrigation projects, flounder – which had largely done what ichthyologists had expected – could have been a small Soviet success story.

Flounder, a flatfish, was unlike any native species. When visiting Tastübek, I met Qydyrbai, who, in his booming voice, told me and his cousin Samalbek about the first time flounder was caught:

> '87, October '87. Ah, no, flounder was released in September '84, in '87 it began to be seen. Elubai was a fisherman, this was the first fisherman to catch a flounder. Then he came and showed it to my

father: '*Agha*, what is this fish? It looks like a tortoise.' Then my father said: 'This fish was released by KazNIIRKh.'

Qydyrbai explained that a man had come to their house from Alma-Ata in 1984, telling them that flounder had been released into the Aral, from the Pacific Ocean. He went on: 'So, he brought in one flounder. The next day my brother laid a net and seven fish were caught. Then my brother – the whole family was scared – my brother said, "If I die I die …" and fried it and ate it. Tasty. So.' Samalbek was confused, having thought, like many in the region, that the Danes had introduced flounder. Qydyrbai corrected him:

> In '96 the Danes came. Autumn '96, at the end of September they came. So. Kurt, Knud, Henrik, Ruud. Four of them came. Then they began. They gave the people nets, Danish nets. They brought a re-frigeration unit. Clothes. They brought everything except for boats. Clothing, life-rings, anchors, life-jackets, rubber boats, nets, needle and thread, crates, basins, seines, they brought all the equipment to give us. Only boats they didn't bring, they brought everything else.

Samalbek's confusion is not uncommon: memories closely link the Danes and the flounder, two foreign arrivals that together reshaped local worlds. However, the Danish project did not respond just to the presence of the flounder but also, as Qydyrbai's narrative suggests, to the disintegrating fishery.

In February 1991, on the orders of the fisheries ministry, there had been an 'experimental catch' of flounder.[6] That year approximately 50 tonnes were caught, the following year more than 100 tonnes (Landsforeningen Levende Hav 1998). However, just as the flounder population reached a size where it could form the basis of a fishery, the fishery itself began to unravel. With the demise of the command economy, the webs of dependency between people and things sustained across Soviet space were becoming disentangled. Ocean fish landed in Russian ports no longer crossed the new border into Kazakhstan. State subsidies evaporated, making trips to other lakes increasingly infrequent. Equipment and boats urgently needed repair. Aralrybprom limped on, bartering fish for fuel, foodstuffs, goods and services; only zander from delta lakes, which was exported to Germany, brought in cash.[7] Official catches fell: by 1995, just a little freshwater fish from delta lakes was caught. Fishermen were paid infrequently, in livestock, equipment or cheap foodstuffs like margarine.[8]

Most development workers, drawn by the famous disaster, saw a ruined environment and ruined fishery. There was a double dissonance between administrative and local worlds: seeing a dead sea, development workers were blind both to the economic crisis that exacerbated the ecological crisis, and to the lifeworlds of flounder, mussels and worms that made up what was, even amid the ruins, a living sea. For this to change, the flounder needed to be enrolled in human relations. This is where the Danes came in.

Kurt Christensen first visited the Aral in 1991. As a grassroots activist, he had been invited to Alma-Ata (now Almaty) to foster environmental activism in Kazakhstan. When I talked with him on Skype after my fieldwork, he explained how, as a former small-scale fisherman, he travelled to Aral'sk to witness the famous disaster, which resonated with his experience in Kattegat of fishing grounds damaged by agricultural pollution and trawling. In the 1980s he and other fishers had formed an NGO, Landsforeningen Levende Hav (LLH; Society for a Living Sea), to stand up for small-scale fishers. The NGO worked on the principle that only those suffering from environmental mismanagement can protect their environment. He was also concerned about what humans were doing to the planet, and was following the Nevada-Semipalatinsk movement, an antinuclear movement linking the USA and Kazakhstan. While in Aral'sk he heard the familiar refrain: if everyone who had visited the Aral had brought a bucket of water, the sea would be full again.

On his return Kurt wrote an article critical of the disaster narrative: so many publications talked about the disaster but ignored the people still living there. He also criticised the delegations which seemed to offer people hope, but simply reproduced the view of their position as hopeless (Christensen 1996 [1991]). Determined to do something, in 1994 he returned with others from LLH. Staying in kolkhoz Zhambul (Zhalangash village), they were told that the sea was not dead, but was teeming with flounder. However, nets needed repair and replacement. The kolkhoz chairman showed them a Russian book from 1936 that mentioned the Danish seine net, designed for catching flatfish, and asked if it could be used on the Aral.

Such were the now legendary beginnings of the project 'From Kattegat to the Aral Sea', which established a commercial flounder fishery. Kurt found international organisations obstructive. They suggested moving people away or providing some other (unspecified) livelihood. So LLH organised a delegation of fishermen to Denmark, where they were introduced to small-scale cooperatives. The Kazakhs talked about the Aral's problems, but also about the flounder; they explained that the situation was not as catastrophic as portrayed, and that many of their problems were logistical (Sørensen 1996). Articulating this point helped mobilise funds from Danida, the Danish agency for international development, and in 1995 a 'Protocol of Our Common Aims' was signed with Kazakhstani partners, including Aralrybprom.

The Danes recognised that the primary obstacle to catching flounder was lack of equipment and money. They also recognised the infrastructural difficulties: processing facilities were far off, and the sea's new shoreline was inaccessible by road; motorised transport was scarce, so most fishermen could only reach the sea by camel. There were difficulties in marketing flounder to a population accustomed to freshwater fish. Many feared flounder's monstrous appearance. Locals joke about people in the market asking for 1 kg of black flounder and 1 kg of white flounder.

Given these obstacles, and given the uncertainty regarding the sea's future, the Danes adopted a step-by-step approach. The first step was to prove that the flounder could be an object of fishery. Flounder, whose cooperation was key to the nascent project's viability, were enrolled in human relations in three ways (Knudsen 2014; Lien 2015). First, in a one-month trial fishery near Tastübek in 1996, four Danish fishermen instructed Kazakh fishermen in the catching and primary treatment of flounder. The seabed proved too muddy for Danish seines, but flounder could be caught with gillnets, which Aral fishermen were familiar with. So flounder were enrolled as a viable object of a fishery. Secondly, the fish were processed in Aral'sk and sold in the market, where a stall demonstrated how flounder is cooked in Denmark. A cookery competition was organised among the town's cafés. As Kurt told me, the flounder's diet of the mussel *A. ovata* made it even tastier than Danish flounder. The monstrous fish thus became a viable foodstuff and commodity. Finally, a biological test established that the flounder were exceptionally clean, far cleaner than Danish flounder. Altogether, flounder exploded the vision of the sea as dying.

Rebuilding a fishery

The Danes found Aralrybprom, especially the director, Aimbetov, less cooperative. While it had been agreed that Aralrybprom would provide transport to and from the sea, this did not materialise since fuel was a scarce resource that was used as a means of payment. Worse still, a year into the project fishermen were still not being paid in cash, despite the Danes forwarding money. So they began to bypass Aralrybprom, encouraging fishermen to set up their own cooperatives and limited liability partnerships (LLPs). In 1998 Aralrybprom finally went bankrupt. The new juridical bodies became the main channel for Danish aid: registering as a cooperative or partnership was the condition for receiving equipment. While this was a pragmatic response to Aralrybprom's demise, it also aligned closely with LLH's philosophy of fishermen taking responsibility for their environment. The Danes envisaged a break from the hierarchical Soviet system that constrained lower-level agency: fishermen would decide for themselves when and where to fish, and would engage in processing and marketing. When they set up workshops to repair engines, they insisted that fishermen pay. When I talked with Kurt, he stressed the centrality of personal responsibility: the aim was to inculcate a sea change in consciousness.

As Aralrybprom materially disintegrated, the hegemony of Soviet institutions fragmented. New juridical forms and the language of personal responsibility conformed to the neoliberal discourse reshaping post-socialist societies. However, the Danes were not part of a homogeneous process of 'hegemonic reconstruction' (Brandtstädter 2007). They recognised what most aid ignored: that 'transition' was experienced as the collapse of material conditions for taking responsibility for one's own life. Rather than engaging in grand plans of transformation, they started from the here and now, seeing that just a little material provisioning could bolster livelihoods, despite the ecological devastation. Nor were they part of a homogeneous transnational apparatus of governmentality. They may have come from the 'centre' of the post-Cold War world, but the waters of Kattegat were peripheral in EU space: as with the Aral, economic marginalisation was accompanied by environmental vulnerability. Moreover, Kurt's support for the Nevada-Semipalatinsk movement suggests a planetary concern at odds with the moralising othering of the mainstream disaster narrative.

Accordingly, the fishery that was rebuilt diverged from the sorts of hegemonic reconstruction seen elsewhere in postsocialist space. Organising cooperatives, the Danes worked through villagers with social capital who could act as local leaders. In Aqespe they worked with the famous labour hero and Party member Narghaly (described affectionately by Kurt as 'an old dictator'); in Bögen with the former director of the state fishery, Äskerbek, and with Zhaqsylyq, an ex-fisherman now working as a livestock herder for the fishery (*malshy*); in Tastübek with Düzbai, another fisherman turned herder; and in Qaratereng with Batyrkhan, who had previously worked in provisioning.[9] Postsocialist rural change elsewhere in Kazakhstan has been characterised as 'accumulation by dispossession', as former managers leveraged their authority to take advantage of privatisation (Toleubayev et al. 2010). In the Aral region, it is widely assumed that, in particular, the Aralrybprom director, Aimbetov, enriched himself from the enterprise's collapse. However, although local leaders were sponsored by the Danes, the pattern of class differentiation attested elsewhere in Kazakhstan was less marked. The nascent flounder fishery offered scant opportunity for profit, and there was little else to accumulate: key productive capital, notably livestock and boats, had been distributed as pay, while processing plants, without any fish to process, had been demolished and scrapped. Indeterminate, precarious, with an uncertain future, the sea did not promise a reliable source of value to be accumulated.

The second phase of the Danish project, 1999–2000, established receiving stations around the sea. As flounder promised a small-scale, sustainable fishery supplying local markets, the Danes foresaw processing being carried out near fishing grounds – not unlike the 1920s vision which was steamrollered by collectivisation (see Chapter 1). Most importantly, the Danes worked with local partners to establish the NGO Aral Tenizi, based in Aral'sk. State control was lax: many fishermen were unregistered, and much of the catch went undeclared. So NGO workers would tour villages, gathering data about catches, nets and vessels. The NGO also acted as an umbrella organisation, agreeing prices, seasons, amounts to be caught. Democracy was key:

> The focus of Aral Tenizi as well as of LLH is the sea, and in order to protect the common interests of all parties living from and by the sea, conflicting interests must be accorded. NGO Aral Tenizi is aiming to be an independent and democratic organisation with numerous national and international contacts and projects. (Landsforeningen Levende Hav 1999)

According to this conception of democracy, conflict is inevitable, but a democratic forum can rationally align interests and find compromises. Simultaneously, local women established, with Danish support, another NGO, 'Aral Aielderi' ('Aral women'), which worked on environmental projects: saving juvenile fish; planting trees; reopening canals to small lakes; training schoolteachers to teach children about the environment. Schools would have an *ekologicheskii ugolok* (ecological corner), echoing the Bolshevik practice of installing a *krasnyi ugolok* (red corner) for propagating Communist ideology.

Both NGOs were staffed largely by women who had worked in middle management in Aralrybprom in the 1980s and 1990s. Aral Tenizi's first president was Aqshabaq, whom we met in Chapter 3 reminiscing about Soviet-era Aralrybprom. She first got involved with the Danes while working in Aralrybprom, and went on collaborating with them after its bankruptcy. During my fieldwork, she was working for another chronically failing fish plant (see Chapter 7) and, when I talked with her, would reminisce happily about her time working for Aral Tenizi. Her narratives are well rehearsed: fishermen had absolutely no hope before the Danes came, but through the NGO's work, she recounts proudly, they regained a sense of dignity.

Baqytzhamal had worked in Aralrybprom from 1988. In the late 1990s her husband gained villagers' trust by setting up a small fish receiving centre, distributing flounder and lake fish in Russia, and settling up with fishermen in cigarettes and groceries. Baqytzhamal describes her time at Aral Tenizi helping fishermen register, creating databases about fishermen, boats and nets. She did not, she stresses, share this database with state inspectors. She also stresses fishermen's trust in her, and their honesty with her, in contrast to their attitude to inspectors. She looks back on that time favourably: although fish today are more abundant, there was less state control in the past. For Baqytzhamal, NGO activism provided an alternative to the hierarchical structures of the state.

Aral Tenizi's most influential member was Zhannat, who, like Baqytzhamal, came of age in the perestroika era. A former Komsomol (Communist Youth League) member and energetic organiser, she left her job as a physics teacher to participate in the NGO. In the 2000s she studied applied ecology in Almaty. She has worked with foreign specialists, contributing to Food and Agriculture Organization and World Bank reports on fisheries in Kazakhstan (Timirkhanov et al. 2010; World Bank 2005). She sees a continuity between her Komsomol activism and her NGO activism, linked by the feeling that 'we can build a fair society'.

Whereas Aqshabaq talks mainly about 'raising the economic level' of fishermen, in my conversations with Baqytzhamal and Zhannat, they both, like Kurt, talked about the importance of responsibility, democracy and sustainability. However, there are subtle differences: Kurt emphasises personal responsibility; he is unconcerned about the structure of the juridical body. For Zhannat and Baqytzhamal, on the other hand, infused with perestroika visions of rebuilding socialism, cooperatives were preferable to LLPs, because of the collective decision-making and sense of shared property; they had been impressed by these features in the Danish fisheries. Arguably, what they saw in the Danish cooperatives was an idealised vision of the kolkhoz, where people lived in harmony with each other and with their environment.

Flounder, then, were not only to provide livelihoods. They were, amid Soviet ruins, to participate in a hegemonic reconstruction of a sustainable and democratic fishery. This hegemonic reconstruction was located within the 'transnational apparatus of governmentality' (Ferguson and Gupta 2002) shaping post-Cold War power relations – but its shape was driven by local trajectories, by the lively interactions between mussels, flounder and fishermen, between Nordic individualists and perestroika dreamers. The transition from *krasnyi ugolok* to *ekologicheskii ugolok* nicely illustrates the resonances and translations in these encounters.

However, these visions would be frustrated, ironically, by the improving environment. As Figure 5.4 (page 149) shows, over the early 2000s, even without a dam, salinity levels fell. Bivalve molluscs became scarcer as the sea grew fresher, to the detriment of the flounder that fed off them. By contrast, freshwater fish, including zander, began to be caught again on the sea (Aladin and Plotnikov 2008). After the World Bank dam project was confirmed in 2001, the assemblage that made up the Small Aral seemed less indeterminate. With the expected construction of a more substantial dam, a further freshening of the sea could be anticipated, and with it, a further shift in species composition. If flounder supported a vision of a small-scale industry supplying local markets, zander promised lucrative export markets. As Kurt put it, they promised dollars. They had been romantic in their initial preference for the small-scale, Kurt told me, so they shifted their priorities, establishing in the third phase of the project (2000–4) a processing plant in the former state bakery in Aral'sk. Kambala Balyk[10] was to help fishermen process and market their catch, and to provide sustainable financing for Aral Tenizi.

Stabilising the Small Aral and materialising sovereignty

Thanks to the renewal of relations between fishermen and flounder over the late 1990s, the sea emerged as a living sea. Rather than a poisoned ruin of the Soviet past, it was a sea that could offer something for the future for local people. For the World Bank, it was now worth saving. When the Syr Darya Control and Northern Aral Sea (SYNAS) project was eventually confirmed in 2001, the project appraisal document stressed the successes of the earlier dams and widespread local approval of the Danish project. Moreover, a pre-investment study had identified that fishing was still important to the local economy and was seen as having potential for growth (World Bank 2001). The project, funded by a $64.5 million World Bank loan, was designed by international consultants together with Kazgiprovodkhoz, once a prestigious arm of Minvodkhoz, but now a nonstate, underfunded cooperative. The aim was to stabilise the Small Aral at 42 m asl.

The low dyke, built over 2003–5 by a Russian company, stretches 13 km across the former Berg Strait, holding the Small Aral in place (Figure 5.9). It is just 4–6 m high, its crest standing at 44.5 m asl, more than a metre higher than the sea level in April 1999 that had breached the previous dyke. Along the top of the dyke runs a gravel road. On the downstream, southern side, the dyke is steep, but on the northern side it slopes gently, like a beach, down to the sea, to minimise wave erosion. Moreover, while the dyke's core is sand mixed with limestone, it is lined with a 30-cm concrete shell, which blocks water from seeping through and undermining the dyke. Since even this more secure structure would remain vulnerable to spring floods, a discharge facility was installed across the channel with nine concrete gates, 5.6 m high and 5.3 m wide. When the sluices are open, the gates can release up to 110 m^3/s. Below the sluices is a concrete spillway to prevent undermining, with concrete

Figure 5.9 Kökaral dyke under construction, 2004. Southern slope of dyke. The dam and sluice gates have yet to be installed. The cliffs of the former Kökaral island are visible in the background. Photograph by Vincent Robinot.

deflectors to slow the speed of water flow. Additionally, hydraulic infrastructure was restored along the Kazakh reaches of the Syr Dariya to guarantee a constant water flow and minimise losses to desert sinks. This element of the project was subject to delays, which the World Bank blamed on old 'Soviet' practices in the Committee for Water Resources (successor to Minvodkhoz) and increasing costs of materials amid Kazakhstan's oil-fuelled construction boom (World Bank 2011). Delays were also due to water levels in the river exceeding predictions, as the high-water climate cycle continued.

Yet, while upstream hydraulic infrastructure was delayed, the sea itself – for the same reason – filled far more rapidly than predicted, reaching the 42 m mark in just nine months, rather than the projected 10 years. The sea was now 15–20 km from Aral'sk (Figures 5.10 and 5.11). Once restoration of upstream hydraulic infrastructure was eventually completed, losses to desert sinks were reduced to nearly zero, while the construction of a sluice at Aghlaq allowed the restoration of Lake Tūshchy, near Bögen. The fall in salinity levels accelerated, and freshwater fish – including carp, bream and zander – migrated downstream from the Syr Dariya, rapidly re-establishing populations in

Figure 5.10 Restored Aral Sea, 2013. Source: US Geological Survey, https://eros.usgs.gov/image-gallery/earthshot/kazakhstan-north-aral-sea, accessed 3 June 2021.

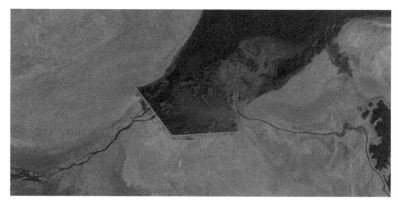

Figure 5.11 Kökaral dam and Syr Dariya delta, 2013. Source: US Geological Survey, LandLook Viewer, https://landlook.usgs.gov, accessed 3 June 2021.

Figure 5.12 A selection of the aquatic fauna of the Small Aral following its restoration. Drawing by Amelia Abercrombie, after Zenkevich (1956). 1. Chironomid larvae, 2. Polychaete worm *N. diversicolor*, 3. Bivalve mollusc *C. isthmicum*, 4. Bivalve mollusc *A. ovata*, 5. Bream, 6. Carp, 7. Roach, 8. Zander.

the freshening sea (Figure 5.12). Not all indigenous species returned: shemaya and barbel remain very scarce, while ship sturgeon, on which the World Bank (2001) had premised the economic benefits of the project, remains absent, because its migration routes along the Syr Dariya are blocked by dams. Long-term changes in the benthic fauna continued, with salt-tolerant bivalve molluscs retreating and other species returning. By 2013 midge larvae, valuable fodder for fish like bream, would make up about 30% of the zoobenthos biomass (Plotnikov et al. 2016). The biggest losers of the sea's return were flounder. In addition to increasing competition for food, the low salinity levels made it increasingly difficult for flounder to reproduce.

The high-water years which filled the sea so quickly brought a further complication. Once the sea level reached its target, water brought down in spring floods was surplus. The possibility of building the dyke higher had been considered, but, given the low-water years of the 1990s, there was no guarantee that the sea would be filled at this level. Moreover, the cost of an additional dyke on the other side of the former Kökaral island rendered the project prohibitively expensive (Aladin and Plotnikov 2008). So every year water is released through the sluices, taking fish and fry together into the remnants of the Large Sea. The problem provokes bitterness from the local director of the fisheries research institute, KazNIIRKh, who argues that a fish ladder should be installed. My informant at Kazgiprovodkhoz, however, claims that a fish ladder, aside from being expensive, would not guarantee the return of all the fish.

Kazgiprovodkhoz engineers remain sanguine about this problem, describing the results of SYNAS-1 as 'intermediate/transitional' (*promezhutochnye*). Indeed, owing to the project's rapid success, the World Bank was, unusually, willing to fund a second phase, involving further restoration of delta lakes. It also involved a feasibility study for further rehabilitation of the Small Aral Sea, a point of considerable contention. One variant would raise the existing dyke to bring the sea level to 48 m asl. The other would create a new waterbody in Saryshyghanaq bay, near Aral'sk, at elevation 50 m asl, which would almost bring the water back to the port. This would be fed by a canal from the river near Qamystybas. Regional authorities favour the first variant: they do not want to divide up the sea still further. International consultants and, now, Kazgiprovodkhoz favour the two-level variant. My informant in Kazgiprovodkhoz explained that, if there was enough water to fill it, of course the one-level variant was preferable. But the dyke might take 10 years to build, and another 30 to fill. While there is enough water today, there is no guarantee that there will be in 40 years' time as populations grow and water demands increase. Uncertainty is compounded by climate change, as shrinking glaciers in the Tien Shan may reduce flow in the Syr Dariya.

Whatever the uncertainties over the lost fish and the sea's future, with the construction of a concrete dam the assemblage of water, salt, aquatic flora and fauna that made up the Small Aral became less indeterminate, less precarious, less vulnerable to the vicissitudes of climate and upstream water politics. The sea's stabilisation gave the World Bank a photogenic success story. In contrast to the famous images of ships rusting in the desert, pictures of the restored sea evoke rebirth and renewal. International media reports like the *National Geographic* article cited above juxtapose Soviet unsustainable mismanagement with the modest, competent approach of the World Bank. In this sense, the dam materialises new post-Cold War hegemonic formations, in which the World Bank is a technocratic institution of government, sitting above the state (Ferguson and Gupta 2002). The story reads as a rare success story of transition to globalised transnational governance.

Locally, however, the dam materialises a rather different sort of hegemonic reconstruction: Kazakhstani sovereignty, embodied in the president. If the indeterminate Aral of the 1990s was suspended between waste and value, the restored, determinate sea is, as an object of value, enrolled in the teleology of the state (cf. Alexander and Sanchez 2019). Children are taught about Nazarbayev's concern for the region. Through posters like those in Figures 5.1 and 5.2 (pages 141–2), the dam is enlisted in what Laszczkowski (2016) calls the 'propaganda of emotion' through which the Kazakh state is projected to its citizens. In post-Soviet Central Asia, as around the world, dams are a powerful form of nation-building (Bromber et al. 2015; Féaux de la Croix 2016; Suyarkulova 2015). The control of water – a mutable substance that epitomises raw nature – is a particularly spectacular materialisation of technopolitical power (Féaux de la Croix 2012). The technopolitical mastery of the state is deployed to reverse the disaster left by the Soviet project, and a peripheral region is integrated into the state by the benevolent desires of the president. The poster in Figure 5.2 characterises Kökaral as *ghasyr zhobasy*, a translation of the Russian *proekt veka*, 'the project of the century', the phrase used for the Siberian rivers scheme. If a project is about appropriating a chunk of the future, this promises, in Soviet fashion, a very large chunk of the future.

Of course, the Kökaral project is on a far smaller scale than the Siberian rivers scheme, or indeed big dam projects elsewhere in Central Asia. There is a modest simplicity about the project: holding in place a fragile assemblage, rather than dramatically reshaping landscapes by blocking or diverting vast volumes of water. Ironically, the pictures do not show the water of the Small Aral that is contained, but the surplus water that is released, water that will be lost. However, the images work through associations: concrete and the president together channel the power of the water, securing the future. The messy, contingent processes which went into assembling the dam, including the World Bank's role, are occluded from this vision. In this hegemonic reconstruction, the dam becomes a 'matter of fact' (Latour 2004), a singular entity through which the state acts on nature, the permanence of concrete embodying the permanence of the Kazakh state.

Indeed, the dam is often related to Kazakhstan's *egemendïk*, 'sovereignty'. When I asked why the central state did not assign money in the 1990s, I was told that Kazakhstan was still a young country then. Kökaral thus embodies mature statehood, where the encompassing reach of the centre is fully realised. Indeed, Kazakhstani sovereignty is sometimes the telos of narrative progressions, the next stage after Communism. Infrastructures, however, are unruly: not only do material processes exceed the control of planners, but infrastructures further 'become entangled with a variety of local hopes, desires, fears, and contestations in ways that are themselves consequential' (Reeves 2017, 716). The following chapters explore the dam's divergent results across the region: while fishing villages benefit to varying degrees from rising catches, fish largely bypass Aral'sk, rendering the restored sea marginal to the town. Many in Aral'sk have never seen the restored sea, which remains far from the town; hardly anyone has seen the dam itself, remote and inaccessible as it is. As a result, how people relate to the dam can diverge from the official 'propaganda of emotion'.

I had expected that the loss of fish would be a matter of dissatisfaction to fishermen. However, although they also deemed a fish ladder necessary, they insisted that it was a problem to be resolved *zhoghary*, 'higher up'. After all, despite the losses through the dam, fish today are abundant. As fishermen extract fish from the restored environment and translate them into money, the dam provides the solid background conditions which enable life to go on: it is not an object of contestation. In locating the solution 'higher up', fishermen highlight the limits of local agency. In Aral'sk the dam is more controversial, even among those unconnected with the fisheries. Many complain that the sea does not reach the former port, because the dam was not built high enough: the connection is incomplete. Indeed, some townspeople claim that the project has achieved *nothing*, because there are no jobs in fisheries in the town. This further leads to accusations of corruption on the part of the bureaucrats and engineers responsible. These accusations form part of a broader discourse of corruption and marginalisation, which in Chapter 7 I relate to Aral'sk's place in post-Soviet Kazakhstan. After all, though Kökaral materialises the reach of the state, it does not integrate the region into anything resembling the incorporating grid of Soviet space. If the 1990s was a period of hegemonic and material fragmentation, the reconstruction that has followed is felt to be incomplete.

As such, while the state is materialised through the dam, the unruliness of materials can simultaneously undermine the state, and its promised future. When I was talking with a pair of teachers, they were privately critical of the president wanting his stamp on everything. Pointing to local involvement in the early dams, they insisted that the idea had come from 'the people'. The encroachment of sovereignty from afar on the local world was presented as unwelcome. But after distancing the president from the dam, they immediately commented on the fish being swept through the dam to their death. The dam's promise of solidity, containment, and rebirth is frustrated. If the first comment dissociated the dam from state-building, with the second the dam became a vehicle for critiquing the state.

SYNAS-2 was getting under way during my fieldwork, and everyone expected that a decision on the two variants was imminent. Most were unclear about the details: there is a desire for a single sea, but residents of Aral'sk also have a strong desire for the water to reach the town – and few recognise the incompatibility of these desires. If the present dam is felt to be incomplete, its very incompleteness becomes the site where future interventions are desired: a fuller, more encompassing state will restore the connection between Aral'sk and the sea, and make the marine landscape whole again. In autumn 2013 the president was to visit Aral'sk. Everyone expected that he would make the decision, and the thought of the sea returning to Aral'sk assumed substance. Selected parts of the town were spruced up: some roads were repaved; streetlamps and road safety signs were installed; photographs of generic watery locations were put up around the shabbier parts of the town. But the president did not come, and no decision was made.

As people speculated about the president's non-arrival, imaginings of personalised sovereignty went askew. One account started from the president's ill health (a controversial topic), before veering into regional politics (Nazarbayev was offended at Medvedev and Putin), terminating in a critique of Kazakhstan's economic dependency on Russia. If sovereignty is imagined in the figure of Nazarbayev, it is imagined as all too human, and international relations are reduced to interpersonal relations between presidents. The president's non-arrival became a joke: would that he would promise to come every year, and the town would get an annual makeover! If Kökaral, as the 'project of the century', materialises the new hegemonic formation of Kazakhstani statehood, it can always be held up to critical scrutiny. As we saw in Chapter 3, memories of the sea's regression are caught up in nostalgic memories of the command economy. So too, the hopes and fears attached to the ongoing project of the sea's restoration are entangled with affective orientation to the political economy of independent Kazakhstan. They are not straightforwardly enrolled in the state's 'propaganda of emotion' (Laszczkowski 2016).

Becoming a postsocialist sea

The new dam may have rendered the Small Aral assemblage materially less indeterminate, but that was not the end of the story: the fishery was also part of the assemblage. Entangled in postsocialist property relations and management practices, the restored sea would become a rather different sort of entity from the Soviet sea that had receded, which is key to understanding the divergent outcomes of the sea's restoration across the region. In this final part of the chapter, I show how the restored sea has participated in a hegemonic reconstruction that, unlike developments in the early postsocialist years, more closely aligns with regional patterns. After all the uncertainty and instability of the 1990s and early 2000s, the Aral was stabilised as an object of value, and the introduction of private property rights (albeit combined with state control) accelerated the hitherto limited socioeconomic differentiation in the region, as the myriad cooperatives and small LLPs gave way to a few large-scale operators.

In 2005 this did not seem inevitable. Before the dam's construction, the indeterminacy of the Small Aral assemblage included also legal uncertainty surrounding its status as a property object and object of state management. What sort of an entity the restored sea would become, and the shape of the hegemonic reconstruction it would participate in, was open. Thus, although SYNAS-1 was primarily technical, the project was accompanied by a vision for how the restored sea would be enrolled in human relations. Recognising the economic constraints on rebuilding a fishery, World Bank staff mobilised a parallel $1.9 million grant from the Japanese Social Development Fund (JSDF). 'Community-based Aral Sea fisheries management and sustainable livelihoods' was drafted by foreign consultants in collaboration with Aral Tenizi and managed by the SYNAS team. The project involved infrastructural measures, including investments in roads and quays; radio communication for fishermen; an ambulance for one village; a water lorry for another village; medical supplies; and sleeping quarters near the sea. It also involved sub-grants for local businesses to diversify incomes. But the project's main goal was to create a sustainable fishery: human relations with the restored environment were to undergo a hegemonic reconstruction, with fishermen actively involved in resource management. In terms of this central goal, the project was a failure, and the hegemonic reconstruction that ensued would take a very different form, ultimately marginalising Aral Tenizi's role as an agent of change.

While the dam was being built, the Fisheries Committee (the former ministry now subordinated to the Ministry of Agriculture) was preparing a new legal framework for Kazakhstani fisheries, which had been in crisis since the 1990s. Amid the disintegration of state enterprises like Aralrybprom and legal uncertainty over property rights, official catches across the country had collapsed. A World Bank (2005) report, with contributions from Zhannat from Aral Tenizi, found that most fishermen were unregistered, and actual catches were up to four times higher than declared catches. The report, which was presented to the Fisheries Committee in 2003, blamed the verticality of the system: quotas were allocated to small companies and sold on to individual brigades. As quotas were expensive, fishermen would buy a quota for one tonne and then fish as much as they could. Efforts at enforcement only alienated fishermen further. Moreover, total quota sizes were arbitrary: research into stocks was only carried out on two lakes in the whole country. The report made recommendations for the new law about fisheries management, including piloting co-management on the soon-to-be-restored Aral.

The JSDF project responded directly to this report. Its centrepiece was co-management. Cooperatives would become co-management organisations, which would register legally and work with KazNIIRKh and the inspectors. They would help decide how much could and should be caught. Fish would be bred in growing ponds, and village processing workshops would be developed. With top-down Soviet-style management relegated to the past, fishermen were to be reconstituted as environmentally-minded subjects. In a hegemonic reconstruction based on 'communities' and 'sustainability', fishermen were to care about, and take responsibility for, the resource; the vertical authority of the state was to be replaced with horizontal collaboration between fishermen and inspectors. If the project, ultimately, failed, this would seem to relate to Brandtstädter's (2007) 'dissonance' between World Bank notions of sustainability and local priorities. However, the JSDF project was not only linked to the World Bank's work on SYNAS-1, but was also the outcome of the work of the NGO Aral Tenizi. 'Sustainability' and 'community', watchwords of neoliberal governance, also resonated with Zhannat and Baqytzhamal's vision of the idealised kolkhoz.

Managed by state officials involved in the SYNAS project, the JSDF project was slow to start. Prepared in 2005, the project was not approved by the relevant state organs until 2008. Even once started, bureaucrats were slow in disbursing funds, so that by 2011, when the project should have been finished, only 22 per cent of the funds had been disbursed. Furthermore, without a central coordinator, most of the money was spent supporting the management teams. Some infrastructure was, eventually, delivered: wagons were placed near the sea for sleeping quarters – some are used, others lie empty; most fishermen today have radios connecting them with the shore; some stretches of road were upgraded. Sub-grants were distributed, to little effect: in Bögen today, an unfinished petrol station stands idle; in Qaratereng, equipment for breeding sturgeon lies unopened in the hatchery. Most importantly, co-management was never trialled, and none of the planned training ever took place. Part of the problem was staffing: the charismatic Zhannat left Aral Tenizi in 2008 to live in Finland. Meanwhile, the fish plant, Kambala Balyk, built to guarantee the NGO's financial viability, went bankrupt in 2011. As Aral Tenizi was left without any source of funding, Baqytzhamal went to resurrect the factory.

Most importantly, while the JSDF project was being prepared, the legal uncertainty surrounding the sea had been resolved, and the postsocialist sea was assuming a more determinate form, one that was not conducive to co-management. Shortly after the World Bank recommendations were presented to the Fisheries Committee, a new legal framework was elaborated (Timirkhanov et al. 2010, 44). The hierarchical system remained, and exclusive access rights defined to particular areas of water. In 2006, therefore, the Small Aral, like other major waterbodies, was divided into plots (Kaz.: *uchaske*/Ru.: *uchastok*). While the sea remained state property, plots were put out to tender for 10 years to a 'nature user' (Kaz.: *tabighat paidalanushy*/Ru.: *prirodopol'zovatel'*).[11] Nature users, which are either cooperatives or, more commonly, LLPs, have the right to exploit their plot up to an annually defined limit of catch per species, their quota; they employ fishermen and provide boats; and they are obliged to deliver a fisheries development plan. All these responsibilities would previously have been carried out by the state fishery or the kolkhoz. The JSDF project was designed in 2005, under the old system. By the time it was confirmed in 2008, the tender system had already been in place for two years, which precluded trialling co-management.

The new law consolidated two subtly different versions of the sea. On the one hand, the sea is an object of environmental management: fish are a scarce resource, and private interests must be managed by the state through allocating quotas, or 'virtual fish' (Minnegal and Dwyer 2011), limiting the number of real fish that can be caught. Accordingly, fisheries development plans include environmental measures such as clearing weeds. On the other hand, the sea is a property object where fish are commodities that are to fuel future development, and fisheries development plans also include costly infrastructural measures: installing refrigeration units, buying new boats, and building receiving stations, sleeping quarters and roads to the sea. Although fisheries development plans show continuities with Soviet planning, their formal logic is to make nature users behave like good capitalists: profits are to be reinvested to further growth. Despite the congruence between management by numbers and the commodification of nature, there is a formal tension: if virtual fish are scarce, profits are too low to make investments; and if investments are made but virtual fish do not increase, there is a risk of overcapitalisation.

On most plots on the sea, tenders were initially won by local leaders who had worked with the Danes. Aral Tenizi's factory, Kambala Balyk, gained one plot. In Bögen, however, the tender was won by Amanbai, from the town of Qazaly, who had no previous connection to fisheries. The former Aralrybprom director, Aimbetov, did not bid, focusing instead on opening a processing plant in the old Aralrybprom building. The new system did not dispel the problems raised in the World Bank report. Indeed, the tender process lacked transparency and was ruled unlawful by the General Prosecutor's Office (Naumova 2012; Timirkhanov et al. 2010, 45–6). With little capital, nature users had difficulty keeping up with the extensive financial obligations in their development plans. The tension between sea-as-management-object and sea-as-property-object was heightened by the constraints nature users faced. If in Soviet times plan fulfilment was constrained by material shortages, fulfilment of fisheries development plans was constrained by lack of money and credit. Infrastructure like refrigeration units required credit, and falling behind with payments jeopardised the future of the enterprise. Hence nature users kept prices for fish low and avoided registering fishermen officially. Crucially, the formal tension between development plans and scarce 'virtual fish' created an incentive to fish above quotas, ignoring virtual fish. A 2010 Food and Agriculture Organization report, again coauthored by Zhannat, estimated that less than 30 per cent of catches was reported, with high levels of illegal export (Timirkhanov et al. 2010, 1, 53).

Over the years several nature users, unable to keep up with their obligations, had their plots confiscated. As plots were left empty, fishermen in the villages of Aqespe, Tastübek and Qarashalang could not fish legally unless someone from Aral'sk bought a temporary licence to organise a brigade. Another nature user, LLP Asta, consistently failed to fulfil its obligations, including installation of a freezer, and, it is widely understood, only kept the plot through the director's personal connections with the inspectors. Eventually, in 2014, at the end of my fieldwork, new tenders were granted on the empty plots, and LLP Asta's plot was also reassigned. Six plots were awarded to Aimbetov, former director of Aralrybprom. With his factory in Aral'sk, which meets EU standards, Aimbetov now had an opportunity to consolidate his business, although his obligations for so many plots were expensive, and many doubted his capacity to exploit the remote plots in the west of the sea. Amanbai, building on his successful fishery in Bögen, won the other two vacant plots. Thus, as small-scale operators have given way to larger players, the trend resembles what happened earlier in the postsocialist period elsewhere in rural Kazakhstan (Shreeves 2002; Toleubayev et al. 2010).[12]

This process has also seen the decline of Aral Tenizi as an agent of change. Given the unresolved problems, Zhannat continued to draft projects to trial co-management. However, with Zhannat in Finland, and Baqytzhamal running Kambala Balyk, their influence in the NGO was waning. The new director, Aina, had previously worked in the judiciary, and had initially been invited to advise fishermen on legal rights. The contrast between Baqytzhamal and Aina is evident in their respective offices: Baqytzhamal takes pride in sitting with a mess of papers around her, the accountant in the same office, while Aina sits authoritatively at the centre of a desk below a picture of the president, with everything tidy and ordered. Aina explained the role of the NGO to me as follows: 'We do projects to improve the condition of the fishermen. They receive benefits from our projects.'

During my fieldwork, Baqytzhamal was fired from her post as director of Kambala Balyk, a moment that marks the final demise of plans for co-management. The story of her dismissal speaks powerfully of the form that hegemonic reconstruction has taken as the new system has been consolidated. Her dismissal centred on her mortgaging the factory to pay for a refrigeration unit, in line with her obligations under the development plan. In summer 2013, she fell behind with loan repayments when a criminal investigation was opened against her for overfishing flounder. The case dated back to April: although she had a quota for 15 tonnes of flounder up to 10 April, she had not received any; the inspectors pressurised her to record that she had caught some, saying that she would receive a lower quota next time otherwise. She made a mistake, recording 13 tonnes before, and 2 tonnes after 10 April, when she did not have a quota. Picking up on the mistake, the inspectors took the case to the prosecutor's office. Baqytzhamal insisted that she had been pressurised by the inspectors to come up with a number, and had made an honest mistake; in any case, she argued, the mistake had not damaged the state, since, with flounder dying out in the freshening sea, the quota has been free since 2007. Eventually, Baqytzhamal wrote to the Fisheries

Committee in Astana, who issued a reprimand to two senior inspectors in Aral'sk.

In this episode, a gap is evident between the formal institution of virtual fish as tools of environmental management, and their practical deployment in the informal exercise of power. Boundaries between the different versions of fish are blurred, as personal connections allow some nature users to ignore virtual fish while others are pursued for the same practice. The consequences of this muddy relationship between virtual fish and real fish will be explored in the following chapter.

In the meantime, Baqytzhamal was banned from fishing, and could not keep up with the loan repayments. After the case was dropped in November 2013, the factory began to operate again and the outstanding debt was paid off. However, in January 2014 there was a quarterly meeting in Bögen of the Aral Tenizi board, including senior fishermen and Aral Tenizi staff. Baqytzhamal was accused of mortgaging the factory for the purpose of embezzlement. While she suggested that an audit commission should investigate, they demanded to see all the relevant documents at once. She had left the paperwork in Aral'sk. Baqytzhamal suspected a hidden agenda behind this denouncement, and felt that she had been tricked into going to Bögen without the relevant paperwork. She remarked bitterly that this was the upshot of teaching the fishermen democracy: that they elected to sack her. Arguably, at stake in the whole saga were different ways of doing politics: Baqytzhamal's insistence on procedure was trumped by a reality of politics as backstage intrigue and denunciation, extending across state and nonstate institutions.[13]

Conclusion

The hegemonic fragmentation and reconstruction that I have narrated in this chapter has been interwoven with material disintegration and restoration. It was the powerful materiality of the disaster, seen through the lens of post-Cold War power relations, that first drew development actors to the region, and set the path that hegemonic reconstruction in Central Asia would take. The high-water years in the 2000s, the impermeability of concrete, the cooperation of fish migrating downstream and reproducing in the freshened sea: all were crucial to the very rapid success story whereby the dam came to materialise Kazakhstani statehood. The material stabilisation of the sea has further driven the hegemonic reconstruction of the fishery, but one far from the various hopes of World Bank planners, Danish activists or Aral Tenizi. Apart from

Narghaly and Äskerbek, who have died, during my fieldwork all those sponsored by the Danes still occupied positions of authority in their villages. In the long term, then, the Danish project bolstered their social capital, putting them in strategic positions to benefit from the sea's return and the new management system. Local leaders, who now are either nature users themselves or have close connections to nature users, today reproduce their social capital through their position on the board of Aral Tenizi.

Amid the material instability and legal uncertainty of the immediate postsocialist years, a small-scale fishery emerged, facilitated by the efforts of the Danes and their colleagues in Aral Tenizi. If the region did not see the level of social differentiation and accumulation by dispossession attested elsewhere in postsocialist Eurasia, this relates to the multiple forms of indeterminacy, which precluded the sea's integration into circuits of value extraction. Yet, by the time of my fieldwork, the dam had stabilised the sea level, guaranteeing the sea's existence into the future; and the legal uncertainty surrounding the sea had been resolved. The ensuing hegemonic reconstruction was also driven by the changing species composition of the sea; the materiality of zander in particular, as I explore in the following chapter, has entangled the newly determinate sea with lucrative transnational markets. As the sea, stabilised and more determinate, has thus become integrated into circuits of value extraction, a few large players have come to dominate the fishery, mirroring patterns elsewhere in postsocialist Kazakhstan and beyond.

Given the continuities between Soviet and post-Soviet hierarchical management, the return of the sea has not been accompanied by the sea change in consciousness that Zhannat and Baqytzhamal hoped for. Zhannat and Baqytzhamal have consistently dreamed of an equitable, open and democratic fishery, a small-scale, artisanal fishery where every village has growing ponds and villagers are involved in processing. In one telling moment, Zhannat told me that co-management might not make the fishermen richer, but at least they would not be slaves. Whereas fishermen have a practical preference for the sea being held by a single factory, Zhannat and Baqytzhamal have a strong moral sense that it should be held in common. When I was talking with Baqytzhamal after her dismissal, she reminisced about her and Zhannat's dreams for the fishing industry: there would be roads and quays; fishermen would wear special clothing; they would neatly pack fish into boxes and unload them onto quays. As it is, she said, they just haul the fish in through the mud in sacks. Her environmentalist vision gave way to a yearning for order, formality, visibility. As we see in the next chapter, such principles – on which the success of co-management would depend – are anathema to most fishermen.

Notes

1   What is commonly described as the 'Kökaral dam' is in fact a dyke stretching across the former Berg Strait with sluice-gates in the middle to release water into a channel to the south. The Kazakh *böget* and Russian *plotina* may both signify either dam or dyke. For the most part, I use the more usual term 'Kökaral dam'.
2   Efforts to preserve part of the Large Sea failed when a discharge facility to provide its eastern part with water from the Amu Dariya was destroyed in floods (Aladin et al. 2009, 181). Nevertheless, though the situation around Moynaq remains bleak, some interventions there have been positive. Internationally funded efforts to restore Amu Dariya delta lakes and create artificial wetlands have been fairly successful, though new waterbodies suffer from highly variable inflow (Micklin 2014b, 376–8). Pollution from agriculture remains a serious problem for the fisheries (Karimov et al. 2005). Meanwhile a German-funded project has successfully stabilised 2,000 km^2 of dried-up seabed through phytomelioration (Micklin 2014b, 378).
3   As social scientists argue, neither water nor ethnicity are in themselves drivers of conflict. Such projects, misrepresenting and reshaping local categories, have often heightened inequalities (Heathershaw and Megoran 2011; Reeves 2014, 94–100; Thompson and Heathershaw 2005).
4   This is broadly typical of aid to Central Asia and wider postsocialist space, which often exacerbated problems and entrenched elites (Babajanian et al. 2005; Pétric 2005; Wedel 1998, 86–7; Werner 2000).
5   Baltic herring had also survived, but, as a planktophage, did not compete with flounder.
6   Prikaz po proizvodstvennomu ob'edineniiu 'Aralrybprom' No 78r, 14 February 1991, AFGAKO, f. 4, op. 2pr, d. 923, ll. 143–4.
7   Bank spokesperson A. Doskabilova, Aralrybprom president A. Aimbetov, and chief accountant M. Tleulesov, 'Akt proverki o postavkakh ryboproduktsii snachala 1996 goda do 1 iunia t.g.', 12 June 1996, AFGAKO, f. 4, op. 2pr, d. 986, l. 11.
8   Such practices were common in rural Kazakhstan (Toleubayev et al. 2010, 358).
9   It is striking that both Zhaqsylyq and Düzbai had worked as herders in state enterprises. This position may have been strategically useful, offering access to fodder supplies, which, given the importance of private livestock to livelihoods, would have been a 'manipulable resource' (Humphrey 1998), enhancing the social capital of those controlling it. Similarly, Batyrkhan, working in provisioning, would have controlled various manipulable resources.
10 *Kambala* is Russian for 'flounder', also used in Kazakh; *balyq* is Kazakh for 'fish'.
11 Though nature users are also obliged to act as environmental managers, the term, dating from Soviet times, implies a utilitarian vision of nature.
12 Aimbetov won Asta's plot near Zhalangash, one near Qarashalang, one in Saryshyghanaq bay (near Aral'sk) and three in Shevchenko bay in the west; Aimbetov won the other half of Saryshyghanaq bay and the plot near Tastübek.
13 Cf. Richardson (2015), who describes the failure of a World Bank community-based conservation project in the Ukrainian Danube delta: project managers' liberal practice of openness was trumped by a local political context of intrigue and denunciation.

6
Zander and social change in Bögen

In spring 2014 Aral fishermen from several villages, and one group from Shardara reservoir, near Shymkent in south Kazakhstan, had permission to fish at Kökaral. Being near the spawning grounds in the Syr Dariya mouth, this is normally a forbidden zone, but fish will be lost through the dam at this time of year, so fishing is allowed for a brief period. I stayed with Bögen fishermen, who were camping in UAZ jeeps and GAZ-66 trucks. They had permission to catch 12 tonnes between 1 and 9 April. Every morning, after washing hands and faces in the cold morning air and drinking tea, fishermen set off in their Soviet-era boats through dense reeds to haul in their nets in the fresh northerly breeze. I stayed behind with a few older fishermen, including my host Zhaqsylyq. Zhaqsylyq would fiddle with the wireless, tuning in to invisible global connections (including English-language news about separatist unrest in Ukraine and the missing Malaysia Airlines flight in the South China Sea), while fishermen were extracting fish which would plug them into transnational markets.

From midday the fishermen would trickle back in. Usually someone would catch a large carp, which was boiled and shared out. At around four o'clock fishermen would bring in their catch, lugging sacks of fish through the shallows and over the muddy foreshore to the ZiL truck, where the driver and I would heave them into place. Fishermen then headed out again to lay their nets, returning as darkness was falling. Supper would be tinned meat, or fried fish with roe. On several occasions, the Bögen fish receivers were approached surreptitiously by fishermen from another village. Muttered negotiations were held a few metres away from the main camp. The next morning a few sacks of fish would mysteriously appear by the Bögen ZiL truck. For official purposes, these were recorded as the ZiL driver's catch. After supper, exhausted bodies would relax, huddling together for warmth, wind-burnt faces animated as fishermen discussed the movement of ice floes and where they had laid their nets.

After four days the weather deteriorated: the northerly wind picked up, bringing snow, sleet and rain. The fish were not moving around, owing to the cold weather. Moods became fractious. Nets were disappearing. While the wind and ice were evidently wreaking havoc, there were suspicions of theft (*ūrlyq*) by fishermen from other villages. Nevertheless, Bögen fishermen were catching reasonable quantities of fish, and were on course to catch about 12 tonnes, their quota. But it was decided to go home early. *Balyq zhoq*, Zhaqsylyq said to me curtly: 'no fish'. Then he added: *Tistï zhoq, aqsha zhoq*, 'No zander, no money'. In driving rain, we hauled boats over the mud and lifted them onto the roofs of the trucks, pouring cold muddy water over ourselves in the process. The Shymkent lorry got stuck in the mud. Another lorry got stuck trying to haul it out. Everyone agreed: it was *bardak*, 'chaos'.

The incident illustrates three points about the contemporary fishery. First, fishing is a way of life, an identity, involving embodied skill, environmental knowledge and masculine camaraderie. It is not a way of life for everyone: one young man present at Kökaral, Ghalymbek, is studying to become a *fizkul'tura* (physical education) teacher, and is fishing temporarily to earn some ready money. He would not want to fish forever, he said, because of its toll on health. For others, though, the fact that fishing is 'heavy work' (*auyr zhūmys*) is a source of pride. Most fishermen in Bögen plan to fish in the future, and plan for their sons to do so as well.

The second point is the pervasive invisibility. As ethnographers explore, fishing involves detailed environmental knowledge about an underwater reality invisible to the human eye (Hoeppe 2007; Howard 2017; Knudsen 2008; Vermonden 2013). However, the human elements of a fishery are also hard to see, and to regulate. According to my informants, the Kökaral expedition descended into *bardak* because outsiders were there. Invisibility, however, pervades the fisheries, frustrating attempts at regulation and shaping relations between fishermen and fish receivers. We closed the previous chapter with Zhannat and Baqytzhamal's yearnings for order and visibility. These are anathema to most fishermen. According to the proverb, *Balyqshy aitpaidy rasyn, künde alady bïr asym*, 'The fisherman doesn't tell the truth, every day he takes one portion'. Invisibility offers fishermen opportunities to 'take a portion' within a hierarchical, inequitable system.

Finally, the incident illustrates the significance of zander (Figure 6.1), which is caught in abundance, far above official quotas.[1] Previously fishing, as a way of life, met the gridded time and space of the plan; today it meets the elastic time and space of global markets. Fishing today is not, as in Soviet times, accompanied by social entitlements, so money itself assumes greater value. Fish are ascribed wildly divergent values according to their spatial reach on transnational markets. Zander, a predator with lean, white meat, is popular in filleted form in Europe, making it far more valuable to Aral fishermen than other fish. Fattier fish like bream can be marketed smoked or cured across the former USSR but, with little processing infrastructure in the Aral region, its value remains low. Moreover, prices, especially of zander, fluctuate over time as currencies fluctuate in relation to exogenous events. Crisis in the Eurozone in the early 2010s halved the price of zander. By contrast, the price of zander rose in early 2014 when, with the Kazakhstani economy under pressure from Western sanctions against Russia, the tenge was devalued to keep oil exports competitive.

In Chapter 4, we saw how an ethic of sharing was overlaid in the colonial and Soviet periods with an understanding of fish as commodities. Today the latter understanding predominates, particularly for zander, which is not rated locally as a foodstuff. Zander is described as *zhūmysymyz*, 'our work/job'; a characteristic greeting at the receiving station is *Balyq qalai? Tïstï bar ma?* ('How is the fish? Is there zander?'). On the

Figure 6.1 Zander. Drawing by Amelia Abercrombie, after Zenkevich (1956).

basis of zander, during my fieldwork, fishermen earned 150,000 KZT or more per month. Fishermen cannot fish all year round: in May fishing is banned while fish are spawning; in summer fish would spoil before reaching the factory; and for some weeks in spring and autumn, fishing is impossible while ice is melting or forming. Nevertheless, this is considered good money in a region where most salaries are around 45,000–60,000 KZT per month – bucking the trend of rural impoverishment characteristic of postsocialist Eurasia (Leonard and Kaneff 2002; Toleubayev et al. 2010; Trevisani 2010; Zanca 2010).

Chapter 5 showed how the restored sea has been entangled in postsocialist property and management regimes. Here I address the relationship between environmental and social change, focusing on Bögen. Two questions guide my analysis: why is zander caught in such high quantities, and how are the newly abundant postsocialist fish transforming social relations? This requires attention both to the formal

Figure 6.2 Meirambek, fish receiver, shows off a huge zander, spring 2014. Source: author.

property regime and to how it is enacted in practice. I also look beyond the property relations to explore the fishery as a 'socioeconomic system', encompassing markets, technologies and so on (Campling et al. 2012; Durrenberger and Pálsson 1987; Howard 2017). I therefore follow the social lives of the fish once they are extracted from the water (Figure 6.2), including their afterlives as money. If Chapter 4 looked at how the chronotope of the plan reproduced and transformed that of *tughan zher*, here we see how the market sustains and transforms local practices of social reproduction and regimes of value.

Local perspectives on the fishery

The current system, formally mixing state and private regulation, rests on assumptions akin to Hardin's (1968) influential thesis of the 'tragedy of the commons': because individuals acting rationally in their own best interests collectively produce results that are worst for everyone, fishing effort must be restrained either by state management or private property, or both, as on the Aral. Yet in practice fishing effort is not restrained: everyone acknowledges that above-quota fishing is pervasive. For inspectors and scientists, the problem is inadequate enforcement of the current system. Zaualkhan, the director of the Aral'sk branch of KazNIIRKh, blames inspectors, contending that Kazakhstan is in 'a transitional period' (Ru.: *perekhodnoi period*); in future, when the law functions better, the system will be properly regulated. Inspectors agree that regulation is inadequate, but blame lack of funding. Conversely, Zhannat and Baqytzhamal, advocating co-management, blame the fishery's hierarchical structure, which excludes fishermen from resource management. Were ordinary fishermen included, they argue, they would have an incentive to conserve the resource. This aligns with theoretical perspectives from new institutionalist economics (especially Ostrom 1990) which, bolstered by empirical findings of anthropologists (e.g. McCay and Acheson 1987), suggest that both state and private control can create incentives for unsustainable resource use.

The ethnography below plots a course between these two explanations, showing how management is enacted in practice, involving neither a direct implementation of formal rules nor their negation.[2] As we shall see, value formation plays a critical role in the practical enactment of the management regime. While Zaualkhan thinks about the present as a deviation from an ideal form that will be reached in the future, when the state will successfully regulate private interests, I instead examine what is there now, the social processes through which categories of 'state' and 'private' emerge.

Overlapping with these explanations for above-quota fishing are two contrasting stereotypes of fishermen among Aral'sk residents, often voiced by the same people. In one vein, fishermen are impoverished, exploited, alienated from resource management, paid a pittance for their labour. Alternatively, they are getting rich (richer than ordinary people in Aral'sk!), motivated only by greed, caring nothing for the future; cheap Chinese nets have made fishing too easy, resulting in a 'tragedy of the commons'.[3] Both stereotypes are simplifications, reductionist views of the village from the town, which tell us more about the concerns of townspeople than about the lives of villagers. Nevertheless, I find them useful for thinking through the transformations in social relations which have followed the sea's return.

The first stereotype, implying class differentiation between fishermen and nature users, matched my pre-fieldwork expectations. I expected to find accumulation by dispossession, as Toleubayev et al. (2010) attest all over rural Kazakhstan. As Shreeves (2002) found in new private farms in Kazakhstan, I expected that labour would be increasingly commodified, disembedded from social relations as well as social entitlements. From the wider literature on postsocialist agrarian change, I expected a sense of exploitation in the extraction of surplus value and appeals to moral economy (Hann 2003; Hivon 1998). From ethnographies of fishing that show how differential access to quotas drives social inequality, I also expected resistance to quotas (Helgason and Pálsson 1997; Minnegal and Dwyer 2011).

However, the picture is more varied across the Aral region, and the ongoing transformation is more complex than a uniform process of 'disembedding'. In his ethnography of decollectivisation in Uzbekistan, Trevisani (2010) finds heterogeneous outcomes: while there is differentiation between peasants and private farmers, there is further differentiation within the peasant class between those with and without access to land via kinship networks. I will suggest something similar here, though the position of those lacking networks is less bleak than in the Uzbekistani case, because resources are abundant. Indeed, while quotas should create scarcity, in practice they are ignored so that there is no sense that fish are owned while still in the water, and relations are shaped by the abundance of real fish, not by the artificial scarcity of quotas.

The second stereotype speaks of the moral ambivalence about money in Aral'sk: zander are seen as easy money which corrupts local society, dissolving social ties, increasing individualist self-interest and damaging the environment.[4] Yet, while long-term social ties between fishermen *are* being weakened, this relates to the technologies money has facilitated, not to money itself. Generally, I found much less moral ambivalence about money in Bögen than in Aral'sk. The stereotype of fishermen as greedy individualists concerned only with the present ignores the local uses of money in sustaining ritual expenditure. If zander connect fishermen to the time and space of global capitalism, once translated into money, they are a means of reproducing local society. At the same time, this money is transforming patterns of ritual expenditure, as elsewhere in Central Asia. Zander's migrations to Poland and Germany produce comparable effects to Central Asian labour migration to urban centres in Kazakhstan and Russia (Reeves 2012; Trevisani 2016): as local economies become increasingly monetised, 'local structures of value' (Reeves 2012, 122) are transformed. This intersection of chronotopes of market and *tughan zher* is critical to understanding the above-quota fishing.

Management by numbers

Since 2006 the state has devolved use rights for 10 years over different plots of the sea and lakes to private juridical bodies ('nature users'). Nature users buy all fish caught on their plot at their prices, and should monitor for poachers. They provide boats but not nets or fuel. Fishermen therefore characterise the system as 'private' (*zheke*), expressing the absence of connection with the state which once provided boats, fuel and equipment. They associate the sea being private with the division into plots, which, except for Qaratereng fishermen who fish fertile waters near the delta, is regarded as an inconvenience.[5] However, the state, in the form of the Inspectorate, is by no means absent, monitoring the banned season during spawning time and the banned fishing zone in the Syr Dariya estuary. Nature users should also mediate between fishermen and the state, paying pension contributions and social tax. They also have, as we saw in Chapter 5, a series of obligations towards the state, codified in fisheries development plans. The inspectorate therefore monitors nature users, and it monitors fishermen themselves directly. Nature users have the right to fish up to an annually defined quota per species, which they purchase from the inspectorate.

Quotas are based on scientists' assessments of biomass and fertility of spawning stock. More fertile, freshwater plots nearer the delta receive proportionally higher quotas than saltier plots. As numbers, quotas perform both representative and constitutive functions (Verran 2010): they represent how many fish can be removed without damaging the future of the resource, and they constitute a form of property, 'virtual fish' (Minnegal and Dwyer 2011).[6] Nature users are obliged to purchase their entire quota from the state, but they can choose when to take it. Virtual fish thus establish a relationship between nature users, the state and actual fish in the sea. This relationship, endorsed by the seeming objectivity of scientific knowledge, is both financial and regulatory.

Yet, as representations, numbers are imperfect. Accuracy of fish stock assessments is seldom better than a range of 30 per cent (Acheson et al. 1998, 396).[7] In the Aral context, there are further complications. Zaualkhan stresses the role of pure science, but he also stresses KazNIIRKh's financial constraints. Even the building of the institute, once in a prime seaside location, is crumbling. Independent ichthyologists are sceptical about the quality of KazNIIRKh's work. Moreover, Zaualkhan told me that, because he knows over-quota fishing happens, it is better to set quotas low. Understanding the present as 'transitional', he partakes in, and reproduces, a system where formal rules do not work. Meanwhile cynics in Aral'sk remark that KazNIIRKh is partly funded by nature users and, since they will overfish anyway, lower quotas suit them as they cost less. Moreover, the allocation of quotas by inspectors is flexible. The root of Baqytzhamal's problems lay in this point: she was told that if she did not record 15 tonnes of flounder, she would receive a lower quota next time. This makes little scientific sense, but is linked to a different view of property, a moral sense that property must be exploited. Here the quota is more like a Soviet plan, a target rather than a limit.

There is therefore a mismatch between virtual fish and real fish. Lampland (2010), discussing early socialist Hungary, argues that false numbers are not necessarily deviations from a formal system, but are part of the process of formalisation: better to deploy wrong numbers in the right manner than to have no numbers at all. From this perspective, Zaualkhan's numbers matter less as a representation of reality than as an enactment of a management system founded on the abstraction of nature as numbers. Current practices thus reproduce hierarchies of scientific knowledge over fishermen's knowledge. No one believes that fishermen's knowledge has any value for management, despite academic arguments to the contrary (Johannes et al. 2000; Pálsson 1994). Even as they fail as representations, numbers constitute the hierarchical system.

Nevertheless, the failure of numbers as representation also matters. Institutions need certainty, which depends on trust in the objectivity of science (J. Wilson 2002). While numbers are always produced socially, in this context, the awareness of the social pressures and constraints within which they are produced undermines faith. The management system is constituted on an arbitrary foundation. If no one believes that the numbers which constitute virtual fish adequately represent fish in the sea, virtual fish are not respected. Virtual fish therefore only establish a financial relation between nature users and the state; the regulatory aspect of the relationship exists in form only. Fish play their part here in the corrosion of trust in the quota system: although everyone knows that quotas are not respected, catches (and quotas) have grown year on year. The formal institution of scarcity through virtual fish has little meaning.

The Bögen fishery

I turn now to how abstract categories of 'nature user', 'state' and 'fishermen' are instantiated in concrete social relations and practices in Bögen (von Benda-Beckmann et al. 2006). Bögen fishermen work for Amanbai, a businessman from Qazaly, about 100 km away; before 2006 he had no connection either to Bögen or to fishing, having made his money in rice in the 1990s. Most of Bögen depends on fishing for a living, although fishing households also keep some livestock (sheep, horses, camels), which remains a marker of social status, and can be translated into money if necessary for ritual expenditure. A few families make most of their livelihood from livestock, though some family members may sometimes fish. There are jobs for women only in the school and the nursery, and most women do not have formal jobs. There are four or five informal 'shops' in the village, selling groceries from Aral'sk or Qazaly at a healthy profit.

Bögen fishermen fish in plot number 8, with about 30 km of shoreline and a total quota of around 800 tonnes a year. There are three receiving stations, the main one at Shaghalaly, 12 km from Bögen over dried-up seabed. The other receiving stations are smaller, and fishermen from nearby inland villages fish there. Initially, poaching was common, and Amanbai faced competition from illegal traders (Ru.: *kommersant*) in the village, but today there is little poaching on the sea. This is partly because of better security along the shore, but it also relates to Bögen fishermen's compliance: the fishing operation is well organised, with fishermen paid in cash every day and weather forecasts provided; fuel and nets are sold at the receiving station. Amanbai has also, in line with his development plan obligations, installed a refrigeration plant on the outskirts of the village, staffed almost entirely by people from Qazaly.

Other development plan obligations, such as building a pontoon and receiving station, remain unfulfilled.

The figures mediating Amanbai's relationship with Bögen fishermen are the two fish receivers (*priëmshchiki*) at Shaghalaly: Zhaqsylyq and Meirambek. Zhaqsylyq, in his late fifties, is a former fisherman who rose to prominence, as we saw, through Aral Tenizi; he started working as a *priëmshchik* in 2012. Zhaqsylyq is the eldest brother of a large family; while other families have dispersed as family members have moved away to Aral'sk or further afield, all Zhaqsylyq's younger brothers also live in the village. Zhaqsylyq's three sons still live at home and also fish. One daughter is married to a camel-herder, and when camels are brought into the village and sold to villagers for meat, they are slaughtered in Zhaqsylyq's pen. His wife Gulzhamal and daughter-in-law (*kelïn*) Gulnar informally sell groceries out of the house. The family has 30 angora goats and a prestigious hybrid *nar* camel.

Meirambek, in his thirties, is Amanbai's nephew; he moved to Bögen in 2006. In 2009 Zhaqsylyq's youngest daughter, Danagul, married Meirambek, putting Zhaqsylyq into a relation of *qūda* with Amanbai. Beyond Zhaqsylyq's formal legal role as Amanbai's employee, his authority within the fishery depends both on his social capital within the village and on this kinship connection with Amanbai; meanwhile, Meirambek and Amanbai too gain acceptance by association with Zhaqsylyq's family. Meirambek has 11 horses roaming the steppe with the village livestock, and keeps some sheep in Zhaqsylyq's fold. Beyond his immediate kin in the village, there are many others of the same *ru* (lineage) as Zhaqsylyq, Zhamanköz. Other *ru* in the village, such as Zhangbai and Teke, are also related, being subdivisions of the larger Külïk *ru*.[8]

Zhaqsylyq projects his authority through his imposing posture and unwaveringly stern gaze. Although not averse to physical work when alone or with close family, when others are around he barks orders, rarely demeaning his dignity by engaging in manual work. He has a strong sense of propriety: most people, even his contemporaries, are afraid to drink in front of him. He often remains aloof from conversations, exuding authority through not engaging. But he is also capable, at appropriate moments, of boisterous banter, relaxing his dignity to generate a different sort of respect through mischievous humour. By contrast, Meirambek is consistently energetic and garrulous, always putting himself at the centre of everything. Whatever the context, Meirambek's boisterous sense of humour asserts his centrality, often at the expense of weaker group members or outsiders – drunks, fishermen from other villages, me.

The relation between fishermen and receivers thus goes beyond the sale of fish. Nevertheless, fishermen are aware that the system is hierarchical – and there is no expectation that it should be otherwise. Whereas the official catch translates not only into pay for fishermen, but also into pension contributions, the unofficial, over-quota catch does not. Fishermen report that their pension contributions are 3,000 KZT a month, which is considerably less than 10 per cent of the 150,000 KZT per month they earn. Their attitude is one of not asking questions. Indeed, there is, as we see below, a sense of complicity between fishermen and receivers.[9]

In general, fishermen must obtain formal permission from Meirambek to fish. Nevertheless, it is sometimes possible to fish without permission and not receive censure. Aikeldï, in his late forties, has a reputation of being a drinker, joker and hard-working fisherman. He lives near Zhaqsylyq and Meirambek, and sometimes fishes with Zhaqsylyq's sons. In spring 2014 persistent ice floes and strong winds made fishing dangerous, so Meirambek was not giving permission. Aikeldï informed him that he was going to lay his nets anyway. Meirambek did not try to dissuade him. When Aikeldï returned, he told Zhaqsylyq's eldest son over a bottle of vodka about where the fish were and the state of the ice – information which was later relayed on to Zhaqsylyq and Meirambek. Fishing in the banned season is also tolerated, so long as fish are sold to the plant.

Negotiations are always possible. One winter's day, Meirambek was patrolling the ice. He came across a group of fishermen from Amanötkel. Although they were on good terms with Meirambek, they did not have permission. While they should have been fined, instead they gave Meirambek a sack of fish. Lake Tūshchy, near Bögen, is full mainly of pike, which is of very little commercial value. On one occasion, I met some Bögen fishermen fishing there who told me that they would sell their catch to local *kommersanty*; they had no fear of Meirambek – as a relative (Ru.: *bratishka*, 'little brother'), he would not punish them for fishing there, although, they implied with a lewd gesture, fishing on the sea without permission would be another matter.

By contrast, when I accompanied Meirambek to the lake another time, we found two men, unknown to Meirambek, laying their nets through the ice beside an ancient Ural motorcycle. Meirambek, dressed in his state-issued camouflage suit, puffed himself up and demanded to see their documents. They did not have any. Meirambek declared that they should have requested permission. To their discomfort, he took a photo of them. The older of the two men had an air of quiet dignity. Addressing Meirambek as *sen* ('you' addressed to an equal or junior), he talked quietly, patiently and at length, as if telling a story. He asserted their right to fish in various ways: *bïz qazaqpyz*, 'we are Kazakhs'; *men aqsaqalmyn*, 'I am an *aqsaqal* (white-beard/elder)'; *bïz tengïzde auladyq, bïz dariiada auladyq*, 'we have fished on the sea, we have fished on the river'; *kölïmïz*, 'our lake'. He told Meirambek at length about his various kin across the region. As the man talked, Meirambek's demeanour altered: he listened patiently, his head bent slightly down, nodding, occasionally asking for clarification, addressing him with the respectful *sïz*. At one point he interjected to ask the man's *ru*, before relapsing again into deferential silence. But the old man proved unable to find a connection to Meirambek. After about 15 minutes of conversation, Meirambek read out an official statement, though more patiently and respectfully. He also gave them his phone number so that next time they could request permission from him. He then dictated a confession for the old man to write out, so that the inspectors could impose a fine.

At stake were competing claims to the right to fish. Meirambek's claim, bolstered by the state authority of the camouflage uniform, appealed to the law. But the old man, drawing attention to his white beard, challenged this authority through appeal to different normative frameworks: ethnicity, seniority and kinship. As his narration of past fishing experience reproduced a relation between persons and places, he laid a claim to the right to fish based on quite different categories from the formal rules. Ultimately, the authority of the camouflage costume and badge won. Had the old man found a kinship connection, the outcome may have been less clear.

Some weeks later I saw these two men again, fishing with Meirambek's permission on the sea. At Shaghalaly, and at Amanbai's other sites, there are fishermen from other villages working informally as hired workers. They do not receive boats or pension contributions. In this context of informal labour, labour is abstracted even from the meagre social benefits which should formally accompany it. The labour of these informally hired fishermen, lacking affective connections to Zhaqsylyq or Meirambek, is therefore more fully commodified than that of the Bögen fishermen. In winter, if they have UAZ jeeps, they can fish as much as anyone else. At other times of year, however, they must use their own boats, which are often small 'lake boats' made of corrugated iron, often without motors. Such boats, dangerous in open waters, cannot travel far out to sea; nor can they hold much fish.

I visited one of Amanbai's new plots in spring 2014. It is in Saryshyghanaq bay, close to Aral'sk itself, and fishermen had come from Aral'sk, Qambash, Qazaly, even from Shymkent. They received no pension contributions and no boats: they would fish here, I was told, as long as there was work, then they would move elsewhere. One group described themselves, with much hilarity, as 'nomadic' (*köshpengdï*): a mobile fishing proletariat, their labour thoroughly commodified. Strikingly, it was only in this context that I heard complaints about the prices of fish, on the basis that they 'are not worth the labour' (*engbegï tūrmaidy*): exploitation becomes visible when labour is fully commodified. For most Bögen fishermen, the process of commodification of labour is incomplete. To the extent that it is abstracted, exchanged for money, it is a commodity. But the relationship is more than purely economic – and they could not be easily fired. Different fishermen can relate to Zhaqsylyq and Meirambek in different ways, as kin, neighbour or fellow fisherman; and they construe the relationship, at least in part, in those terms.[10]

Extracting and commodifying fish

Arriving one winter's day in Bögen from Aral'sk, I was surprised to find Zhaqsylyq's house full of men tucking into a camel *quyrdaq*. A commission had come from the capital to inspect the fisheries. Because everyone uses monofilament, 'Chinese' nets (*qytai au*), they had all stayed at home: *qūlaghymyz bar*, 'we have ears', I was told. Instead of going fishing, they had stayed in the village to slaughter camels brought for sale by Zhaqsylyq's son-in-law. Threatened by an external authority, fishermen and receivers acted together. Like explosive and electrocution devices, which are not used on the Aral, monofilament nets are illegal. Being cheap, they are readily discarded, left in the sea or on the shore. If fishermen cannot find them, it is not a major loss, and the nets get tangled on the seabed. Once stuck, they do not decompose. So abandoned nets go on catching fish. Because they are illegal, if unknown vehicles ever approach the shore, fishermen hastily throw all their nets into the boat and cast off; but otherwise there is no attempt to conceal their use.

In Knudsen's (2008) ethnography of the conflicts between the practical knowledge of fishers and the expert knowledge of scientists in Turkey, he finds contrasting views on the sonar: fishers insist that it damages fish, while the scientists insist that it has no negative impact. While the scientists simply see it as a piece of technology, Knudsen proposes that fishers' knowledge about the sonar constitutes a moral commentary on technology and social inequality. By contrast, with Chinese nets, rather than a clash of knowledge systems, there is a disavowal of knowledge, as in the following conversation:

William:	Why don't they give permission [to use them]?
Küntughan:	I don't know. If they are left in the water they don't decompose, they say, there's a storm or whatever and they can't be pulled out … fish come and get stuck, they say, and they rot. When that fish rots, it pollutes the water, they say. Then diseases spread from it, they say. Therefore it's forbidden to lay those nets.

After disavowing knowledge, Küntughan actually gave a full explanation, but at one remove, as someone else's knowledge. On another occasion, I pressed a young Bögen fisherman as to whether he thought they were harmful. He replied: 'Harmful, it's said … but [broad grin] they catch fish well (*ziangdy deidï ghoi, bïraq balyq tüseidï*, lit. "the fish enter them")'. He thereby delimited two domains of knowledge, claiming knowledge about the technology in the practice of fishing, but not about the technology's long-term effects. In contrast to the meanings of the sonar to Turkish fishers, for Aral fishermen Chinese nets *are* just pieces of technology. As in Chapter 4, agency with respect to the environment is felt to be elsewhere. Here this point is empowering: the hierarchical form of the current system constrains fishermen not to think about resource management; at the same time, awareness of the wide gulf between form and reality means that rules can be readily ignored. Indeed, agency is dispersed beyond the fishermen who actually use the nets: although their import is banned, they can be imported as nets for catching birds, and, while in Aral'sk they are sold covertly, in Qazaly they are sold openly in the market.

Chinese nets, which can be laid by just two or three people, have led to a downsizing in fishing units. Moreover, the need for cooperation between households has also declined as rising incomes have enabled more households to acquire UAZ jeeps, facilitating access to the sea. In 'the time of flounder' (*kambala kezïnde*), most access to the sea was by camel, and people would camp in groups by the shore. This matched wider trends in early postsocialist Central Asia where the maintenance of wide social networks was a crucial survival strategy amid economic breakdown (Kandiyoti 1998; Werner 1998). Today households are becoming more self-sufficient and less dependent on networks of friends and relations.

The fishing unit we saw in the introduction was an unusually large unit, involving Zhaqsylyq's sons, a brother-in-law (*bazha*), two cousins and a neighbour. While the journey to the sea was a squash, the UAZ effectively levelled differences between its owners and the other fishermen. But by the following spring Bolat had bought his own UAZ, and he, Aikeldï and Zhüman had formed a new unit. Mūkhtar was on military service, and Zikön and Maqsat were joined by their cousin Aibek, Müsïlïm's son, and a brother-in-law (*zhezde*) from Qoszhar. Another large unit was Nauryzybai's (Figures 6.3 and 6.4). Nauryzybai is in his early twenties. In early 2013 Nauryzybai drove his family UAZ to the sea with various maternal relatives collectively referred to as *naghashy*: two cousins and two uncles who had recently started fishing. The following year he was fishing with just one cousin, and with another cousin on his

Figures 6.3 and 6.4 Nauryzybai and colleagues, winter 2013. Source: author.

father's side who is fishing temporarily. So while the gradual increase in UAZ ownership could represent increased differentiation between villagers, the flexible formation of fishing units helps spread the benefits more widely. There is little sense that the owner of the UAZ is in command. In the long term, however, increasing UAZ ownership is reducing the importance of these horizontal ties between fishermen.

In the Introduction we saw the interplay of skill, local environmental knowledge, cooperation and hierarchy in the intricate process of laying nets through the ice. Nets of 45–50 mm are preferred for catching zander, but the Chinese net is not particularly discriminating, unlike the seine nets used in Soviet times. The process of hauling nets in (*au qarau*, 'to look at the nets') is more straightforward than laying them. Two holes are made in the ice with a *lom*, heavy work performed by junior fishermen. The net is retrieved with a hook and attached to a piece of string, which pays out down the first hole as the net is hauled through from the second. Fishermen extract the fish from the net, trying not to tear the net (not easy with low-quality Chinese nets!). This tends to be accompanied by conversation and improvised singing. Once all fish have been removed, the net is pulled back through from the first hole with the string.

Fish are thrown unceremoniously onto different heaps: bream, roach, zander, asp. This is the commercial catch, which will be handed in to the fish receivers. The least onerous work of putting fish in sacks falls to the oldest person present. There will also be a few small flounder, sabrefish and possibly also carp, catfish, pike; perhaps some of the exotic introductions from the 1960s, silver carp or belyy amur. Because their numbers are small, fish receivers do not take them. The smaller ones are added to the heap of bream where they will hopefully go unnoticed by fish receivers, while larger ones are put on one side. In winter the catch is driven straight to the receiving station at the end of the day, at 9 or 10 p.m. In spring and autumn fishermen haul in their nets in the morning, and then they go ashore and extract the fish, put them in sacks and clean their nets. In the afternoon they take the catch round to the receiving station either by UAZ or by boat, before going out to lay their nets again in the evening.

As we follow the fish to the receiving station, other sorts of negotiation become evident, encapsulated in the proverb: 'The fisherman doesn't tell the truth, every day he takes one portion (*bïr asym*).' This proverb is told with a smirk, reflecting the informality that is integral to fishing as a way of life. The exact wording is telling: '*asym*' is a pot's worth of food, the amount of meat needed for a *besbarmaq*. That is, the fisherman does not tell the truth because he is taking some of his catch home to feed his household. It is not the same as taking some to sell to a *kommersant*. Not telling the truth is legitimated – within reason.

The receiving station consists of a set of Soviet-era scales and a Soviet-era ZiL truck (Figures 6.5 and 6.6). Zhaqsylyq chats affably with the older fishermen; Meirambek jokes with all and sundry. Formally, the

Figure 6.5 Receiving station, Shaghalaly, spring 2014. Source: author.

Figure 6.6 Receiving station, winter 2013. Zhaqsylyq is on far left; Meirambek operates the scales. Source: author.

relation between the receivers and fishermen is a monopsony, but the formal relation is fraught by uncertainty about what is and is not seen. Fishermen may haul in their nets and take their boat to a reedy bit of shoreline some kilometres from the receiving station, where they put the fish into sacks. One or two sacks may go into their UAZ. As the proverb suggests, they will take home the noncommercial fish, and maybe also a sack of bream or asp for domestic consumption. They then transport the commercial catch by boat to the receiving station. Zhaqsylyq and Meirambek, who are busy all day receiving fish, are unable to patrol the entire shore. It is also not practical to check that every sack contains what fishermen claim it contains. Zander are generally obvious, their pointy heads tearing the sack and sticking out of the sides. But a sack of bream will almost certainly also contain some flounder and other noncommercial varieties.

The fishermen unload the sacks of fish and pile them onto the scales. Fish are now valued as commodities as they are known in a new way, quantified by weight. Since this quantification rests not only on technology, the scales, but also on the fish receivers' deployment of the technology, the process by which fish become commodities is embedded in social relations. The receivers ask what is in each sack, but they do not check. They also do not ask what is in the UAZ. Once the scales are loaded, one of the fish receivers adjusts the balance and reads off the weight (Figure 6.7). Meirambek operates the scales deftly; Zhaqsylyq tends to be clumsier. However, I only saw the result challenged once, when Zhaqsylyq, sliding the measure slightly too far, aroused an angry shout of *Eeee, boldy, eeee!* ('Hey! That's enough! Hey!') – but there was no one else about, and Zhaqsylyq ignored it. On another occasion, a zander was rejected from the lorry because it was mangled; it was reweighed and its value deducted. Another fisherman who was looking on shouted, although it was not his catch, 'It's just one!' Meirambek replied: 'Yes, but that's 500 tenge!' Since everyone knows that what is visible is partial, the production of knowledge must always be negotiated. These minor incidents indicate the 'social pressure' (Hivon 1998) involved in these negotiations: the receivers' capacity to exploit their position is limited by their need to maintain trust. While the social pressure failed in these very minor cases, I did not see more serious challenges to the receivers' authority in Bögen. Indeed, fishermen usually ignored the operation of the scales.

While there are social pressures on the receivers, there are limits too on what fishermen can get away with. Not telling the truth may receive censure. Informal rules, albeit backed up by the formal authority of the camouflage uniform, shape relations between receivers and fishermen.

Figure 6.7 Meirambek weighs the catch, winter 2013. Source: author.

One day Zhaqsylyq was outraged to find that an entire sack of zander had been rejected by factory directors as it was full of juveniles, some 20 cm long. This is formally forbidden, as juvenile fish should be put back, but Zhaqsylyq's outrage was financial. Too small for filleting, the fish had been rejected by the factory: they have no value as commodities. Zhaqsylyq pays fishermen himself, before being reimbursed at the factory, so he was out of pocket. That day, this sack was left near the scales, a few fish spilling out, and Zhaqsylyq drew attention to it as fishermen came in. Eventually the presumed guilty party arrived, and was sternly reprimanded by Meirambek and Zhaqsylyq, who stressed that the factory would not receive fish under 400 g. They did not mention the formal rule that juvenile zander under 38 cm should be put back. The fisherman defended himself, saying that he had laid 45-mm nets like everyone else, but he did not deny handing in undersized fish, nor did he dispute the cost of the sack being deducted from his day's earnings. When he left, he made a point of saying a friendly goodbye to Zhaqsylyq, but Zhaqsylyq ignored him.

With a last act of shared labour, two fishermen heave the sacks into the lorry (Figure 6.8), perhaps with a helping shove from a third. Their brief relationship with the fish is severed. The cost is calculated, and deductions are made for fuel or nets purchased from Meirambek. The money is handed over to a senior member of the fishing unit (not

Figure 6.8 Loading the ZiL, spring 2014. Source: author.

necessarily the owner of the UAZ). During my fieldwork, bream and roach, which formed a large proportion of the catch, cost consistently less than 100 KZT/kg. Asp ranged from 100–170 KZT/kg. But the bulk of fishermen's earnings came from zander: zander was 250 KZT/kg when I first arrived in winter 2013, and 500 KZT/kg by spring 2014, after the currency devaluation. The later social lives of the commodity fish explain the divergent value that fishermen extract from them.

Fish from factory to market

The commodity fish now travel in the ZiL across the dried-up seabed to the small refrigeration plant outside the village, where 50 people, nearly all from Qazaly, work. Sacks are hauled out of the lorry and slit open to reveal their contents. Exhausted men, working through the night, lug sacks of fish a few metres onto the scales. Zander are transferred into crates and loaded into a modern container lorry for transport to Qazaly. Bream, roach and asp are taken into the factory, where they are washed in long baths before being fished out by strong-armed women and young men. From here they undergo sorting (*sortirovka*; Figure 6.9), as a different group of women knows them fleetingly as sizes. Then they are frozen. Later, a group of young men and women joking and laughing together will package them.

While the *sortirovka* is proceeding, factory bosses are adding up the figures, checking the weights against those recorded by the fish receivers. They also draw up official documentation, again translating fish into numbers. According to inspectors, it is here that a mismatch appears, as fish caught above quota is not reported. With just 10 inspectors, equipped with three UAZ jeeps, one Niva and two boats, they stress the difficulties of regulating reporting. Keeping two sets of records, one by the shore and one at the factory for the inspectors, is routine. Out of the water, fish lead double lives: as commodified frozen meat, and as official numbers which, again, perform both representative and constitutive functions (Verran

Figure 6.9 *Sortirovka*, fish plant, Bögen, spring 2014. Source: author.

2010). These numbers misrepresent the real fish, but they also constitute the relationship between nature users and the state.

From one perspective, then, the lack of state oversight is exploited by private actors. However, above-quota fishing also stems directly from the formal tensions in the property regime explored in Chapter 5. Given the acute financial constraints facing nature users, there is a strong incentive to fish above quotas. Indeed, the reliance on credit to fulfil fisheries development plans means that factories and refrigeration units are not built on the proceeds of fish which have been caught, but on the proceeds of future fish. Fish, translated into money, pay off the debt incurred in building the factories where they are processed. This in turn drives nature users' high demand for fish, especially zander, which exceeds the limited 'virtual fish' they are assigned.

Let us return to the plant for the next stage in the social lives of the fish. Because most factories in the region do not do large-scale smoking and curing, the frozen bream, roach and asp are then loaded again into modern container lorries, bypassing Aral'sk, for export to Russia, where they will be processed, before finally being sold to consumers. Eventually, our Aral bream may be known as flavour and texture by beer drinkers in a bar somewhere in Russia. Meanwhile zander caught in Amanbai's waters are on their way to Qazaly, where they will be filleted and coated in an ice glaze in Amanbai's factory, which has an EU export code. In this form, they travel across Kazakhstan into Russia and eventually to Poland, Germany and Turkey. However, not all the zander caught in the Aral is processed in this way. For most of my fieldwork, Amanbai was the only nature user who had a processing factory fitting European standards as well as plots on the sea. Above-quota fish cannot be bought and sold legally, and factories without plots on the sea are obliged to buy fish with documentation. So the above-quota zander is mysteriously exported in frozen form and processed elsewhere in Kazakhstan or in Russia. Critically, it therefore bypasses Aral'sk, to the dismay of townspeople, as we see in Chapter 7.

As fish cross international borders, customs officials know them by code and documentation. Arriving in Russia, crates of fish are now stamped with different codes. Fish lying packed in lorries continue their double lives, as frozen meat, a commodity with exchange-value, and as official numbers mediating a relationship with customs officials (Figure 6.10). In the course of their migrations, the zander meet other Kazakhstani zander and are repackaged, eventually arriving in German and Polish supermarkets labelled as 'zander from Kazakhstan'; they will then become entangled in central European taste, cuisine and sociality.

Figure 6.10 Fish in the back of the ZiL, spring 2014. Source: author.

Demand for Kazakhstani zander in the EU is high, because the country's freshwater bodies are relatively deep and clean, so the fish is of high quality. This final stage is crucial: high consumer demand maintains high prices.

Above-quota fishing, therefore, depends on fish's valuation on distant markets. McGoodwin (1991) argues that when markets for fish are local, aggregate demand is finite; when fish feed regional and global markets, demand is infinite, creating incentives to fish without end. However, if, like Latour's (1993) railways, markets are local at every point, extraction is driven by the sum of locally contingent processes of value formation. The divergent spatial reach of different fish depends on fluctuating prices in Germany and Russia, as well as the processing infrastructure in the Aral region. It also rests on the 'atmosphere of intrigue' (Anderson 2002, 161) surrounding sale of above-quota fish, which is created both by the formal tensions in the management system and by the obfuscation with which it is enacted. At each stage in fishes' social lives, there is a new form of abstraction or (mis)translation. Nature users' official statistics mystify the actual number of fish in the lorry, while the supermarket price mystifies everything that has gone before it. Meanwhile, at each stage of abstraction in fish's migrations from sea to European supermarkets, value is extracted. Together, these processes drive the high extraction of fish from the sea. However, while agency is dispersed, intensive fishing also depends on fishermen themselves. In the next section, therefore, I explore how fishermen relate to the resource that their livelihoods depend on.

'The fisherman dreams for the day'

Fishermen do not share the vision of scarcity on which regulation is premised. As the proverb goes, 'the sower dreams for the year, the fisherman dreams for the day'. From day to day, fish are unreliable: *bïrde bolady, bïrde bolmaidy* ('sometimes there are, sometimes there aren't'). Laying nets is a project (*zhoba*): knowledge is imprecise; only God knows if there are fish here. But in the longer term, according to the dominant view, fish are abundant. Narratives of past abundance are a guide to future abundance: recall how Zhūbatqan's narrative in Chapter 4 about the sea sustaining the starving in the 1930s was prompted by my question as to whether there would be fish *in the future*. Fishermen also draw on their own experience: every fish lays a million eggs, so of course there will be fish in the future. If there is water, there will be fish, and everyone is confident that there will be water, especially if the dam is raised. Images of natural abundance thus sustain a 'politics of the present'. Though it is characteristic of hunter-gatherer societies, Day et al. (1999) identify such a politics among marginalised people in a range of contexts.

As I have suggested, in contrast to animal herding, catching fish has a certain immediatism, producing a sense of nature's bounty, as Astuti (1999) describes for the Vezo of Madagascar in her contribution to Day et al.'s (1999) volume. Whether fishing for immediate consumption, for the plan or for the market, relations with fish are impersonal and transitory, unlike those with livestock. The politics of the present has also been reproduced by the hierarchical structure of both Soviet and post-Soviet fisheries, which constrain fishermen not to worry about the resource. Indeed, they express their lack of interest in quotas with a dismissive expletive. The history of environmental change further explains this point. Villagers have known the resource become scarce, but they know that the fish died out because the sea dried up, which was nothing to do with their actions. Over recent years, fish populations have been growing rapidly despite intensive fishing, reproducing an image of nature as inherently abundant.[11]

There are, however, dissenting voices. Some younger people are concerned about the possible development of oil – again, a threat to the resource from non-fishermen. Others express concern about the current intensive fishing, saying that only Allah knows if there will be fish in future. Düzbai, a senior fisherman in Tastübek, who now works as a fish receiver for Amanbai, is the only figure in a position of authority that I talked to who showed real anxiety about the future of the resource. He contrasted the modern fishing without limit to the past, when fishermen would return from Balqash with little money but content with what they had received. When I asked whether there would be zander in the future, he replied quietly: 'I don't know … I'm not God!' (*Bilmeimïn … Qūdai emespïn*). To ensure fish in the future, he said, the sea must be properly monitored and controlled; Chinese nets must not be used; limits must be respected; the banned season must be enforced. He blamed the sea's division into plots, arguing for a single factory with domain over the whole sea. Such anxiety is suppressed in the narratives of every fish laying a million eggs and of past abundance. While these narratives derive from experience, they also serve the social function of justifying fishing today without concern for the future. They constitute an ideology of the present, legitimising intensive fishing.

However, if Aral fishermen share a politics of the present with hunter-gatherers and other marginalised groups, there are, of course, important differences. Hunter-gatherers are famous for not working hard (e.g. Sahlins 1972), whereas Aral fishermen work very hard. This is partly because of the limited fishing seasons and the unpredictability of the weather. The Soviet valorisation of labour also helps explain why. But Düzbai also contrasts a Soviet past of moderation with a present dominated by money. To dig deeper into why fishermen work so hard, I turn now to the role of fish in local structures of value, showing how different sorts of fish reproduce and transform social relations in different ways, over different timescales.

Fish in Bögen

Let us return to the fishermen as they arrive home after a day's fishing. In my first winter in Bögen, Zikön and his fellow fishermen would gather in Zhaqsylyq's *sarai* to divide up fish, sort nets and relax over drinks. The non-commodity fish were divided not by individual fisherman, but by household. A large carp would go to Müsïlïm, as he was the oldest. Catfish would be sliced evenly, each household taking a share (Figure 6.11). Most of this fish is for household consumption; but some may also be given to relatives elsewhere who do not fish, entering long-term reciprocal relations. Furthermore, claims may be made on fish – mostly by relatives or friends but sometimes even by someone completely unconnected, where there is no long-term reciprocity. They may thus enter short-term immediate relations with no expectation of return: the hunter-gatherer practice of shares, whereby economic value is not assigned to nature's bounty, persists where fish have low monetary value. Although there is a

Figure 6.11 Aikeldï divides up a catfish, winter 2013. Source: author.

sense that a gift of fish need not be reciprocated, most often, if fish is given to someone unconnected, vodka may be offered in return, but not money.

Despite the persistence of practices of sharing, there is no anxiety about the commodification of fish, particularly the translation of zander into lots of money. This is in striking contrast to E. Wilson (2002) and Nakhshina's (2011; 2012) discussions of post-Soviet fisheries in the Russian Far East and Far North respectively: both describe communities where commodification is perceived to come from outside, and is resisted as immoral, contradicting local ethics of sharing. In both those examples, the object of contestation is salmon, which has high market value *and* is prized locally. By contrast, zander is not rated by Kazakhs. Popular in Europe for its leanness, it is unpopular among Kazakhs for the same reason: fat and oil are rated highly in Kazakh diet. The same material feature entangles zander in different ways in different regimes of value: with high monetary value but low local culinary value, zander is readily commodified by Aral fishermen.

While the non-commodity fish would be divided according to household, money from commodity fish would be divided equally among individual fishermen. At this moment they are all equal individual economic actors: they are momentarily disembedded. Some of this money would be consumed immediately, as the individual economic actors now took turns to buy drinks, reproducing sociality between fishermen. Zikön, Aikeldï and Müsïlïm would drink vodka, while Bolat and Zhüman would drink beer (Mūkhtar and Maqsat did not drink in front of their seniors). However, most of the money is handed over to wives or mothers, and fishermen are no longer individual economic agents, but are embedded in their household. Indeed, when in Bögen outside fishing seasons, I would be called on to buy drinks and cigarettes; the litany was always the same: 'no fish, no money'. When they were fishing again, I was promised, they would reciprocate. Evidently, they had no money which was not earmarked for household expenditure. The money that fish are associated with is specifically ready money.

Fish, money and social reproduction

It is November 2013. There is an air of excitement as fishermen return from the sea: Ghalymbek's wedding (*toi*) is approaching. Over the next day, which is grey and windy, the air thick with dust, men are slaughtering livestock in preparation for the feast, the vodka flowing freely, while women are busy preparing inside the newly built family house. The day of the *toi* is cool and breezy. Beneath pale blue skies, the face of the bride, who is from Shymkent, is revealed, while a poet improvises with a dombra (a type of lute), singing about the wedding guests, who give a small gift of money. Not only are villagers present, but also Külïkter from further afield, from Aral'sk and Qyzylorda. The day includes various formal meals and a lot of informal drinking on the sidelines, culminating in the *svad'ba* (Ru.: wedding) in the evening: 1980s Soviet singers like Iurii Shatunov, Boney M. and modern Kazakh pop music blare from a sound system as everyone dances together, vodka continuing to flow on the sidelines. Then a master of ceremonies invites a series of *tilekter*, brief speeches wishing the couple well, from Zhaqsylyq, Aikeldï, Gulnar and others, including the new *qūda* from Shymkent. As the master of ceremonies celebrates the presence of so many Külïkter and Zhamanközder, the wedding promises the continuation of the *ru* into the future. The wedding is a key moment in the reproduction of *tughan zher*, which today hinges on the intersection of abundance in the sea with transnational markets.

Fishing thus sustains this ritual economy which reproduces society over time. This is not its only significance. Money is also saved for investment in productive capital such as UAZs and GPS finders. Money, by facilitating access to these technologies, has brought some freedom in reducing the importance of affective ties and obligations. The importance of networking as a survival strategy, crucial in the 1990s (Kandiyoti 1998; Werner 1998), is declining as households become more self-sufficient. However, the role of money in ritual expenditure is crucial to understanding social change in Bögen. It also marks a key difference from the presentism explored by Day et al. (1999): while the Vezo, for example, living for the moment, transcend durational time (Astuti 1999), most Aral fishermen are committed to the long-term order of social reproduction. If the fisherman dreams for the day, his family dreams for the next wedding. The influx of money through fishing has led to the increasing monetisation of this ritual economy. Indeed, weddings now cost 1–2 million KZT. Bridewealth (*qalyng*), which used to involve transfers of livestock from the groom's to the bride's family, is now usually cash – with figures of 100,000–150,000 KZT cited as normal, sometimes higher. Money is also required for building new houses (essential if a wedding is approaching), with a house costing 2–3 million KZT. When I was roped into housebuilding projects in Bögen in summer 2013, everyone emphasised the cooperation and reciprocity involved in housebuilding: through enlisting other villagers in the institution of *asar*, collective help, people rally support in advancing their project. But housebuilding is also competitive; houses are judged on size and style, with *evro-tip* (European-style) preferred – that is, fronted with factory bricks, with PVC windows and new furniture. Because of all these factors, however much zander is caught, there is never enough money.

Overlapping explanations have been put forward for conspicuous ritual consumption in post-Soviet Central Asia. As financial capital is turned into symbolic capital, it reproduces and cements social differentiation (Kandiyoti and Azimova 2004; Koroteyeva and Makarova 1998). Accordingly, this long-term order in which society itself is reproduced is not only about solidarity, but is also the site of competition between households; as society is reproduced, it is differentiated. For Trevisani (2016), in Uzbekistan an 'instrumental mode' of ritual rationality is thus replacing a 'communitarian mode'. In a different vein, in her discussion of migrant remittances in Kyrgyzstan, Reeves (2012) argues that ritual expenditure allows migrants both to affirm presence back home and to maintain networks that are crucial for navigating neoliberal labour markets abroad. Given the ongoing embeddedness of the fishery, social networks are still important in Bögen too. However, as I have shown, horizontal ties between households are becoming less salient, while the vertical ties between ordinary fishermen and Zhaqsylyq and Meirambek remain crucial. Networking still matters, but there is an asymmetry in the connections: Zhaqsylyq and Meirambek are considerably less dependent on other fishermen than vice versa. As Botoeva, discussing the effects of an influx of money from hash on a rural Kyrgyz village, concludes: 'monetization of gift giving transforms social networks into more layered and stratified dependencies' (2015, 545).

In Bögen, therefore, society is becoming differentiated as it is reproduced. At one extreme, there is Tolpash, a little older than Zhaqsylyq. He has no relatives in the village; his siblings left years ago; and his only son now works in Qazaly, although the youngest son is expected to live with his parents. He is not excluded from the fishery: he and two other elderly fishermen in a similar position fish in a boat provided by Amanbai. But his house is old and crumbling. His wife complains about the cost of groceries and the amounts charged by *kommersanty* in the village. Most families are much better off than this: with several members of the household fishing, it is possible to maintain a reasonable standard of living.

At the other extreme, Zhaqsylyq's family has benefited most from the return of the sea: the position of fish receiver is lucrative; and all the sons fish. In summer 2013 preparations were being made for the family's new house: 3,000 bricks were to be made. Zhaqsylyq's *bazha* Müsïlïm and his sons were helping mix sand and clay. Müsïlïm stressed that they were helping as they were *aghaiyn*, 'relatives'. What no one voiced was that Müsïlïm, who lives in Amanötkel, depends on Zhaqsylyq for access to the fishery. The following summer the new house was to be built, and soon Mūkhtar, once returned from the army, was to get married. The extensive financial capital the family accumulates in turn reproduces their symbolic capital, the wedding in the large new house serving as a performance of their new prominence.[12]

Conclusion

The restored sea, then, is transforming local social relations. As money from zander feeds the ritual economy, natural abundance intersects with opaque transnational markets to reproduce *tughan zher*. There are superficial parallels with Carsten's (1989) account of a Malay village where fishing is a hierarchical, competitive activity, and the money earned from it attracts moral discomfort; however, as the money is symbolically 'cooked', it feeds into the reproduction of household and community, an order governed by reciprocity. Carsten's case study is an important instance of what Bloch and Parry (1989), contesting assumptions of a 'great divide' between gift societies and commodity societies, or between embedded and disembedded economies, characterise as a divide *within* societies, between a short-term order based on competitive self-interest and a long-term order over which society itself is reproduced.

On closer examination, the Aral case diverges from Carsten's study. After all, the everyday practice of fishing is marked by various forms of cooperation and claims based on social ties. Furthermore, different fish, with different material qualities, enter very different practices of exchange. Crucially, as elsewhere in Central Asia, the long-term order is characterised by competitive accumulation of symbolic capital. Helgason and Pálsson (1997) question Bloch and Parry's (1989) assumption of a great divide within societies, proposing instead the metaphor of a single moral landscape, crisscrossed with different patterns of exchange and different moralities. While there are some processes of disembedding within the Aral region, if less advanced in Bögen itself, this is neither a transition from one sort of society to another, nor even a shift in emphasis from the long-term order of social reproduction to short-termist self-interest. Rather, this moral landscape is reshaped as the physical landscape is integrated into the time and space of contemporary capitalism. So too, the social relations that are reproduced within this moral landscape are being transformed as fishermen are differentiated from *priëmshchiki* and nature users, and as Bögen fishermen are differentiated from hired fishermen from other villages. Zander, in their entanglements with technologies of extraction (boats, nets, jeeps), with formal and informal property relations, and with transnational markets, are driving these transformations. During my fieldwork, as resources were abundant, no one was excluded from fishing, despite differential access to boats and other means of production. Were that to change, evidently the hired fishermen would be laid off first.

The stereotypes with which we began thus both contain a grain of truth. There is certainly social differentiation, though this is uneven (in some contexts, fishermen are more exploited than in others), and fishermen certainly are concerned about making money, because it is through money that social status is reproduced. At the same time, fishing is also a way of life, an identity – and the different forms of sociality at sea, at the receiving station and in the village cannot be reduced to competition between households.

Likewise, neither account of above-quota fishing is wholly wrong: it is neither that there is too much regulation, nor that there is too little; rather, above-quota fishing must be explained through the overlapping formal and informal norms, and the opaque market, which together shape how management is enacted in practice. The materialities of fish, in the context of different sorts of consumer demand and processing infrastructure, shape different spatial trajectories and thus different patterns of value formation. Agency for above-quota fishing is dispersed across the whole fishery, as a socioeconomic system (Campling et al. 2012). Even within Bögen, the intricate and shifting moral landscape does not support a reading of a 'tragedy of the commons', a free-for-all of self-interested individuals. Nor is it a 'tragedy of the private', where a select few profit to the exclusion of others. The intersections of *tughan zher* and the postsocialist market entangle everyone in the rush for zander. Critically, the more zander are caught, the further social reproduction is monetised. As zander transform local society, they create further incentives for fishermen to go on catching them in ever greater quantities.

Notes

1 During my fieldwork, total allowable catch for all species was just over 4,000 tonnes, of which 10 per cent was zander. However, from my observations, zander made up 30–50 per cent of the fish received.

2 I have related the Aral fisheries to the 'tragedy of the commons' versus 'tragedy of the private' debate in greater depth elsewhere (Wheeler 2017).

3 This latter stereotype is far from unique to the Aral. As Howard (2017, 7) stresses, the stereotype of fishers as greedy and destructive ignores the market forces that structure fishing practices.

4 As Bloch and Parry (1989) stress, such perspectives, often taken for granted by theorists, are a widespread response to processes of commodification.

5 In practice, boundaries are not respected, though considerations of fuel and distance limit encroachments.

6 Unlike individual transferrable quotas (ITQs) in the West, which can be traded as commodities, in Kazakhstan quotas can only be purchased by nature users from the state.

7 Quotas in the West are widely critiqued: scientists increasingly argue that fish populations are chaotic or stochastic, so simply regulating quantity of fish caught is a blunt instrument compared to parametric management, that is, regulating gear and introducing banned seasons and zones (Larkin 1977; Ludwig et al. 1993; Pitchford et al. 2007; Wilson et al. 1994). However, KazNIIRKh also assesses fertility of spawning stock, so their assumptions are not, in theory, as simplistic as those critiqued by the authors cited; moreover, a banned season and banned zone should both support the reproduction of fish populations.

8 While people can make claims on *rulas*, fellow clan members, there is no sense that a *ru* is a corporate entity forming the basis of the organisation of production. For this point, cf. Isakov and Schoeberlein (2014) on Kyrgyzstan, and Trevisani (2007) on Uzbekistan.

9 In other post-Soviet fisheries too, regulations are flouted, but the necessity of a hierarchical structure is not contested (King 2003; Nakhshina 2012; E. Wilson 2002).

10 Of course, embeddedness does not automatically translate into easier labour relations: in the village of Zhalangash, the nature user, LLP Asta, which lost its plot in 2014, was run by a former fisherman, who failed to fulfil obligations to provide boats, and was accused of making deductions from pay to subsidise quotas.

11 Comparative evidence supports this argument: Finlayson and McCay (1998) show that a paradigm shift in understanding the Atlantic cod fisheries only happened when stocks became scarce; Acheson et al. (1998) show how memories of overfishing produce social pressure for restraint even decades later.

12 Similarly, Batyrkhan, nature user in Qaratereng, who has also built a lavish new house with bricks from Almaty, held a huge feast in honour of his recently deceased son, involving sports contests, with cash prizes given to winners.

7
Aral'sk today: fish, money, *ekologiia*

In summer 2013 I was roped into a school project in Aral'sk. The schoolchildren, aged between 10 and 14, were making a film about their region for a national competition. In the film they were to show a foreigner the sights of the town, with one of their teachers, Gulnar, translating into English. We began at a large white monument of a square-rigged sailing ship (Figure 7.1), near the station (although no such ships ever sailed on the Aral). It took several takes to get everyone in position, but eventually we could begin the dialogue. Following my instructions, I asked the children to tell me about this ship. One boy piped up his rehearsed lines: 'Our region is primarily a fishing region, but the Aral Sea dried up (*tartylyp ketken*), and this monument is to commemorate our fishermen.' But one of the teachers shouted from the sidelines that we would have to start again: 'The sea is coming back (*tengïz qaityp kelïp zhatyr*)! Say that the sea is coming back!' A few more takes (the cameraman's patience wearing thin) and the boy had got his lines right, and Gulnar translated for my benefit: 'The children think that the sea is coming back.'

The rest of the tour presented Aral'sk to a putatively global audience. It was instructive for both what was and what was not included. We steered clear of the Soviet-era Hotel Aral, despised by locals and visitors alike. We spent much time on the wide, clean central square, the site of the town and raion akimats and several banks. Some other schoolchildren were putting on a performance of traditional dancing accompanied by dombra (a type of lute). A drunk shuffled past smirking. One of the boys with the dombra told me that there would be a concert in Astana, conjuring up a connection between Aral'sk and the capital. We also filmed a Soviet-era monument of a fisherman.

We next followed the road towards the station, where Aral'sk's few apartment buildings are located – elegant if crumbling two-storey buildings, and of no interest to our tour; we also, like most inhabitants,

Figure 7.1 *Aqkeme* (white ship), autumn 2013. Source: author.

ignored the mosque, which is on the same road. Our goal was the town museum, where we examined some traditional jewellery. We did not look at exhibits about the sea, or about Soviet times. We then visited a local jeweller, before heading for Independence Square. Formerly salt marsh, the square centres on a tall monument surrounded by some parched flowerbeds. Unlike the central square, which is frequently traversed by people on their business about town, no one walks across the centre of Independence Square, and it is something of a vacuum amid its surroundings. Around the flowerbeds, mud and dust give way to broken tarmac. One side is lined with workshops offering car repair and welding; on the other side taxi drivers vie for custom; beyond is the bus station, with Soviet-era buses serving local villages and long-distance second-hand French coaches. Beyond the bus station is the bustling bazaar, selling local meat, fish, dairy and wool products; fruit and vegetables from southern Kazakhstan; and tat from China. Of all this, we just filmed the monument at the centre of the square.

We then drove round the town, along pot-holed roads and rutted tracks of saline mud and sand, to look at glossy new monuments of Kazakh national heroes, which are also sites for wedding photos. We ended at a small sports complex near the former harbour, which had recently been opened by a local businessman as a gift to the town. The dried-up seabed lying just beyond did not feature in the film. Nor did we visit any of the former Soviet enterprises examined in Chapter 3. In a sense, Aral'sk is a microcosm of Kazakhstan as a whole: pockets of shiny newness purporting continuity with a distant pre-Soviet past, amid expanses of decay. Visitors mostly perceive the decay, but it was the newness that the children and their teachers wanted to display. In her ethnography of the nuclear town of Kurchatov, another remote Kazakhstani town scarred by its Soviet legacy, Alexander (2020, 4) writes of 'a desire to be known, to be on the map' for something other than what the town is notorious for. The children's film spoke of a similar desire.

It is a desire that is often frustrated. The boy's mistake at the beginning of the tour speaks of the sea's marginality to Aral'sk today. Not only is the sea marginal to Aral'sk: Aral'sk is also marginal to contemporary Kazakhstan's oil-based economy. Moreover, Aral'sk inhabitants are aware, often through intimate experience of ill health, of ongoing ecological problems. As residents juggle local pride with anxieties about unseen particles in the air and about economic insecurity, integrity is felt to be threatened at different scales: the integrity of the imagined community of the nation and that of local society; the integrity of persons, both moral and physical. This chapter therefore asks how subjectivities are shaped in relation to the environment. In particular, I am interested in the feel of living in Aral'sk, the corporeal sensations created by the environment, its 'material affects' (Laszczkowski 2016; Mazzarella 2009; Navaro-Yashin 2012).

As we saw in Chapter 5, while posters of Kökaral enrol the restored sea in the state's 'propaganda of emotion' (Laszczowski 2016), the sea's distance from the town is a source of frustration and dissatisfaction with the new hegemonic formation that the dam materialises. Most people are aware of the sea's partial restoration and talk positively about improvements to the climate and flowers that have returned. Many hope that the sea level will be raised further, which will be good for the people (*khalyq*) and allow tourism to flourish in the town. At the more pessimistic extreme is Svetlana Mikhailovna, my Russian landlady, who declared firmly that the sea's return was 'drips' (*kapli*), doing very little to resolve the town's problems. In general, however, there is ambivalence, and few imagine their or their family's future as connected with the sea. After all, if the official 'propaganda of emotion' relies on the positive affects emanating from the restored marine environment, this is frustrated by the sheer inaccessibility of the sea to most of the town's residents. The nearest point on the sea is the boggy and reedy shallows at the north end of Saryshyghanaq bay, about 20 km away, and access is only possible by four-by-four. Summer days out for swimming, beer and shashlyk are generally to Lake Qamystybas, which, though further, can be reached by tarmac road. Beyond the physical incompleteness of the connection between the town and the sea, the opacity of the fishery and the peculiar shape of the market (see Chapter 6) further marginalise Aral'sk from the restored sea, meaning that the sea's return has not translated into large-scale employment. Hence the comparison of Soviet times with today, and hence the sense that the sea's return holds limited meaning for the town: there is a failed connection between the town and the sea.

At the same time, like Alexander's (2020) informants in Kurchatov, Aral'sk residents continue to be affected by what they describe as *ekologiia*, ecological problems that affect the human body. As people complain about the extreme summer heat, the dust, the salt in the air that can be tasted in the mouth, there is a sense that *ekologiia* acts, that it might account for headaches, high blood pressure (*davlenie*), tiredness or low mood. For many, however, *ekologiia* poses a threat to their local pride, and some, feeling no ill health, question whether *ekologiia* exists. After all, unlike in Almaty or Astana, there is no air pollution from traffic or factories. In the second half of the chapter, therefore, I explore how, in Navaro-Yashin's (2012, 18) words, 'the environment exerts a force on human beings in its own right'. I will show how subjectivities take shape in the intersection, in the body, of the materiality of the environment with material conditions of economic insecurity. Though I assume that material affects can shape local subjectivities, I do not regard these affects emanating from the environment as prediscursive or presocial.[1] Certainly, the penetration of particles of salt and dust reveal the material vulnerability of the body, its porosity and continuity with the world around. Nevertheless, I assume, in Bakhtinian vein, that this body is also rooted in a social reality. Experiences of *ekologiia*, which vary across different bodies, are always already located in the multiple, shifting ways of talking about it.

Marginality and threatened integrity

Where previously Aral'sk was incorporated into the grid of the command economy, post-Soviet economic transformations, driven by optics of 'seeing like an oil company' (Ferguson 2005), have differentiated space again, marginalising Aral'sk in a new form of uneven development (Smith 1984). These sea changes in the economy generate concerns about lack of employment, shortage of money, and corruption – concerns which feed the nostalgia we saw in Chapter 3. Indeed, there is a perception that there is 'no work' in Aral'sk, except in the state sector – the akimat, schools and hospitals. State employees benefit from the *ekologicheskaia zarplata*, 'ecological salary', the extra pay granted in an ecological disaster zone.

However, despite wilder estimates, Aral'sk is not beset with unemployment and stagnation. It benefits from its position on key transport routes. During my fieldwork, the trunk road passing the town was being upgraded in a massive World Bank project to connect Western China with Western Europe, providing some temporary work in the town. Most important, now as throughout the town's history, is the railway. The railway is a source of jobs itself, and it also provides access to jobs, for those with and without educational capital, in shift work on oilfields in Aqtöbe oblast to the north and Qyzylorda oblast to the south. Such work allows people to stay living in Aral'sk, where land is abundant and housing relatively cheap. People also migrate further afield to Almaty or Astana on a longer-term basis. For example, Edïge needed to raise money to get married and renovate the family house, so moved to Almaty where he worked for international companies; he returned to look after his mother when she was ill.

There is also informal work in the bazaar and in construction around the town. Ownership of a vehicle opens limited economic opportunities: any car can be used as a taxi; a UAZ van can be used for ferrying wedding parties to distant villages, or for collecting fish for *kommersanty*, or even for taking tourists to the sea (if one has an acquaintance in the NGO); a KAMAZ truck is useful for transporting building materials. Some families keep livestock, though increasingly few as the cost of feed rises. Finally, growing numbers of people from Aral'sk fish in the nearby Saryshyghanaq bay, especially after these plots, which had previously not been exploited, were assigned to nature users at the end of my fieldwork in early 2014.

The perception that there is no work in Aral'sk, then, alludes both to the sense that economic opportunity is elsewhere and to the form of work: the predominance of temporary, informal jobs rather than the major enterprises and job security remembered from the Soviet era. Even access to the formal sector depends on personal connections and, often, bribes. There are also constant complaints about the cost of everyday goods relative to salaries, especially after the currency was devalued in February 2014.[2] High prices are partly put down to the town's remoteness. Only meat is relatively cheap because of the livestock in the region. By contrast, fish, of which there is very little in the bazaar, is considered scandalously expensive. Indeed, much of the fish in the bazaar is suspected to be Caspian fish: Aral fish shows its freshness by the glint in its eyes.

Within this context of marginality and financial constraint, overlapping discourses seek to make sense of Aral'sk's new place in the world. One day as we were drinking tea, a TV news story reported that a swarm of locusts had devastated land in Aqtöbe oblast. When I asked where they had come from, the reply (as I half-expected) was: 'I don't know ... from China probably. Everything bad comes from China.' There are stories about Chinese nets invading Kazakhstan and Russia and destroying the environment; accounts of sweets infected with worms and bananas with HIV coming from China; and complaints that China takes everything out of Kazakhstan without giving anything back. Not only oil and minerals flow to China: even the abandoned ships on the dried-up seabed, local heritage which, people stress, should have been preserved, are scrapped and sent to China. Another threat from the outside is the cosmodrome at Baikonur, which is leased to Russia: this is viewed as the source of contemporary environmental problems, and national integrity is felt to be threatened as Russian rockets spew their waste onto Kazakh soil, just as Kazakh lands were treated as *terra nullius* during Soviet times. The most common theme is corruption at all levels. Discourse about corruption veers from the local to top-level bureaucrats (Ru.: *chinovniki*) in Kazakhstan to global corruption. The money motive is imputed everywhere: the dam was not built higher because of the corruption of Kazgiprovodkhoz; local scientific institutions like the fisheries research institute, KazNIIRKh, or Barsakelmes nature reserve are, apparently, motivated only by money, to the detriment of science; any official or NGO projects are dismissed as money-laundering; love of money, apparently, drives fishermen to take reckless risks, while greedy nature users exploit the fishermen.

Such discourses, veering between the plausible and implausible, speak of an anxiety about the unseen movement of things. Inferences are made about an opaque world based on known effects. These inferences and speculation are not abstract forms of reason: speaking subjects draw on the different discourses available to them – Soviet discourses about the evils of money; Kazakh Islamic thinking about moderation (*qanaghat*); media stories. The forms of reasoning do not follow logical steps, hence the slippage between the plausible and the bizarre, especially when it is the integrity of the nation that is felt to be at stake. However, as Pelkmans (2006, Chapter 7) argues, such discourses rightly highlight core effects of postsocialist transformations – which transitologists would dismiss as side effects. Concerns about integrity reflect the different sorts of outside forces – flows of commodities and money – that shape and constrain people's lives in Aral'sk.

Fish factories

During my fieldwork, fish were scarce not only in the bazaar, but also in factories around the town, which is why the fishing industry is marginal to most townspeople, providing few jobs. Crucially, above-quota fish cannot be sold openly. Factories in Aral'sk are liable to checks from the prosecutor's office, and thus face cripplingly high prices for material to process. Indeed, as one factory director told me, buyers must pay separately for fish and for documentation, through which 'black fish becomes white fish'. Without documentation, it is possible to smuggle fish out of the region for processing elsewhere, as crates can be restamped with different codes. Anderson (2002, 161) finds in 1990s Siberia that, despite high local demand for meat, the market is shaped by an 'atmosphere of intrigue' which channels meat in certain directions so this demand is not satisfied. Similarly, despite local demand for fish as food and as a source of jobs, the 'atmosphere of intrigue' that we saw in Chapter 6 shapes the market so that fish do not reach Aral'sk.

After Aralrybprom went bankrupt, it was sold off and dismantled. In 2007 Aimbetov, the last director of Aralrybprom, bought the derelict shell, 'for kopecks'. Assisted by a state loan, he restored the factory for 100 million KZT, and in 2010 the factory started production as Aral Servis, employing about 50 people. Until winning a tender for six plots on the sea at the end of my fieldwork in 2014, Aimbetov only had a small plot on the river, which limited his access to fish for processing. The main production is zander fillets, and the factory meets EU standards. But, during my fieldwork, very little of the old building was used: there was no smoking or curing, although such production is popular across the Commonwealth of Independent States (CIS). Given the lack of fish, the output of zander was very low during my fieldwork, with the factory only exporting 104 tonnes of zander fillet in 2012, though this has apparently changed since Aimbetov acquired plots on the sea in 2014.

There are a few other small fish plants, including Kambala Balyk, which employs about 20 people. Aimbetov's main competitor in the town is Atameken,[3] near the shipyard and the old military town. Fenced off from a road running alongside a stagnant lake, this shiny, futuristic building is unlike anything else in Aral'sk (Figure 7.2). Indeed, it purports to be the only such processing plant in the CIS. Atameken was originally part of Atameken Holding Company, owned by a wealthy businessman originating from the Aral region; the holding has interests in construction, real estate, import-export and engineering across Kazakhstan and an international office in Paris. The factory, Atamekenrybprom, was built in

2009 and cost $12 million, of which half was a state loan (Redaktsiia 'Novaia Gazeta' – Kazakhstan 2012). The factory is equipped with modern Korean technology, including an instant freezer, machinery for mincing offcuts and a smoking-chamber. But the first time the smoking-chamber was used, it filled up with smoke; the manufacturers have promised to repair it but have not yet done so. Today the factory produces some smoked fish on a small scale, unofficially, for the local market. Atameken also acquired an EU standard code in 2012 and exports zander fillets to Germany and Turkey. The factory was built with a capacity of 6,000 tonnes output, and was to employ 300 workers. It has never run anywhere near capacity. Lacking a plot on the sea, it must buy fish from other nature users. In 2012 just 500 tonnes were processed – including fish bought from Balqash and the Caspian. Just 75 people work in the factory, and payment of salaries is fraught. In 2013 the manager was fired. It was reclaimed by state authorities and new buyers were sought.

Atameken occupies an ambiguous place in Aral'sk. Architecturally, it resembles the futuristic glass buildings of Astana, and generates similar positive affects to those Laszczkowski (2016) finds there. People would praise its beauty and modernity and, as a Westerner, I would be asked if I had seen it. 'Even the director looks like a foreigner!' beamed my friend Mira (referring to the director who was later fired). 'Atameken' means 'fatherland', and, as a public–private partnership equipped with up-to-date foreign technology, the factory embodied Aral'sk's place in the glossy new global Kazakhstan, integrating the restored environment of the Small Aral Sea into the booming economic space of the country and

Figure 7.2 Atameken fish factory, autumn 2013. Source: author.

transnational markets. Fish were to play their part in this transformation, bringing jobs to a depressed region. So, when people talk about the fishing industry in the town, they usually talk about Atameken, not 'the old *rybokombinat*' (Aral Servis). Unsurprisingly, some older people criticise such a major enterprise factory not being state-run. When Svetlana Mikhailovna announced that there is no benefit to the town from the sea, it was because the factories were privatised, so all the profit goes 'to one person': her complaint reflected Soviet assumptions about the evils of private property. Most people, though, are more impressed by the external form than they are concerned about the ownership structure.

However, the hopeful affect exuded by the factory's material appearance is contradicted by its chronic failure. There is a widespread expectation that all the fish caught on the sea should end up in Atameken – and frustration that this does not happen. The failure of fish to reach Atameken represents a failed connection between the town and the restored sea, which speaks of Aral'sk's place in Kazakhstan as a whole. Rumours swirl around the factory. Recall the invisibility that pervades fisheries even when fish are out of the water: people in Aral'sk know that the sea has been restored, and they can see that some people are getting rich from it while the wider town stagnates, but everything in between is opaque. Rumours provide a means of reasoning in the absence of clear knowledge (Alexander 2009b). So, people complain that the fisheries inspectorate in Qyzylorda (headed by a man from Qazaly) rigged the tender so that all the fish should go to Qazaly, rather than Aral'sk.[4] However this decision was made, it is certainly true that Amanbai has three plots on the sea, and all his fish go for processing in his factory in Qazaly. Qazaly is nearer both Bögen and Qaratereng than Aral'sk, but as Aral'sk is the historical centre of the fishing industry, its marginalisation is resented.

There are also extensive rumours, encouraged by media reports (e.g. Naumova 2012), that *kommersanty* come to buy fish from poachers, and that the fish mysteriously disappears out of the region unprocessed. The provenance of these *kommersanty* varies – often they are said to come from Shymkent, the crime capital of Kazakhstan and source of all rumours about anything bad; sometimes from the Caspian or from Aqtöbe; and sometimes from abroad, from Russia or Georgia. On this view, Atameken is failing to deliver its promises because of penetration of the region by the outside. This forms part of the wider discourse about danger from the outside outlined above. However, if those complaints speak of Aral'sk's place within Kazakhstan, the factory itself is not exempt from criticism. It is also suspected of carrying on more production than is declared, cleaning and reselling without processing. People switch between praising the factory's beauty and criticising the high turnover of directors who simply pocket the money, buy a fancy Japanese four-by-four and leave. In this register, the factory management is not victim but agent: the factory does not provide jobs in the town because its directors are only interested in their personal profit.

There is a final point which no one mentions: if quotas were respected, less than 500 tonnes of zander would be caught per year, which would not translate into any more factory jobs than there are today.[5] However, zander makes up only about 10 per cent of the total allowable catch: the rest is not processed in the region, despite high demand for smoked and cured fish in the CIS. Developing infrastructure like smoking-chambers (or fixing the faulty one in Atameken's case) requires capital, and given the difficulties of raising capital for investment, all the factories are geared only to processing zander, the most profitable sort of fish.

Across post-Soviet space, shiny new buildings (or new façades) gesture towards bright futures, leaving the grey Soviet past behind. In Pelkmans' account of 1990s Ajaria, even when standing empty, new buildings are central to imagining the transition to a better future: though vehicles of dissatisfaction with the status quo, empty buildings are 'early signs of that turn for the better, of a future of fulfilled dreams' (Pelkmans 2006, 207). In this vein, one well-educated young state employee who had worked in Almaty explained Atameken's problems as intrinsic to the transitional present: though optimistic about the capitalist future, he argued that more state oversight is needed to ensure that factories like Atameken work properly.

However, in a more common register, the factory embodies a present which is felt to be stable, not a system-in-formation but a fully formed system where corruption is intrinsic. Indeed, in other ethnographic accounts, the failures of new buildings undermine the straightforward temporal progression they seem to promise. Alexander (2020, 12) describes how Kurchatov locals see an unfinished nuclear technopark, supposed to embody a positive nuclear future, as a 'ruin', aligning it with the wastes of the Soviet past. Atameken's finished form does successfully break with the Soviet past. However, the frustration of the promised future speaks of a wasted present that contrasts negatively with the positive memories of the ruined enterprises that we saw in Chapter 3. For Laszczowski's (2016) informants in Astana, while shiny new buildings exude positive affects that are enrolled in the 'propaganda of emotion', binding the nation-state together around the capital, these same buildings also carry affects of sterility and fakeness that imbue the emergent political reality with instability. In the case of Atameken, there is rather an affective dissonance between the hope exuded by the building's exterior and the knowledge of the emptiness inside, which speaks of a disordered present; a dissonance between the factory's promise to put Aral'sk on the map of global Kazakhstan and the failed connection between the town and sea, the failure of the restored sea to integrate the town into wider economic spaces.

Indeed, the disordered present can point towards a darker future, as when I was talking to my landlady Ornyq, who told me about some Russian businessmen who had stayed with her four years earlier. There were lots of fish then, she said. I was surprised and asked if there were not plenty of fish now. She gave a dismissive click. Why are there not fish now? I asked. Because, she replied swiftly and confidently, they divided the sea up, and now they just fish and fish, only thinking about money. In a lull in her tirade, I said that the future of the industry was a key question for my research, at which she said instantly: 'There is no future.' She blamed the absence of the state: there should be a state factory, state control. I said something about the inspectors, but she was dismissive: you just take a licence, and fish and fish; some just get a licence because their cousin is a minister, and there is no control – everyone only thinks about money. She concluded by noting that there is corruption everywhere – Africa, France and especially in Kazakhstan. While Ornyq's pessimistic account was contradicted by evidence of growing catches, the connections she made – between money, corruption and environmental degradation – were not unusual in Aral'sk, and find particular expression in discussions of *ekologiia*.

Ekologiia and money

Soon after returning to Aral'sk in June 2013, not long before the filmed tour of the town, I had been looking round the town for myself one sunny, breezy day. My walk was cut short by the rapidly rising wind. Soon the air was thick with swirls of dust and sand whipped up from the street. Whichever way I turned, the wind blew directly in my face, stinging my eyes; there was sand in my mouth, nose and ears, and I felt as though I was sweating sand. Barely able to see or to direct my body in a straight line, I floundered back to my accommodation, foggily aware, through the haze, of people around me walking about their business as if as normal, faces uncovered. Indeed, locals would tell me that, as former nomads, 'we've got used to it' (Kaz.: *üirenïp kettïk*; Ru.: *my privykli*), in contrast to the Russians, who had to leave. Such moments were, however, rare during my fieldwork, as dust storms have become less frequent over the years. Even so, even on some calmer days people feel that there is something wrong with the weather, and I would often be asked if I noticed *ekologiia*. I would usually reply in the negative: after all, the many glorious sunny days were welcome to a native of 'foggy Albion', and, aware of the negative connotations of *ekologiia*, I was keen not to offend my hosts. Looking back over my fieldnotes, however, I find comments like the following from times when I was feeling low and isolated:

> As often in Aral'sk, I have this frustrating thing of feeling ill with very few or minor symptoms – hard to tell whether it's to do with the climate, the food[6] or just my general feeling of discontent.

Many of my informants struggled with similar questions. Serious illnesses – problems with lungs, kidneys or stomach – are readily ascribed to *ekologiia*, but with milder conditions too, headaches or even low mood, *ekologiia* is often posited as the cause. Yet for others, who feel healthy, the environment does not exert such agency, and sometimes, keen to dispel the stigma that comes with it, they question whether *ekologiia* exists. Affect, after all, is indeterminate: material agency is relational, affecting different bodies in different ways. Because of this indeterminacy, *ekologiia* is shrouded in ambiguity and uncertainty. The agency of matter, a theoretical question for social scientists, is also a question of acute concern to my informants. It is in how people make sense of *ekologiia*'s impact on their bodies, I suggest, that local subjectivities emerge.

Below, I sketch out the everyday lives of some key informants in Aral'sk, showing how *ekologiia* affects their lives and how they talk about it. In most everyday usage, *ekologiia* is explained not by the sea's regression but by the rocket launches from Baikonur. Although kidney problems are also related to the polluted water which inhabitants drank for decades (Elpiner 1999), it is more common to blame present problems in the atmosphere. After all, clean drinking water has been available in Aral'sk since 1990, and was piped to individual households in the late 1990s. Amid concerns about broken connections and threatened integrity, drinking water infrastructure created a powerful new connection between state and citizens. But such connections are noticed when they are broken, as Alexander (2007) finds when infrastructure was privatised in 1990s Almaty. They attract less comment when they are present, as 'matters of fact', predictable in their effects (Latour 2004). *Ekologiia* is a problem in the present: the dust particles are a 'matter of concern' – unknowable, beyond control, with no clear delineation of cause and effect.

As a matter of concern, fuzzy around the edges, *ekologiia* is inseparable from the concerns about integrity that we saw above. After all, environmental problems and the political-economic transformations of post-Soviet Kazakhstan intersect in their effects on individual bodies. In Alexander's (2009a) account of Almaty in the chaotic move away from state socialism in the 1990s, she describes how scandals connect influxes of foreign companies, rural migrants and viral infections, the discursive connections between them suggesting a homology between the economic and the ecological. Similarly here, as the unseen circulation of money and commodities materially shapes everyday social relations, and as unseen materialities affect individual bodies, *ekologiia* is experienced as already connected with concerns about money and corruption.

Ecological citizenship

Sasha and Svetlana Mikhailovna[7] live in a house near the station, where they have a flourishing kitchen garden. They have three children, two in Togliatti and one in Almaty. The daughter in Almaty is a successful journalist, while the daughter in Togliatti is undergoing financial difficulties, and some of the money from my rent was sent to help her out. Svetlana Mikhailovna worked in a nursery, and has received her pension since retirement, but does not feel that its value matches the labour she gave the state over the years – nor does it match the ever-rising cost of everyday goods. When the region was declared an *ekologicheskii raion*, retirement age was lowered, but this was cancelled on independence, so she had to continue working. Sasha kept working in the shipyard until it went bankrupt in 1995 when he was 45. From then until he could draw his pension in 2013, his only income was from repairing car batteries, for which he is known around town as *akkumuliator Sasha*; he claims that people trust him more than they would a Kazakh to do a good job.

While they do not have relatives in the town, both Sasha and Svetlana Mikhailovna talk about how respected they are, and the importance of mutual aid, which they relate to Kazakh hospitality, implicitly opposing this to the uncaring state. They are invited to Kazakh festivals like Nauryz, and reciprocate at Russian holidays. When I first arrived to stay, neighbours were helping Sasha get coal in for the winter, which was rewarded with a drinking session. Sometimes their friends help pay for medicine. A neighbour sometimes assists them by printing official documents, which may be reciprocated with fish. Indeed, fish play an important role in maintaining these relationships. Sasha is renowned for curing roach, bream, sabrefish and so on, and for making *khe*, a Korean fish salad; he sends some to their daughters, but most is for renewing relations with friends around Aral'sk. Sasha still goes hunting and fishing whenever possible, departing with gun, rubber boat and vodka, and returning with game and fish. He also relies on fishermen friends in villages, including Tolpash in Bögen. On one occasion a rather tipsy Sasha told me at length how Tolpash had sent them fish; if in the future Tolpash was not fishing for some reason, Sasha would send him a sack of flour: 'Exchange (*obmen*) … that's how we live.' But if, he went on, rubbing his fingers together, Tolpash had to go to the *kommersanty* in the village, then it would be expensive. Sasha would often use Tolpash as an example of the immorality and exploitation in the current fisheries. In his accounts of such everyday practices, Sasha contrasted relationships of delayed reciprocity with those mediated by monetary exchange.

While the couple painted a rosy picture of their integration into the town, the support they received was necessarily limited. Help could be rallied getting the coal in, but the cost of coal would eat up a month's pension. In the past they have had electricity and phone cut off for nonpayment. Furthermore, while giving fish is important for maintaining reciprocal relations, getting hold of fish is not straightforward, but dependent on help from acquaintances. My research needs were a help here: a few times my *komandirovochnye raskhody* (business-trip expenses) covered trips for both of us to go to Tastübek.[8] Once, I paid Sasha's acquaintance Almatbek to take us in his UAZ, a trip which highlighted Sasha's dependence. His friend in Tastübek had moved to Aral'sk and, like me, Sasha was awkward about demanding fish from people he did not know. We had to rely on the self-confident Almatbek, who had relatives in the village, to get people to give us fish. Thus, through Almatbek's social capital, we returned to Aral'sk with a good haul, to be divided evenly between Almatbek and Sasha. However, back in Aral'sk, before the fish were divided up, neighbours and relatives of Almatbek took their share before the division was made. At that point, the larger fish all went to Almatbek.

Neither Sasha nor Svetlana Mikhailovna is in good health. Sasha's troubles date from a motorcycle accident on a hunting trip, when he dislocated his shoulder. Svetlana Mikhailovna has extensive kidney problems, which she blames on drinking polluted water in the past, and she recently underwent a month's private treatment in Almaty, paid for by their journalist daughter. They are also sensitive to the health problems of others: Sasha will greet people in Kazakh with elaborate enquiries about their health. Svetlana Mikhailovna drinks milk for her health. She and Sasha used to buy it from trusted neighbours, but as these neighbours no longer keep cows, they buy from more distant sellers, who water the milk down. They have told the sellers, and asked if they are not ashamed ('Allah is watching'), but to no avail. Svetlana Mikhailovna characterises this as 'robbery' (*voruiut*), the same idiom she and Sasha use to talk about the behaviour of high-up officials. As corruption impinges on local society, it affects Svetlana Mikhailovna's own bodily wellbeing.

Svetlana Mikhailovna talks about how *ekologiia* affects her on a daily basis. Whenever a rocket is launched, she notes wearily that the weather has changed, a headache has started and her blood pressure has gone up. As she once explained to me, the sea used to absorb the pollutants in the air, but without the sea, there is no greenery, and no natural filtration. She continued that no one grew anything because Kazakhs are lazy, there was just bare steppe (*golaia step'*), and that is why it was made an *ekologicheskii raion*, and the pension age was set at 55 for women – the provision that was cancelled after the Soviet collapse, leaving her to work for several more years.

Svetlana Mikhailovna's complaints echo the Russian tradition of cosmic forces arrayed against the hapless individual, and she frequently argues on the phone with pensioner friends in Russia about how much worse her lot is than theirs. They also draw on Soviet understandings of the proper relation between state and citizen. For Svetlana Mikhailovna, the term *ekologicheskii raion* implies rights and entitlements accruing to its inhabitants, a sort of 'ecological citizenship' resembling the 'biological citizenship' afforded to Chernobyl victims who could prove a connection between cancer and radiation (Petryna 2002). However, the *ekologicheskii raion* only entails extra salary for state employees. It does not entail an addition to Svetlana Mikhailovna's pension, or any recognition of her health problems, in contrast to the Chernobyl case. Her outlook is one of certainty: epistemological certainty that *ekologiia* exists and is responsible for her ill health, and moral certainty that the state is failing to honour its obligations towards her.[9] Environmental affects, corporeally felt, shape Svetlana Mikhailovna's subjectivity as they are apprehended as *ekologiia*, with its connotations of victimhood, rights and entitlements. The headache and rising blood pressure she feels when rockets go off are bodily reminders of her victimhood, of a world set against her.

'Ekologiia must be everywhere'

Ornyq works in school administration. Her husband Samat is a veterinary inspector, for which he is assigned a Niva (Lada four-by-four), and their unmarried son Zhakön works in the land registry in the akimat. Ornyq has two sisters and a brother, and their households are closely connected, often sharing meals and childcare. Her brother, Ertai, in his fifties, retired early as an invalid, suffering from kidney problems, like Svetlana Mikhailovna and many others. The *kelïn* (daughter-in-law) in Ertai's household is roped into household duties for all the siblings, especially when guests are round. While the immediate family is close-knit, Ornyq complains about the financial obligations towards more distant kin at ritual occasions. Ertai recently took out a major loan for his daughter's wedding, and told me ruefully about the competitive aspect of ritual expenditure.

Although all three household members work, like everyone else Ornyq talks a lot about financial constraints, especially the impossibility of saving. In late perestroika, they had been saving up for a prestigious Volga, but when newly independent Kazakhstan switched from the rouble to the tenge, their money became worthless – since then, she said, they have not trusted banks. The family recently purchased an Audi on credit; they are paying back 40,000 KZT a month. While the Niva is used for Samat's work, the Audi is a status marker for the family. Whenever possible, Zhakön drives very fast around Aral'sk with his friends listening to Enrique Iglesias at full volume. However, he is also at his mother's beck and call, driving her every day to and from work, and he may be called upon late into the evening to buy her beer and sunflower seeds (*semechki*). Once the debt for the Audi is paid off, they plan to install a septic tank for an indoor bathroom.

Because of the credit repayment schedule, the household's finances were stretched. A further complication emerged while I was there: Ornyq had, unbeknown to Samat, lent 150,000 KZT to her sister's colleague, who had lent it to another woman whom Ornyq did not know. When the debtor had trouble repaying the money, Ornyq spent the evening on the phone to both women applying as much pressure as possible. The whole episode gave her a severe headache and sent her blood pressure (*davlenie*) up. The situation was resolved in the end, though I am not sure how. As such loans allow people to avoid the punitive rates of commercial lenders, money, as in other postsocialist settings, does not weaken social networks but puts them to new uses (Ledeneva 2006; McGuire 2014; Wanner 2005). However, because of the complication that arose when the money was lent outside Ornyq's immediate network, the effect was to corrode trust.

Samat goes on regular work trips to Qaratereng. As he cannot drive, he is driven by Ornyq's brother, Ertai. Ornyq and Ertai's mother was from Qaratereng, so these trips are a means of maintaining relations with kin in the village. Hence Ertai and Samat often return with the car laden with fresh fish, which are distributed among close kin in Aral'sk or cooked in a *besbarmaq* or *qarma*. Ornyq avoids buying fish in the market as it is overpriced and not fresh. Like many others in Aral'sk, she waxes lyrical about the quality of Aral fish and meat, emphasising the beneficial effects of the salt in both the sea and the pastures. She told me proudly how her husband is not, despite his age, wrinkled, because he drinks *sorpa* (meat stock). Local pride is thus rooted in shared meals of tasty meat and fish, as well as dairy products like *shūbat* and *qymyz*.

Alongside this positive bodily engagement with regional products, Ornyq is also acutely aware of *ekologiia*. Once she asked me over tea about health problems in the UK. I talked a bit, then asked about Aral'sk. The health in the town is bad, she said: lots of asthma because of the constant wind and dust, and lots of *davlenie* and heart disease. But then she asked if that wasn't the case all over the world. I made a noncommittal sort of noise, at which she declared that she had heard that was the case, before concluding, 'So *ekologiia* must be everywhere.' While Svetlana Mikhailovna insisted on the specificity of her fate in an *ekologicheskii raion*, Ornyq balanced her local pride with her awareness of *ekologiia* by denying that *ekologiia* singled the region out.

We talked a bit about drinking water, but our conversation was cut short by a news report on the TV showing a rocket exploding shortly after take-off, near Aral'sk. Ornyq was outraged. She told me angrily how this had happened last year too. Her relatives nearer Baikonur had seen a cloud of smoke, and immediately everyone's blood pressure went up. The Kazakhstan government insisted that there was no risk to health. 'But they get paid €50 million a year,' she pointed out cynically, 'and of course, that's all money in the pocket (Ru.: *den'gi v karmane*).' She then told me again how everyone in Aral'sk has high blood pressure, saying how her brother Ertai had recently collapsed, and had been lucky to survive.

As with remarks about Chinese goods infecting Kazakh children, national and bodily integrity are at stake. However, while the remarks about China were based on lurid rumour, this was rooted in direct experience: the dramatic newsflash broadcast across her kitchen, and her brother's health crisis. But much too is opaque: the high-level circulation of money and the unseen environmental forces. As Ornyq posits connections between official corruption, ecological damage and personal health, the integrity of Kazakh national territory is threatened by a corrupt government leasing out land to Russia, which threatens the local environment and her brother's bodily health. If '*ekologiia* is everywhere' downplayed the capacity of the environment to mark the region out as cursed, here the shared experience of *davlenie*, entangled in a discourse about rockets and national betrayal, shapes an intersubjective sense of a region vulnerable to outside forces.

'Everything now depends on money'

Elmira and Samalbek are in their late thirties. Elmira was born in Qyzylorda but moved to Aral'sk in 1990 as her parents divorced and her mother was from Aral'sk. Samalbek's father is from Tastübek and now works in Atyrau, on the Caspian, in a state organ, but will return to his *tughan zher* on his retirement. Elmira's time is full looking after their six children; Samalbek works for the railway as a security guard. The family used to put tourists up via a contact in the NGO; during my fieldwork they were supplementing their income by housing an engineer working on the Western China to Western Europe road. He lived in the house, while they were squashed into the *sarai* (shed or summer quarters). Samalbek has recently upgraded to a newer and larger UAZ, with which he maintains close contact with his cousin Qydyrbai in Tastübek, who is a source of fish, camel meat, fermented camel milk (*shūbat*), saiga antelope meat and seagull eggs.[10]

Samalbek has two brothers and an older sister, Mira. She and her husband Zhūmakhan, the son of a former fisherman, are both religiously observant, saying namaz (ritual prayers), and fasting in Ramadan; he attends mosque every Friday. When the two families share a *besburmaq*, Zhūmakhan is called on to say a prayer. Mira has a law degree from an Almaty university, but has chosen to devote her time to childcare. Zhūmakhan was offered shift work in a Chinese company, but it would have cost him a bribe of 90,000 KZT.[11] He refused, he said, on religious grounds, but also because he would need credit to pay the bribe. Zhūmakhan once told me how his ancestors had fled to Karakalpakstan during the famine, but he concluded his narrative by saying that, despite the repression, Stalinist times were better than today, because there was work, and you did not need to pay a bribe to get it. So Zhūmakhan works informally as a welder, mostly making doors and gates. Materials are brought by bus from a depot in Türkïstan, south of Qyzylorda, but as all metal is priced the same, he has to be on the lookout for metal which is *brak* ('waste, defective materials') or *kitaiskii* ('Chinese').

Mira and Zhūmakhan's children, like Samalbek and Elmira's, study in a Russian-language school, which is oversubscribed, economic opportunity being felt to depend on Russian language. The family watch Russian TV, and Zhūmakhan talks about the whole family moving to Russia, where he thinks there are more economic opportunities. However, if Mira and Zhūmakhan's situation is insecure given the instability of his work, they are bolstered by their relationship with Samalbek. Indeed, during my fieldwork Mira and Zhūmakhan moved to a larger house, for which Samalbek gathered a loan from all his neighbours. Unlike the corrosion of trust that took place with Ornyq's loan, this seemed more successful, at least for as long as I was there.

Mira and Zhūmakhan's daughter has Marfan syndrome, a growth disorder, and Mira speculates as to whether *ekologiia* is the cause, which seems unlikely as it is genetic. They receive some state support for medical bills, and Mira stresses that she is grateful to Allah that they are alive today when such medical care is available. Mira herself often feels tired and unwell, and wonders if *ekologiia* is behind this. After all, the wind blows from spring and all through the summer, whipping up sandstorms that 'irritate us all': 'We think that *ekologiia* acts, but we don't know … Allah knows.'

One Friday I was having lunch with Mira, when Samalbek came round with some fish from Tastübek. Samalbek teased his sister by expressing surprise that they had a foreigner for lunch on a Friday. After some banter, he declared that he preferred whatever faith would allow him to make money, at which his sister hit him with a rolled-up magazine. Over lunch Samalbek asked with interest whether I noticed *ekologiia*. I said that I wasn't particularly aware of it, and asked him what he thought. He talked about the extreme summer heat and winter cold, but did not attach much importance to it. I asked if it was worse when they were younger. He responded that they had not noticed anything. Then after a pause, he told me, part-reflectively, part-humorously (with a good deal of showing off to his giggling sister), how, when they were little, they would play all day long outside (no TVs or computers back then!); when they fell and cut themselves, they did not have time to go inside, so they would just sprinkle some sand on it and carry on playing – and they would heal. But at some point, he said, the sand 'lost its quality', perhaps because of *ekologiia*. Evidently, the siblings' different ways of speculating about *ekologiia* relate to their differing bodily engagement with the environment. The time Samalbek spends outdoors in Tastübek with his cousin precludes a sense of pollution or ruination, while Mira, spending most of her time indoors, is more sensitive to the irritation of the weather.

After this I asked whether they had seen TV programmes in the 1990s which showed Aral'sk as the epicentre of an ecological disaster. They had – and were unimpressed. Samalbek said scornfully that you can find impoverished *babushki* (Ru.: 'grandmothers') everywhere in the world. Of course there are a few in Aral'sk, so the film-makers picked on them, waited three or four days for a sandstorm and then made their film. While not denying that sandstorms happen, Samalbek questioned how such material effects are enrolled in a discourse of catastrophe, a discourse which itself threatens the integrity of the region in which he feels pride. At this, Mira interjected that deformed children are sometimes born in the maternity hospital – that is so scary, she said. Samalbek instantly replied that such things happen everywhere. Justifying his assertion, he first cited the Nuclear Polygon in Eastern Kazakhstan, but then said that they happen everywhere. Mira agreed at once, saying: 'Yes, because nowadays everything depends on money.' Samalbek concurred, and a heated discussion ensued, largely about people being paid to donate blood.

The citation of the Nuclear Polygon suggests a link to critiques about Kazakh territory being used as *terra nullius* for Soviet projects. Instead, the conversation veered into more global issues. After all, this conversation occurred more than two decades after the end of the USSR, at a time imbued with global crises shaped by new geopolitical ambiguities. As with Ornyq's '*ekologiia* must be everywhere', the generalisation away from the local signals a refusal to single the region out. Strikingly, while Samalbek and Mira differed in their bodily feeling of the weather, and thus in their speculation about *ekologiia*, they concurred about money. If *ekologiia* is indeterminate in its affects, money is an ever-present concern in everyone's everyday life – even if much of its circulation is unseen and unknowable.

Ethnographers of postsocialist societies have suggested that discourse about the corrosive effects of money, including rumours and conspiracy theories, is a means of coming to terms with what money is under capitalism (Oushakine 2009; Ries 2002; Verdery 1996, Chapter 7). For Oushakine (2009, 90), people living through postsocialist transformations fail to see money as a medium of exchange or a store of value, taking it instead 'as a condensed metaphor of change itself'. Yet, in post-Soviet Kazakhstan, which has seen major bouts of inflation and devaluation of currency, money is hardly a reliable store of value. Nor is money an abstract, impersonal medium of exchange; rather, it is tangled up with informal interpersonal relations, from the ritual economy through various shades of grey to straightforward bribery (Humphrey 2002, Chapter 6; Humphrey and Sneath 2004; Ledeneva 2006; McGuire 2014; Rigi 2004; Wanner 2008).

In such contexts, money is not a metaphor but a metonym of change. It is one tangible facet, present in everyday life, of opaque and incomprehensible change at different scales, which has reshaped spaces and transformed moral orders – and, as such, it is money that is used to reason about such change, as a pressing local concern that also ties the region into volatile global market relations. It is in this sense, I think, that we should approach Mira's 'Because nowadays everything depends on money'. Within this worldview, *ekologiia*, as a threat to bodily integrity, is not specific to Aral'sk, or indeed to Kazakhstan, as a toxic legacy of Soviet-era dispossessions; rather, it is symptomatic – through unspecified, inferred connections – of a new world order for which money is a metonym.

The spectre of oil

If Mira and Samalbek were doubtful, others deny that *ekologiia* exists altogether. Daniiar, whom we met in Chapter 3 bringing fish from all corners of the USSR, regularly goes on illicit fishing trips (Figure 7.3). As he keeps this fish for personal consumption or to help out friends like Sasha, he characterises these trips as strictly moral, while the formal fishery is, like everything else in Daniiar's vision of the contemporary world, scored with greed and corruption. In his seventies, Daniiar is in rude health, and is particularly strident about the absence of *ekologiia*, arguing, with some justification, that the prevailing wind is from the north, so most of the dust and salt from the dried-up seabed is blown away to the south. In Almaty, by contrast, the air is dirty and water recycled. Again, the integrity of the local is at stake, threatened not by *ekologiia* itself but by the discourse about it. When I asked him about the characterisation of Aral'sk as a disaster zone, he replied furiously:

> When they start extracting oil from here, *then* it will be catastrophe … in Atyrau – have you been there? There aren't even ants there, not just no birds, there aren't even ants, no ants; not just no cockroaches, NO ANTS! My relative lives there, and I look – there *aren't even ants*, THOSE are catastrophic effects … dirty … the atmosphere …

'But no one talks about that,' I murmured. He went on: 'But of course, it's just money money money, they don't think about their own health, just money money money.' Not only is pollution elsewhere: it is also a threatened future, where lust for money threatens the integrity of nature and human health. If mainstream narratives link the Aral catastrophe to Soviet socialism, Daniiar turns this on its head by putting disaster discourse into dialogue with Soviet moralising about the evils of money.

Daniiar is not alone in fearing that oil will threaten the integrity of the local environment; nor is he alone in mixing this with the money motive. For some, concern about oil is embedded in worries about Kazakhstan's relationship with other countries, especially China. For Zhūmakhan, oil extraction will turn Aral'sk into a truly *ekologicheskii raion*; when that happens, the family will have to leave. However, this is not the only way of thinking about oil. In 2002 NGO workers asked schoolchildren to draw the past, present and future of the Aral region. For the past, they imagined the sea full; the present showed dried-up seabed, skeletons of fish and rusting ships; their visions of the future included a

Figure 7.3 Daniiar, with dried fish, autumn 2013. Source: author.

full sea, but also oil rigs, and Aral'sk was a thriving town full of large buildings. Unlike Daniiar's apocalyptic vision, the children imagined oil as part of a possible bright future for the town. The exercise of making schoolchildren draw past, present and future was repeated while I was there. This time there were no oil rigs. Indeed, I did not hear much about oil while I was there: if rumours and media reports had been rife 10 years previously, they were not when I was there, and oil was imagined, in all its ambivalence, elsewhere.

Bright futures

Ecological change, as we have seen throughout this book, does not come alone. Entangled with a market marked by invisibility and intrigue, the sea's return has had variegated effects, and modernist assumptions that fish will bring a high-employment industry are confounded by the opaque realities of a financially constrained fishery. When invisible particles impinge on bodily health at the same time as unseen flows of money and commodities reproduce Aral'sk's marginality, modes of apprehending the two are connected. The ethnography above casts light on the relationship between ecological affects and local subjectivities. *Ekologiia*, its affects felt in the body, shapes subjectivities through its discursive entanglements, as we saw with Svetlana Mikhailovna's headaches that speak of failed ecological citizenship, or the widespread *davlenie* that, for Ornyq, signals local vulnerability to high-level corruption. At the same time, local pride is rooted in the shared pleasures of consuming Aral fish, meat and dairy products, which are felt to sustain local health. This pride is threatened not only by the bodily experience of *ekologiia*, but also by the stigmatising discourse about it. After all, if, following Bakhtin, discourse is rooted in material social encounters, then discourse too has the capacity to generate negative affects – hence Samalbek's disgust at the films portraying ecological catastrophe.

Both the ecological and the economic define, in different ways, people's place in the world. If living with indeterminacy is to occupy the ambiguous space between waste and value (Alexander and Sanchez 2019), then both *ekologiia* and economic marginalisation pose the question of whether people can live worthwhile lives in Aral'sk. The unseen particles, indeterminate in their agency, and opaque flows of money and commodities together threaten the integrity of the local. Financial insecurity; corrosions of trust; dust in the air; health problems in the body – all are real, but the connections between them are unclear, and the sorts of connections that are made speak of the worldviews with which people negotiate indeterminacy. As my informants grapple with *ekologiia*, questioning its existence or generalising it away from Aral'sk, they assert the value of the local even as they lament its marginalisation within a new world order dominated by money.

The tour with which I opened the chapter and the children's drawings of the future suggest a different mode of imagining Aral'sk, as a site of pride and global interest, without the stigma attached. Although the 2013 depictions of the future did not include oil rigs, many included large modern buildings, including Atameken (Figure 7.4). While I was there, there was also a competition for pupils to think of ways to attract tourists to the town. Most of the projects explained the Aral Sea disaster (*apat*) in terms strikingly similar to the global discourse, though devoid of moral or political content, with at least one drawing on Wikipedia. Their descriptions also avoided the late Soviet fishery that older generations dwell so much on. Local history was felt to be of interest to visitors – but only distant history, not Soviet history. Overall, responses expressed pride and optimism for the region, and many went beyond their brief to imagine a future where unemployment was eliminated through development of light industry, food processing and local crafts. The fishing industry, in the form of Atameken, was present in just one

Figure 7.4 Child's representation of the future, November 2013. Source: author.

presentation. Recent developments in the region – new buildings and monuments in Aral'sk, the Western China to Western Europe road – were included as sources of hope, new connections that would put Aral'sk firmly on the map.

If these imaginings – geared, of course, to the teachers' expectations – represented a town with its economic problems eliminated, some pupils also expressed hope that the stigma attached to the ecological problems for which Aral'sk is known will go away. Most, however, ignored the region's negative connotations altogether, focusing instead on its health benefits – the warm waters of Qamystybas (very few suggested taking tourists to the sea itself); hot springs at Aqespe and Aqbasty; the healing properties of wormwood from the steppe, and of dairy products like *shūbat, qymyz* and *qūrt*. Overall, these projects imagined a future free of the economic and ecological problems that preoccupy so much of the discourse of the town today.

Notes

1 Cf. Mazzarella (2009) and Navaro-Yashin (2012), for whom earlier theorists' insistence that affect is prediscursive and presocial (e.g. Massumi 1995) reinscribes the very mind–body dualism that they purport to overcome.
2 Previously the currency had been devalued in 2009 after the financial crisis. In an economy based on raw commodities, such moves render Kazakhstan's exports competitive, including, as we saw in Chapter 6, zander, while having crippling effects on imported consumer goods.
3 Formally, the factory is no longer called Atameken, but it is still known as such across the town.
4 See Naumova (2012) and Timirkhanov et al. (2010) on the opacity of the tender process.
5 In 2012 the quota for zander was 407 tonnes, out of a total of 4,105 tonnes.
6 Unlike my informants, I found that my body struggled with the diet of fatty, salty meat.
7 Around Aral'sk, Sasha is referred to by the short form of his name, sometimes with a respectful Kazakh ending, 'Sake', while Svetlana Mikhailovna is known by her full name with patronymic.
8 Sasha wanted to complete my expenses claims by *pripiska*, having ample experience of *komandirovki* from when he worked in the shipyard. As the ESRC research allowance constituted a 'hard budget restraint' (Kornai 1978), I felt compelled to refuse.
9 Werner and Purvis-Roberts (2014) find a similar gap between the meagre entitlements for victims of nuclear testing in East Kazakhstan and state narratives which endorse their victimhood.
10 I never saw anyone but Qydyrbai eat seagull eggs, which are tasty, but with a strong odour of fish.
11 For this combination of informal, personalised relations and financial transactions in post-Soviet Kazakhstan, see Oka (2015), Rigi (2004) and Werner (2000).

Conclusion

Large-scale environmental disasters seem to strike with a singular force. When the earthquake or tsunami hits, everyone is affected. These are moments of clarity: as different people are affected to different degrees, the 'revelatory crisis' lays bare structural inequalities, revealing a truth about society (Hoffman and Oliver-Smith 2002). Such, for a few years during perestroika, was the Aral Sea catastrophe: a revelatory crisis that laid bare the failings of the Soviet state. Yet the sea's regression was not given in advance as a catastrophe. Its emergence as catastrophe in the 1980s, culturally recognisable in a distinctively Russian eschatological tradition, took painstaking efforts by activists and scientists, forcing the dried-up seabed and rusting ships into public view. Once established as a catastrophe, it assumed political agency, mobilising protest and hope for systemic change. This formation, however, was not stable. Following the marginalisation of environmental issues in late perestroika and the Soviet collapse, the 'dead' sea became associated with the defunct Soviet project. What the 'revelatory crisis' reveals depends on who is looking.

Entangled in post-Cold War power relations, the same material effects that had constituted catastrophe-as-utopian-hope became disaster-as-vehicle-for-development. Much was obscured from the disaster-as-vehicle-for-development – not least the economic unravelling of post-Soviet space – but in this form too, the Aral assumed political agency, mobilising projects, including, ultimately, the Kökaral dam. We can predict, to varying degrees, material changes in the environment; but what environmental change will become as it is caught up in historical processes is not given in advance, nor will it act in a unitary way.

Indeed, throughout the book, the Aral has emerged as a multiple object, entangled in diverse sets of relations. As a source of unexploited natural wealth, it 'necessitated' the development of infrastructure, sedentarisation and deportations that would maximise labour resources, serving progress through the quantitative growth of fish production. Yet, simultaneously, within the same modernist paradigm, it was an obstacle to progress, a natural aberration, an embarrassing detail on the margins of Soviet Central Asia, its expansive surface area allowing evaporation that wasted precious water resources which could have been used productively in agriculture.

These two 'versions' of the Aral were not equal: the-Aral-as-aberration was sustained by more powerful interests. Again, before the Aral burst into public view during perestroika as a catastrophe, the same material effects, interfering with the interests of regional bosses and fisheries managers, had been a bureaucratic 'problem' of employment and living standards. Precisely because of the dominance of the-Aral-as-aberration, the fact of the regression was sustained as limited, which relied on determined ignorance/ignoring: the crisis could not reveal much if no one was looking. Indeed, this bureaucratic problem was both fact and fiction, as we saw in Chapter 2 when the sharp discrepancy between the limitedness of the bureaucratic fact and the escalating problems experienced by the local population erupted in an angry letter to Gosbank. And yet, even this limited, obfuscatory fact assumed agency: the infrastructural developments and reorganisation of the fishery that it entailed would prove materially consequential for local people so that, looking back, the 1970s and 1980s were not 'catastrophic', but a time of 'Communism'. After all, those around the Aral's shores were part of the entanglement that constituted the-sea-as-economic-value, and through it they were integrated into gridded Soviet space, with its modernist promises of progress. For those who stayed after the sea retreated, the maintenance of the relationship between fishermen, fishing and the state afforded a level of continuity despite the sea's devastating demise.

The Aral thus provides an apt site for re-examining arguments about the emergence of natural entities as multiple. The versions of the Soviet Aral that emerged within different entanglements may all have been real to those caught up in those entanglements, but they were not equal, nor were they equally true. Similarly, the postsocialist sea is both an object of management and a source of economic value. As an object of management, the sea is entangled with virtual fish, regulations, scientists and inspectors; and when virtual fish mediate between nature users and the state, they have, as Lien (2015) would argue, real effects that are irreducible to their status as abstractions. However, the-sea-as-object-of-management is always subordinated to the-sea-as-economic-value, so that virtual fish are both fact and fiction. Their fictional quality itself has real consequences, undermining trust in the system – and shaping an opaque circulation of fish that largely bypasses factories in Aral'sk.

As an object of economic value, the postsocialist sea differs from the Soviet sea that retreated. Abstracted in the gridded time-space of the plan, fish's value was stable and connected with social entitlements, whereas within the flexible time-space of the market, there is limited connection between fishermen and the state, while value varies according to the spatial reach of the commodity fish, and fluctuates over time – hence the present limitless demand for zander. However, to locals, the sea is not just an object of economic value, but also part of *tughan zher*, the sustaining centre that fed 'all people' and saved them from famine. It is in the intersection between *tughan zher* and the-sea-as-economic-value that, where the retreating sea had seen a measure of continuity, the returning sea drives social change. In Chapter 6, I pointed to transformations in the ritual economy that sustains *tughan zher*: as zander monetise the practices of social reproduction, social relations are differentiated as they are reproduced. It is not just the shift from a socialist to a postsocialist sea that matters, but the articulation of this shift with the time-space of *tughan zher*.

Getting used to slow violence

In his account of the 'slow violence' of environmental degradation in the global South, Nixon (2011, 8) calls for environmentalists to interrogate the 'post' in terms like 'postcolonial', 'postindustrial', 'post-Cold War': 'For if the past of slow violence is never past, so too the post is never fully post: industrial particulates and effluents live on in the environmental elements we inhabit and in our very bodies, which are epidemiologically and ecologically never our simple contemporaries.' Alexander (2020) makes a similar argument regarding nuclear pasts in Kurchatov: the material Soviet legacy is not readily contained in the past. However, Nixon leaves open the indeterminacy of material legacies of slow violence. The salt particles lingering in the air from Soviet ruination, the kidneys damaged by polluted drinking water: these are not 'simple contemporaries' of my informants' subjective lives. We are not determined by our environments or our bodies. If the material legacies of past slow violence continue to exert agency in the present, the agency of these 'environmental elements' is entangled with the layers of social, economic and political change in between. The ethnography in the last chapter showed how subjectivities emerged at the intersection between the materiality of the post-Soviet environment and contemporary material conditions of economic insecurity.

Similarly to Stawkowski's (2016) self-professed 'radioactive mutants' claiming to have adapted to radiation, Aral residents claim 'we've got used to' (Kaz.: *üirenïp kettïk*; Ru.: *my privykli*) dust storms and other problems connected with the sea's regression. The word *üireny* literally means 'to learn', and my informants claim that it was their nomadic heritage that helped them adapt – whereas other nationalities had to move away. They seem to highlight a capacity for adaptation and resilience, key concerns in the social science of environmental change (e.g. Adger 2000; Crate and Nuttall 2009). Chapters 2 and 4 brought a new perspective to this literature, suggesting that local resilience depended on, though was not reducible to, the top-down adaptation of the Soviet state. Here, however, I elaborate a rather different perspective on adaptation. Critiquing the focus in much resilience literature on bounded socioecological systems, Hastrup (2009) remarks that local worlds, never the bounded entities they were once assumed to be, are, especially amid large-scale environmental change, increasingly 'perforated'. Resilience, then, is not just about 'practical' adaptation, but also 'a conceptual flexibility in perceiving the temporality or degree of "eventness" of the disaster as variable and contingent' (Hastrup 2009, 28).

For my informants in Aral'sk, the local today is 'perforated' not only by particles of salt found as far away as Japan, but also by the Chinese nets, by the rusting ships – local heritage – exported for scrap, by the stigmatising discourse of *ekologiia*. If, however, these anxieties carry within them a yearning for a more bounded local, this local is not some 'pure' pre-Soviet or precolonial identity, but a local that has been remade repeatedly as inhabitants have got used to, learnt to cope with, multiple perforations. Cast out as waste by the cotton-based project of Soviet modernity in Central Asia, superfluous to the extractive projects of Kazakhstan's contemporary oil economy, inhabitants of Aral'sk occupy an indeterminate space that threatens to become a wasteland (Alexander and Sanchez 2019). To the outside eye, the Aral regression stands out spectacularly, but it came close on the heels of colonial dispossession, collectivisation and famine, mass deportations and two world wars. There was plenty to 'get used to' in twentieth-century Kazakhstan. In Chapter 4, we saw how traumatic memories of collectivisation were not transmitted, arguably a form of 'getting used to' new realities.[1]

Soviet uneven development marginalised the Aral, leaving it vulnerable to the myopia of the cotton vision. Yet the nostalgic discourses we examined in Chapter 3 reconstitute a bounded, knowable Soviet past, sealing off or domesticating, as far as possible, the destabilising memories of the 'bad' Soviet past. The remembered integrity of the local rests on memories of ocean fish integrating Aral'sk into Soviet gridded space, materialising the social contract. After all, when the grid disintegrated, Aral'sk was marginalised anew and subject to new forms of perforation. Recall Ornyq's dreamy vision of the sea returning to the town in Chapter 3: the beach lined with tourists, the factory siren sending people off to proper jobs – in this vision, suspended between past memory and future dream, Aral'sk is made whole (again), secure in its place in the world.

I want to suggest, then, that we rethink the notion of adaptation as the messy, never finished process of 'getting used to' multiple, overlapping processes of perforation that remake local worlds. The sea's retreat and, from the perspective of Aral'sk, failed return is just one form of perforation. As my ethnography has shown, getting used to the material legacies of slow violence is inseparable from getting used to large-scale political-economic transformations. Nostalgic reconstructions of a past when things were whole, despite the ecological devastation, are arguably part of Hastrup's (2009) 'conceptual flexibility'. So too are the discussions and speculations about *ekologiia*. When Mira and Samalbek cast *ekologiia* not as a toxic post-Soviet legacy, but as a symptom of a corrupt contemporary world governed by money, they were perhaps making the claim that there is no further need to get used to the toxic legacy of the Soviet system; it is the new world where 'everything depends on money' that we need to get used to. Note the active work that goes into this separating of times and spaces which, as Alexander (2020) shows, threaten to leak into each other. Samalbek at first put the Aral in the same comparative frame as the Nuclear Polygon, evoking the time-space of the USSR, but immediately he and Mira together generalised *ekologiia* to 'everywhere' and 'now'. This discursive ordering of material affects, times and spaces, I suggest, is part of the ongoing process of adaptation to multiple overlapping forms of change. The claim that 'we've got used to' the problems stemming from the sea's regression – we've absorbed them and integrated them into our daily lives, we've adapted – perhaps represents a claim, albeit contestable, never finalisable, that the slow violence of the past *is* truly past.

The flounder at the end of the world?

Could I, with a nod to Tsing (2015), have entitled this book 'on the possibility of life in state-socialist ruins'? At first sight, there is a parallel between the fishermen emerging from the wreckage of the socialist fishery, who caught flounder from a sea ruined by the scalable projects of Soviet agriculture, and the 'collaborative survival' Tsing describes between Southeast Asian refugees living in a post-progress USA and the matsutake mushrooms that grow in its ruined industrial forests. But on closer inspection, the parallel does not hold. For Tsing, both the matsutake and the economy of picking it are instances of nonscalable relations, ecological and economic, 'erupting' from the ruins of scalable modernity. By contrast, the introduction of flounder to the Aral was a planned, if experimental, intervention. As we saw in Chapter 2, acclimatising new species was also about scalability, about abstracting organisms from their lifeworld entanglements and placing them in new contexts. To be sure, early acclimatisations, notably of stellate sturgeon, had ruinous consequences comparable to other projects of scalability. However, later acclimatisation practices differ from Tsing's account of scalability, which is rooted in the history of the sugarcane plantation, where quantitative expansion rested on the interchangeability of planting stock, 'comparatively self-contained, oblivious to encounter' (2015, 39). They differ too from the linear expansion of Norwegian salmon farms on the basis of anchovy pellets imported from the Pacific (Lien 2015). For Soviet ichthyologists, acclimatisation, while based on utilitarian principles of scaling up the production of commodities, was premised on the encounter between the species and its new environment. Growth of fisheries, serving human progress, depended on attention to the diverse lifeworlds of fish, mussels and worms.

This is not, of course, to suggest that the science was flawless. After all, the polychaete worms introduced in the 1960s may have become part of a rich, salt-tolerant zoobenthos, but they probably also reduced biodiversity by predating midge larvae (Plotnikov 2013). Assessments of postwar acclimatisations across the USSR are frustrated by the fact that lakes were already damaged by agriculture: the science of scaling up was applied in firefighting catastrophic declines in fish populations. Nevertheless, the successful – and expected – growth of the entangled lifeworlds of flounder, mussels and worms highlights the diversity of utilitarian projects of scalability. Certainly, across Central Asia as a whole, environments have been disastrously reshaped by the scalable promises of cotton plantations. Even so, we need more thick description of projects of scalability, highlighting, as we look ahead to Anthropocenic futures, those that have *not* proceeded 'as if the entanglements of living did not matter' (Tsing 2015, 5).

There is a further, more consequential, distinction between the two ethnographic contexts. Tsing's (2015) theory of salvage accumulation provides a compelling account of how capitalist value is extracted from ruination. She separates the 'pericapitalist', nonscalable economic relations between mushrooms, pickers and buyers from the process of inventorisation through which mushrooms are commodified and value extracted, feeding circuits of capital accumulation. Analysing the exchange between buyers and pickers not as a free capitalist market but as a cultural performance of freedom, she argues that, for pickers, mushrooms are not commodities but trophies. Commodification happens later, in the factory where mushrooms are sorted and inventorised. Salvage accumulation, then, predates on pericapitalist, nonscalable economic relations. In contrast to modernist, scalable forms of labour that integrated workers into promises of progress, these mushroom hunters are left picking through the ruins of progress while value is accumulated elsewhere. They are thus emblematic of what Tsing (2015) casts as a contemporary condition of universalised precarity. If the heroes of an earlier age of anthropology were the 'primitive' peoples living in harmony with pristine nature, the heroes of the anthropology of the Anthropocene are the 'collaborative survivalists' who make a living through their entanglements with the lifeworlds of 'third nature', the ruined environments left by modernity.

Central to the theory of salvage accumulation is that commodification happens at the point of inventorisation, not before. This point is beautifully illustrated by an ethnographic detail about discarding small mushrooms. While it is formally illegal to pick them, pickers collect them anyway, and they are discarded by the factory because they are too small for consumers (Tsing 2015, 128). Yet pickers go on selling them to middlemen; after all, as Tsing argues, the 'sale' is a performance of the market, rather than pure capitalist exchange. Compare this to the episode described in Chapter 6, when a fisherman was reprimanded for selling undersized fish. As with the mushrooms, it was formally illegal to have caught juveniles, but the reprimand related to the rule of the factory: they were too small for processing. Unlike Tsing's mushroom pickers, however, the fisherman had the cost of the fish deducted from his pay. Commodification here happens earlier than the moment of inventorisation: it happens in the exchange between fishermen and receivers.

The consequences of this small difference are profound. Certainly, value is extracted elsewhere – by nature users, by intermediaries in Kazakhstan and Russia, by German supermarkets. Certainly, the fishery can be described as a 'pericapitalist' formation where economic practices are embedded in noncapitalist social relations. However, fishing families also have a stake in the value extracted, which transforms relations between people in the region, and between people and environment.

Moreover, while the grand progress metanarrative of Soviet socialism lies in the past, independent Kazakhstan holds out promises of consumerist abundance and private utopias. As the 'project of the century', the Kökaral dam is enrolled in this progress narrative and therefore carries expectations, which are haunted by the all-encompassing 'expectations of modernity'. As these promises intersect with local structures of value, zander's integration into transnational markets offers localised models of progress, whose promise is expected widely, but whose distribution is uneven.

For Tsing (2015), in a world after progress, we are all precarious. That may be so. Yet I remain troubled by Tsing's universalising framing of the anthropology of the Anthropocene. Where localised offers of advancement entangle us in different ways in capitalist relations, we are also, to varying degrees, complicit: German consumers and Kazakh fishermen both have a stake in high levels of zander fishing. Nor are we equally precarious: should zander stocks collapse, Kazakh fishermen would be much more precarious than German consumers. How precarious the zander themselves are remains to be seen. As I write, further environmental restoration is promised as SYNAS-3 gets under way, involving the two-level variant of the sea as well as further rehabilitation of lakes, so perhaps their future too is bright, at least in the near term. As for my human informants in the region, their lives are more precarious than mine, but they are doing rather more than picking through the ruins.

Notes

1   Cf. Kindler (2018, 238), who talks of 'complex processes of adaptation and psychological repression' in the silence and collective forgetting about the famine.

Appendix: sources for fish catches, 1905–80

The table below provides the sources for Figure 1.3 (page 46), which shows fish catches in tonnes in the whole Aral Sea (blue), and in the northern (Kazakh) part of the sea (red), 1905–80. The blue dotted line (1931–80) marks a curve taken from Zholdasova et al. (1998, 233; no data set provided). Data points from other sources are laid out below. The dashed lines (whole sea 1905–9; northern part 1905–30) mark informed estimates.

Years	Source for whole sea	Source for north
1899		Plotnikov et al. (2014, 56)
1909–13, 1921	'Zakliuchenie o vydelenii dolgosrochnogo kredit [sic] dlia nuzhd Aral'skogo gosrybpromyshlennosti (osnovanie: Postanovlenie EKOSO ot 23/IV – 1925 g., prot. No 71)', n.d. but 1925, AFGAKO, f. 4, op. 1, d. 8, 26–9 (26)	
1914–24	Evseev, n.d. but 1925, 'Perspektivnyi piatiletnii plan rybnoi promyshlennosti KazSSR', AFGAKO, fond 4, op. 1, d. 8, ll. 1–17 (7)	

(Continued)

(Continued)

Years	Source for whole sea	Source for north
1929–31	Brigada Obkoma VKPb i Obl KK RKI, 'Vyvody i predlozheniia brigady Obkoma i Obl KK-RKI o rezul'tatakh obsledovaniia Aralrybtresta', n.d. but 1932, AFGAKO, f. 7, op. 1, d. 12, ll. 2–12 (2)	
1930–59		'Fakticheski [sic] vylov ryby po kolkhozami [sic] Aral'skogo Rybakkolkhozsoiuza /soglasno statotcheta/', n.d. but 1960, AFGAKO, f. 4, op. 2, d. 10, l. 77
1939, 1946	Plotnikov et al. (2014, 58)	
1960, 1965, 1970	'Aral'skoe more (sovremennoe sostoianie)', n.d., TsGARK, f. 1130, op. 1, d. 1484, ll. 147–56 (148)	'Aral'skoe more (sovremennoe sostoianie)', n.d., TsGARK, f. 1130, op. 1, d. 1484, ll. 147–56 (148)
1961, 1971–80	Ermakhanov et al. (2012, 7)	
1974		Rybokombinat director K. Sarzhanov, 'Vstrechnye plany na 1975 god Aral'skogo rybokombinata Ministerstva rybnogo khoziaistva KazSSR', n.d. but 1975, AFGAKO, f. 4, op. 1, d. 491, l. 44
1975		R.S. Kuznetsova, Prilozhenie No 10 k prikazu Ministerstva rybnogo khoziaistva Kazakhskoi SSR ot 11 noiabria 1976 goda No 334, 'Ulov ryby – vsego po predpriiatiiam

(Continued)

(Continued)

Years	Source for whole sea	Source for north
		Minrybkhoza Kazakhskoi SSR na 1976–1980 gody', 11 November 1976, AFGAKO, f. 4, op. 1, d. 509, l. 54
1976		Sh.B. Baekeshev, Zakliuchenie po promezhutochnomu otchetu ob issledovaniiakh KazNIIRKha po teme No 100, 'Razrabotat' nauchnye osnovy upravliaemogo rybnogo khozhiaistva Aral'skogo moria', 5 April 1978, TsGARK, f. 1130, op. 1, d. 1898, l. 77
1977		Sh.B. Baekeshev, Zakliuchenie po promezhutochnomu otchetu ob issledovaniiakh KazNIIRKha po teme No 100, 'Razrabotat' nauchnye osnovy upravliaemogo rybnogo khozhiaistva Aral'skogo moria', 5 April 1978, TsGARK, f. 1130, op. 1, d. 1898, l. 77
1978		Letter from Minrybkhoz KazSSR to Minrybkhoz SSSR, 'Informatsiia o khode vypolneniia punkta I prikaza Ministerstva rybnogo khoziaistva SSSR ot 20 iunia 1978 No 273', 29 September 1978, TsGARK, f. 1130, op. 1, d. 1861, ll. 118–19 (119)

Bibliography

Archival documents

Central State Archive of the Republic of Kazakhstan (*Tsentral'nyi gosudarstvennyi arkhiv respubliki Kazakhstana* [TsGARK]), Almaty:

Fond 759, *Kazakhskii kraevoi kooperativno-promyshlovyi soiuz rybakov*
Fond 1130, *Ministerstvo rybnogo khoziaistva Kazakhskoi SSR*
Fond 1137, *Sovet ministrov Kazakhskoi SSR*
Fond 1874, *Glavnoe upravlenie rybnoi promyshlennosti soveta narodnogo khoziaistva Kazakhskoi SSR*

Aral'sk branch of the state archive of Qyzylorda oblast (*Aral'skii filial gosudarstvennogo arkhiva Kyzylordinskoi oblasti* [AFGAKO]), Aral'sk:

Fond 4, *Aral'skii gosudarstvennyi rybopromyshlennyi trest*
Fond 5, *Aral'skoe upravlenie regulirovaniia rybolovstva*
Fond 7, *Pravleniia Aral'skogo rybatsko-kolkhoznogo soiuza*

Secondary sources

Abashin, S. N. 2015. *Sovetskii kishlak: Mezhdu kolonializmom i modernizatsiei*. Biblioteka zhurnala 'Neprikosnovennyi zapas'. Moskva: Novoe literaturnoe obozrenie.

Acheson, James M., James A. Wilson and Robert Steneck. 1998. 'Managing Chaotic Fisheries'. In *Linking Social and Ecological Systems: Management Practices and Social Mechanisms for Building Resilience*, edited by Fikret Berkes and Carl Folke, 390–413. Cambridge: Cambridge University Press.

Adams, Laura L. and Assel Rustemova. 2009. 'Mass Spectacle and Styles of Governmentality in Kazakhstan and Uzbekistan'. *Europe-Asia Studies* 61 (7): 1249–76. https://doi.org/10.1080/09668130903068798.

Adger, W. Neil. 2000. 'Social and Ecological Resilience: Are They Related?'. *Progress in Human Geography* 24 (3): 347–64. https://doi.org/10.1191/030913200701540465.

Aladin, N. V., A. A. Filippov, I. S. Plotnikov and A. N. Egorov. 2000. 'Sovremennoe ekologicheskoe sostoianie Malogo Aral'skogo mor'ia'. In *Fizicheskaia geografiia okeana i okeanicheskoe prirodopol'zovanie na poroge XXI veka: Sbornik nauchnykh trudov*, edited by V. M. Litvin and A. P. Alkhimenko, 79–90. Kaliningrad: Kaliningradskii gosudarstvennyi universitet.

Aladin, N. V. and I. S. Plotnikov. 1995. 'K voprosu vozmozhnoi konservatsii i reabilitatsii Malogo Aral'skogo mor'ia'. *Trudy Zoologicheskogo instituta RAN*, Biologicheskie i prirodovedcheskie problemy Aral'skogo moria i Priaral'ia, 262: 3–16.

Aladin, N. V. and I. S. Plotnikov. 2008. 'Sovremennaia fauna ostatochnykh vodoemov, obrazovavshikhsia na meste byvshego Aral'skogo moria'. *Trudy Zoologicheskogo instituta RAN* 312 (1/2): 145–54.

Aladin, N. V., I. S. Plotnikov and R. Letolle. 2004. 'Hydrobiology of the Aral Sea'. In *Dying and Dead Seas: Climatic Versus Anthropic Causes*, edited by Jacques C. J. Nihoul, Peter O. Zavialov and Philip P. Micklin, 125–57. NATO Science Series: IV: Earth and Environmental Sciences. Dordrecht: Springer Netherlands. https://doi.org/10.1007/978-94-007-0967-6_6.

Aladin, Nikolay V., Igor S. Plotnikov, Philip P. Micklin and Thomas Ballatore. 2009. 'Aral Sea: Water Level, Salinity and Long-Term Changes in Biological Communities of an Endangered Ecosystem – Past, Present and Future'. *Natural Resources and Environmental Issues* 15: 177–83.

Alexander, Catherine. 2002. *Personal States: Making Connections between People and Bureaucracy in Turkey*. Oxford: Oxford University Press.

Alexander, Catherine. 2004a. 'Value, Relations and Changing Bodies: Privatization and Property Rights in Kazakhstan'. In *Property in Question: Value Transformation in the Global Economy*, edited by Katherine Verdery and Caroline Humphrey, 251–74. Oxford: Berg.

Alexander, Catherine. 2004b. 'The Cultures and Properties of Decaying Buildings'. *Focaal* 2004 (44): 48–60. https://doi.org/10.3167/092012904782311263.

Alexander, Catherine. 2007. 'Almaty: Rethinking the Public Sector'. In *Urban Life in Post-Soviet Asia*, edited by Catherine Alexander, Victor Buchli and Caroline Humphrey, 70–101. London: UCL Press.

Alexander, Catherine. 2009a. 'Waste under Socialism and after: A Case Study from Almaty'. In *Enduring Socialism: Explorations of Revolution and Transformation, Restoration and Continuation*, edited by Harry G. West and Parvathi Raman, 148–68. New York: Berghahn Books.

Alexander, Catherine. 2009b. 'Privatization: Jokes, Scandal, and Absurdity in a Time of Rapid Change'. In *Ethnographies of Moral Reasoning: Living Paradoxes of a Global Age*, edited by Karen Sykes, 43–65. New York: Palgrave Macmillan.

Alexander, Catherine. 2020. 'A Chronotope of Expansion: Resisting Spatio-Temporal Limits in a Kazakh Nuclear Town'. *Ethnos* (ahead-of-print): 1–24. https://doi.org/10.1080/00141844.2020.1796735.

Alexander, Catherine and Victor Buchli. 2007. 'Introduction'. In *Urban Life in Post-Soviet Asia*, edited by Catherine Alexander, Victor Buchli and Caroline Humphrey, 1–39. London: UCL Press.

Alexander, Catherine and Andrew Sanchez. 2019. 'Introduction: The Values of Indeterminacy'. In *Indeterminacy: Waste, Value, and the Imagination*, edited by Catherine Alexander and Andrew Sanchez, 1–30. WYSE Series in Social Anthropology. New York: Berghahn Books.

Anderson, David G. 2002. 'The Ecology of Markets in Central Siberia'. In *Ethnographies of Conservation: Environmentalism and the Distribution of Privilege*, edited by Eeva K. Berglund and David G. Anderson, 155–70. New York: Berghahn Books.

Asarin, Alexander E., Valentina I. Kravtsova and Vadim N. Mikhailov. 2010. 'Amudarya and Syrdarya Rivers and Their Deltas'. In *The Aral Sea Environment*, edited by Andrey G. Kostianoy and Aleksey N. Kosarev, 101–21. The Handbook of Environmental Chemistry, 7. Berlin: Springer. http://link.springer.com/chapter/10.1007/698_2009_8.

Astuti, Rita. 1999. 'At the Center of the Market: A Vezo Woman'. In *Lilies of the Field: Marginal People Who Live for the Moment*, edited by Sophie Day, Evthymios Papataxiarchis and Michael Stewart, 83–95. Studies in the Ethnographic Imagination. Boulder, CO: Westview Press.

Bakhtin, Mikhail Mikhailovich. 1981a. 'Forms of Time and of the Chronotope in the Novel: Notes toward a Historical Poetics'. In *The Dialogic Imagination: Four Essays*, by Mikhail Mikhailovich Bakhtin, edited by Michael Holquist, translated by Caryl Emerson and Michael Holquist, 84–258. University of Austin Press Slavic Series, No. 1. Austin: University of Texas Press.

Bakhtin, Mikhail Mikhailovich. 1981b. 'Discourse in the Novel'. In *The Dialogic Imagination: Four Essays*, by Mikhail Mikhailovich Bakhtin, edited by Michael Holquist, translated by Caryl Emerson and Michael Holquist, 259–422. University of Austin Press Slavic Series, No. 1. Austin: University of Texas Press.

Bakhtin, Mikhail Mikhailovich. 1986. 'The Problem of Speech Genres'. In *Speech Genres and Other Late Essays*, by Mikhail Mikhailovich Bakhtin, edited by Michael Holquist and Caryl Emerson, translated by Vern W. McGee, 60–102. University of Texas Press Slavic Series, No. 8. Austin: University of Texas Press.

Bakhtin, Mikhail Mikhailovich. 2019. 'Experience Based on a Study of Demand among Kolkhoz Workers'. *Interventions*. https://doi.org/10.1080/1369801X.2019.1649184.

Balysheva, Anna. 2019. 'Introduction to Mikhail Bakhtin's Article "Experience Based on a Study of Demand among Kolkhoz Workers"'. *Interventions*. https://doi.org/10.1080/1369801X.2019.1585924.

Beckert, Sven. 2014. *Empire of Cotton: A New History of Global Capitalism*. London: Allen Lane.

Beknazarov, Rakhym Agibaevich. 2010. 'Kazakhi severnogo Priaral'ia v XIX – nachale XX vv. (Istoriko-etnograficheskoe issledovanie)'. Avtoreferat dissertatsiia na soiskanie uchenoi stepeni doktora istoricheskikh nauk. Almaty: In-t ist. i etnol. im. Sh. Ualikhanova.

Bennett, Jane. 2010. *Vibrant Matter: A Political Ecology of Things*. Durham, NC: Duke University Press.

Berdahl, Daphne. 1999. '"(N)Ostalgie" for the Present: Memory, Longing, and East German Things'. *Ethnos* 64 (2): 192–211. https://doi.org/10.1080/00141844.1999.9981598.

Berg, Lev Semenovich. 1908. *Aral'skoe more: opyt fiziko-geograficheskoi monografii; s 2 kartami, 6 tabl. i 78 risunkami*. Izvestiia Turkestanskago otdela imperatorskago russkago geograficheskago obshchestva. Sankt-Peterburg: Stasiulevich.

Berka, Rudolf. 1990. *Inland Capture Fisheries of the USSR*. FAO Fisheries Technical Paper, 311. Rome: Food and Agriculture Organization of the United Nations.

Berkes, Fikret. 1987. 'Common-Property Resource Management and Cree Indian Fisheries in Subarctic Canada'. In *The Question of the Commons: The Culture and Ecology of Communal Resources*, edited by Bonnie J. McCay and James M. Acheson, 66–91. Arizona Studies in Human Ecology. Tucson: University of Arizona Press.

Berkes, Fikret and Carl Folke, eds. 1998. *Linking Social and Ecological Systems: Management Practices and Social Mechanisms for Building Resilience*. Cambridge: Cambridge University Press.

Beyer, Judith. 2012. 'Settling Descent: Place Making and Genealogy in Talas, Kyrgyzstan'. In *Movement, Power and Place in Central Asia and beyond: Contested Trajectories*, edited by Madeleine Reeves, 97–110. Thirdworlds. London: Routledge.

Bichsel, Christine. 2012. '"The Drought Does Not Cause Fear"'. *Revue d'études Comparatives Est-Ouest* 43 (1–2): 73–108. https://doi.org/10.4074/S0338059912001040.

Bloch, Maurice, and Jonathan Parry. 1989. 'Introduction: Money and the Morality of Exchange'. In *Money and the Morality of Exchange*, edited by Maurice Bloch and Jonathan Parry, 1–32. Cambridge: Cambridge University Press.

Blommaert, Jan. 2015. 'Chronotopes, Scales, and Complexity in the Study of Language in Society'. *Annual Review of Anthropology* 44 (1): 105–16. https://doi.org/10.1146/annurev-anthro-102214-014035.

Botoeva, Gulzat. 2015. 'The Monetization of Social Celebrations in Rural Kyrgyzstan: On the Uses of Hashish Money'. *Central Asian Survey* 34 (4): 531–48. https://doi.org/10.1080/02634937.2015.1092742.

Boym, Svetlana. 2002. *Future of Nostalgia*. New York: Basic Books.

Brandtstädter, Susanne. 2007. 'Transitional Spaces: Postsocialism as a Cultural Process'. *Critique of Anthropology* 27 (2): 131–45.

Bressler, Michael L. 1995. 'Water Wars: Siberian Rivers, Central Asian Deserts, and the Structural Sources of a Policy Debate'. In *Rediscovering Russia in Asia: Siberia and the Russian Far East*, edited by Stephen Kotkin and David Wolff, 240–55. Armonk, NY: M. E. Sharpe.

Bromber, Katrin, Jeanne Féaux de la Croix and Katharina Lange. 2015. 'The Temporal Politics of Big Dams in Africa, the Middle East, and Asia: By Way of an Introduction'. *Water History* 6 (4): 289–96. https://doi.org/10.1007/s12685-014-0111-9.

Brown, Kate. 2015. *Dispatches from Dystopia: Histories of Places Not Yet Forgotten*. Chicago: University of Chicago Press.

Brown, William Y. 2014. 'A Green Growth Path'. In *Kazakhstan 2050: Toward a Modern Society for All*, edited by Aktoty Aitzhanova, Shigeo Katsu, Johannes F. Linn and Vladislav Yezhov, 149–80. New Delhi: Oxford University Press.

Buchli, Victor. 2007. 'Astana: Materiality and the City'. In *Urban Life in Post-Soviet Asia*, edited by Catherine Alexander, Victor Buchli and Caroline Humphrey, 40–69. London: UCL Press.

Buck-Morss, Susan. 2002. *Dreamworld and Catastrophe: The Passing of Mass Utopia in East and West*. Reprint edition. Cambridge, MA: MIT Press.

Cameron, Sarah. 2018. *The Hungry Steppe: Famine, Violence, and the Making of Soviet Kazakhstan*. Ithaca, NY: Cornell University Press. https://www.jstor.org/stable/10.7591/j.ctt21h4vb7.

Campbell, Ian W. 2012. 'Settlement Promoted, Settlement Contested: The Shcherbina Expedition of 1896–1903'. In *Movement, Power and Place in Central Asia and beyond: Contested Trajectories*, edited by Madeleine Reeves, 65–78. Thirdworlds. London: Routledge.

Campbell, Ian W. 2018. '"The Scourge of Stock Raising": Zhūt, Limiting Environments, and the Economic Transformation of the Kazakh Steppe'. In *Eurasian Environments: Nature and Ecology in Imperial Russian and Soviet History*, edited by Nicholas B. Breyfogle, 60–74. Pittsburgh, PA: University of Pittsburgh Press. https://doi.org/10.2307/j.ctv7r41ms.9.

Campling, Liam, Elizabeth Havice and Penny McCall Howard. 2012. 'The Political Economy and Ecology of Capture Fisheries: Market Dynamics, Resource Access and Relations of Exploitation and Resistance'. *Journal of Agrarian Change* 12 (2–3): 177–203. https://doi.org/10.1111/j.1471-0366.2011.00356.x.

Carrier, James G. 2001. 'Social Aspects of Abstraction'. *Social Anthropology* 9 (3): 243–56. https://doi.org/10.1111/j.1469-8676.2001.tb00151.x.

Carrier, James G. 2012. 'Dollars Making Sense: Understanding Nature in Capitalism'. *Environment and Society: Advances in Research* 3 (1): 5–18. https://doi.org/10.3167/ares.2012.030102.

Carsten, Janet. 1989. 'Cooking Money: Gender and the Symbolic Transformation of Means of Exchange in a Malay Fishing Community'. In *Money and the Morality of Exchange*, edited by Maurice Bloch and Jonathan Parry, 117–41. Cambridge: Cambridge University Press.

Castree, Noel. 2002. 'False Antitheses? Marxism, Nature and Actor-Networks'. *Antipode* 34 (1): 111–46. https://doi.org/10.1111/1467-8330.00228.

Chebanov, Sergey. 2015. 'Ukhtomsy's Idea of Chronotope as Frame of Anticipation'. *Anticipation: Learning from the Past. The Russian/Soviet Contributions to the Science of Anticipation*, edited by Mihai Nadin, 137–50. Cham: Springer.

Christensen, Kurt Bertelsen. 1996. 'Aralsøen: En Menneskeskabt Katastrofe'. Landsforeningen Levende Hav. http://gl.levendehav.dk/projekter/Kasakhstan/en-menneskeskabt-katastrofe1.htm, accessed 4 June 2021. First published in 1991.

Crate, Susan A. 2008. 'Gone the Bull of Winter? Grappling with the Cultural Implications of and Anthropology's Role(s) in Global Climate Change'. *Current Anthropology* 49 (4): 569–95.

Crate, Susan A. and Mark Nuttall, eds. 2009. *Anthropology and Climate Change: From Encounters to Actions*. Walnut Creek, CA: Left Coast.

Cronon, William. 1992. 'A Place for Stories: Nature, History, and Narrative'. *Journal of American History* 78 (4): 1347–76. https://doi.org/10.2307/2079346.

Cruikshank, Julie. 1998. *The Social Life of Stories: Narrative and Knowledge in the Yukon Territory*. Lincoln: University of Nebraska Press.

Dadabaev, Timur. 2010. 'Power, Social Life, and Public Memory in Uzbekistan and Kyrgyzstan'. *Inner Asia* 12 (1): 25–48. https://doi.org/10.1163/146481710792710291.

Das, Veena. 1995. *Critical Events: An Anthropological Perspective on Contemporary India*. Delhi: Oxford University Press.

Davé, Bhavna. 2007. *Kazakhstan: Ethnicity, Language and Power*. London: Routledge.

Davis, Mike. 2001. *Late Victorian Holocausts: El Niño Famines and the Making of the Third World*. London: Verso.

Day, Sophie, Evthymios Papataxiarchis and Michael Stewart, eds. 1999. *Lilies of the Field: Marginal People Who Live for the Moment*. Studies in the Ethnographic Imagination. Boulder, CO: Westview Press.

Dua, Jatin. 2017. 'A Sea of Profit: Making Property in the Western Indian Ocean'. In *Legalism: Property and Ownership*, edited by Georgy Kantor, Tom Lambert and Hannah Skoda, 175–202. Oxford: Oxford University Press.

Dubuisson, Eva-Marie and Anna Genina. 2012. 'Claiming an Ancestral Homeland: Kazakh Pilgrimage and Migration in Inner Asia'. In *Movement, Power and Place in Central Asia and beyond: Contested Trajectories*, edited by Madeleine Reeves, 111–27. Thirdworlds. London: Routledge.

Durrenberger, E. Paul and Gísli Pálsson. 1987. 'Ownership at Sea: Fishing Territories and Access to Sea Resources'. *American Ethnologist* 14 (3): 508–22. https://doi.org/10.1525/ae.1987.14.3.02a00060.

Ellis, William. 1990. 'A Soviet Sea Lies Dying'. *National Geographic* 177: 72–93.

Elpiner, Leonid I. 1999. 'Public Health in the Aral Sea Coastal Region and the Dynamics of Changes in the Ecological Situation'. In *Creeping Environmental Problems and Sustainable Development in the Aral Sea Basin*, edited by Michael H. Glantz, 128–56. New York: Cambridge University Press.

Ermakhanov, Zaualkhan K., Igor S. Plotnikov, Nikolay V. Aladin and Philip P. Micklin. 2012. 'Changes in the Aral Sea Ichthyofauna and Fishery during the Period of Ecological Crisis'. *Lakes & Reservoirs: Research & Management* 17 (1): 3–9. https://doi.org/10.1111/j.1440-1770.2012.00492.x.

Féaux de la Croix, Jeanne. 2012. 'Moving Metaphors We Live by: Water and Flow in the Social Sciences and around Hydroelectric Dams in Kyrgyzstan'. In *Movement, Power and Place in Central Asia and beyond: Contested Trajectories*, edited by Madeleine Reeves, 129–44. Thirdworlds. London: Routledge.

Féaux de la Croix, Jeanne. 2014. 'After the Worker State: Competing and Converging Frames of Valuing Labor in Rural Kyrgyzstan'. *Laboratorium: Russian Review of Social Research* 6 (2): 77–100.

Féaux de la Croix, Jeanne. 2016. *Iconic Places in Central Asia: The Moral Geography of Dams, Pastures and Holy Sites*. Culture and Social Praxis. Bielefeld: transcript-Verlag. https://doi.org/10.14361/9783839436301.

Fehér, Ferenc, Agnes Heller and György Márkus. 1983. *Dictatorship over Needs*. Oxford: Basil Blackwell.

Ferguson, James. 1999. *Expectations of Modernity: Myths and Meanings of Urban Life on the Zambian Copperbelt*. Perspectives on Southern Africa, 57. Berkeley: University of California Press.

Ferguson, James. 2005. 'Seeing Like an Oil Company: Space, Security, and Global Capital in Neoliberal Africa'. *American Anthropologist* 107 (3): 377–82. https://doi.org/10.1525/aa.2005.107.3.377.

Ferguson, James and Akhil Gupta. 2002. 'Spatializing States: Toward an Ethnography of Neoliberal Governmentality'. *American Ethnologist* 29 (4): 981–1002. https://doi.org/10.1525/ae.2002.29.4.981.

Ferguson, Robert W. 2003. *The Devil and the Disappearing Sea: A True Story about the Aral Sea Catastrophe*. Vancouver, BC: Raincoast Books.

Feshbach, Murray and Alfred Friendly. 1992. *Ecocide in the USSR: Health and Nature under Siege*. London: Aurum.

Fine, Ben. 2005. 'From Actor-Network Theory to Political Economy'. *Capitalism Nature Socialism* 16 (4): 91–108. https://doi.org/10.1080/10455750500376057.

Finlayson, A. Christopher and Bonnie J. McCay. 1998. 'Crossing the Threshold of Ecosystem Resilience: The Commercial Extinction of Northern Cod'. In *Linking Social and Ecological Systems: Management Practices and Social Mechanisms for Building Resilience*, edited by Fikret Berkes and Carl Folke, 311–37. Cambridge: Cambridge University Press.

Gardiner, Michael. 1993. 'Ecology and Carnival: Traces of a "Green" Social Theory in the Writings of M. M. Bakhtin'. *Theory and Society* 22 (6): 765–812.

Garvy, George. 1977. *Money, Financial Flows, and Credit in the Soviet Union*. Studies in International Economic Relations, 7. New York: National Bureau of Economic Research.

Glantz, Michael H., ed. 1999a. *Creeping Environmental Problems and Sustainable Development in the Aral Sea Basin*. Cambridge: Cambridge University Press.

Glantz, Michael H. 1999b. 'Sustainable Development and Creeping Environmental Problems in the Aral Sea Region'. In *Creeping Environmental Problems and Sustainable Development in the Aral Sea Basin*, edited by Michael H. Glantz, 1–25. New York: Cambridge University Press.

Gleason, Gregory. 1991. 'The Political Economy of Dependency under Socialism: The Asian Republics in the USSR'. *Studies in Comparative Communism* 24 (4): 335–53. https://doi.org/10.1016/0039-3592(91)90010-4.

Graeber, David. 2015. *The Utopia of Rules: On Technology, Stupidity, and the Secret Joys of Bureaucracy*. New York: Melville House.

Grant, Bruce. 1995. *In the Soviet House of Culture: A Century of Perestroikas*. Princeton, NJ: Princeton University Press.

Gupta, Akhil. 2012. *Red Tape: Bureaucracy, Structural Violence, and Poverty in India*. Durham, NC: Duke University Press.

Hann, Chris M. 2003. *The Postsocialist Agrarian Question: Property Relations and the Rural Condition*. Halle Studies in the Anthropology of Eurasia, Vol. 1. Münster: Lit.

Hardin, Garrett. 1968. 'The Tragedy of the Commons'. *Science* 162: 1243–48.

Harvey, David. 2009. 'The "New" Imperialism: Accumulation by Dispossession'. *Socialist Register* 40 (March): 63–87.

Hastrup, Kirsten. 2009. 'Waterworlds: Framing the Question of Social Resilience'. In *The Question of Resilience: Social Responses to Climate Change*, edited by Kirsten Hastrup, 11–30. Historisk-Filosofiske Meddelelser, 106. København: Det Kongelige Danske Videnskabernes Selskab.

Hastrup, Kirsten. 2013. 'Scales of Attention in Fieldwork: Global Connections and Local Concerns in the Arctic'. *Ethnography* 14 (2): 145–64. https://doi.org/10.1177/1466138112454629.

Hastrup, Kirsten. 2014. 'Nature: Anthropology on the Edge'. In *Anthropology and Nature*, edited by Kirsten Hastrup, 1–26. Routledge Studies in Anthropology, 14. New York: Routledge.

Hastrup, Kirsten and Cecilie Rubow. 2014. 'Introduction'. In *Living with Environmental Change: Waterworlds*, edited by Kirsten Hastrup and Cecilie Rubow, 2–9. London: Routledge.

Heathershaw, John and Nick Megoran. 2011. 'Contesting Danger: A New Agenda for Policy and Scholarship on Central Asia'. *International Affairs* 87 (3): 589–612. https://doi.org/10.1111/j.1468-2346.2011.00992.x.

Helgason, Agnar and Gísli Pálsson. 1997. 'Contested Commodities: The Moral Landscape of Modernist Regimes'. *Journal of the Royal Anthropological Institute* 3 (3): 451–71. https://doi.org/10.2307/3034762.

Herzfeld, Michael. 1992. *The Social Production of Indifference: Exploring the Symbolic Roots of Western Bureaucracy*. Global Issues. Oxford: Berg.

Hitchcock, Peter. 1998. 'The Grotesque of the Body Electric'. In *Bakhtin and the Human Sciences: No Last Words*, edited by Michael Mayerfeld Bell and Michael Gardiner, 85–98. Theory, Culture & Society. London: SAGE.

Hivon, Myriam. 1998. 'The Bullied Farmer: Social Pressure as Survival Strategy?'. In *Surviving Post-Socialism: Local Strategies and Regional Responses in Eastern Europe and the Former Soviet Union*, edited by Frances Pine and Sue Bridger, 33–51. London: Routledge.

Hodder, Ian. 2012. *Entangled: An Archaeology of the Relationships between Humans and Things*. Malden, MA: Wiley-Blackwell.

Hoeppe, Götz. 2007. *Conversations on the Beach: Fishermen's Knowledge, Metaphor and Environmental Change in South India*. New York: Berghahn Books.

Hoffman, Susanna M. and Anthony Oliver-Smith, eds. 2002. *Catastrophe and Culture: The Anthropology of Disaster*. Santa Fe, NM: School of American Research Press.

Holling, C. S. 1973. 'Resilience and Stability of Ecological Systems'. *Annual Review of Ecology and Systematics* 4 (1): 1–23. https://doi.org/10.1146/annurev.es.04.110173.000245.

Hornborg, Alf. 1996. 'Ecology as Semiotics: Outlines of a Contextualist Paradigm for Human Ecology'. In *Nature and Society: Anthropological Perspectives*, edited by Philippe Descola and Gísli Pálsson, 45–62. European Association of Social Anthropologists. London: Routledge.

Howard, Penny McCall. 2017. *Environment, Labour and Capitalism at Sea: 'Working the Ground' in Scotland*. Manchester: Manchester University Press.

Humphrey, Caroline. 1995. 'Introduction'. *Cambridge Anthropology* 18 (2): 2–13.

Humphrey, Caroline. 1998. *Marx Went Away – but Karl Stayed Behind*. Ann Arbor: University of Michigan Press.

Humphrey, Caroline. 2002. *The Unmaking of Soviet Life: Everyday Economies after Socialism*. Culture and Society after Socialism. Ithaca, NY: Cornell University Press.

Humphrey, Caroline and David Sneath. 2004. 'Shanghaied by the Bureaucracy: Bribery and Post-Soviet Officialdom in Russia and Mongolia'. In *Between Morality and the Law: Corruption, Anthropology and Comparative Society*, edited by Italo Pardo, 85–99. Aldershot: Ashgate.

Ianitskii, Oleg Nikolaevich. 1995. 'Evoliutsiia ekologicheskogo dvizheniia v sovremmenoi Rossii'. *Sotsiologicheskie issledovaniia* 8: 15–25.

Ibañez-Tirado, Diana. 2015. '"How Can I Be Post-Soviet If I Was Never Soviet?": Rethinking Categories of Time and Social Change – a Perspective from Kulob, Southern Tajikistan'. *Central Asian Survey* 34 (2): 190–203. https://doi.org/10.1080/02634937.2014.983705.

Ingold, Tim. 2000. *The Perception of the Environment: Essays on Livelihood, Dwelling and Skill*. London: Routledge.

Isakov, Baktybek and John Schoeberlein. 2014. 'Animals, Kinship, and the State: Kyrgyz Chabans Rebuilding Herds and Reorienting Belonging after the Soviet Collapse'. *Anthropology of East Europe Review* 32 (2): 33–48.

Jacquesson, Svetlana. 2002. 'Parcours ethnographiques dans l'histoire des deltas'. *Cahiers d'Asie centrale* 10 (May): 51–92.

Jansen, Stef. 2014. 'Hope For/Against the State: Gridding in a Besieged Sarajevo Suburb'. *Ethnos* 79 (2): 238–60. https://doi.org/10.1080/00141844.2012.743469.

Joffe, Muriel. 1995. 'Autocracy, Capitalism and Empire: The Politics of Irrigation'. *Russian Review* 54 (3): 365–88.

Johannes, Robert E., Milton M. R. Freeman and Richard J. Hamilton. 2000. 'Ignore Fishers' Knowledge and Miss the Boat'. *Fish and Fisheries* 1 (3): 257–71. https://doi.org/10.1111/j.1467-2979.2000.00019.x.

Kalinovsky, Artemy M. 2018. *Laboratory of Socialist Development: Cold War Politics and Decolonization in Soviet Tajikistan*. Ithaca, NY: Cornell University Press.

Kandiyoti, Deniz. 1996. 'Modernization without the Market? The Case of the "Soviet East"'. *Economy and Society* 25 (4): 529–42.

Kandiyoti, Deniz. 1998. 'Rural Livelihoods and Social Networks in Uzbekistan: Perspectives from Andijan'. *Central Asian Survey* 17 (4): 561–78.

Kandiyoti, Deniz. 2002. 'How Far Do Analyses of Postsocialism Travel? The Case of Central Asia'. In *Postsocialism: Ideals, Ideologies and Practices in Eurasia*, edited by Chris M. Hann, 238–57. London: Routledge.

Kandiyoti, Deniz. 2007. 'The Politics of Gender and the Soviet Paradox: Neither Colonized, nor Modern?'. *Central Asian Survey* 26 (4): 601–23.

Kandiyoti, Deniz and Nadira Azimova. 2004. 'The Communal and the Sacred: Women's Worlds of Ritual in Uzbekistan'. *Journal of the Royal Anthropological Institute* 10 (2): 327–49. https://doi.org/10.1111/j.1467-9655.2004.00192.x.

Karimov, Bakhtiyor, Bakhtiyor Kamilov, Maroti Upare, Raymon van Anroy, Pedro Bueno and Dilmurod Shokhimardonov. 2009. *Inland Capture Fisheries and Aquaculture in the Republic of Uzbekistan: Current Status and Planning*. Rome: Food and Agriculture Organization of the United Nations. http://agris.fao.org/agris-search/search.do?recordID=XF2009439831.

Karimov, Bakhtiyor, Helmut Lieth, Mohira Kurambaeva and Irina Matsapaeva. 2005. 'The Problems of Fishermen in the Southern Aral Sea Region'. *Mitigation and Adaptation Strategies for Global Change* 10 (1): 87–103. https://doi.org/10.1007/s11027-005-7832-0.

Karpevich, A. F. 1960a. 'Teoreticheskie predposylki k akklimatizatsii vodnykh organizmov'. *Trudy VNIRO* 43: 9–30.

Karpevich, A. F. 1960b. 'Obosnovanie akklimatizatsii vodnykh organizmov v Aral'skom more'. *Trudy VNIRO* 43: 76–114.

Karpevich, A. F. 1975. *Teoriia i praktika akklimatizatsii vodnykh organizmov*. Moskva: Pishch. prom-st'.

Khan, Azizur Rahman and Dharam P. Ghai. 1979. *Collective Agriculture and Rural Development in Soviet Central Asia*. World Employment Programme. London: Macmillan.

Khazanov, Anatoly M. 2012. 'Pastoralism and Property Relations in Contemporary Kazakhstan'. In *Who Owns the Stock? Collective and Multiple Property Rights in Animals*, edited by Anatoly M. Khazanov and Günther Schlee, 141–57. New York: Berghahn Books.

Kindler, Robert. 2018. *Stalin's Nomads: Power and Famine in Kazakhstan*, translated by Cynthia Klohr. Pittsburgh, PA: University of Pittsburgh Press. https://doi.org/10.2307/j.ctv3znxgm.

King, Alex D. 2003. 'Social Security in Kamchatka: Rural and Urban Comparisons'. In *The Postsocialist Agrarian Question: Property Relations and the Rural Condition*, edited by Chris M. Hann, 391–418. Münster: LIT Verlag.

Knudsen, Ståle. 2008. *Fishers and Scientists in Modern Turkey: The Management of Natural Resources, Knowledge and Identity on the Eastern Black Sea Coast*. New York: Berghahn Books.

Knudsen, Ståle. 2014. 'Multiple Sea Snails: The Uncertain Becoming of an Alien Species'. *Anthropological Quarterly* 87 (1): 59–91. https://doi.org/10.1353/anq.2014.0013.

Kornai, János. 1980. *Economics of Shortage*. Amsterdam: North-Holland.

Koroteyeva, Victoria and Ekaterina Makarova. 1998. 'Money and Social Connections in the Soviet and Post-Soviet Uzbek City'. *Central Asian Survey* 17 (4): 579–96. https://doi.org/10.1080/02634939808401057.

Kosarev, Aleksey N. and Andrey G. Kostianoy. 2010a. 'Introduction'. In *The Aral Sea Environment*, edited by Andrey G. Kostianoy and Aleksey N. Kosarev, 1–9. Berlin: Springer.

Kosarev, Aleksey N. and Andrey G. Kostianoy. 2010b. 'The Aral Sea under Natural Conditions (till 1960)'. In *The Aral Sea Environment*, edited by Andrey G. Kostianoy and Aleksey N. Kosarev, 45–63. Berlin: Springer.

Kostianoy, Andrey G. and Aleksey N. Kosarev, eds. 2010. *The Aral Sea Environment*. Berlin: Springer.

Kotkin, Stephen. 1995. *Magnetic Mountain: Stalinism as a Civilization*. Berkeley: University of California Press.

Krupa, Elena and Olga Grishaeva. 2019. 'Impact of Water Salinity on Long-Term Dynamics and Spatial Distribution of Benthic Invertebrates in the Small Aral Sea'. *Oceanological and Hydrobiological Studies* 48 (4): 355–67. https://doi.org/10.2478/ohs-2019-0032.

Kudaibergenova, Diana T. 2015. 'The Ideology of Development and Legitimation: Beyond "Kazakhstan 2030"'. *Central Asian Survey* 34 (4): 440–55. https://doi.org/10.1080/02634937.2015.1115275.

Lampland, Martha. 2010. 'False Numbers as Formalizing Practices'. *Social Studies of Science* 40 (3): 377–404. https://doi.org/10.1177/0306312709359963.

Landsforeningen Levende Hav. 1998. 'The Aral Sea and Its Fishery: A Project Report'. http://gl.levendehav.dk/uk/a-fishery-project.htm, accessed 4 June 2021.

Landsforeningen Levende Hav. 1999. 'Presentation Dossier – CCR Registration Form for EU Tacis.' http://gl.levendehav.dk/uk/doss-tacis-1999.htm, accessed 4 June 2021.

Larkin, P. A. 1977. 'An Epitaph for the Concept of Maximum Sustained Yield'. *Transactions of the American Fisheries Society* 106 (1): 1–11. https://doi.org/10.1577/1548-8659(1977)106 <1:AEFTCO>2.0.CO;2.

Last, Angela. 2013. 'Negotiating the Inhuman: Bakhtin, Materiality and the Instrumentalization of Climate Change'. *Theory, Culture & Society* 30 (2): 60–83. https://doi.org/10.1177/026327 6412456568.

Laszczkowski, Mateusz. 2011. 'Building the Future: Construction, Temporality, and Politics in Astana'. *Focaal* 2011 (60): 77–92. https://doi.org/10.3167/fcl.2011.600107.

Laszczkowski, Mateusz. 2014. 'State Building(s): Built Forms, Materiality, and the State in Astana'. In *Ethnographies of the State in Central Asia: Performing Politics*, edited by Madeleine Reeves, Johan Rasanayagam and Judith Beyer, 149–72. Performing Politics. Bloomington: Indiana University Press. http://www.jstor.org/stable/j.ctt16gzghd.12.

Laszczkowski, Mateusz. 2016. '"Demo Version of a City": Buildings, Affects, and the State in Astana'. *Journal of the Royal Anthropological Institute* 22 (1): 148–65. https://doi.org/10.1111/ 1467-9655.12338.

Latour, Bruno. 1993. *We Have Never Been Modern*. New York: Harvester Wheatsheaf.

Latour, Bruno. 2004. *Politics of Nature: How to Bring the Sciences into Democracy*. Cambridge, MA: Harvard University Press.

Ledeneva, Alena V. 1998. *Russia's Economy of Favours: Blat, Networking and Informal Exchange*. Cambridge Russian, Soviet and Post-Soviet Studies, 102. Cambridge: Cambridge University Press.

Ledeneva, Alena V. 2006. *How Russia Really Works: The Informal Practices That Shaped Post-Soviet Politics and Business*. Culture and Society after Socialism. Ithaca, NY: Cornell University Press.

Leonard, Pamela and Deema Kaneff. 2002. *Post-Socialist Peasant? Rural and Urban Constructions of Identity in Eastern Europe, East Asia and the Former Soviet Union*. Basingstoke: Palgrave.

Li, Tania. 2014. *Land's End: Capitalist Relations on an Indigenous Frontier*. Durham, NC: Duke University Press.

Lien, Marianne E. 2015. *Becoming Salmon: Aquaculture and the Domestication of a Fish*. California Studies in Food and Culture, 55. Oakland: University of California Press.

Loy, Thomas. 2006. 'From the Mountains to the Lowlands – the Soviet Policy of "Inner-Tajik" Resettlement'. *Internet-Zeitschrift für Kulturwissenschaften* 16. https://www.inst.at/ trans/16Nr/13_2/loy16.htm, accessed 4 June 2021.

Lubin, Nancy. 1984. *Labour and Nationality in Soviet Central Asia: An Uneasy Compromise*. St. Antony's/Macmillan Series. London: Macmillan.

Ludwig, Donald, Ray Hilborn and Carl Walters. 1993. 'Uncertainty, Resource Exploitation, and Conservation: Lessons from History'. *Science* 260 (5104): 17–36. https://doi.org/10.1126/ science.260.5104.17.

Massumi, Brian. 1995. 'The Autonomy of Affect'. *Cultural Critique* 31: 83–109. https://doi. org/10.2307/1354446.

Mazzarella, William. 2009. 'Affect: What Is It Good For?'. In *Enchantments of Modernity: Empire, Nation, Globalization*, edited by Saurabh Dube, 291–309. Critical Asian Studies. New Delhi: Routledge.

McCay, Bonnie J. and James M. Acheson, eds. 1987. *The Question of the Commons: The Culture and Ecology of Communal Resources*. Arizona Studies in Human Ecology. Tucson: University of Arizona Press.

McGoodwin, James R. 1991. *Crisis in the World's Fisheries: People, Problems and Policies*. New edition. Stanford, CA.: Stanford University Press.

McGuire, Gabriel. 2014. 'By Coin or By Kine? Barter and Pastoral Production in Kazakhstan'. *Ethnos* 81 (1): 53–74. https://doi.org/10.1080/00141844.2014.901983.

McMann, Kelly M. 2007. 'The Shrinking of the Welfare State: Central Asians' Assessments of Soviet and Post-Soviet Governance'. In *Everyday Life in Central Asia: Past and Present*, edited by Jeff Sahadeo and Russell G. Zanca, 233–47. Bloomington: Indiana University Press.

Micklin, Philip P. 1988. 'Desiccation of the Aral Sea: A Water Management Disaster in the Soviet Union'. *Science* 241 (4870): 1170–5. https://doi.org/10.1126/science.241.4870.1170.

Micklin, Philip P. 1998. 'International and Regional Responses to the Aral Crisis: An Overview of Efforts and Accomplishments'. *Post-Soviet Geography and Economics* 39 (7): 399–416. https:// doi.org/10.1080/10889388.1998.10641085.

Micklin, Philip P. 2000. *Managing Water in Central Asia*. London: Royal Institute of International Affairs.

Micklin, Philip P. 2007. 'The Aral Sea Disaster'. *Annual Review of Earth and Planetary Sciences* 35: 47–52.

Micklin, Philip P. 2010. 'The Past, Present, and Future Aral Sea'. *Lakes and Reservoirs: Science, Policy and Management for Sustainable Use* 15 (3): 193–213. https://doi.org/10.1111/j.1440-1770.2010.00437.x.

Micklin, Philip P. 2014a. 'Aral Sea Basin Water Resources and the Changing Aral Water Balance'. In *The Aral Sea: The Devastation and Partial Rehabilitation of a Great Lake*, edited by Philip P. Micklin, Nikolay V. Aladin and Igor S. Plotnikov, 111–35. Springer Earth System Sciences, 10178. Berlin: Springer. http://link.springer.com/chapter/10.1007/978-3-642-02356-9_5.

Micklin, Philip P. 2014b. 'Efforts to Revive the Aral Sea'. In *The Aral Sea: The Devastation and Partial Rehabilitation of a Great Lake*, edited by Philip P. Micklin, Nikolay V. Aladin and Igor S. Plotnikov, 361–80. Springer Earth System Sciences, 10178. Berlin: Springer. http://link.springer.com/chapter/10.1007/978-3-642-02356-9_15.

Micklin, Philip P. and Nikolay V. Aladin. 2008. 'Reclaiming the Aral Sea'. *Scientific American* 298 (4): 64–71.

Micklin, Philip P., Nikolay V. Aladin and Igor S. Plotnikov, eds. 2014. *The Aral Sea: The Devastation and Partial Rehabilitation of a Great Lake*. Berlin: Springer.

Minnegal, Monica and Peter Dwyer. 2011. 'Appropriating Fish, Appropriating Fishermen: Tradable Permits, Natural Resources, and Uncertainty'. In *Ownership and Appropriation*, edited by Veronica Strang and Mark Busse, 197–215. Oxford: Berg.

Mitrofanov, V. P., G. M. Dukravets and A. F. Sidorova. 1992. *Ryby Kazakhstana. Tom 5: Akklimatizatsiia, promysel*. Alma-Ata: Gylym.

Mol, Annemarie. 1999. 'Ontological Politics. A Word and Some Questions'. *The Sociological Review* 47 (S1): 74–89. https://doi.org/10.1111/j.1467-954X.1999.tb03483.x.

Mostowlansky, Till. 2017. *Azan on the Moon: Entangling Modernity along Tajikistan's Pamir Highway*. Central Eurasia in Context. Pittsburgh, PA: University of Pittsburgh Press.

Myers, Fred. 1988. 'Burning the Truck and Holding the Country: Property, Time and the Negotiation of Identity among Pintupi Aborigines'. In *Hunters and Gatherers 2: Property, Power and Ideology*, edited by Tim Ingold, David Riches and James Woodburn, 52–74. Explorations in Anthropology. Oxford: Berg.

Nakhshina, Maria. 2011. 'Fish, Bread and Sand: Resources of Belonging in a Russian Coastal Village'. PhD thesis, University of Aberdeen. http://digitool.abdn.ac.uk:80/webclient/Delivery Manager?pid=167800, accessed 4 June 2021.

Nakhshina, Maria. 2012. 'Community Interpretations of Fishing Outside Legal Regulations: A Case Study from Northwest Russia'. In *Fishing People of the North: Cultures, Economies, and Management Responding to Change*, 229–41. Fairbanks: University of Alaska.

Naumova, Zlata. 2012. 'Ryba iz vozdukha v mutnoi vode'. *Novaia Gazeta - Kazakhstan*. http://www.novgaz.com/index.php/2-news/382-рыба-из-воздуха-в-мутной-воде, accessed 4 June 2021.

Navaro-Yashin, Yael. 2012. *The Make-Believe Space: Affective Geography in a Postwar Polity*. Durham, NC: Duke University Press.

Nixon, Rob. 2011. *Slow Violence and the Environmentalism of the Poor*. Cambridge, MA: Harvard University Press.

Nove, Alec and J. A. Newth. 1967. *The Soviet Middle East: A Model for Development?* London: Allen & Unwin.

Oberhänsli, Hedi, Nikolaus Boroffka, Philippe Sorrel and Sergey Krivonogov. 2007. 'Climate Variability during the Past 2,000 Years and Past Economic and Irrigation Activities in the Aral Sea Basin'. *Irrigation and Drainage Systems* 21 (3–4): 167–83.

Obertreis, Julia. 2017. *Imperial Desert Dreams: Cotton Growing and Irrigation in Central Asia, 1860–1991*. Göttingen: V&R.

Oka, Natsuko. 2015. 'Informal Payments and Connections in Post-Soviet Kazakhstan'. *Central Asian Survey* 34 (3): 330–40. https://doi.org/10.1080/02634937.2015.1047154.

Oldfield, Jonathan D. 2005. *Russian Nature: Exploring the Environmental Consequences of Societal Change*. Ashgate Studies in Environmental Policy and Practice. Aldershot: Ashgate.

Ostrom, Elinor. 1990. *Governing the Commons: The Evolution of Institutions for Collective Action*. Political Economy of Institutions and Decisions. Cambridge: Cambridge University Press.

Oushakine, Serguei Alex. 2009. '"Stop the Invasion!": Money, Patriotism, and Conspiracy in Russia'. *Social Research* 76 (1): 71–116.

Pálsson, Gísli. 1994. 'Enskilment at Sea'. *Man* 29 (4): 901–27.

Pedersen, Morten Axel. 2011. *Not Quite Shamans: Spirit Worlds and Political Lives in Northern Mongolia*. Ithaca, NY: Cornell University Press. http://www.jstor.org/stable/10.7591/j.ctt7zcqx.

Peet, Richard and Michael Watts. 1996. 'Liberation Ecology: Development, Sustainability, and Environment in an Age of Market Triumphalism'. In *Liberation Ecologies: Environment, Development, Social Movements*, edited by Richard Peet and Michael Watts, 1–45. London: Routledge.

Pelkmans, Mathijs. 2006. *Defending the Border: Identity, Religion, and Modernity in the Republic of Georgia*. Culture and Society after Socialism. Ithaca, NY: Cornell University Press.

Pelkmans, Mathijs. 2013. 'Ruins of Hope in a Kyrgyz Post-Industrial Wasteland'. *Anthropology Today* 29 (5): 17–21. https://doi.org/10.1111/1467-8322.12060.

Penati, Beatrice. 2013. 'The Cotton Boom and the Land Tax in Russian Turkestan (1880s–1915)'. *Kritika* 14 (4): 741.

Peterson, Maya K. 2019. *Pipe Dreams: Water and Empire in Central Asia's Aral Sea Basin*. Studies in Environment and History. Cambridge: Cambridge University Press. https://doi.org/10.1017/9781108673075.

Pétric, Boris-Mathieu. 2005. 'Post-Soviet Kyrgyzstan or the Birth of a Globalized Protectorate'. *Central Asian Survey* 24 (3): 319–32. https://doi.org/10.1080/02634930500310402.

Petryna, Adriana. 2002. *Life Exposed: Biological Citizens after Chernobyl*. In-Formation Series. Princeton, NJ: Princeton University Press.

Pianciola, Niccolò. 2004. 'Famine in the Steppe: The Collectivization of Agriculture and the Kazak Herdsmen 1928–1934'. *Cahiers du monde russe*, 137–92. https://doi.org/10.4000/monderusse.8681.

Pianciola, Niccolò. 2019. 'Cossacks and Sturgeons: Fisheries, Colonization, and Science around the Aral Sea (1873–1906)'. *Journal of the Economic and Social History of the Orient* 62 (4): 626–73. https://doi.org/10.1163/15685209-12341490.

Pianciola, Niccolò. 2020. 'The Benefits of Marginality: The Great Famine around the Aral Sea, 1930–1934'. *Nationalities Papers* 48 (3): 513–29. https://doi.org/10.1017/nps.2019.22.

Pine, Frances. 2015. 'Living in the Grey Zones: When Ambiguity and Uncertainty Are the Ordinary'. In *Ethnographies of Grey Zones in Eastern Europe: Relations, Borders and Invisibilities*, edited by Ida Harboe Knudsen and Martin Demant Frederiksen, 25–40. London: Anthem Press.

Pine, Frances, Deema Kaneff and Idis Haukaness. 2004. 'Introduction: Memory, Politics and Religion: A Perspective on Europe'. In *Memory, Politics and Religion: The Past Meets the Present in Europe*, edited by Frances Pine, Deema Kaneff and Idis Haukaness, 1–29. Münster: Lit Verlag.

Pitchford, Jonathan W., Edward A. Codling and Despina Psarra. 2007. 'Uncertainty and Sustainability in Fisheries and the Benefit of Marine Protected Areas'. *Ecological Modelling* 207 (2–4): 286–92. https://doi.org/10.1016/j.ecolmodel.2007.05.006.

Plotnikov, I. S. 2013. 'Izmenenie vidovogo sostava fauny svobodnozhivushchikh bespozvonochnykh (Metazoa) Aral'skogo moria'. *Trudy Zoologicheskogo instituta RAN* 317 (S3): 41–54.

Plotnikov, Igor S., Nikolay V. Aladin, Zaualkhan K. Ermakhanov and Lyubov V. Zhakova. 2014. 'Biological Dynamics of the Aral Sea Before Its Modern Decline (1900–1960)'. In *The Aral Sea: The Devastation and Partial Rehabilitation of a Great Lake*, edited by Philip P. Micklin, Nikolai V. Aladin and Igor Plotnikov, 41–76. Springer Earth System Sciences, 10178. Berlin: Springer. http://link.springer.com/chapter/10.1007/978-3-642-02356-9_3.

Plotnikov, Igor S., Zaualkhan K. Ermakhanov, Nikolai V. Aladin and Philip Micklin. 2016. 'Modern State of the Small (Northern) Aral Sea Fauna'. *Lakes and Reservoirs: Science, Policy and Management for Sustainable Use* 21 (4): 315–28. https://doi.org/10.1111/lre.12149.

Pohl, Jonathan O. 2007. 'A Caste of Helot Labourers: Special Settlers and the Cultivation of Cotton in Soviet Central Asia: 1944–1956'. In *The Cotton Sector in Central Asia: Economic Policy and Development Challenges*, edited by Deniz Kandiyoti, 20–36. Proceedings of a conference held at SOAS, University of London, 3–4 November 2005. London: School of Oriental and African Studies.

Post, Jennifer C. 2007. '"I Take My *Dombra* and Sing to Remember My Homeland": Identity, Landscape and Music in Kazakh Communities of Western Mongolia'. *Ethnomusicology Forum* 16 (1): 45–69. https://doi.org/10.1080/17411910701276369.

Privratsky, Bruce G. 2001. *Muslim Turkistan: Kazak Religion and Collective Memory*. London: Routledge.

Redaktsiia 'Novaia Gazeta' - Kazakhstan. 2012. 'More bez khoziaina'. *Novaia Gazeta - Kazakhstan*. http://www.novgaz.com/index.php/2-news/557-море-без-хозяина, accessed 4 June 2021.

Reeves, Madeleine. 2012. 'Black Work, Green Money: Remittances, Ritual, and Domestic Economies in Southern Kyrgyzstan'. *Slavic Review* 71 (1): 108–34. https://doi.org/10.5612/slavicreview.71.1.0108.

Reeves, Madeleine. 2014. *Border Work: Spatial Lives of the State in Rural Central Asia*. Ithaca, NY: Cornell University Press.

Reeves, Madeleine. 2017. 'Infrastructural Hope: Anticipating "Independent Roads" and Territorial Integrity in Southern Kyrgyzstan'. *Ethnos* 82 (4), 711–37. https://doi.org/10.1080/00141844.2015.1119176.

Reznichenko, Grigory Ivanovich. 1989. 'My znaem, chto nyne lezhit na vesakh'. *Novyi mir* 5: 182–94.

Richardson, Tanya. 2014. 'The Politics of Multiplication in a Failed Soviet Irrigation Project, Or, How Sasyk Has Been Kept from the Sea'. *Ethnos* 81 (1): 125–51. https://doi.org/10.1080/00141844.2014.940990.

Richardson, Tanya. 2015. 'On the Limits of Liberalism in Participatory Environmental Governance: Conflict and Conservation in Ukraine's Danube Delta'. *Development and Change* 46 (3): 415–41. https://doi.org/10.1111/dech.12156.

Ries, Nancy. 2002. '"Honest bandits" and "Warped People": Russian Narratives about Money, Corruption, and Moral Decay'. In *Ethnography in Unstable Places: Everyday Lives in Contexts of Dramatic Political Change*, edited by Carol J. Greenhouse, Kay B. Warren and Elizabeth Mertz, 276–315. Durham, NC: Duke University Press.

Rigi, Jakob. 2004. 'Corruption in Post-Soviet Kazakhstan'. In *Between Morality and the Law: Corruption, Anthropology and Comparative Society*, edited by Italo Pardo, 101–18. Aldershot: Ashgate.

Rumer, Boris Z. 1989. *Soviet Central Asia: "A Tragic Experiment"*. Boston, MA: Unwin Hyman.

Sahlins, Marshall. 1972. *Stone Age Economics*. Chicago: Aldine-Atherton.

Sandywell, Barry. 2000. 'Memories of Nature in Bakhtin and Benjamin'. In *Materializing Bakhtin: The Bakhtin Circle and Social Theory*, edited by Craig Brandist and Galin Tihanov, 94–118. St Antony's Series. London: Palgrave Macmillan. https://doi.org/10.1057/9780230501461_6.

Scott, James C. 1990. *Domination and the Arts of Resistance: Hidden Transcripts*. New Haven, CT: Yale University Press.

Scott, James C. 1998. *Seeing like a State: How Certain Schemes to Improve the Human Condition Have Failed*. New Haven, CT: Yale University Press.

Seliunin, Vasilii. 1989. 'Vremia deistvii'. *Novyi mir* 5: 213–41.

Shreeves, Rosamund. 2002. 'Broadening the Concept of Privatization: Gender and Development in Rural Kazakhstan'. In *Markets and Moralities: Ethnographies of Postsocialism*, edited by Ruth Mandel and Caroline Humphrey, 211–35. Oxford: Berg.

Sievers, Eric. 2003. *The Post-Soviet Decline of Central Asia: Sustainable Development and Comprehensive Capital*. London: RoutledgeCurzon.

Sigman, Carole. 2013. 'The End of Grassroots Ecology: Political Competition and the Fate of Ecology during Perestroika, 1988–1991'. *The Soviet and Post-Soviet Review* 40 (2): 190–213. https://doi.org/10.1163/18763324-04002006.

Simpson, Edward. 2013. *The Political Biography of an Earthquake: Aftermath and Amnesia in Gujarat, India*. Society and History in the Indian Ocean. London: Hurst.

Small, Ian and Noah Bunce. 2003. 'The Aral Sea Disaster and the Disaster of International Assistance'. *Journal of International Affairs* 56 (2): 59–73.

Smith, A. L. 2004. 'Heteroglossia, "Common Sense," and Social Memory'. *American Ethnologist* 31 (2): 251–69.

Smith, Neil. 1984. *Uneven Development: Nature, Capital and the Production of Space*. Oxford: Blackwell.

Sorabji, C. 2006. 'Managing Memories in Postwar Sarajevo: Individuals, Bad Memories, and New Wars'. *Journal of the Royal Anthropological Institute* 12 (1): 1–18.

Sørensen, Gert Lynge. 1996. 'Danish Fishermen to Help Revitalize the Aral Sea'. *Danish Environment, Internet Edition*. http://www.statensnet.dk/pligtarkiv/fremvis.pl?vaerkid=534&reprid=0&filid=103&iarkiv=1, accessed 16 June 2016; website no longer accessible 8 June 2021.

Spoor, Max. 1993. 'Transition to Market Economies in Former Soviet Central Asia: Dependency, Cotton and Water'. *The European Journal of Development Research* 5 (2): 142–58. https://doi.org/10.1080/09578819308426591.

Stawkowski, Magdalena E. 2016. '"I Am a Radioactive Mutant": Emergent Biological Subjectivities at Kazakhstan's Semipalatinsk Nuclear Test Site'. *American Ethnologist* 43 (1): 144–57. https://doi.org/10.1111/amet.12269.

Suyarkulova, Mohira. 2015. 'Between National Idea and International Conflict: The Roghun HHP as an Anti-Colonial Endeavor, Body of the Nation, and National Wealth'. *Water History* 6 (4): 367–83. https://doi.org/10.1007/s12685-014-0113-7.

Teichmann, Christian. 2007. 'Canals, Cotton, and the Limits of De-colonization in Soviet Uzbekistan, 1924–1941'. *Central Asian Survey* 26 (4): 499–519. https://doi.org/10.1080/02634930802018240.

Teichmann, Christian. 2018. 'Leviathan on the Oxus: Water and Soviet Power on the Lower Amu Darya 1920s–1940s'. In *Eurasian Environments: Nature and Ecology in Imperial Russian and Soviet History*, edited by Nicholas Breyfogle, 97–112. Pitt Series in Russian and East European Studies. Pittsburgh, PA: University of Pittsburgh Press.

Tett, Gillian. 1994. '"Guardians of the Faith": Gender and Religion in an (Ex) Soviet Tajik Village'. In *Muslim Women's Choices*, edited by Camillia El-Solh and Judy Mabro, 128–51. Providence, RI: Berg.

Thompson, Chad D. and John Heathershaw. 2005. 'Introduction'. *Central Asian Survey* 24 (1): 1–4. https://doi.org/10.1080/13648470500049925.

Thompson, E. P. 1967. 'Time, Work-Discipline, and Industrial Capitalism'. *Past & Present* 38: 56–97.

Timirkhanov, Serik, Boris Chaikin, Zhannat Makhambetova, Andy Thorpe and Raymon van Anrooy. 2010. *Fisheries and Aquaculture in the Republic of Kazakhstan: A Review*. FAO Fisheries and Aquaculture Circular, No. 1030/2. Ankara: Food and Agriculture Organization of the United Nations.

Toleubayev, Kazbek, Kees Jansen and Arnold van Huis. 2010. 'Knowledge and Agrarian De-collectivisation in Kazakhstan'. *Journal of Peasant Studies* 37 (2): 353–77. https://doi.org/10.1080/03066151003595069.

Tolybekov, Sergali Esbembetovich. 1959. *Obshchestvenno-ekonomicheskii stroi kazakhov v XVII-XIX vekakh*. Alma-Ata: Kazakhskoe gosizd-vo.

Trevisani, Tommaso. 2007. 'After the Kolkhoz: Rural Elites in Competition'. *Central Asian Survey* 26 (1): 85–104. https://doi.org/10.1080/02634930701423509.

Trevisani, Tommaso. 2010. *Land and Power in Khorezm: Farmers, Communities, and the State in Uzbekistan's Decollectivisation*. Halle Studies in the Anthropology of Eurasia, v. 23. Berlin: LIT Verlag.

Trevisani, Tommaso. 2014. 'The Reshaping of Cities and Citizens in Uzbekistan: The Case of Namangan's "New Uzbeks"'. In *Ethnographies of the State in Central Asia: Performing Politics*, edited by Madeleine Reeves, Johan Rasanayagam and Judith Beyer, 243–60. Bloomington: Indiana University Press. http://www.jstor.org/stable/j.ctt16gzghd.18.

Trevisani, Tommaso. 2016. 'Modern Weddings in Uzbekistan: Ritual Change from "above" and from "below"'. *Central Asian Survey* 35 (1): 61–75. https://doi.org/10.1080/02634937.2015.1114781.

Tsing, Anna Lowenhaupt. 2015. *The Mushroom at the End of the World: On the Possibility of Life in Capitalist Ruins*. Princeton, NJ: Princeton University Press.

Turmagambetov, M., D. Turmagambetov and M. Utarkulov. 1968. *Aral'skii rybokombinat*. Alma-Ata: Ministerstvo rybnogo khoziaistva Kazakhskoi SSR.

UNEP. 1993. 'Diagnostic Study for the Development of an Action Plan for the Conservation of the Aral Sea'. Nairobi: UNEP (United Nations Environment Programme). https://wedocs.unep.org/bitstream/handle/20.500.11822/30348/Aral_Sea.pdf?sequence=1&isAllowed=y, accessed 4 June 2021.

Verdery, Katherine. 1996. *What Was Socialism, and What Comes Next?* Princeton, NJ: Princeton University Press.

Vermonden, Daniel. 2013. 'Reproduction and Development of Expertise within Communities of Practice: A Case Study of Fishing Activities in South Buton'. In *Landscape, Process and Power: Re-Evaluating Traditional Environmental Knowledge*, edited by Serena Heckler, 205–29. Berghahn Books.

Verran, Helen. 2010. 'Number as an Inventive Frontier in Knowing and Working Australia's Water Resources'. *Anthropological Theory* 10 (1–2): 171–8. https://doi.org/10.1177/1463499610365383.

Voeikov, Aleksandr Ivanovich. 1949a. 'Chelovek i voda: sposoby pol'zovaniia vodoiu i ikh geograficheskoe raspredelenie'. In *Vozdeistvie cheloveka na prirodu: izbrannye stat'i*, 127–49. Moscow: Gos. izd-vo geogr. lit-ry. First published in 1909.

Voeikov, Aleksandr Ivanovich. 1949b. 'Oroshenie Zakaspiiskoi oblasti s tochki zreniia geografii i klimatologii'. In *Vozdeistvie cheloveka na prirodu: izbrannye stat'i*, 157–78. Moscow: Gos. izd-vo geogr. lit-ry. First published in 1908.

von Benda-Beckmann, Franz, Keebet von Benda-Beckmann and Melanie Wiber. 2006. 'The Properties of Property'. In *Changing Properties of Property*, edited by Franz von Benda-Beckmann, Keebet von Benda-Beckmann and Melanie Wiber, 1–39. New York: Berghahn Books.

Walters, Patrick. 2010. 'Aral Sea Recovery?'. *National Geographic*. http://news.nationalgeographic.com/news/2010/04/100402-aral-sea-story/, accessed 4 June 2021.

Wanner, Catherine. 2005. 'Money, Morality and New Forms of Exchange in Postsocialist Ukraine'. *Ethnos* 70 (4): 515–37. https://doi.org/10.1080/00141840500419782.

Watson, Rubie S. 1994. *Memory, History, and Opposition under State Socialism*. Sante Fe, NM: School of American Research Press.

Wedel, Janine R. 1998. *Collision and Collusion: The Strange Case of Western Aid to Eastern Europe, 1989–1998*. New York: St Martin's Press.

Weiner, Douglas R. 1988. *Models of Nature: Ecology, Conservation, and Cultural Revolution in Soviet Russia*. Indiana-Michigan Series in Russian and East European Studies. Bloomington: Indiana University Press.

Weiner, Douglas R. 1999. *A Little Corner of Freedom: Russian Nature Protection from Stalin to Gorbachëv*. Berkeley: University of California Press.

Weinthal, Erika. 2002. *State Making and Environmental Cooperation: Linking Domestic and International Politics in Central Asia*. Cambridge, MA: MIT Press.

Werner, Cynthia. 1998. 'Household Networks and the Security of Mutual Indebtedness in Rural Kazakstan'. *Central Asian Survey* 17 (4): 597–612.

Werner, Cynthia. 2000. 'Gifts, Bribes, and Development in Post-Soviet Kazakstan'. *Human Organization* 59 (1): 11–22. https://doi.org/10.17730/humo.59.1.w2582tqj18v3880p.

Werner, Cynthia and Kathleen Purvis-Roberts. 2014. 'Cold War Memories and Post-Cold War Realities: The Politics of Memory and Identity in the Everyday Life of Kazakhstan's Radiation Victims'. In *Ethnographies of the State in Central Asia: Performing Politics*, edited by Madeleine Reeves, Johan Rasanayagam and Judith Beyer, 285–310. Bloomington: Indiana University Press. http://www.jstor.org/stable/j.ctt16gzghd.18.

Wheeler, William. 2016. 'Aral-88: Catastrophe, Critique and Hope'. *The Slavonic and East European Review* 94 (2): 295–324. https://doi.org/10.5699/slaveasteurorev2.94.2.0295.

Wheeler, William. 2017. 'Fish as Property on the Small Aral Sea, Kazakhstan'. In *Legalism: Property and Ownership*, edited by Georgy Kantor, Tom Lambert and Hannah Skoda, 203–33. Oxford: Oxford University Press.

Wheeler, William. 2019. 'The USSR as a Hydraulic Society: Wittfogel, the Aral Sea and the (Post-) Soviet State'. *Environment and Planning C: Politics and Space* 37 (7): 1217–34. https://doi.org/10.1177/2399654418816700.

Wilson, Emma. 2002. 'Est' zakon, est' i svoi zakoni: Legal and Moral Entitlements to the Fish Resources of Nyski Bay, North-East Sakhalin'. In *People and the Land: Pathways to Reform in Post-Soviet Siberia*, edited by Erich Kasten, 149–68. Berlin: Dietrich Riemer.

Wilson, James. 2002. 'Scientific Uncertainty, Complex Ecosystems and the Design of Common-Pool Institutions'. In *The Drama of the Commons*, edited by Elinor Ostrom, Thomas Dietz, Nives Dolsak, Paul C. Stern and Susan Stonich, 327–59. Washington, DC: National Academies Press.

Wilson, James A., James M. Acheson, Mark Metcalfe and Peter Kleban. 1994. 'Chaos, Complexity and Community Management of Fisheries'. *Marine Policy* 18 (4): 291–305.

Wittfogel, Karl August. 1957. *Oriental Despotism: A Comparative Study of Total Power*. New Haven, CT: Yale University Press; Oxford: Oxford University Press.

Woodburn, James. 1982. 'Egalitarian Societies'. *Man* 17 (3): 431–51. https://doi.org/10.2307/2801707.

World Bank. 1995. *Aral Sea Basin Program Phase 1: Progress Report No. 1*. Washington, DC: World Bank. http://www.ircwash.org/sites/default/files/822-USSR-AS95-13110.pdf, accessed 4 June 2021.

World Bank. 1997. *Kazakstan: Syr Darya Control and Northern Aral Sea Project*. Washington, DC: World Bank. http://documents.worldbank.org/curated/en/1997/09/694172/kazakstan-syr-darya-control-northern-aral-sea-project, accessed 4 June 2021.

World Bank. 1999. 'Annual Review of Environment Matters at the World Bank'. Washington DC: World Bank.

World Bank. 2001. *Project Appraisal Document on a Proposed Loan in the Amount of US $64.5 Million to the Republic of Kazakhstan for the Syr Darya Control and Northern Aral Sea Phase-I Project, May 11, 2001.* Washington, DC: World Bank. http://www-wds.worldbank.org/servlet/WDSContentServer/WDSP/IB/2001/06/07/000094946_01051804010622/Rendered/INDEX/multi0page.txt, accessed 4 June 2021.

World Bank. 2005. *Innovations in Fisheries Management for Kazakhstan.* Washington DC: World Bank. http://documents1.worldbank.org/curated/en/401031468047413143/pdf/313830KZ0ENGLISH0updated0fisheries.pdf, accessed 4 June 2021.

World Bank. 2011. *Kazakhstan: First Phase of the Syr Darya Control and Northern Aral Sea Project.* Washington, DC: World Bank. http://documents.worldbank.org/curated/en/2011/06/15404043/kazakhstan-first-phase-syr-darya-control-northern-aral-sea-project, accessed 4 June 2021.

Yurchak, Alexei. 2005. *Everything Was Forever, Until It Was No More: The Last Soviet Generation.* In-Formation Series. Princeton, NJ: Princeton University Press.

Zanca, Russell G. 2010. *Life in a Muslim Uzbek Village: Cotton Farming after Communism.* Case Studies in Cultural Anthropology. Belmont, CA: Wadsworth.

Zenkevich, L. A. 1956. *Moria SSSR, ikh fauna i flora.* Izdanie 2-e, dopolnennoe. Moskva: Uchpedgiz.

Zholdasova, I. M., L. P. Pavlovskaya, A. N. Urasbaev, E. Adenbaev and S. K. Lubimova. 1998. 'Biological Bases of Fishery Development in the Water Bodies of the Southern Aral Sea Region'. In *Ecological Research and Monitoring of the Aral Sea Deltas: A Basis for Restoration*, edited by S. Bruk, D. Keyser, J. Kutscher and V. Moustafaev, 213–33. UNESCO Aral Sea Project: 1992–1996 Final Scientific Reports. Paris: UNESCO.

Zonn, Igor S. 1999. 'The Impact of Political Ideology on Creeping Environmental Change in the Aral Sea Basin'. In *Creeping Environmental Problems and Sustainable Development in the Aral Sea Basin*, edited by Michael H. Glantz, 157–90. New York: Cambridge University Press.

Zonn, Igor S. 2002. 'The Caspian Sea: Threats to Its Biological Resources and Environmental Security'. In *The Security of the Caspian Sea Region*, edited by Gennady Chufrin, 69–82. Oxford; New York: Stockholm International Peace Research Institute.

Zonn, Igor S., Michael H. Glantz, Aleksey N. Kosarev and Andrey G. Kostianoy. 2009. *The Aral Sea Encyclopedia.* Berlin: Springer.

Index

Abashin, S. N. 14, 55, 88n8, 138
above-quota fishing 168, 170, 182–3, 185
  agency of fishermen in 197–9, 205
  causes of 179–80, 195–7, 204–5
  and fish factories 212, 215
  prosecution for 171–2
  of zander 176–7, 196
abstraction
  and discourse 57–8, 64n40, 66, 77
  and environmental damage 10, 30, 125
  of natural entities 10, 29–31, 32, 121,
    138–9, 182, 197, 232
  of space 34–5n4, 99–100, 122, 130
abundance
  as chronotope 127–8
  and fishing practices 39, 119, 180,
    198–9
  and hunter-gatherer practices 31, 129,
    198, 199
  and memories of the Aral 93–4, 98–9,
    127–8, 131
  and property 128, 180
  and Soviet ideology 47
  Soviet times remembered as 93–4, 109,
    115, 133
acclimatisation of new species 52, 69–71,
    88n10, 190, 236
accumulation by dispossession 41–2, 157,
    173, 180
adaptation 15–16, 119, 140n16, 234–5
  top-down 87, 138, 234
affect 208–9, 213–14, 215–16, 220, 228
  indeterminacy of 217, 225
Aghlaq 21, 79, 161
Aladin, N. V. 147–8, 150
alcohol
  beer and dried fish 25, 112, 196
  and celebrations 18, 201
  and everyday sociality 17, 112, 117, 132,
    184, 201, 208, 221
  and fishing 23, 185
  as gift 105, 116n2, 200, 218
  vodka mitigating *ekologiia* 8, 16
Alexander, Catherine 104, 208, 209, 215,
    217, 218, 233, 235
Almaty (formerly Alma-Ata) 16–17, 92, 154
  emigration to 117, 210
Amanötkel 19, 22, 76, 185, 203
Amu Dariya 2, 36, 42, 99, 121
  delta and delta lakes 3, 35n5,
    90n36, 145, 174n2

Anthropocene, anthropology of the 236–8
apparatus *see* bureaucracy, Soviet
Aqbasty 21, 77, 86, 230
Aqespe 19, 230
  environmental degradation in 124
  famine in 128
  fishery 77, 135, 156, 170
Aqshatau, Lake 19, 73, 78–9, 134
Aqtöbe 78, 117, 214
Aral-88 expedition 58–60, 94, 231
Aralgosrybtrest 45, 53
Aral region
  colonisation of 39, 129
  geography 18–21
  immigration to 40–1, 50, 103, 127–8
  meat and dairy products in 9, 127, 210,
    222, 228, 229
  pride in 7, 99–100, 112, 117, 206–8, 209,
    222, 225, 228–30
  saltiness of 9, 19, 127, 222
  as *zona ekologicheskogo bedstviia* (ecological
    disaster zone) 8, 210, 218, 220, 227
Aralrybprom 77–86, 104–10, 153, 155–6, 158
  bankruptcy of 127, 156, 212
  see also Aral Sea fisheries
Aral Sea
  as ancestral property 5, 7, 119
  biodiversity of 2, 52, 63n27, 69–70
  as biologically dead 143, 147, 150, 231
  division into Large and Small Seas 2, 143
  dried-up seabed 2–3, 22, 36, 123, 126–7,
    207, 226
  exploration of 19, 39
  geological history of 36, 52
  and leisure 94, 100–1, 109, 111, 115, 208
  as multiple object 11–12, 60–1, 169–70,
    231–3
  partial restoration of 3, 93, 141–3, 147–50,
    159–63, 206, 208
  previous regressions of 36, 123–4, 125
  salinity levels 2, 57, 69–71, 94, 147 *see also*
    Small Aral Sea, salinity levels
  as shipping route 42, 52, 57, 97, 147
  southern shore 3, 35n5, 47, 67
  as wasteful 42, 45, 61, 231–2
  water balance 54, 60, 89n28, 147
Aral Sea Basin Program 145, 150
Aral Sea fisheries 2, 9–10, 31–3
  contraction following sea's regression 65,
    67
  financial difficulties of 53, 80–6, 170–1

future of 127, 198–9, 216, 238
industrialisation of 48, 50–1
invisibility of 32, 48–9, 214, 173–4, 175–6, 192–3, 214
mechanisation of 48, 52, 53, 65
post-Soviet collapse of 143, 153, 155–6
and property relations 144, 167–72, 178–9, 181–7, 204–5
reorganisation following sea's regression 9, 65, 67, 77–8, 79–80, 84, 134–7
and transnational markets 10, 25, 33, 153, 177, 196–7, 201, 233
Tsarist development of 39–41
see also fisheries management; fishing
Aral Sea regression *see also* disaster
  as bureaucratic problem 9, 66–8, 72–3, 82, 87, 232
  fish populations, effect on 2, 57, 65, 69–70, 74
  global visions of 2–3, 93, 142–3, 145, 225
  health effects of 3, 59, 68, 92–3, 112, 217, 219–20, 233 *see also* ekologiia
  and international development 3, 141–7, 154, 231
  justification of 2, 56–8, 121
  and Kazakhstani state 16, 141–2, 164
  local meanings of 6–7, 84, 110–14, 117–19, 121–2, 138–9 *see also* emigration as response to sea's regression
  and political economy 32–3, 55–8, 67–8, 93–5, 119–20, 126–7, 143, 154, 231–3
  and salinisation of pastures 126–7 *see also* Aral Sea, salinity levels
  Soviet responses to 56–8, 65, 66–7, 69–80, 87, 96, 122 *see also* Aral Sea fisheries, reorganisation of following sea's regression; *pereselenie*, relocations following sea's regression
Aral'sk
  cost of living in 210, 219
  demographics of 51, 88n6, 97, 103
  economy of 18, 97, 99, 207, 209–10, 223–4
  fish factories in 97–8, 101, 107–9, 110, 170, 171, 212–16
  fish in 98–9, 109, 210, 211–13, 214–15, 219, 222, 226
  industrial character of 50–2, 93–4, 97–101
  military bases 54, 101–2, 109, 115
  port 51–2, 78, 97, 163
  relocations to 72, 76
  shipyard 52, 78, 99–101, 218
  as transport hub 40, 42, 50–2, 97, 109, 210
  urban fabric of 5, 18, 97–103, 206–8
  views on fishery in 180–1, 196, 214, 216, 219
  views on restored sea in 165–6, 206, 208–9, 235
  see also drinking water, in Aral'sk
Aral Tenizi 3, 107, 157–9, 167–9, 171–2, 173–4
asar (*hashar*) 22, 45, 202
Astana (now Nūr-Sūltan) 17, 18, 35n7, 187, 206, 210, 213
Astuti, Rita 198

Atameken fish factory 212–16, 229–30
atherines 69, 70, 152
Azov Sea 40, 70, 71

Baikonur 8, 54, 111, 211, 222–3 *see also* ekologiia, and rocket launches
bailyq 38–9, 93, 117, 131, 138 *see also* abundance
Bakhtin, Mikhail Mikhailovich 8, 27–31, 57–8, 68, 84, 119 *see also* chronotope; discourse, monologic; speech genres
Balqash, Lake
  fish from in Aral'sk 213
  fish populations in 80, 137
  memories of fishing on 117, 118, 136–7, 199
  sending of Aral fishermen to 80, 82, 83, 87
Barsakelmes nature reserve (*zapovednik*) 52, 63n28, 211
Berg, Lev Semenovich 40, 52
Berg Strait 97, 147, 148, 150, 160
besbarmaq 18, 22, 125, 223
  fish 25, 190–1, 222
Black Sea 101, 113 *see also* Azov Sea
boats
  access to 129, 130, 153, 169, 181, 186–7, 204
  distributed as pay 157
  types of 118, 186
Bögen 5, 20–1, 68–9, 111, 117, 169
  contemporary social relations in 201–3
  famine in 47, 128, 130–1
  fishery 156, 170, 175–6, 183–94, 214
  fish factory 77, 80, 117, 133, 139, 194–6
  inhabitants' protests 122, 134
  pastures 126–7
Bolsheviks 13, 43, 157
Brandtstädter, Susanne 143, 146, 168
bream
  catches of 65, 69, 74
  as commercial fish 192, 194
  as food 25, 190, 192, 196
  on other lakes 80
  processing of 177, 195, 196, 219
  recovery of 161, 162
Brown, Kate 13, 34n4, 62n2, 101
Buck-Morss, Susan 10, 14, 43
bureaucracy, Soviet 44, 54–5, 57–8, 65–9, 121–2 *see also* Aral Sea regression, as a bureaucratic problem; bureaucratic discourse; command economy
bureaucratic discourse
  centripetal tendencies of 56–8, 61
  constraints on 58, 67–9, 81–2
  limits of 84–6
  redundancy of 66, 88n4

camels
  as meat 184
  pastures for 19, 127
  as property 123
  as working livestock 5, 129, 155, 188
Cameron, Sarah 12, 39, 47

INDEX 257

canals 37, 45, 54, 59, 113 *see also* irrigation
capitalism
    in the Aral region 108, 181, 204
    as endpoint of post-Soviet
        transition 106–7, 145, 215, 225
    and environments 10, 25, 32, 236–8
carp
    catches of 69, 74, 190
    as food 18, 25, 175
    and prestige 69, 199
    recovery of 161
    stocking of lakes with 78, 79, 80, 137
Carsten, Janet 203–4
Caspian Sea 36, 42, 54
    aquatic fauna of 52, 64n34
    fishery 64n34, 79
    fish from in Aral'sk 210, 213
    relation to the Aral 52, 110–11
catfish 99, 190, 199
Central Asia
    colonisation of 39
    cotton economy in 13, 41–2, 50, 55, 59,
        146
    environmental history of 12–13, 37, 43–5,
        62n3, 66
    environmental problems in 10, 13, 14,
        35n5, 59, 236
    ethnography of 13–15
    labour migration in 181, 202
    labour surplus in 55, 75
    modernisation of 12–15, 42–5, 54, 60–1,
        67, 120, 138
    as postcolonial 12–13, 38
    post-Soviet aid to 145, 146, 172, 174n2
    relationship to Soviet centre 13–14, 38,
        44–5, 54–5, 87
    social networks in 180–1, 188, 201–2
    Tsarist 13, 37, 41–2
Chechens 50, 128
Chernobyl 3, 6, 58, 145, 220
China
    Kazakhstan's relations with 18, 211, 222,
        227
    as source of nets 7, 25, 27, 211, 234
Christensen, Kurt 154, 156, 158, 159
chronotopes 28–31, 119, 181 *see also*
        abundance, as chronotope; plans,
        Soviet, as chronotope; *tughan zher*,
        as chronotope
Civil War, Russian 5–6, 43, 99
clans *see ru*
climate
    of Aral region 2, 209, 226
    change 163
    effect of sea's regression on 2–3
    effect of Small Aral restoration on 208
    and living conditions 124, 209, 224
    and sea levels 36, 54, 150, 161, 172
    see also ekologiia; weather
Cold War 3, 145, 159, 164, 231
co-management 47, 168–9, 171, 173–4, 179
collective farms *see* kolkhozy, fishing
collectivisation 12–13, 19, 30, 43–4, 47–50,
        131–2
    memories of 120, 130–1, 234
    see also famine; kolkhozy, fishing

command economy
    centralisation of 11, 43–4, 48, 57, 61–2, 87
    and limits of centralised control 11, 44, 49,
        78–9, 134
    money in 81
    redistribution within 13, 44–5, 62, 67, 87,
        119
    see also plans, Soviet; shortage economy;
        state socialism
Communism
    ideology of 129, 157
    as a historical stage 93, 120, 132–3, 165,
        232
Communist Party 60, 67, 103, 111, 112–13
cooperatives 45–7, 154, 156, 158–9, 167,
        168
corruption, discourses about 106, 209, 211,
        218, 220
    and Baikonur 222–3
    and fishery 211, 215–16
    and Small Aral restoration 165, 211
Cossacks, Ural 39–40
cotton cultivation
    as cause of Aral Sea regression 2–3, 54–8,
        59–60, 110, 112, 142, 234
    and clientelism 54–5, 59
    and coercive labour relations 13, 55, 59,
        62n3
    and cotton scandal 59
    environmental effects of 54–5, 59, 62n1,
        236
    global history of 41–2, 62n1
    and manufacturing 41–2, 50, 61, 97
    as modernity in Central Asia 13, 45, 59,
        234
    post-Soviet dependence on 146
    Tsarist development of 41–2
'creeping environmental problems' 55, 73
'critical events' 5, 7, 66, 77, 93

dams 15, 37, 162, 164 *see also* Kökaral dam
Danes 3, 9, 143–4, 153–8, 172–3
Demeuov, Narghaly 79, 135, 156
dependency
    within command economy 48–9, 61, 67,
        87, 153
    within contemporary fishery 202–3
    and entanglement 25–6, 60
    modernisation and transformations
        of 37–8, 39, 41, 45, 55
    resource 25
    theory 38
deportations *see pereselenie*
devaluation of tenge 177, 194, 210, 225,
        230n2
development *see* Aral Sea regression, and
        international development; Central Asia,
        post-Soviet aid to; postsocialism, and
        international development; uneven
        development
disaster 2–3, 58–60, 142–7, 154, 172, 229,
        231–2
    anthropology of 5–6, 58, 231
    sea's regression not recognised as 55–6,
        66, 232
    as stigmatising 6, 93, 225, 226–7

discourse 27–8, 67–9, 95–6
  monologic 57–8, 113, 143
  see also Bakhtin; bureaucratic discourse;
    speech genres
drinking *see* alcohol
drinking water 19, 53, 60, 74, 76, 79
  in Aral'sk 18, 96, 217
  polluted 76, 217, 219–20, 233
  in villages 21, 76, 133, 167
dust storms 2–3, 68, 216–17, 224–6, 234
    see also climate; weather

ekologiia
  and Aral Sea regression 8, 92–3, 126, 139,
    217
  debates about 8–9, 126, 217–18, 222,
    224–8, 235
  and health 8, 209, 217, 220, 222–5
  and rocket launches 8, 111, 217, 220,
    222–3
  and subjectivities 209, 217–29, 233
embeddedness and disembedding
  economic 180, 192, 200–1, 203–4,
    205n10, 237
  of nature 35n13, 48
emigration as response to the sea's
    regression 3, 84, 117, 184
  decisions about 123–6
  of non-Kazakh population 67, 97,
    122
  official relocations 72, 76, 122–3
  see also pereselenie, relocations as a
    response to the sea's regression
employment
  contrasts between past and present 77,
    101, 106–7, 109, 114–15, 209
  effect of sea's retreat on 59, 72, 74–6
  and post-Soviet unemployment 7,
    145
  Soviet provision of 72–80, 84–5, 99–101,
    104–10, 134
  and Soviet social contract 45, 72–3, 84, 87,
    104–7
  see also fish processing, and employment
entanglement 10, 24–6, 31
  discursive 8, 28, 228
  lifeworld 10, 26, 29–31, 43, 236
  and multiplicity 232–3
environmental anthropology 10, 26–8
environmental change
  and the body 28
  multiplicity of 9, 33, 231–3
  political agency of 9, 231–2
  and political-economic change 15–16, 28,
    32–3, 114, 228
  and social change 3, 9–10, 178–9, 233
  and subjectivities 16, 28, 208–9
Europe, zander exports to 7, 26, 153, 177,
    196–7
  effects on local society of 25, 181
  and EU-code factories 196, 212–13
  and fishing practices 197, 238
famine 30, 47–8
  Aral saving people from 127–8, 233
  flight from 47, 128, 131, 223
  historiography of 12–13

social forgetting of 128, 130–1, 140n7,
    234, 238n1
  in Volga region 5, 129
Féaux de la Croix, Jeanne 15
Fehér, Ferenc, Agnes Heller, and György
    Márkus 11, 44
First World War 15, 42–43
fish
  as commodities 32, 129–30, 136, 138, 177,
    192–7, 200–1, 237–8
  as food 25, 109, 127, 153, 190–1, 199
  as gifts 68–9, 185, 199–200
  immediatism of 31, 38–9, 198–9
  and money 25, 31, 129, 137–8, 180,
    199–201
  perishability of 31–2, 39, 178
  recovery of 148, 150, 161–2
  and sharing 31, 35n15, 129, 177, 199–200
  social life of 179, 194–7
  virtual *see* quotas, and virtual fish
  see also Aral Sea regression, fish
    populations, effect on
fisheries
  in Kazakhstan 64n34, 167–8
  and markets 197
  post-Soviet 200, 205n9
  as socioeconomic systems 179, 205
  Soviet 53, 54, 64n34, 88n4
  see also Aral Sea fisheries; fisheries
    management; fishing
Fisheries Committee 167–8, 171–2
fisheries development plans 169–70, 171,
    181, 183–4, 196
fisheries inspectors
  constraints on 179, 195
  informal practices of 170, 171–2, 214, 216
  and monitoring of fishery 26, 78, 158, 181,
    186, 232
  and quotas 171–2, 182
fisheries management
  and agency of fishermen 45, 167, 179, 182,
    185, 187–8
  perceived failures of 134, 157, 170,
    179–80, 199, 216
  post-Soviet changes to 157, 169–70, 181–2
  and regulation of fishing practices 26, 188,
    193
  science of 182–3, 205n7
  Soviet 52, 54, 64n34, 134
  Tsarist 39–40
  see also quotas
Fisheries Ministry, Kazakh *see* Minrybkhoz
    KazSSR
Fisheries Ministry, Soviet *see* Minrybkhoz
    USSR
fish farms *see* lakes, Syr Dariya delta
fishing 22–4, 175–6, 190
  agency in 48–9, 134–6, 156 *see also*
    management of fisheries, and agency of
    fishermen
  anthropology of 24–5, 176, 180, 205n11
  and informal practices 53, 190–3
  as labour 25, 32, 48–9, 134–7, 186–7, 199
  for markets 32–3, 177, 197, 199
  without permission 78, 134, 185–7, 226
  for plans 32–3, 134–7

pre-colonial 38–9
and skill/local knowledge 22–4, 176, 187–8, 190, 198
and social entitlements 33, 48–50, 181, 185, 186–7, 233
technologies of 23, 39, 118, 129, 133, 155
see also nets; UAZ jeeps
units 188–90, 204
as a way of life 24, 132–3, 175–6, 190–1, 200–1, 204
see also above-quota fishing
fish processing 31–32, 35n16, 39, 194–6
cost of investment in 170, 196, 215
cottage production 45, 213, 219
and employment 33, 74, 76, 77–8, 104–110, 133, 212–15, 228
filleting 25, 177, 193, 196, 212–13
and ice 31–2, 39
refrigeration 52, 74, 80, 86, 153, 169–70, 171, 183, 196
and salt 31–2, 39, 62n7
smoking/curing 45, 177, 196, 213, 215
see also Aral'sk, fish factories in; Bögen, fish factory; Qaratereng, fish factory
flounder
catching of 153, 154, 155, 235–6
and Danes 3, 9, 153, 154–7, 159
dying out of 159, 162, 171
fishery 3, 143, 153, 155–7, 158–9, 171, 188
as food 153, 155
introduction of 71, 151, 152–3, 236
and Small Aral restoration 9, 143, 145, 159

Germans, Volga 50, 128
Germany *see* Europe, zander exports to
Glantz, Michael H. 55
gobies 69, 70, 71, 152
Gosbank 80–6, 90n51, 105
Gosplan 73, 75, 76–7, 82
governmentality, transnational 143–4, 146, 156, 159
Grant, Bruce 15
gridded space 13, 30, 34n4, 132
Aral region's integration into 9, 54, 87, 232–3
disintegration of 143, 235
nostalgia for 94, 109, 115, 165, 235
and vulnerability 121

Hardin, Garrett 179
Hastrup, Kirsten 16, 140n16, 234, 235
health *see* Aral Sea regression, health effects of; *ekologiia*, and health
herring, Baltic 69, 70, 174n5
Herzfeld, Michael 57–8
Hodder, Ian 26, 55
homeland *see tughan zher*
hope
and catastrophe 59–60, 64n44, 231
and Danish project 154, 157
for sea's return 93, 123, 125–6
and Small Aral restoration 120, 208, 214, 216
house-building 22, 49, 202–3
Howard, Penny McCall 25, 205n3

Humphrey, Caroline 132, 140n12
hunter gatherers *see* abundance, and hunter-gatherer practices
hydroelectricity 145, 146, 148

ichthyologists, Tsarist and Soviet 40, 52
and acclimatisations 69–71, 88n10, 152, 236
indeterminacy
and indeterminate assemblages 143, 147, 159, 163
of material agency 217, 225, 228–9, 233
and postsocialism 16, 144, 234
and progress 59
and property rights 144, 167
and value 16, 157, 164, 173, 228–9, 234
infrastructure
and difficulties posed by sea's retreat 74, 155
electricity 21, 53, 76, 133
and imagination 165–6
as incorporating Aral region into Soviet space 37, 60–1
investments in as response to Aral Sea regression 72, 74–7, 133, 232
and post-Soviet aid projects 167, 168–9
roads 19, 210, 230
see also dams; drinking water; fish processing; hydroelectricity; irrigation; Kökaral dam; railway
irrigation
as cause of Aral Sea regression 2–3, 38, 59, 71, 110, 111, 121
and clientelism 55, 59
and command economy 44, 55, 59–60
and expertise 13, 54–5
and forced labour 44
inefficiency of 44–5, 56, 59–60
and legitimacy of Soviet rule 13, 54
medieval 36, 42
post-Soviet dependence on 145
pre-Tsarist Central Asian practices of 38, 43
Tsarist interest in 42
Islam
and environmental awareness 92–3, 198, 199
Kazakh practices of 18, 124–5, 139n1, 139n4, 211, 223
and Sovietisation 14–15, 139n4

Japan 8, 86, 118, 234

Kalinovsky, Artemy M. 55, 64n33, 88n7, 88n18
Kalmyks 50, 128, 137
Kambala Balyk 159, 169, 170, 171–2, 212
Kandiyoti, Deniz 14
Karakalpaks 38
Karakalpakstan 63n18
and Aral Sea regression 35n5, 67, 121
cotton exported from 42, 97, 109
and famine 47, 223
fishing industry 49
Karpevich, A. F. 63n27, 69–71, 88n11

Kazakhs
arrival in Aral region 38
and diet 200
historical adaptability of 8–9, 17, 38, 216–17, 234
as nation 16, 17, 103, 211, 222–3
relations with other nationalities 97, 112, 128, 218, 220
see also collectivisation; Islam, Kazakh practices of; *ru*; *tughan zher*
Kazakhstan
colonisation of 39
multiethnic composition of 17
nuclear testing in 16, 154, 225, 235
official histories in 17, 35n6, 96, 140n7
political economy 17–18, 93, 166, 208, 209, 218, 230n2
pre-Soviet heritage 17, 207–8, 229
as sovereign state 16, 92, 96, 120, 165, 238
see also Kökaral dam, and Kazakhstani sovereignty
Soviet legacy 15–16, 18, 234–5
as *terra nullius* 211, 225
see also China, Kazakhstan's relations with; oil, and Kazakhstani economy
Kazakhstan-2030 strategy 14, 17, 21
Kazakhstan-2050 strategy 14, 17, 21, 35n7
Kazalinsk *see* Qazaly
Kazgiprovodkhoz 160, 163, 211
KazNIIRKh 52, 163, 168, 179, 182, 205n7, 211
Kazsovmin 71, 73, 74–6, 79, 134
Kindler, Robert 12–13, 48, 140n7, 238n1
kinship
and attachment to the land 124–6
and collectivisation 131–2
and organisation of fishery 184, 188–90, 203, 204
see also ritual economy; *ru*; social reproduction
Kökaral, former island of 132, 147, 175–6
Kökaral dam 3, 160–6, 174n1, 238
complaints about 165–6, 211
construction of 160–1
early incarnations 143, 147–51, 159
and Kazakhstani sovereignty 113, 141–2, 144, 164–6, 208
positive effects of 161–2
as 'project of the century' 142, 164, 165, 238
kolkhozy, fishing 48–50, 53, 127, 130, 159
see also collectivisation
kommersanty
and cost of groceries 203, 219
and fish 183, 185, 191, 210, 214
Koreans 50, 111–12, 128
Kornai, János 11, 72–3, 81 *see also* shortage economy
kulans 63n28, 126
Kyrgyzstan 144–5, 146, 148

lakes, Syr Dariya delta 19–21, 71, 82, 122
fish farms on 72–6, 78–9
post-Soviet fisheries on 134, 153
pre-colonial economy around 19, 38–9
rehabilitation of 161, 163, 238
resettlements from 47

Landsforeningen Levende Hav 154, 156, 157
Large Aral (South Aral) 3, 147, 163, 174n2
Laszczkowski, Mateusz 164, 213, 215–16
Lenin's letter 5–6, 99, 115, 128–30
Lien, Marianne E. 11–12, 15, 27–8, 35n16, 62n7, 232
lifeworld *see* entanglement, lifeworld
livestock
confiscation of 12, 30, 47, 48, 128, 130
distributed as pay 153, 157
vs. fish 31, 38–9, 62n4, 198
household ownership of 18, 26, 72, 75, 126–7, 183, 184, 210
state/kolkhoz ownership of 80, 127, 156
see also Aral region, and meat and dairy products; camels; ritual economy, livestock in
living standards
and Aral Sea regression 66, 68, 72–7, 87, 104, 122, 232
and fishing 49, 138
and irrigation/cotton 45, 54
in Soviet Central Asia 13, 38
see also state socialism, social contract of

Makhambetova, Zhannat 158–9, 168–71, 173
material agency
and affect 217
of Aral Sea 124, 127–8, 138
and Aral Sea regression 110–11, 147
and Small Aral restoration 148, 150, 172
theories of 25–6
'matters of fact' vs. 'matters of concern' 58, 66, 144, 164, 217–18
melioration of water-bodies 45, 52, 65
memory
as commentary on the present 95, 101, 105–8, 113, 114–15
and dark Soviet past 103–4, 111–13
and nostalgia 94–7, 109–10, 113–14, 120, 234–5
politics of 95–6
transmission of 92, 115, 120–1, 139
see also famine, social forgetting of
Michurin 70, 112
Minrybkhoz KazSSR (Fisheries Ministry of Kazakh SSR) 54, 68, 73, 78–80, 81–4, 122, 153
Minrybkhoz USSR (Soviet Fisheries Ministry) 61, 64n36, 71–2, 76, 78
Minvodkhoz KazSSR (Ministry of Land Reclamation and Water Management of Kazakh SSR) 76–7, 78, 122
Minvodkhoz USSR (Soviet Ministry of Land Reclamation and Water Management) 62, 71
modernity
in Central Asia 12–15, 55, 96, 120, 121, 136, 140n10 *see also* Central Asia, modernisation of; cotton, as modernity in Central Asia
and environmental ruination 2, 10, 15, 59, 235–7
'expectations of' 13, 55, 94, 238
'orderly' 101–2
Soviet 10–11, 59, 60–1

INDEX   **261**

modernisation *see* Central Asia, modernisation of

money
anxiety about 105–6, 180–1, 199, 225–7, 235
and postsocialism 221–2, 224, 225–6, 230n11
and ritual expenditure *see* ritual economy
see also fish, and money

Mostowlansky, Till 13–14

Moynaq 3, 67, 97, 174n2

multiplicity of nature/natural entities 11–12, 15, 30–1, 232–3 *see also* Aral Sea, as multiple object; environmental change, multiplicity of

Myers, Fred 31

National Geographic 142–3, 163–4

nature
mastery of 3, 10, 13, 37, 42–3, 164
modernist paradigms of 10, 11, 26–7, 36
Soviet ideology of 43, 47, 111–12, 114
see also abstraction, of natural entities; embeddedness and disembedding, of nature

nature users 169–70, 174n11, 181–3, 196, 205n10

Nazarbayev, Nursultan 17, 35n7, 141–2, 164, 166

nets
'Chinese' (monofilament) 7, 26, 27, 180, 187–8, 190, 199
gillnets 22–4, 155
provision of 48, 130, 139, 144, 153, 154, 181, 183
seines 33, 136, 154, 155, 190

nostalgia *see* memory, and nostalgia

Ob' *see* Siberian rivers project

Obertreis, Julia 13, 45, 54, 58, 62n3

ocean fish 9, 80, 87, 133, 153
irregular delivery of 80, 82, 83, 85, 107–9
and local identity 109, 117
procurement of 81, 83, 104–6
and social contract 95, 96, 104, 107, 114, 235

oil
in Aral region 19, 198, 226–8
and employment 210
and environmental problems 14, 226–7
exports of 177, 211
and Kazakhstani economy 14, 16, 17, 35n7, 177, 208, 209, 211, 234

Oushakine, Serguei Alex 225

overfishing *see* above-quota fishing

Peet, Richard and Michael Watts 11

Pelkmans, Mathijs 104, 211, 215

pensions 218–20
and fishing 181, 185, 186–7
and nostalgia 94, 96

pereselenie (deportation/relocation)
deportations to Aral region 39, 47, 50, 103, 111, 112, 128, 234

deportations/relocations elsewhere in Central Asia 44, 63n11, 89n18
relocations following sea's regression 72, 73–6, 87, 89n18, 122–3, 125

perestroika 77, 86, 158
and Aral Sea disaster 3, 9, 58–60, 95, 111–12, 144–5, 231

perforation 8, 16, 129, 234–5

Peterson, Maya K. 13, 45, 62n2, 62n3, 62–63n9

Pianciola, Niccolò 38–9, 47, 62n4

pike 5, 78, 185, 190

plans, Soviet
central imposition of 12, 43–4, 47, 67, 81
as chronotope 29, 119, 127, 139, 179
fulfilment of 48–9, 59, 81–2, 83, 86
and homogenisation of space 32–3, 60, 233
memories of 107–8, 134–7
negotiation of 68, 82, 88n7
post-Soviet continuities with 170

poaching *see* fishing, without permission

political ecology, of socialism and postsocialism 10, 11, 38, 67–8, 120

Polygon *see* Kazakhstan, nuclear testing in

postsocialism
and economic breakdown 146, 148, 153–4, 155–6, 188
and international development 143–4, 145–6
and nostalgia *see* memory, and nostalgia
and social networks 188, 201–2, 221–2
rural 144, 156–7, 171, 173, 174n8, 178, 180
and socioeconomic differentiation 144, 156–7, 173
as transition 106–7, 143, 145, 146, 156, 179, 182, 215

precarity 143, 147–8, 157, 163, 237–8

Privratsky, Bruce G. 125, 139n4, 140n10

progress 10, 59, 231–2, 235–8

proverbs 31, 32, 190–1, 198

Qamystybas 19
fish farm 74–5, 78
and leisure 208–9, 230
station 129

Qarashalang 5, 21, 79, 92

Qaratereng 5, 21, 76, 120, 169
fishery 126, 156, 181, 205n12, 214
fish factory 78, 80, 133
relocations from 124, 125
relocations to 72, 125, 126

Qasqaqūlan 21, 126, 139n5, 189

Qazaly
and colonisation of Central Asia 39
and contemporary fishery 25, 170, 183, 186, 194–6, 214
migration to 117, 124, 203
Soviet fishing industry in 77, 78, 80

Qoszhar 19, 136

Qūlandy 76, 77, 86

quotas
allocation of 171, 181–3
individual transferable quotas (ITQs) 205n6

and inequality 180
scientific basis 168, 181–3, 205n7
and virtual fish 169, 170, 172, 182, 196
see also above-quota fishing; fisheries
management
Qyzylorda, emigration to 124, 201
Qyzylorda obkom/oblispolkom 73–6

railway 40–1, 42, 52
and employment 210
and famine 47
and transport of fish 5, 40–1, 61, 80
Raiym, kolkhoz 19, 53, 79, 127
Raiym, Lake 19, 39, 134, 136
Reeves, Madeleine 96, 165, 181, 202
religion *see* Islam
resettlement *see pereselenie*
resilience 16, 115, 122–7, 138–9, 143
and pastoral economy 38–9
theories of 119–20, 140n16, 234
resistance 15, 72, 88n8, 120, 134
Reznichenko, G. I. 58–60
rice cultivation 2, 61, 74, 76, 110, 121
in Qyzylorda oblast 74, 76, 122–3, 124,
125
Richardson, Tanya 12, 174n13
ritual economy 221, 226
money from fishing in 25, 138, 181, 201–3,
233
livestock in 138, 183, 202
ru 19, 125, 186, 205n8
in Bögen 20, 184, 201
and collectivisation 131–2
Russia
emigration from Aral'sk to 97, 224
and Kazakhstan 166, 177, 211, 223
marketing of Aral fish in 158, 196–7,
214
textiles industry 42, 50
Russians 112, 117, 129, 217, 218–20

saiga antelopes 63n28, 223
salinisation *see* Aral Sea regression,
salinisation of pastures
salinity *see* Aral Sea, salinity levels; Small Aral
Sea, salinity levels
salt *see* Aral region, saltiness of; fish
processing, and salt
salvage accumulation 236–7
Saryshyghanaq bay 40, 97, 208
fishery 174n12, 186–7, 210
and SYNAS–II 163
scalability 10–11, 43–4, 61–2, 235–6
and acclimatisations 70, 88n10, 236
of fisheries 31–2, 35n16, 52, 61
Science and Technology Studies (STS)
11, 12
Scott, James 38, 56, 62n3, 67, 68
seaweed *see shalang*
Second World War 50, 52, 113, 127–8, 131
sedentarisation *see* collectivisation
Seliunin, Vasilii 60, 64n44
shalang (seaweed) 22, 25–6, 137
ships 52, 53, 65, 118
exported for scrap 211, 234
shipyard *see* Aral'sk, shipyard

shortage economy
and bureaucratic competition 11, 44, 53,
59, 60, 67
and dysfunction of fishing industry 81–6
and informal practices 48–9, 105–6, 109,
131–2
and investment hunger 72–3, 74
see also command economy; state socialism
Shymkent 175, 176, 186, 201, 214
Siberian rivers project 37, 61–2
cancellation of 58, 110, 113–14
and employment provision 55
as 'project of the century' 164
as solution to Aral Sea regression 71, 110,
112, 113–14, 146
slow violence 233–5
Small Aral Sea (North Aral) 3
biodiversity of 151–2, 154, 159, 161–2
salinity levels 148–50, 159, 161–2
stabilisation of 147–50, 159–61
social reproduction 138, 179, 201–5, 233
socio-ecological systems 119, 140n16
Soviet Union
collapse of 7, 60, 93–4, 110, 144–5
as dreamworld 114
environmental management in 43–5, 54–5,
59, 145, 146, 164 *see also* fisheries
management, Soviet
environmental protest in 58, 60, 231
military-industrial complex 54, 101
repression in 50, 103, 111, 114, 223
as time-space 94, 143, 235
see also state socialism
speech genres 68
affordances of 82
and emergence of Aral Sea problem 73,
74–5, 77, 87
limits of 84
and speech will 67, 86
stagnation era 54–5, 67, 81–83
remembered as 'Communism' 132–3, 232
Stalin 103, 111–12, 113–14, 128, 130–1
Stalinism 47, 111, 223
state socialism
and personal connections 68–9, 103,
105–6, 109, 115, 116n2
social contract of 9, 13, 45, 72–3, 84, 87,
116n1 *see also* ocean fish, and social
contract
and Soviet welfare state 13, 67, 88n18, 103
urbanist values of 45, 59, 94, 96
see also command economy; political
ecology, state socialist and postsocialist;
postsocialism; Soviet Union
Stawkowski, Magdalena E. 16, 234
sturgeon
and acclimatisations 52, 70
on Caspian 64n34
failure to return to Small Aral 162, 169
as gift 68
Tsarist fishery of 39–40, 43
sustainability
of fisheries 3, 157, 158, 159, 168, 179
Soviet Union and 44, 145, 164
see also Aral Sea fisheries, future of; Soviet
Union, environmental management in

INDEX   263

swimming *see* Aral Sea, and leisure
Syr Dariya 2, 121
in colonial period 39, 42
delta 40, 73, 145, 148, 175–6, 181 *see also*
lakes, Syr Dariya delta
hydraulic infrastructure on 19, 79, 148,
161
as source of drinking water 19, 79
and stabilisation of Small Aral 147–8, 150,
161–3
water volume in 76, 79, 89n28, 89n30,
148
Syr Darya Control and North Aral Sea Project
(SYNAS) 150, 159–64
and Japanese Social Development Fund
project 167–8
second phase of 163, 166, 238

Tajikistan 89n18, 105, 144–5, 146
Tastübek 19, 219, 223
fishery 156, 170
and flounder 152–3, 155
technopolitics 142, 164
Teichmann, Christian 44–5, 62n3
Tien Shan 2, 163
Togliatti 97, 218
toi see ritual economy
tragedy of the commons 179, 180, 205
transition *see* postsocialism, as transition
Trevisani, Tommaso 35n6, 116n1, 180, 202
Tsing, Anna Lowenhaupt 10–11, 14, 35n14,
43, 235–8 *see also* scalability
tughan zher
as chronotope 29, 119, 125, 139
and environmental change 120, 124–7,
233
and ethnographies of Kazakhs 125, 139n4
and postsocialist markets 201, 203, 205,
233
Sovietisation of 127, 131–2, 138–9
Turkmenistan 47, 54, 144–5
Tūshchy, Lake 19, 161, 185–6

UAZ jeeps 21, 22–3, 186, 188–9, 201
Üialy 21, 72, 77, 111
United Nations Environment Programme
(UNEP) 145
uneven development
capitalist 16, 64n45, 209
state-socialist 38, 60–2, 87, 119, 234
USSR *see* Soviet Union
Uzbekistan 47, 99, 105
and cotton 13, 59, 144–5
and Aral Sea regression 121
see also Aral Sea, southern shore
Üzyn Qaiyr 21, 72, 77

Virgin Lands programme 16, 17
vodka *see* alcohol
Voeikov, Aleksandr Ivanovich 42, 45, 57
Vozrozhdenie Island 2, 47, 54, 101
vulnerability 38
of body 209
to cotton/irrigation complex 61, 115,
119–20, 121–2, 234
within imperial space 39, 43
within post-Soviet space 223, 228
within Soviet space 47, 61, 87
of Small Aral Sea environment 147, 163

water *see* drinking water; irrigation; nature,
mastery of; Wittfogel, Karl August
water scarcity and conflict 145, 146, 174n3
weather 209, 216–17, 224
and fishing practices 49, 175–6, 178, 185,
199
and Small Aral restoration 148, 150
see also dust storms
weddings *see* ritual economy
Weinthal, Erika 63n11, 146
Wittfogel, Karl August 44, 114
World Bank *see* Syr Darya Control and North
Aral Sea Project
wormwood 19, 230

Yrghyz Lakes 79, 134, 137

Zaisan, Lake 80, 134, 137
zander 25–6, 176–8
catches of 69, 74
export 196–7, 212
materiality of 25, 173, 177, 191, 200
monetary value of 153, 159, 176–7, 200,
233
on other Kazakhstani lakes 80, 137
processing 193, 196, 212–13, 215
recovery of 159, 161
and social change 180–1, 204–5, 238
transnational markets for 7, 25–6, 153,
177, 181, 238
Zhalangash 19, 53, 154, 174n12, 205n10
Zhambul, kolkhoz 53, 107, 127, 154
and Lake Aqshatau 79
and Lake Balqash 80
zhūt 38, 39
zoobenthos 52, 150, 151–2, 159, 162, 236
A. ovata 70, 71, 151
Chironomidae 70, 150, 162, 236
C. isthmicum 71, 88n12, 151
N. diversicolor 70, 71, 151, 236
P. elegans 69, 151
zooplankton 52, 69, 70
C. aquaedulcis 70

Milton Keynes UK
Ingram Content Group UK Ltd.
UKHW051308200923
429049UK00033B/279